THE EMERGENCE OF BRITAIN'S GLOBAL NAVAL SUPREMACY

The War of 1739–1748

Richard Harding

THE BOYDELL PRESS

First published 2010
The Boydell Press, Woodbridge
Reprinted in paperback and transferred to digital printing 2013

ISBN 978 1 84383 580 6 hardback
ISBN 978 1 84383 823 4 paperback

The Boydell Press is an imprint of Boydell & Brewer Ltd
PO Box 9, Woodbridge, Suffolk IP12 3DF, UK
and of Boydell & Brewer Inc.
668 Mount Hope Ave, Rochester, NY 14620-2731, USA
website: www.boydellandbrewer.com

A catalogue record for this book is available from the British Library

The publisher has no responsibility for the continued existence or
accuracy of URLs for external or third-party internet websites referred to in
this book, and does not guarantee that any content on such websites is,
or will remain, accurate or appropriate

This publication is printed on acid-free paper

THE EMERGENCE OF BRITAIN'S GLOBAL NAVAL SUPREMACY

The War of 1739–1748

Contents

For My Parents, James and Kathleen Harding

Illustrations

Figures

Maps

Plates (between pages 214 and 215)

Tables

Preface

This is not a comprehensive history of the war that lasted from 1739 to 1748, nor even of Britain's part in it. It is not able to encapsulate all the recent work on the emergence of 'Britishness' in the eighteenth century. Nor is it possible to build in an analysis of the war and its impact on parliamentary activity.[1] It is an attempt to show how the naval war was intimately tied up with domestic political and European diplomatic imperatives. It tries to explain how and why decisions were made, and how the wider war shaped the naval contribution, as much as vice versa. The Seven Years War was not a re-run of the war of 1739-1748 with more competent personnel. The situation was very different from the 1750s, but the lessons that were learned between 1739 and 1748 were powerful and provided the basis for the emergence of Britain's global naval supremacy just over a decade later.

This work has been many years in gestation. I am extremely grateful to Dr Philip Woodfine, whose advice and comments have much improved this work. The opinions and any errors that remain are entirely my own. I owe a debt to archivists at local and national archives for making it a pleasure to visit and work with their collections. The quotations from the Cumberland Papers held in the Royal Library at Windsor are from the microfilms made of these papers in 1968 and are used by gracious permission of Her Majesty Queen Elizabeth II. The papers of the Fourth Duke of Bedford are used by kind permission of the Duke of Bedford and the Trustees of the Bedford Estates. The Chatsworth Manuscripts, from the Devonshire Collection, are used by kind permission of the Duke of Devonshire and the Chatsworth House Trust.

This work has its origins in an interest in eighteenth century British politics and administration, encouraged by Professor Aubrey Newman of the University of Leicester. That interest was further honed by the friendly criticism of Graham Gibbs of Birkbeck College, who patiently guided me through a doctoral dissertation almost twenty five years ago. Professor Jeremy Black has, over many years, done more than anyone to encourage me to continue

---

1   R. Connors, 'Pelham, Parliament and Public Policy, 1746–1754', unpublished PhD thesis, University of Cambridge, 1993.

to work on the questions of mid-eighteenth century diplomatic history. The interest stayed alive because of the patience of my wife Anne and daughters Rebecca and Hannah, for whom seapower has been a constant, if no doubt occasionally irritating, companion. I owe them all a great debt of thanks.

Richard Harding

Note on Dates: England used the Julian calendar at this time (old style), which was eleven days behind the Gregorian calendar used in Western Europe (new style) and New Year's day fell on 25 March rather than 1 January. Throughout, old style is used except where specifically noted as New Style by (n.s.). The new year is assumed to start on 1 January.

Introduction

From the early years of the eighteenth century the sea played an important part in how Britons' defined themselves. 'Fenced in with a wall which knows no master but God only', the diverse peoples of the British Isles, with all their differences, clearly perceived themselves as separate from their European neighbours.[1] The Civil Wars (1642–1648, 1649–1651) and the Anglo-Dutch Wars (1652–1654, 1665–1667, 1672–1674), established a confident Protestantism and a notion of political liberty that provided the ideological underpinning that supported the development of the British state into the eighteenth century. The navy was an essential part of this ideological construct. Under the Cromwellian Protectorate (1653–1660) the English gentry had experienced the oppressive power of armies, which they were determined never again to endure.[2] Navies could not impose such domestic oppression and the navy of the short-lived English republic also demonstrated that properly supported English ships could preserve the sea as a natural defence, protect the growing wealth of English maritime commerce and even project power far enough to damage enemies in the Baltic, Mediterranean and the Americas.[3] After 1660 the restored Stuart monarchs maintained the navy, and preserved the political notion that a strong navy was the basis of national defence, mercantile prosperity and political liberty.[4]

By 1688 the English navy was not as large as that of France, but it had shown itself to be extremely formidable. Unlike either France or the United Provinces (modern Netherlands), England did not have exposed land borders and this seemed to put England with an unusually happy position. The navalist idea

---

1   Quoted in L. Colley, *Britons: Forging the Nation, 1707–1837*, Yale, New Haven, 1992, 17. See also P. Stallybrass, 'Time, Space and Unity: The Symbolic Discourse of the Faerie Queene', in R. Samuel (ed.), *Patriotism: The Making and Unmaking of British National Identity*, London, 1989, iii, 199–214.

2   L.G. Schwoerer, *No Standing Armies!*, Baltimore, 1974.

3   B. Capp, *Cromwell's Navy: The Fleet and the English Revolution, 1648–1660*, Oxford, 1989.

4   J.S. Wheeler, *The Making of a World Power: War and the Military Revolution in Seventeenth Century England*, Stroud, 1999. For an overview of the navy at that time, see J.D. Davies, *Pepy's Navy: Ships, Men and Warfare, 1649–1689*, Barnsley, 2008.

that England could invest in powerful naval forces, which would not pose a threat to domestic political liberties, but at the same time could effectively defend her borders at sea and project its power to enemy coasts and trade throughout the western hemisphere, was extremely attractive.

While Charles II (1660–1685) and James II (1685–1688) had been on the throne, they had not been directly threatened by growing power of Louis XIV of France. However, when William of Orange came to the throne, as William III in 1688, his concern for the borders of his Dutch territories forced the English to accept that the war which formally broke out in 1689 (Nine Years War, 1689–1698), would be a continental as well as a naval war. While neither William nor his ministers would abandon either the continental or maritime war in favour of the other, the issue provided an important rhetorical dividing line between the political groups throughout William's reign. To many in England, William's campaigns in Flanders reinforced the notion that continental wars were primarily in the interests of foreign powers, while a maritime war was unquestionable of benefit to England.[5] This seemed to suggest that the King and his 'court' were the driving force behind the continental war, while the maritime war was advocated by the 'country', as exemplified by its natural rulers, the English gentry. The Whigs had championed William's invasion in 1688 and so became predominantly associated with the continental strategy, while the Tories held more firmly to an English maritime war. So the approach to war and the role of the navy became entangled in the party political rhetoric of the early eighteenth century and the broader idea of a dichotomy of interest between court and country.[6] By 1700 the suspicion that a foreign monarch would divert English resources to his or her own ends, was so deeply held that, when it became clear that the preferred successor to the childless William would be the heirs of the Princess Sophia of Hanover, an Act of Settlement (1701) was passed insisting that 'in case the Crown and imperial dignity of this Realm shall hereafter come to any person, not being a native of this Kingdom of England, this nation be not obliged to engage in any war for the defence of

---

5   D.W. Jones, *War and Economy in the Age of William III and Marlborough*, Oxford, 1988; J.A. Johnson, 'Parliament and the Navy, 1688–1714', unpublished PhD, University of Sheffield, 1968; T.J. Denman, 'The Political Debate over Strategy, 1689–1712', unpublished PhD, University of Cambridge, 1985. See also, J.C.D. Clark, 'Protestantism, Nationalism and National Identity', *Historical Journal*, xliii (2000), 249–276, particularly p. 251.

6   H.T. Dickinson, *Liberty and Property: Political Ideology in Eighteenth Century Britain*, London, 1977, 91–118.

any dominions or territories which do not belong to the Crown of England, without the consent of Parliament'.[7]

The debates about the virtues of continental and maritime war continued during the War of Spanish Succession (1701–1713). Once again the rhetorical divisions were clear, with Tories generally supporting a maritime, American or Mediterranean policy, in contrast to Whig support for the campaign in Flanders. As in the previous war, the practical policy differences of Whig and Tory ministers were not at all as clearly divided.[8]

At the end of the war, the Grand Alliance, led by Austria, Britain and the United Provinces had succeeded in curbing the ambitions of an aging Louis XIV. British resources had been used in all theatres to force France to spread her efforts.[9] By 1712, the Tory ministry of the time had seen the diplomatic logic of ending the war. However, to do so it had to unilaterally negotiate a suspension of hostilities in Flanders and effectively abandoned her allies. Peace was eventually achieved, but the abandonment was to remain a bitter memory for the Whigs and for George, Elector of Hanover, who was one of those allies and who was shortly to succeed to the British throne as George I.[10]

The Peace of Utrecht was completed during 1713, but the Tory ministry did not last much longer. It fell on the death of Queen Anne in August 1714. The residual Tory loyalty to the Stuart succession, was too ambiguous for the Elector of Hanover, and he turned exclusively to the Whigs for his ministers. In looking back on the war, the Whigs could condemn the Tories' unilateral armistice in Flanders, but overall the war had achieved British aims: the Protestant succession had been accepted by France and Spanish independence from France and Austria had been maintained. This had been achieved by exhausting campaigns in Flanders, Spain and Italy and at sea. However,

---

7   Act of Settlement (1701) c. 12 and 13 Will 3, III. William's immediate heir, Princess Anne, daughter of James II, also had no living heirs, after her son the Duke of Gloucester died in 1700. See G.C. Gibbs, 'Accession to the Throne and Change of Rulers: Determining Factors in the Establishment and Continuation of the Personal Union', in R. Rexhauser, in R. Rexhauser (ed.) *Die Personalunionen von Sachen-Polen 1697–1763 und Hannover-England 1714–1837: Ein Vergleich*, Wiesleben, 2005, 241–274.

8   Jones, *War and Economy*, op. cit; Johnson, 'Parliament and the Navy', op. cit.; Denman, 'Political Debate', op. cit.; J.B. Hattendorf, *England and the War of Spanish Succession: A Study of the English View and Conduct of Grand Strategy, 1702–1712*, New York, 1987.

9   Ibid., 265–270. The term 'British' is now employed to recognise the Union of the England and Scotland in 1707.

10 B.W. Hill, 'Oxford, Bolingbroke and the Peace of Utrecht', *Historical Journal*, xvi (1973), 241–263.

Britain had also captured Gibraltar (1704), Minorca (1708) and by the peace treaty, gained concessions in the West Indies and Nova Scotia near the mouth of the St Lawrence River. These were clearly the results of sea power. The Royal Navy emerged from the war twice the size of the French fleet. This was largely because of the collapse of the French navy in the middle of the war. The structure of the British fleet had also changed so that besides the great ships of the line with three gun decks that formed the backbone of the battlefleet in home waters, there were more two-deck, 70-gun ships, better suited for sustained operations in distant waters.[11] Allied to the Dutch, the British achieved an overwhelming advantage at sea. After the peace there was no power that could match the British Royal Navy.

The first decades of the eighteenth century were a period in which this new naval superiority was to be tested. The early years of George I's reign (1714–1727) were dominated by the Great Northern War (1701–1721) in which the interests of Hanover were intimately tied up. The war primarily concerned the fate of the Swedish empire as varying coalitions struggled to balance their own interests with those of Sweden and the emerging power of Russia. Britain had its own interests in the Baltic, particularly access to naval resources from the eastern Baltic, such as wood and pitch. However, from the first British politicians were concerned about the possibility that George was using British resources for his Hanoverian dominions in breach of the Act of Settlement of 1701. On four occasions a British fleet was sent to the Baltic to protect British interests. It was an impressive display of naval power to be able to maintain squadrons of men of war at a distance from home ports in disputed, if not hostile waters. Although the deep-draughted warships almost certainly had an impact on the behaviour of the belligerents, they were ill suited to shallows and archipelagos of the eastern Baltic. By 1720 George had come to accept that the political cost in Britain of employing the fleet in this way was not worth the contribution that the squadrons made.[12] The ships had not been put to the test of combat, but they had had an impact on events and they had demonstrated again that British naval power could be exercised in distant waters.[13]

---

11   J. Glete, *Navies and Nations: Warships, Navies and State Building in Europe and America, 1500–1860*, 2 vols, Stockholm, 1993, i, 241; B. Lavery, *Ship of the Line*, London, 1983, i, 71.

12   D.D. Aldridge, '*Admiral Sir John Norris and the British Naval Expeditions to the Baltic Sea, 1715–1727*, Lund, 2009.

13   J.J. Murray, *George I, the Baltic and the Whig Split of 1717*, London, 1969.

The other region that disturbed the European peace was Italy. The price the new Bourbon King of Spain, Philip V, had paid for obtaining the throne was the loss of Spain's Italian and Flemish lands to the Austrian Habsburgs. Whereas the later could be dismissed, the loss of Naples was a blow that neither Philip nor his Italian wife, Elizabeth Farnese, were willing to accept. In 1717 Spanish naval and land forces took Sardinia from the Savoyards. To stop further threats to the Utrecht settlement, France, Britain and the United Provinces decided to act. A squadron of 20 ships of the line was sent out to the Mediterranean under Admiral Sir George Byng. He arrived too late to stop the Spanish landing on Sicily, but he met their fleet of 12 line of battle off Messina on the 31 July 1718. As the Spanish fleet withdrew Byng gave chase, caught and comprehensively destroyed that force.[14] Byng continued to assist the Austrians in the re-conquest of the island. In January 1719, France and Britain declared war on Spain and a French army advanced over the Pyrenees. A small British force was landed at Vigo without opposition. The Spanish forces facing the French army began to crumble and Philip was forced to come to terms. In October the Spanish garrison on Sicily surrendered and the war came to a close. While the French campaign in northern Castile was probably decisive, the role of naval power in this short war was highly visible to contemporaries. Byng's crushing victory, his support of Austrian operations on Sicily, the landing at Vigo and the defeat of a Spanish attempt to invade Scotland, in support of a Jacobite rising, were clear naval contributions to the Spanish defeat.

The perception of Spain's vulnerability to seapower was reinforced in 1726. Spain and Austria came together to advance their mutual objective to adjust the Utrecht settlement. For Spain this still meant the recovery of her Italian domains and Gibraltar. The siege of Gibraltar lasted from February to June 1727, but the Spanish were unable either to take the landward fortification or blockade the town in the face of British naval forces operating out of Gibraltar.[15] The British sent squadrons to Cadiz and to the West Indies to blockade the treasure fleets. Admiral Francis Hosier's squadron, sitting off Porto Bello, suffered catastrophic losses from yellow fever, but the overall effect of the blockade was to bring Spain and Austria to the negotiating table.

---

14 T. Corbett, *An Account of the Expedition of the British Fleet to Sicily in the Years 1718, 1719 and 1720*, London, 1739.

15 R. Harding, 'A Tale of Two Sieges, Gibraltar 1726–7 and 1779–1783', *Transactions of the Naval Dockyards Society*, ii, (2006), 31–46.

After each of these wars treaties with Spain addressed another important point of friction in Anglo-Spanish relations. Periodically, since 1713 British merchant ships trading in the Caribbean had been seized by Spanish coast guards, the *gardacostas*. The Spanish claimed that these ships were smuggling goods in and out of Spanish imperial territories. The British merchants claimed they were legal traders, intercepted in the course of their legitimate commerce. The Treaty of Seville in 1729, which ended the 1726–1727 conflict, established plenipotentiaries to settle the differences over these depredations. In 1730, when Spain appeared to be delaying matters, reprisal orders were sent the squadron in the West Indies to act vigorously against Spanish interests. The rapid resumption of negotiations was perceived, in British eyes, as another example of the successful influence of naval power.

By the end of 1737 the Anglo-Spanish dispute over the depredations was reaching a crisis. British opinion was becoming increasingly belligerent. Some basic assumptions had become entrenched and were leading Britain towards war: Spain was at fault; Britain could win a war at sea; the naval war would be effective; Spain knew this was case; and, finally, merely threatening war would force her to negotiate seriously. In the popular imagination, naval power would bring Spain rapidly to heel.

War was declared by Britain on 23 October 1739. Hostilities ended nine years later and a definitive commercial treaty, settling the issues at the root of depredations crisis, was not concluded until 1750.[16] The Anglo-Spanish war had become subsumed in another, larger war over the Austrian Succession (1740–1748) that consumed Europe. After all this time, naval and continental campaigns had not shattered the Spanish empire nor modified their pretensions to protect their colonies from interlopers. The war had opened with massive expectations of quick victory based on naval power. It ended with failures and disappointments. In the last full year of the war (1747), two major naval victories (the First and Second Battles of Finisterre) failed to have any practical impact on French or Spanish policy.

Yet, just 13 years later, at the end of the Seven Years War (1756–1763), British naval power had crushed the Franco-Spanish naval forces, devastated their maritime commerce and had captured the most significant parts of their colonial empires. The troubling question of why naval power had failed to deliver the victory expected between 1739 and 1748, was replaced by a new question – how had Britain established itself so quickly as the pre-eminent

---

16   J.O. McLachlan, *Trade and Peace with Old Spain, 1667–1750*, Cambridge, 1940, 132–141.

world naval power? In the course of answering this latter question, the failure of 1739–1748 could be explained simply by inferring the reverse of the successes of 1759–1763. The ideology of the maritime war, which assumed a natural British advantage, if not invincibility, had been in the political arena for about 100 years previously and to contemporaries its failure in the 1740s could be only explained by the incompetence or obstruction of ministers, administrators, senior officers and even the King, George II. There was no systemic failure of sea power, just its poor application in specific circumstances. The War of Jenkins Ear (against Spain) and the War of Austrian Succession, were left as a minor background note, largely irrelevant to the dominant trajectory of British global power. The figure of William Pitt dominates Britain's contribution to the Seven Years War. Pitt depended on his personal magnetism for his power within parliament. This magnetism was also important in linking him in the minds of contemporaries with victory. Generations of biographers and historians, from Horace Walpole onwards, have largely followed this association of Pitt with victory. Guided by the vision and application by a new generation of politicians and service men like Pitt, George Anson, James Wolfe and many others, the true potential of balancing sea power and continental involvement became obvious.[17] In the 1740s seapower had been wasted, by incompetence and muddled thinking.[18]

Recently, historians have given us a more nuanced picture of the 1740s. The unrealistic expectations of naval power in the 1730s and the impact this had on ministers have been charted by Philip Woodfine.[19] The importance of decisions and the choices available to ministers at any given time have been

---

17 For example, see H. Walpole, *Memoirs of the Reign of George II*, London, 1846, iii, 156; B. Williams, *The Life of William Pitt, Earl of Chatham*, London, 1915, i, 379; B. Tunstall, *William Pitt, Earl of Chatham*, London, 1938, 170, 215; P.D. Brown, *William Pitt, Earl of Chatham*, London, 1978, 139. Although Pitt's personal role continues to dominate the popular general histories of the Seven Years War, recent historians and biographers have been careful to place Pitt more precisely in the context of the British military and naval war effort. The clearest expression of Pitt's role as the strategic director of the war can be found in J.S. Corbett, *England in the Seven Years War*, 2 vols, London, 1907.

18 The fullest, and still the best, coverage of British naval war of 1739–1748, by H.W. Richmond, places the blame squarely on the political leadership of the time. See H.W. Richmond, *The Navy in the War of 1739–48*, 3 vols, Cambridge, i, 112; iii, 252.

19 P. Woodfine, 'Ideas of Naval Power and the Conflict with Spain, 1738–1742', in J. Black and P. Woodfine (eds), *The British Navy and the Use of Naval Power in the Eighteenth Century*, Leicester, 1988, 71–90; P. Woodfine, 'Horace Walpole and British Relations with Spain, 1738', *Camden Miscellany*, xxxii, Royal Historical Society, 1994, 277–311.

highlighted by Jeremy Black.[20] The fact that despite what contemporaries felt, the war of 1739–1748 was a success in that it contained French power in Europe has been cogently argued by Brendan Simms.[21] Robert Harris has described the way in which the war was rationalised by contemporaries through political propaganda.[22]

We now have a much better view of the war of 1739 to 1748, but it still invites re-examination. Why naval power failed to fulfil expectations needs to be understood. It was not just that British expectations were unrealistically high so the victories were less spectacular than anticipated. Contemporaries were disturbed by the navy's failure to make a decisive impact in any theatre, but far worse, they were staggered by the periodic loss of control in some regions and horrified by the threat of French invasion in 1744–1745. It is important to understand why this happened and what was done to rectify the situation if we are to understand how the British state built up its resources to win the decisive victories of 1759–1762. What emerges is not so much incompetence or obstruction as people trying to manage a continually changing war in a complex political and diplomatic environment.

---

20 J. Black, *America or Europe? British Foreign Policy, 1739–1763*, London, 1997.

21 B. Simms, *Three Victories and a Defeat: The Rise and Fall of the First British Empire, 1714–1783*, London, 2007, 352–354.

22 B. Harris, A., *Patriot Press: National Politics and the London Press in the 1740s*, Oxford, 1993.

1

The Route to War, 1738–1739

On Tuesday 23 October 1739 heralds made their way from St James Palace to the Royal Exchange to proclaim King George II's declaration of war upon Spain. Bells peeled out across the City and the stocks which had been languishing on Exchange Alley began to rise.[1] Preparations for war had commenced in June, but the British ministry was not united on the wisdom of the war.[2] The King and his First Lord of the Treasury, Sir Robert Walpole, only reluctantly came to accept the need for war. Walpole is famously said to have commented on hearing the bells peeling out across London that they now ring their bells, but they will soon wring their hands.[3] In the end, neither George II nor Walpole could resist the popular logic of war: that British sea power would make the war swift, cheap, relatively bloodless and have an positive impact on British power and reputation that would transform Britain's place in the world.

These expectations were exaggerated. Sea power did not bring Spain to a quick or humiliating peace. By 1741 Britain was engaged in a far bigger War of Austrian Succession, which entailed a major commitment of land and sea forces in European campaigns. By 1744 France and Britain were at war and the conflict entered a critical phase as fears of French invasion and a dangerous Jacobite rebellion diverted British efforts to home defence. By the beginning of 1748 the original Anglo-Spanish dispute seemed to have faded into insignificance.

The navy recorded some remarkable achievements. Vice Admiral Vernon's capture of Porto Bello in 1739 became the first truly popular

---

1   W. Coxe, *Memoirs of the Life and Administration of Sir Robert Walpole, Earl of Orford*, London, 1816, vol. 4, 111–112.

2   The best narrative of the Anglo-Spanish negotiations leading to war is P. Woodfine, *Britannia's Glories: The Walpole ministry and the War with Spain*, Woodbridge, 1998.

3   Coxe, *Walpole*, op. cit., 111.

imperial conquest.[4] Commodore George Anson's circumnavigation of the world (1740–1744) and his capture of a rich galleon off the Philippines, was applauded and admired.[5] Anson's and Hawke's two victories against French squadrons, called the First and Second Battles of Finisterre (May and October 1747) demonstrated that the Royal Navy was capable of catching and beating its enemies.[6] However, this was intermixed with many failures that undermined public faith in the navy and naval power. Furthermore, the long-term impact of the naval blows was limited. Just as after the War of Spanish Succession (1701–1713), French colonial trade recovered and flourished. The original causes of the war, free passage of trade in the West Indies, were finally addressed after the peace, but without much concession from Spain. At the end of the war, observers could not say that the hopes of 1739 had been realised.

Nevertheless, over the nine years some important things had happened. British forces and the government had gained substantial experience of intensive warfare, which had not been seen since 1713. Much had been learned about converting naval force into maritime power that could have a direct and immediate impact on European diplomacy. Troops had been sent to Flanders, the West Indies, North America and India. Americans had been raised to fight in the Caribbean and North America. The navy had campaigned continuously against the combined naval power of France and Spain across the world. Forces had been raised, supplied, sustained and reinforced. The administrative machinery of government was tested in new ways. A new generation of politicians, administrators, diplomats and military men all learned their trade in this difficult war.

The Origins of the War: Domestic Political Background

In October 1739, Sir Robert Walpole had been Chancellor of the Exchequer and First Lord of the Treasury for over eighteen years.[7] As a Whig who had

---

4   K. Wilson, *The Sense of the People: People, Culture and Imperialism in England, 1715–1785*, Cambridge, 1995, 65.

5   G. Williams, *The Prize of All the Oceans: The Triumph and Tragedy of Anson's Voyage Round the World*, London, 1999, 219–235.

6   R. Mackay, *Admiral Hawke*, Oxford, 1965, 87–88.

7   There are many biographies of Walpole. J.H. Plumb's is the most detailed, but he did not complete the third volume, ending his account in 1734, *Sir Robert Walpole*, 2 vols, London, 1956 and 1960; H.T. Dickinson, *Walpole and the Whig Supremacy*, London, 1973; B. Kemp, *Sir Robert Walpole*, London, 1976; B.W. Hill, *Sir Robert Walpole*,

entered parliament in 1701, Walpole quickly learned the ways of House of Commons and the court. He survived Whig and Tory intrigues as he steadily advanced his career. In June 1720 he had managed to return to the ministry as Paymaster General, but it was the South Sea Bubble Crisis that burst in the autumn of 1720 that propelled him into the senior posts of First Lord and Chancellor of the Exchequer in April 1721. Once in power, he continued to show the financial and political acumen that had underpinned his rise. His grasp of parliamentary management was formidable and his relations with the court were deftly managed. The fractious relationship between George I and his son the Prince of Wales made the impending succession a time of acute anxiety for Walpole, but despite expectations, he continued in office after the accession of George II in June 1727.

However, no politician remains in power for many years without accumulating enemies. The Tories were excluded from office, but remained a significant group in the House of Commons. Walpole's own rise was facilitated by divisions among the Whigs on foreign policy and these divisions remained to be exploited.[8] Ambitious Whigs who were excluded from power formed a loose grouping who ached to replace Walpole. By the mid-1730s, men such as William Pulteney, and John, Earl Carteret, had become a focus for this group of politicians.[9] Rallying points for these excluded Whigs could come from dissident nobles. In July 1737 relations between George II and his son, Frederick Prince of Wales, broke down. The Prince left the court and set up his political home at Carlton House. Around him, dissident Whigs formed an active opposition group.[10] Viscount Cobham, the Earl of Stair, the Earl of Chesterfield and the Duke of Bedford were other nobles who provided support for opponents of Walpole. They all had personal reasons for their opposition to Walpole, but what held them together, and to a limited degree allowed them to encompass the Tories, was the idea of 'patriotism'. There had long been the belief that the natural order of the 'country', the landed squirearchy, was being undermined by the 'court' which, in pursuing its European wars, was distorting social relations and threatening domestic liberty by corruption and the promotion of new monied interest.[11] This was

London, 1989; J. Black, *Walpole in Power*, Stroud, 2001, are all good short accounts of his life.

8   R. Sedgwick, *The House of Commons, 1715–1754*, 2 vols, London, 1970, i, 33–50.

9   B.W. Hill, *The Growth of Parliamentary Parties, 1689–1742*, London, 1976, 189–216.

10   A.S. Foord, *His Majesty's Opposition, 1714–1830*, Oxford, 1964, 128.

11   Dickinson, *Liberty and Property*, op. cit., 163–192. The country ideology never translated

given a new impetus after 1725 when Lord Bolingbroke returned to England from France. He had been one of Queen Anne's last Tory secretaries of state. He became the focus for Tories and nostalgic Whigs who looked back to a mythical, purer constitution, before ministerial corruption had tainted the political system. Over the next 15 years intellectuals, poets, playwrights and political hacks, provided a critical commentary on the policies of Walpole's ministry.[12] While 'patriotism' did not attract a consistent and committed body of politicians, it was capable of absorbing the general principles of Tories or Whigs and it did translate into a coherent, if limited, series of measures to limit the corrupting power of the court. These included shorter parliaments, a place bill to exclude crown office holders from the Commons and a reduction in the standing army.

More numerous than career politicians in or out for office, were the independent MPs. They were not naturally party men, but local gentry who generally held the prerogatives of crown and parliament to be sacrosanct. They were likely to have deeply held assumptions about the limits of both bodies and deep suspicions of anyone challenging either. Although 'patriot' ideology could not bind them to leaders, it did provide a superficial explanation for Walpole's ability to hold on to power. By the mid-1730s, opposition newspapers, pamphlets and prints were presenting Walpole as the corrupt 'Great Man' who had used court patronage to engross political power for himself. Not only was he distorting the natural order of British society, but he was even suspected of being in the pay of France.[13] Since 1734 Walpole's

---

into a coherent party programme, but was capable of accommodating anti-court feelings of Whigs and Tories. See D. Hayton, 'The "Country" Interest and the Party System, 1689–c1720, in C. Jones (ed.), *Party and Management in Parliament, 1660–1784*, Leicester, 1984, 36–85; J.B. Owen, 'The Survival of Country Attitudes in the Eighteenth Century House of Commons', in J.S. Bromley and E.H. Kossmann (eds) *Britain and the Netherlands*, iv, Hague, 1971, 42–69.

12   I. Kramnick, *Bolingbroke and his Circle: The Politics of Nostalgia in the Age of Walpole*, Ithaca, 1968; Q. Skinner, 'The Principles and Practice of Opposition: The Case of Bolingbroke versus Walpole, in N. McKendrick (ed.) *Historical Perspectives: Studies in English Thought and Society*, London, 1974, 93–128; W. Speck, '"Whigs and Tories Dim their Glories": English Political Parties under the First Two Georges', in J. Cannon (ed.) *The Whig Ascendency: Colloquies on Hanoverian England*, London, 1981, 51–76; J.C.D. Clark, *Revolution and Rebellion: State and Society in England in the Seventeenth and Eighteenth Centuries*, Cambridge, 1986, 136–144; G.C. Gibbs, 'Newspapers, Parliament and Foreign Policy in the Age of Stanhope and Walpole', in *Melanges Offerts á G. Jaquemyns*, Brussels, 1968, 293–315; Foord, *His Majesty's Opposition*, op. cit., 113–216.

13   W.T. Laprade, *Public Opinion and Politics in Eighteenth Century England to the Fall of Walpole*, New York, 1936, 344–387. See also M.D. George, *English Political Caricature*

grip on power had weakened, but while his friends in government, the 'Old Corps' Whigs held together and they were able to convince the independent members that their policies preserved political and fiscal stability at home and safety from foreign enemies or the extortions of Hanoverian ambitions, Walpole's position was not in great danger.[14] The problem was that by 1737 these members were becoming uneasy that so far as the Spanish depredations were concerned.

The other very significant factor in the political situation was the King himself.[15] George II came to the throne in 1727, aged 43. Like his father, he had a military training and a deep attachment to the Electorate of Hanover. This sensitivity to Hanover was shared by the political classes in Britain, but for very different reasons. Fear of distortion of policy in the interests of a foreign state was deeply held and easy to exploit.[16] Both George and Walpole were astute enough to realise that the King had to balance the demands of his British kingdom with the needs of his Hanoverian Electorate.[17] However, success in this relied on the ability to explain British policy in parliament in relation to Hanoverian interests. From the 1720s, partly because calculations for Hanoverian safety had to be incorporated into foreign policy decisions, it was possible for the opposition to taint Walpole with an unpatriotic Hanoverianism.[18] During the 1740s, the need to explain the Hanoverian dimension of British policy became even more vital, but because of changing circumstances in Europe, Walpole's successors found it increasingly difficult to carry it out, leading to serious problems in 1744–1745.[19]

to 1792, Oxford, 1959, particularly 87–93 and associated reproductions.

14   For parliamentary management in this period, see. G.C. Gibbs, 'Parliament and Foreign Policy, 1715–1731', MA thesis, University of Liverpool, 1953.

15   The best biography of George II is J. Black, *George II: Puppet of the Politicians?*, Exeter, 2007. See also, J.B. Owen, 'George II Reconsidered', in A. Whiteman, J.S. Bromley and P.G.M. Dickinson (eds) *Statesmen, Scholars and Merchants*, Oxford, 1973, 113–134.

16   G.C. Gibbs, 'English Attitudes towards Hanover and the Hanoverian Succession in the First Half of the Eighteenth Century', in A.M. Birke and K.Kluken (eds) *England und Hannover*, Munchen, 1986, 33–51.

17   N. Harding, 'Sir Robert Walpole and Hanover', *Historical Research*, lxxvi (2003), 164–188.

18   J. Black, *Parliament and Foreign Policy in the Eighteenth Century*, Cambridge, 2004, 66–7 .See also, J. Black, 'Hanoverian Nexus: Walpole and the Electorate', in B. Simms and T. Riotte (eds) *The Hanoverian Dimension in British History, 1714–1837*, Cambridge, 2007, 10–27.

19   Harris, *A Patriot Press*, op. cit.

The King was head of the executive, and George played his part to the full. He understood the difference between his constitutional position in Hanover and in Britain. He also understood the mechanics of the relationship with his British ministers. Nevertheless, the dual role of King and elector created tensions. Eighteenth-century government was a very personal activity. It was carried out through meetings between monarch and ministers.[20] The court was a vital political venue. It was the place where matters of patronage were determined, and where signals of political approval or disapproval were most acutely observed. It was where policy was discussed, sometime with ostentatious public display, and at other times confidentially.[21] Relationships worked best when monarch and ministers could share similar views on subjects, but they could still work when they were of differing opinion. They worked far less well when monarch and ministers could not meet. This was what happened when George left Britain to spend the summer months in Hanover. The physical distance between monarch and ministers was to play an important part in shaping policy at critical times during the war.

By the end of 1737, the King and his ministry were satisfied with each other. Walpole had established himself firmly in the King's favour very soon after the latter's accession to the throne, but trouble was brewing. The split of the Prince of Wales from the King's household by September and the death of Queen Caroline in November, who was seen as one of Walpole's staunchest supporters at court, were sending ripples of concern through the corridors of power. Walpole's colleagues in office were also beginning to show signs of discontent. Among the Whigs of the Old Corps was a small inner group of trusted friends who were the key supporters of Walpole's ministry. They were experienced and capable politicians, mustering formidable parliamentary support either by interest or skills of parliamentary management. The Secretary of State for the Southern Department, the Duke of Newcastle, had been in post since 1724. Newcastle controlled a substantial parliamentary interest of about 14 parliamentary seats.[22] His parliamentary influence and his experience in office gave him increasing confidence and during 1737 there were growing disagreements between him and Walpole over foreign policy. Newcastle's brother, Henry Pelham, had been Paymaster General since 1730 and was

---

20   J. Black, *George II*, op. cit., 18–24.

21   H. Smith, *Georgian Monarchy:Politics and Culture, 1714–1760*, Cambridge, 2006, 59–115; 194–239; 'The Court in England, 1714–1760: A Declining Political Institution?', *History*, xc (2005), 23–41.

22   R. Browning, *The Duke of Newcastle*, New Haven, 1975, 28–35.

an important spokesman in the Commons.[23] The death of Lord Chancellor Talbot in February 1737 opened the way for Lord Chief Justice Philip, Baron Hardwicke, an old ally and great friend of Newcastle to assume this key post. The other Secretary of State (for the Northern Department) was William Stanhope, Baron Harrington, another protégé of Newcastle's who had come into office in 1730. Although Walpole was undoubtedly head of the ministry and in the King's favour, events at court, within the ministry and in parliament were conspiring to de-stabilise his power.

Economics and Ideology

The origins of the war with Spain lay in the West Indies. Spain's massive American empire had excited the envy and greed of Europeans ever since the sixteenth century. Despite her claim to monopoly, Spain could do little about English, French and Dutch encroachments on her colonial possessions and in 1670 Spain finally conceded the legitimacy of English settlements in the Caribbean.[24]

Although the War of Spanish Succession had many objectives for the British, the security of trade to the Caribbean was certainly one of them. The Treaty of Utrecht in 1713 confirmed the exclusion of France from Spanish colonial trade.[25] It also confirmed the transfer of the *Asiento*, from France to the British South Sea Company for 30 years. This was a contract to supply 4800 slaves annually to the Spanish Empire. It also carried with it the right to send one ship a year of 650 tons (originally 500 tons) to the Spanish American ports to trade at the fairs.[26]

The Caribbean was one of the most valuable trade sources. After 1660 sugar had supplanted tobacco as the most valuable bulk crop and production expanded dramatically in the first years of the eighteenth century (Table 1.1).

---

23 J. Wilkes, *A Whig in Power: The Political Career of Henry Pelham*, Evanston, 1964; D.G. Barnes, 'Henry Pelham and the Duke of Newcastle', *Journal of British Studies*, i (1962), 62–77.

24 W.G. Bassett, 'The Caribbean in International Politics, 1670–1707', unpublished PhD thesis, University of London, 1934; L. Horsfall, 'British Relations with the Spanish Colonies in the Caribbean, 1713–1739', unpublished MA thesis, London, 1936, 18.

25 R.S. Villalabos, 'Contrabando Frances en el Pacifico, 1700–24', *Revista Historica Americana*, li (1961), 49–80.

26 Horsfall, *British Relations*, op. cit., 35; A.S. Aiton, 'The Asiento Treaty as Reflected in the Papers of Lord Shelburne', *Hispanic American Historical Review*, viii (1928), 167–177.

Table 1.1 Sugar imports into Britain (annual averages)

Year	Volume (tons)	Import growth (%)	Ships employed
Pre-1640	Nil		
1663–1669	7,400		
1683	18,202		143 ships
1699–1700	18,550	+19	
1701–1710	18,902	+3.8	149 ships
1711–1720	28,122	+49	221 ships
1721–1730	38,512	+37	303 ships
1731–1740	41,069	+7	323 ships

Source: I. Steele, *The English Atlantic, 1675–1740*, Oxford, 1986, p. 286, table 2.4; R. Davis, 'English Foreign Trade, 1660–1740', in W.E. Minchinton (ed.) *The Growth of English Overseas Trade in the Seventeenth and Eighteenth Centuries*, London, 1969, 81.

The sugar trade supported other valuable trades, notably slaving and shipping. The West Indies and slave trades were carried on in medium-sized vessels of about 150 to 200 tons burden and the rising volume of trade provided a boost to construction and associated maritime industries. These ships were not large enough to defend themselves against well-armed Spanish *gardacostas* (coast guards), but there were enough owners to create a political storm back in Britain. The expanding Caribbean trades also supported a growing number of small vessels trading out of the North American colonies.[27]

Apart from the South Sea Company's 'annual' ship, the Spanish colonies were closed to all but Spanish merchants trading through the *Casa de Contratacion* at Cadiz or, from 1728, though the Caracas Company sailing from Guipuzcoa for La Guaira and Porto Cabello in modern Venezuela. Since the early seventeenth century, Spanish trade had been organised annually around two great fleets.[28] The *Galeones* sailed from Cadiz to Cartagena de las Indias. After watering, this fleet sailed up the coast to Porto Bello, where the fair would be held. Colonists paid for goods in silver mined at Potosi, in modern Bolivia, which had been brought by ship from Lima to Panama and then by pack horse across the peninsula over the Royal Road. The *Galeones*

---

27   Hunter to Newcastle, 24 Dec. 1730. Governor Hunter of New York claimed the number of ships trading annually to Jamaica had increased from 5–6 before 1710 to over 200 in 1730. (quoted in Horsfall,, *British Relations*, op. cit., 173).

28   G. Walker, *Spanish Politics and Imperial Trade, 1700–1789*, London, 1979, 1–15, 67–92.

then made their way back to Spain, taking the winds and currents out of the Caribbean through the Gulf of Florida, past Havana.

The *Flota*, the other great fleet, left Cadiz for the coast of Mexico. It entered at the latitude of Puerto Rico. The trade fair was held at La Vera Cruz, financed by the output of the Mexican silver mines. Once loaded with silver, the *Flota* made its way to Havana to replenish and repair before returning to Spain. From the late seventeenth century the system worked only imperfectly.[29] The irregular sailing of these fleets left the Spanish colonists lacking the European manufactured products they desired and for which they had ready money to pay. For the growing number of British merchants and ships' masters trading in the West Indies, the temptations and opportunities for illegal trading to Spanish ports was too much. British and Dutch interlopers regularly traded to the Spanish colonies, but as Spain began to re-assert her monopoly, clashes were bound to escalate.[30] In the years immediately after 1713 the activities of the *gardacostas* were tolerated. After nearly 20 years of continuous warfare and with the region infested with pirates it was difficult to contain. However, as time passed their interference with legitimate British trade was increasingly resented, especially as the rate of seizures seems to have been increasing. Seventy-seven British ships were seized by *gardacostas* between 1713 and 1731, 27 of which (34 per cent) were taken after 1727.[31] Merchant pressure and diplomatic attempts to resolve the problems started almost from the conclusion of Utrecht, but always foundered on the Spanish demand for the restitution of Gibraltar, Spanish refusals to concede land or privileges or fears of French reaction.[32] The conclusion of the war between Britain (in alliance with France and the United Provinces) and Spain, 1718–1721 resolved nothing concerning the West Indies. During the early 1720s, British trade with Old Spain flourished, but the situation in the West Indies deteriorated. The Spanish squadron at Havana, *la Armada del Barlovento*, was re-established. The more aggressive Dutch and French smuggling was met with more determined action by the Spanish *gardacostas*. The British logwood settlements along the coast of the Bay of Campeachy were suppressed. Private trade between British colonies in the West Indies was becoming depressed.

---

29   Ibid., 228–229.

30   G.H. Nelson, 'Contraband Trade under the Asiento, 1730–1739', *American Historical Review*, li (1945), 55–67.

31   Horsfall, *British Relations*, op. cit., 202.

32   S. Conn, *Gibraltar in British Diplomacy in the Eighteenth Century*, New Haven, 1942.

In 1725 the Caribbean issue became caught up in a revival of war in Europe. Austria and Spain had allied to settle their claims in Italy. France and Britain, with the United Provinces and Prussia, joined together by the Treaty of Hanover, to stop them. The British plan was to cut the supplies of silver that flowed from the Americas to Madrid. Admiral Jennings was to blockade Cadiz, while Vice Admiral Francis Hosier blockaded Porto Bello. The devastation of Hosier's squadron by yellow fever during 1726 became legendary and played its part in the future of Anglo-Spanish relations, but on the whole, the restraint showed by both nations made it easier to come to terms during 1727. The question of navigation in the Caribbean still could not be resolved and it was agreed to put it to a commission, which would consider the whole matter.

The peace of 1727 seems to have marked an important turning point in Anglo-Spanish relations. The complaints and petitions of the West Indian merchants continued between 1727 and 1730, but the counter-balancing concern for trade with Old Spain, which had characterised earlier negotiations, had diminished. An alternative means of infiltrating the Spanish colonial markets was to sell to Spanish merchants at Cadiz, who sent the goods on the annual fleets. However, this was the only legitimate point of access by French merchants to the Spanish markets and by 1730, the struggle with them for dominance in the Cadiz trade had been lost. Furthermore, the trade itself was less profitable as the Spanish turned to other means of supplying their colonies. Register ships were being sent periodically to fill the gaps when the annual fleets did not sail. The Caracas Company, set up in 1728, also began to fill the gap, as well as providing more *gardacostas*. By 1730 it seemed that the future of both the legitimate British West Indian trades and merchant aspirations to penetrate the Spanish American markets were to be resolved together by solving the problem of depredations by the *gardacostas*. However, by this time both sides had catalogues of complaints that they could justifiably raise to complicate and delay affairs. In February 1732 a new treaty was signed by which Spain would restrain its *gardacostas* and Britain would cease protecting the interloping trade.

However, the chances of this new treaty resolving the points of dispute soon slid away. The collapse of the Anglo-French Alliance in 1731 and the Family Compact between France and Spain in 1733 created a new diplomatic constellation in which Spain was less dependent on British goodwill and Britain was no longer bound to treat Spain gently for fear of angering France. Despite being tangled up in the War of Polish Succession between 1733 and 1738, Spain was in no mood to comply with British concerns and continued to tighten regulations on trade.[33] At the same time the public mood in Britain was becoming increasingly belligerent. The perception of the importance of the West Indies, and of Jamaica in particular, had been rising in the public mind during the 1720s. Now, in the mid-1730s, Jamaica was going through a difficult period both because of internal problems and the trading situation. Additional pressures on this critical point for British prosperity could quickly lead to crisis, but 1735 and 1736 passed quietly in the West Indies. Illegal trading continued, but despite increasing *gardacostas* presence, there was little interruption to legitimate British trade.

However, in 1737, with peace preliminaries for the war in Europe in the offing, the situation deteriorated suddenly.[34] Six ships were taken by *gardacostas* during the year and there was a furious outcry among the London merchant community. In October 1737 news from the West Indies arrived in Bristol that three more British ships had been seized by the Spanish. Without waiting for any confirmation, a petition of 150 merchants was raised and presented to the Privy Council.[35] About half the petitioners had direct interests in the Caribbean. The participation of the other half is indicative of the growing general concern among the merchant community. Since the early 1720s the rapid recovery of France from the wars of the previous decades had been noted.[36] French merchants now dominated the trade in Old Spain. French West Indian sugars were driving out British sugars from European markets. Between 1730 and 1740 sugar production on St Domingue doubled.[37] The War of Polish Succession seemed in London to be ending with yet more French success. Spain also benefited from the peace with the cession of Naples and Sicily to Spain from Austria. British trade to Northern Europe and the Levant seemed more under threat than ever.

The dispute over navigation in the Caribbean hit at the vital interests of Spain and Britain. Spain was determined to preserve the trade monopoly to its colonies. For Britain the essence of the case was easily summarised and proclaimed in the press with increasing intensity during 1738. The West

---

33 Horsfall, *British Relations*, op. cit., 232–235.

34 The course of events is best followed in P. Woodfine, *Britannia's Glories*, op. cit.

35 Library of Congress, Vernon-Wager Mss, microfilm reel 91, 139–140, Wager to Bladen, 2 Nov. 1737.

36 C. King, *The British Merchant*, London, 1721, passim.

37 P. Butel, 'France, the Antilles and Europe in the Seventeenth and Eighteenth Centuries: Renewals of Foreign Trade', in J.D. Tracy (ed.) *The Rise of the Merchant Empires*, Cambridge, 1990, 153–173.

Indies trade was not only 'a very beneficial Branch of British Commerce, but the very being of our Colonies absolutely depending on it; for if the Spaniards should be allowed to search our Ships … it will be giving up the Sovereignty of those Seas, and in Effect the Sugar Islands'. The depredations were 'the most flagrant Rapine and Villainy that ever was committed by Subjects of one Nation on the another in Amity with them'. Since the reign of Elizabeth, sea power was the infallible means for Britain to deal with threats like this from Spain or the Dutch. Spain was weak and the press hinted darkly that the failure to use this powerful weapon against the Spanish could only be attributed to 'Persons of figure and Character in the World' who were encouraging the Spanish to humiliate and weaken Britain.[38]

Nevertheless, both the British and Spanish government continued to seek a resolution to the problem. Finally, a settlement was agreed at the Convention of the Pardo, signed on 31 December 1738. Spain was to pay £95,000 compensation to merchants who have suffered depredations. The South Sea Company was to pay £68,000, which was owed to Spain in import duties. [39] The date for Spain to pay the compensation was 25 May 1739. The Convention came to Parliament in early March 1739. It was met with a torrent of opposition in both Houses. Petitions and instructions came in from constituencies, urging their members not to vote for the Convention. Besides the threat the Convention posed to the very heart of colonial commerce, comparisons between this craven compromise with Spain and their Elizabethan and Cromwellian forebears highlighted the insult to British honour. The Convention passed the Commons by just 28 votes. This was far more dangerous than the previous major crisis of Walpole's administration, the Excise Bill in April 1733. Then, Walpole had recovered his position simply by dropping the bill. In 1739 this was not an option. If the Convention failed, the ministry would be compelled to act.

As the weeks passed, the fate of the Convention rested on the willingness of the South Sea Company to pay its part of the bargain and the courts on both sides to act with restraint. In the event this did not happen. The British ministry, under intense public pressure since 1738 to show vigour in its negotiations with Spain, stopped the withdrawal of the naval squadron from the Mediterranean.[40] The Spanish court reacted with offended pride.

---

38   For examples of press reaction, see *The Gentleman's Magazine* (1738), 39, 147, 152, 217, 292, 296.

39   The negotiations are best followed in P. Woodfine, *Britannia's Glories*, op. cit.

40   L.G. Wickham Legg, 'Newcastle and he Counter Order to Admiral Haddock, March 1739',

The South Sea Company strenuously denied its liability, insisting that compensation for its losses be adjusted by Spain first. The Company took full advantage of a new seizure of a merchant ship by *gardacostas*, as grounds for refusing to accept the agreement.[41] Philip V, angered by the attitude of the Company and apparent bad faith by the British in seeming to use its naval forces to put Spain under duress, let the date for payment of the compensation pass without action. When 25 May passed without payment, there were immediately calls in Parliament for action. Walpole still hesitated, but others in the Cabinet now agreed that action must be taken.[42] Eventually, the ministry agreed that a reinforcement of ships would be sent to the West Indies. At home the fleet would be mobilised under the command of the Admiral of the Fleet, Sir John Norris. To man the fleet there was an immediate embargo, preventing the sailing of merchant ships until the navy was manned. Regiments were augmented. Governors in the Americas were authorised to issue letters of marque and reprisal, permitting merchants to fit out private warships to capture Spanish vessels.[43] On 8 June orders were sent out to the commanders of British squadrons in the West Indies and the Mediterranean to commit hostilities against Spain.[44] War had not yet been declared, but the Duke of Newcastle, ordered the British ambassador in Spain, Sir Benjamin Keene, not to enter into any more negotiations. The King was now committed to action and it was time for Keene to prepare to come home.[45]

The chance for peace was rapidly slipping away. Sir Robert Walpole, who remained anxious about the uncertainty of war, was an increasingly isolated figure. Dispirited and fractious since the death of his second wife

English Historical Review, xlvi (1931), 272–274.

41 E.G. Hildner, 'The Role of the South Sea Company in the Diplomacy Leading to the War of Jenkins' Ear, 1729–1739', *Hispanic American Historical Review*, xviii (1938), 322–341. For the role of the South Sea Company in the broader Anglo-Spanish trade dispute, see V.L. Brown, 'The South Sea Company and Contraband Trade', *American Historical Review*, xxxi (1925–6), 662–678; V.L. Brown, 'Contraband Trade: A Factor in the Decline of Spain's Empire in America', *Hispanic American Historical Review*, viii (1928), 178–189; A.S. Aiton, 'The Asiento Treaty', op. cit.; G.H. Nelson, 'Contraband Trade', op. cit.

42 B(ritish) L(ibrary), Add. Ms., 32982, f. 64, Hardwicke to Newcastle, 1 June 1739.

43 TNA, SP42/22, f. 487, Proclamation to encourage seamen, 15 June 1739; SP42/69, Instructions to Commodore Brown, 15 June 1739; CO137/56, Newcastle to Trelawney, 15 June 1739; BL, Add Ms 32692, f.75, Privy Council to Newcastle, 15 June 1739.

44 TNA, PRO, SP42/22, Newcastle to the Admiralty, 8 June 1739.

45 BL, Add. Ms, 32801, f. 71, Newcastle to Keene, 14 June 1739.

in March 1738, and at odds with the Pelhams, he was losing his authority in the ministry and with it his ability to manage the Commons. The arguments for war, based on economic necessity, the intransigence of Spain and a belief in the overwhelming effectiveness of British naval power were, by the summer of 1739, unanswerable. A key element in Walpole's argument for peace was the doubtful outcome of any war.[46] He argued that even if the trade to America were secured by war, which could not be guaranteed, the trade to Old Spain and the Mediterranean would certainly be placed in great danger. However, this argument collapsed as the public and decision makers convinced themselves that naval power would defend British interests and compel Spain to make a rapid peace.

Another factor that had played an important part in British policy since 1714 and which seems to have faded at this time was the fear of a Jacobite rebellion. Although the last armed Jacobite rising had been crushed in 1715 Walpole was obsessed that Jacobitism was only dormant, waiting for the opportunity to raise its head again. Any hostile power could use the Jacobites to destabilise the Hanoverian monarchy. The Spanish had tried to stimulate a rising in 1719 by a landing in Scotland. Preventing foreign powers aiding the Jacobites was an important objective of foreign policy throughout the period from 1688 to 1746. A great deal of effort was put into gathering intelligence of known Jacobites and their sympathisers in foreign courts.[47] Inevitably, war aroused fears of Spain encouraging a Jacobite rising. In the past the Jacobite spectre had served Walpole well, but during the months leading to war it did not feature as a strong argument against the conflict.[48] In part this owed to the complex make-up of the intense and organised campaign against Walpole. Led by patriot Whigs, it was based on the maxim that the country needed true patriot Whiggery not Popery and Jacobitism, yet it relied on support from Tories, whom Walpole would never allow to shake off the taint of Jacobitism. Why Walpole and the Old Corps did not use the fear of Jacobitism, or attempt to brand the whole opposition as Jaco-

---

46 For example, see the speeches attributed to him in the debates on the bill for securing trade to America (5 and 12 May 1738) in W. Cobbett, *Parliamentary History*, x (1737–1739), 816, 835.

47 P.S. Fritz, 'The Anti-Jacobite Intelligence System of the English Ministers, 1715–1745', *Historical Journal*, xvi (1973), 265–289; P. Monod, *Jacobitism and the English People*, Cambridge, 1989.

48 G.V. Bennett, 'Jacobitism and the Rise of Walpole, in N. McKendrick (ed.) *Historical Perspectives: Studies in English Thought and Society*, London, 1974, 70–92.

bite, is unclear, but it was not a strong card to play in the light of the rhetoric and assumption of overwhelming naval power. While British naval power dominated the waters of Europe, no foreign power could provide effective aid to rebels.

This dominant faith in naval power was fundamental to the argument for war. Mid-eighteenth-century Britain was not a society rich in information.[49] Political debate tended to revolve around general principles rather than detailed analyses of situations. The role of ideology in the public political arena was, therefore, important. It provided certainties that could be easily expressed and understood in different media such as debate, journalism, theatre, street plays and graphic prints.[50] The debates from early in 1738 provide a good illustration of this. The first significant debate took place on 3 March 1738 on the Spanish depredations. The occasion was the presentation of petitions to the House by merchants, owners and masters of some ships that had been seized by Spanish gardacostas in 1728 and 1729. The opposition moved that it was impossible to discuss the cases or advise the King without access to the papers exchanged by British and Spanish ministers. The ministers resisted this, pointing out that Spain would view the disclosures as a step towards war and would not trust the confidentiality of further exchanges with ministers. Without the detailed information debates depended upon rhetorical dexterity, exploiting generally held assumptions. Walpole argued that the true interest of Spain dictated an eventual accommodation with Britain by quoting a supposed Spanish proverb 'Peace with England and war with the world besides'.[51] The opposition were forced to rely on equally general propositions, such as the belief that war would be best avoided by acting vigorously to convince Spain that the British were serious. The ministry could counter that such measures would only convince Spain and the rest of Europe that Britain meant to declare war, thus bringing war and the general hostility of Europe a step closer.[52] The debate slid from a focus on the petitions to the possibility that debate would, in itself, lead to war.

Likewise, debate about the conduct of a war was informed by general-

---

49 For an overview of intelligence in this period, see, J. Black, 'British Intelligence in the Mid-Eighteenth Century Crisis', *Intelligence and National Security*, ii (1987), 209–229.

50 See for example E.L. Avery and A.H. Scouton, 'The Opposition to Sir Robert Walpole, 1737–1739', *English Historical Review*, lxxxiii (1968), 331–336.

51 Cobbett, *Parliamentary History*, op. cit., x (1737–1739), 585.

52 Ibid., see particularly the speeches of William Windham (613–622). For a rebuttal of Windham's theme, see Walpole's speech on 12 May (828–835).

ised beliefs. A leading member of the opposition Whigs, William Pulteney, opening the debate on a bill for securing the trade to America, argued that, 'In the event of war, I believe, no gentleman doubts that it must in our part be a sea war.'[53] No further discussion on the principle was required as it was, indeed, axiomatic to the House. Rather, the case had to be made that Britain would win a sea war; that war would be effective and that Spain could not counter-balance British success by diplomatic or military action elsewhere. Over 18 months, the opposition made this case with great success.

They were able to do this by blending deeply-held assumptions about the navy with the experience of the last 50 years. The navy had a powerful historical resonance as the force that defended the kingdom against the threat of invasion and preserved its political liberties. By the 1730s, the feats of the Elizabethan and Cromwellian navies were common currency in the political debate.[54] The more recent experience of the Nine Years War and the War of Spanish Succession confirmed confidence in the effectiveness of British naval power. The prestige of the Royal Navy and expectations of its success fuelled a growing pressure for war as addresses and memorials were sent from the cities of London, Lancaster, Liverpool, Bristol, Glasgow and Edinburgh.[55]

By 1737 there appeared to be substantial evidence that Spain was vulnerable to British naval power. This capped the basic assumptions underpinning the belligerent British attitude – that Spain was at fault; that Britain could win a war at sea; that the war would be effective; that Spain knew this was case and, finally, merely threatening war would force her to negotiate seriously. During the debate on the merchants' petitions on 3 March 1738 all these arguments were rehearsed. Walpole emphasised the unpredictability of the outcome of a war, but never challenged those assumptions. Just over three weeks later, on 30 March, as the petitions went before a committee of the Whole House, the opposition put forward a much more aggressive case against Spanish infringements of treaties dating back to 1670, demanding that a squadron should be sent to the West Indies to halt the depredations. The opposition could argue that such action would be effective either as a deterrent to Spain or in combating the *gardacostas*. Walpole was thrown back on claiming such action would inevitably cause open war leading to the destruction of one

---

53   Ibid., 812.

54   Ibid., 680, William Pulteney, 30 March 1738. See also C. Gerrard, *The Patriot Opposition to Walpole*, Oxford, 1994.

55   Wilson, *The Sense of the People*, op. cit., 141.

or other nation. Behind this claim was the implicit notion that whoever won, France would be the ultimate beneficiary.[56]

Walpole's most powerful argument for peace was that successful action would bring down the hostility of other nations upon Britain. During the War of Polish Succession Walpole had successfully maintained British neutrality. However, the apparent success of France in this war had caused great concern. For those hostile to Walpole, this neutrality was evidence that he had betrayed his country. Even those more disinterested could not ignore the fact that not only had Walpole lost the, perhaps unnatural, alliance with France which existed between 1716 and 1731, but had also forfeited the support of the traditional ally Austria. The two Bourbon monarchies, Spain and France had come together in alliance in 1733, and Britain appeared dangerously isolated. Britain had a defensive treaty with the United Provinces dating back to 1678, but this could not be relied upon if Britain attacked Spain. The wealth of the Spanish Indies was a prize many nations coveted and the Utrecht settlement was largely based on an acceptable division of the Spanish lands, riches and opportunities. If British action appeared to upset this balance there was no telling what might happen.

While Walpole was open to accusations of failing to conduct foreign policy effectively over the previous 10 years, he was, in the current situation regarding Spain, in a strong position, which was difficult for the opposition to counter. During the debate on the depredations on 3 March 1738, Walpole had opposed the call for papers related to the negotiations partly on the grounds that it would cause a breach with Spain and 'our coming to an immediate rupture with Spain might unite several powers against us, and in that case, surely, it would be madness in us to call for any papers, or to make any step which might hasten that rupture'.[57] Walpole returned to the point on 12 May claiming that war in which private property was handed to the captors would not only put the interests of British merchants at risk, but would make half of Europe our enemies or cold friends.[58] It was an argument that was never effectively countered, but in the welter of other arguments, the threat of isolation or even active hostility from other powers, was dismissed. The maritime war could be won, would be effective and the other powers of Europe would have to accept it.

---

56   Cobbett, *Parliamentary History*, op. cit., x (1737–1739), 561–729.

57   Ibid., 587.

58   Ibid., 830.

Necessity, Urgency and Honour

By the spring of 1739 the arguments were very finely balanced. The ministry's position, based on the need to preserve other branches of trade and the impact war might have on the other powers of Europe, had not been effectively countered by the opposition, but the ministry had not overcome the basic assumptions of the opposition case that a maritime war was necessary and likely to be effective.

All negotiations have their own unique dynamic, determined by the particular situation of the negotiators. The death of Queen Caroline, the death of Walpole's wife, the mental instability of Philip V all played their parts. The performance of diplomats and politicians was critical. Mistakes were made and dangerous intransigence was demonstrated by both sides, ultimately culminating in the failure of the Convention. The opposition in Parliament or in the country at large did not dictate the course of events. However, what it did was to undermine the case for peace. There was no single event, upon which the opposition latched, that destroyed the negotiations. Jenkins' Ear played a very small part indeed.[59] The merchant petitions of 1737 and 1738 were the occasions for the debates rather direct stimuli for decisive shifts in policy. However, during the course of these debates the ministry could not deploy decisive arguments against the opposition. The ministry was forced to agree with all the principal premises put forward by the opposition. Spanish behaviour was intolerable. The American trade was vital. A maritime war against Spain could be won and would be effective. Its own counter argument of the uncertainty of war, and that hostilities would certainly bring on a full scale war, were soundly based, but contained two important hostages. First, it appeared to accept that nothing could be done until the last extremity. Second, it seemed to put into French hands the fate of Britain's American trade.[60] At a time when it was agreed that national reputation and economic strength were under threat, neither argument

---

59   The case of Captain Robert Jenkins' Ear was well known to the public. His ship the Rebecca had been plundered and Jenkins supposedly mutilated off Havana in 1731. Once war had broken out the capture of the gardacosta who cut off the ear was reported at least twice, but during the critical months of 1738–1739 the broader arguments of national reputation and power were far more significant. In March 1738 he was summoned to attend the House of Commons, but there is no evidence that he turned up. He captained an East Indiaman to Bombay and died there in 1743. See *New Oxford Dictionary of National Biography*.

60   For an overview of Anglo-French relations, see J. Black, *Natural and Necessary Enemies: Anglo-French Relations in the Eighteenth Century*, Athens, Georgia, 1986, 1–35.

promised any satisfactory settlement of the dispute. A ministry that could not present a coherent justification for policy was unlikely to hold together and, by late May 1739, it did not. The Secretary of State for the Southern Department, the Duke of Newcastle, saw that the arguments were unanswerable and attitudes in both courts would not be changed fast enough to prevent serious electoral problems in 1741. Just before Spain failed to pay the compensation, news arrived of new commercial and defensive treaties between Spain and France in the wake of the engagement of Don Philip with Louise Elizabeth, daughter of Louis XV. It was unlikely that Spain was going to be more tractable in the foreseeable future.[61] The growing closeness of the Bourbon courts made the threat of French intervention more pronounced, but by this time the arguments of urgency and necessity had taken firm root. That war was preferable to a bad peace was an argument employed by the opposition in 1738, but now it was accepted by ministers such as Newcastle, the Duke of Grafton (Lord Chamberlain) and the First Lord of the Admiralty, Sir Charles Wager.[62] Wager, the professional naval advisor to the King and council, was convinced that only vigorous action would now resolve the dispute with Spain and that Britain was better placed than ever before to bring about a just and quick peace.[63]

On the evening of 1 June 1739 Walpole attended a meeting with the Lord Chancellor, the Baron Hardwicke. Hardwicke described him as melancholic, arising as he thought 'from a fixed opinion in many and from a suspicion in some of his friends, that nothing would be done against Spain, that this might be discerned from the differences in our Division upon matters relative to that great affair'.[64] Walpole conceded that Spain had broken the Convention, Britain could act in good faith and the action had to start now. Nothing could be worse than Spain suddenly consenting to pay the £95,000 as it would be attended with accusations of a private treaty. The Cabinet met on the 3 June to agree measures.[65] Notice was sent to the merchants in Spain

---

61   P. Vaucher, *Robert Walpole et la Politique de Fleury (1731–1742)*, Paris, 1924, 292–293.

62   BL, Add Ms 32692 (Newcastle Papers), f. 97, Grafton to Newcastle, 1 July 1739, Lib of Congress, Vernon-Wager Mss, reel 91, 139–140, Wager to Bladen, 2 Nov. 1737.

63   BL Add 19036, ff. 7–9, Spanish Forces, June 1739.

64   BL, Add Ms32692, f. 64, Hardwicke to Newcastle, 2 June 1739.

65   The Cabinet Council had evolved in the seventeenth century as a smaller, more manageable group of advisors to the monarch than the Privy Council. In the last years of Walpole's administration it had become common for a very small group of trusted ministers and advisors to discuss business and agree policy before submitting them to the Cabinet. These

and an immediate press to man the warship was ordered. Admiral Haddock in the Mediterranean and Commodore Charles Brown in the West Indies were ordered to commit hostilities. Eight regiments in Ireland were ordered to England. Walpole could not bring himself to make these proposals to the Cabinet and it was left to the Duke of Newcastle. They fell short of a formal declaration of war, but there was no doubt that a naval war had begun.

meetings usually took place in the houses of ministers, rather than state buildings. Subsequently, this group has been called an 'inner Cabinet'. See H.W.V. Temperley, 'The Inner and Outer Cabinet and Privy Council, 1679–1783', *English Historical Review*, 27 (1912), 682–699; R.R. Sedgwick, 'The Inner Cabinet from 1739 to 1741', *English Historical Review*, 34 (1919), 290–302.

2

Mobilisation and the Outbreak of War, June–October 1739

Mobilisation and Diplomacy

On the evening of 3 June, the die had been cast and Britain was committed to hostilities with Spain. Over the following days the orders went out from the secretaries of state's offices for preparations to begin. Bringing the fleet up to operational standard was not an easy process in the eighteenth century. One of the vital resources for mobilising the fleet was manpower. The navy drew its seamen from the maritime communities of the kingdom as and when it needed them. However, in early summer, with maritime commerce at its annual peak of activity, there were few unemployed seamen lingering ashore. A further problem was that while the wages of seamen in the Royal Navy were fixed, those in merchant service fluctuated with the market conditions. Generally, merchant wages were higher than those in the navy, and the sudden additional demand for seamen from the Royal Navy, would, inevitably, place an upward pressure on wage rates, further widening the pay gap between the navy and the merchants. This was well understood and the state possessed legal instruments of coercion and encouragement to meet such emergencies as this. On the 5 June the Admiralty issued press warrants to naval officers to begin manning the fleet. Shortly afterwards, on the 11 June, orders were sent to all ships' masters prohibiting them from releasing men from the service until further notice.[1] On the 15 June a proclamation was issued providing an additional bounty to encourage seamen to enlist freely in the navy.[2] On the following day, the Privy Council approved an Admiralty request for an embargo on all shipping leaving British ports

---

1   TNA Adm3/43 (quoted in Baugh), 8 and 11 June.
2   TNA, SP42/22, f. 487, Proclamation, 15 June 1739.

until the fleet was manned.[3] The rapid response of the government in taking these measures was not just a recognition of the time it would take, but also an attempt to make the most of popular support for the war before the economic effects of an embargo began to bite on the merchant community, further destabilising the political situation.

While the basic logistical orders were being sent out, the ministry had to address the emergent diplomatic situation. Walpole had lost the political battle against the war, but his main argument – the impact it would have on the wider diplomatic position – had not been countered or discredited. The ministry now had to live with a very ambiguous diplomatic situation as the war began to take shape. Britain's relations with Spain had become much clearer. On 14 June, Newcastle wrote to the envoy extraordinary in Madrid, Benjamin Keene, that 'as all sort of correspondence will probably be soon at an end between the two crowns, Mr Castries and you may be preparing your affairs to return home'.[4] However, he was not to return until ordered. In the meantime he was to report on Spanish naval strength, on their army and on any rumours about plans to invade Britain. Newcastle had received rumours from Galicia that an army of 7,000 troops on was aboard transports. Keene was to discover their purpose and advise on whether it was best to attack Spain in Europe or the West Indies.[5] Within a month Keene made an impressive report. Outside the Spanish Court, Keene reported that opinion was pessimistic about the possibility of French intervention in their favour. The Spanish army numbered 70,000, supported by an unspecified number of militia. The 7,000 in Galicia were to reinforce the defence of that region. Cadiz was solidly defended, but the main fear of the Spanish court was for Majorca and they were preparing six battalions to be sent to that island. The Spanish navy would not venture out unless it was certain that it would not meet superior numbers of British ships. He concluded 'In regard therefore to Europe my lord I am sorry to say that, according to my poor lights, there is no

---

3   Acts of the Privy Council, p. 630, 16 June 1739. In order not to interfere with other preparations for getting the fleet to sea, ships in the service of the Victualling Board, the Ordnance Board and the Customs Service were excluded from this embargo.

4   BL, Add Ms 32801, f. 67, Newcastle to Keene, 14' June 1739. Abraham Castries was the consul at Madrid and joint plenipotentiary with Keene negotiating the Convention of the Prado.

5   Ibid., f. 71, Newcastle to Keene, 14 June 1739, 'Most Private'.

great probability of our striking home a blow as every good subject of His Majesty must long after … America, therefore, my lord, is where we can do them much and important damage.' Keene believed the Spanish were unimpressed by British threats of arming privateers, but they feared for the *Flota*, which was due to leave Havana on 10 August, 'without which succours this country must linger and perish'.[6] On 3 August Keene reported growing confidence in the Spanish Admiralty. Expectations of French support were beginning to rise and they now wanted to attack Admiral Haddock's squadron in the Mediterranean. Their own ships were not well equipped. They had six line of battle ships at Ferrol in Galicia and 12 poorly supplied ships of the line in Cadiz. However, they calculated that Haddock had only six large and four small ships with him, which was broadly correct.[7]

From Britain's perspective, one of the most important courts to manage was that of Portugal. Portugal was one of Britain's oldest allies, and had played an important part in British calculations ever since British fleets began long-term operations in the Mediterranean during the 1670s.[8] Lisbon was an important port for both merchant and naval shipping to and from the Mediterranean. Lisbon enabled the British to run short-leg convoy and packet services to the Mediterranean, thus getting ships back on station more quickly than if the outward bound service had run as far as Gibraltar or Port Mahon. Even letters to the commander-in-chief Mediterranean would change vessel at Lisbon.[9] However, in a war with Spain, Portugal was in immediate danger of invasion. French overtures in recent months also complicated any calculation the ministry made about the level of Portuguese support.[10] Newcastle ordered the envoy extraordinary at Lisbon, James O'Hara, Baron Tyrawly, to explain the reasons for the military preparations to King Joa V and encourage him to accept a defensive alliance. The Portuguese were well aware of the significance of British sea-power in their diplomatic calculations. In 1735 a British

6   Ibid., f. 117, Keene to Newcastle, 14 July 1739.

7   Ibid., f. 156, Keene to Newcastle, 3 August 1739. This was not officially a *Flota*, but it was referred to as such by the British.

8   J.S. Corbett, *England in the Mediterranean: A Study of the Rise and Influence of British Power within the Straits, 1603–1713*, 2 vols, London, 1904, vol. ii, 143–315.

9   TNA, SP89/40, f. 38, Newcastle to Tyrawly, 8 June 1739.

10   TNA, SP89/40, f. 35, Tyrawly to Newcastle, 23 May 1739; f. 48, Tyrawley to Newcastle, 11 July 1739.

squadron had been instrumental in defusing a Spanish–Portuguese crisis. Since then, disputes between Portugal and Spain over the boundaries of their colonies around the River Plate in South America remained tense, and Newcastle believed that an offer of British naval support to break the continuing Spanish blockade of San Sacramento would be attractive to the Portuguese.[11] Throughout the summer Tyrawly coaxed the Portuguese towards a convention but could not obtain more than a strict neutrality based on the May 1703 treaty, which permitted British ships to use the Tagus.[12]

The other ally whose support was important was the Dutch. Since 1678 the British and Dutch had been tied by a defensive alliance. However, a war with Spain posed problems. While they had a mutual interest in containing French ambitions in Flanders, Anglo-Dutch relations were cool. The British and Dutch were intense commercial rivals. The Dutch were as concerned about the Spanish *gardacostas* as the British, but had found a satisfactory *modus vivendi*. War threatened to upset the fragile balance of interests in the Americas. There was also a lingering resentment among the Dutch stemming from unilateral British negotiations at the end of the War of Spanish Succession.[13] Since 1734 the British ambassador to the Hague was Sir Robert Walpole's brother, Horatio. However, during the growing crisis with Spain he was often absent supporting his brother in domestic political clashes, and affairs in the United Provinces were handled by his secretary, Robert Trevor. Trevor signalled Dutch concern at the growing crisis in May, but Horatio's hurried return at the end of June could do nothing to convert the Dutch to support. The Dutch were completely opposed to the war and were determined to remain resolutely neutral.[14]

Walpole had been broadly right. Rather than welcoming the British attempts to end Spanish interference with legitimate trade, other powers

---

11   Ibid., f. 42, Newcastle to Tyrawly, 21 June 1739.

12   Ibid., f. 127, Tyrawly to Newcastle, 16 January 1739/40. The progress of this negotiation during the year can be followed in detail in this volume of papers.

13   For a narrative of the Anglo-Dutch aspect of those negotiations, see R. Geikie and I.A. Montgomery, *The Dutch Barrier, 1705–1719*, Cambridge, 1930. For a wider view of this diplomatic relationship, see H. Dunthorne, *The Maritime Powers, 1721–1740: A Study of Anglo-Dutch Relations in the Age of Walpole*, New York, 1986.

14   BL, Add Ms 32801, f.8, Trevor to Newcastle, 20 May 1739; TNA, SP 78/221, 115–8, Newcastle to Waldegrave, 13 Aug. 1739 o.s. See also Dunthorne, *The Maritime Powers*, op. cit., 310–318.

were hostile. Neither of Britain's potential allies supported her in the enterprise. However, far more important was the attitude of Britain's major adversary France. France was the great power of Western Europe. Behind British fears for their trade in the Americas lay a fear of French commerce expanding to match her political ambitions. Even as a neutral power, France could have a major impact on events. If France joined Spain in the war, then the results could be catastrophic. France, under the guiding hand of the elderly Cardinal Fleury, had no wish for war. The War of Polish Succession had only just ended without much tangible gain for France. Conversely, France would not permit Britain to adjust the balance of power in the Americas. Fleury was a masterful diplomat, who had shown during the previous 10 years that he was more than a match for the British ministry. As the Anglo-French alliance, which formed the basis of stability in Western Europe since 1716, began to crumble in the late 1720s, Fleury adroitly repositioned French alliances, leaving Britain without firm allies in Europe. However, the British had one important advantage in that since 1734 they had a spy in the French diplomatic service, François de Bussy, a clerk in the Ministry of Foreign Affairs. Bussy had been recruited in 1734 by the British ambassador at Versailles, the Earl of Waldegrave. Waldegrave was irritated by Bussy's constant demands for more money, but quickly came to realise that Bussy was a reliable, well informed and forthcoming informant.[15] By 1739 Bussy was vital in Waldegrave's attempts to discover Fleury's intentions.

On 7 June Newcastle wrote to Waldegrave warning him that negotiations with Spain had failed and that hostilities were being prepared. He instructed Waldegrave find out from Bussy what Fleury's intentions might now be. He was to reassure Fleury, but, at the same time, to organise a spy network to watch the French ports and report on French recruiting of troops in Ireland. Keene had reported from Madrid that a new Family Compact between France and Spain was to be concluded following the marriage agreement between the two branches of the family. Waldegrave was ordered to report anything he heard about this and, of course, the perennial issue of Jacobites.[16] Bussy proved frustratingly vague. Waldegrave did his best to gather his own intelligence, but he was never able to get to the bottom of Fleury's intentions. Throughout June and July Waldegrave reported that Fleury would keep France neutral in the coming conflict,

---

15 E. Cruickshanks, '101 Secret Agent', *History Today*, April (1969), 273–276; Vaucher, *Robert Walpole*, op. cit.

16 TNA SP78/220 (State Papers – France), f. 228, Newcastle to Waldegrave, 7 June 1739.

but hinted at allowing French privateers to go out under Spanish colours.[17] Fleury skilfully punctuated his claim to desire neutrality with threats. The seizure of a French merchant ship the *Viege de Grace*, he claimed, would give the pro-war faction in France more vigour.[18] Fleury's preference for neutrality was founded on a belief that there would be no war and that Britain would not actually take action against Spain. The treasure ships reported at Havana were expected back in Europe shortly and he claimed that as two thirds of the cargo was French owned he did not expect the British to interfere in it. Waldegrave knew that the ships would be seized and did not hide this from Fleury. The danger of Fleury basing his discussions with Waldegrave on erroneous assumptions, deliberately or not, was not lost on the ministry in London.[19]

Up until mid-July intelligence reports Waldegrave gathered from French ports reinforced the impression that Fleury was not prepared for war. There was little activity in the naval arsenals and, as in Britain at this time of year, about two-thirds of the trained naval crews were away on merchant voyages.[20] Keene's reports that the French ambassador in Madrid had told Spain that France would not assist in a war was further comforting news. This outlook began to change in the latter part of July. Keene reported that the French ambassador in Madrid had claimed that France would join Spain. A few days later Waldegrave reported that 'there seems to be a perfect arrangement made between this court and the Court of Madrid'. Fleury denied it, but a day later he was hinting that an alliance with Spain had been concluded.[21] A week later, Fleury was again denying the claims of the French ambassador at Madrid and claiming that a war would be ruinously expensive, but Waldegrave was by now unconvinced. On 3 August when the King finally agreed to the recall of Keene from Madrid, Newcastle also believed that war with France

---

17   Ibid., f. 248, Waldegrave to Newcastle, 26 June 1739; f. 271, Waldegrave to Newcastle, 3 July 1739.

18   Ibid., ff. 38–43, Waldegrave to Newcastle, 1 August 1739 n.s.

19   Ibid., ff. 276–8, Newcastle to Waldegrave, 28 June 1739 o.s.; SP 78/221(State Papers – France), ff. 9–12, Waldegrave to Newcastle, 22 July 1739 ff. 49–63, Newcastle to Waldegrave, 27 July 1739 o.s. especially f. 52.

20   TNA, SP 78/221 (State Papers – France), ff. 26–27, Waldegrave to Newcastle, 28 July 1739.

21   BL, Add Ms 32801 (Newcastle Papers- Diplomatic), f. 170, Waldegrave to Newcastle, 8 August 1739 n.s.; SP 78/221 (State Papers – France), ff. 64–67, Waldegrave to Newcastle, 9 Aug. 1739. n.s.

could be very close and ordered Waldegrave to step up his spy network, particularly on the French ports.[22]

While the British ministry were bracing themselves for war with Spain and France, Fleury was actually trying to prevent a war. His plan was to intimidate Britain by threatening action, but without committing himself to Spain, whose King, he feared, wanted war.[23] In London the impact of this shifting policy in France was to induce some hesitancy within the ministry, but no let up in the preparations. The seizure of the *Vierge de Grace* was the occasion for more aggressive French representations in London. Much more trouble could be expected if the navy managed to capture the Spanish ships heading back from Buenos Aires, laden with goods, many of which were French owned. On 26 July the inner group of ministers met at Walpole's house to consider what should be done about French goods on the Buenos Aires ships.[24] It was agreed that Newcastle should reassure Fleury that French goods would be returned on the payment of whatever customs duties they would have paid to the Spanish.[25]

By early August it was accepted that France would probably intervene. This did not prevent the King agreeing, on 3 August, to the declaration of war on Spain, but the atmosphere was clearly changing. On the next day, Hardwicke urged a reconsideration and delay at least until Count de Cambis, the new French envoy, arrived in London.[26] The extent in the change was evident on the 9 and 10 August. On those days Newcastle had two long meetings with George II concerning the war. He reported to Hardwicke that 'we take it for granted that France will join with Spain and that we think be attacked at home'. The King's attention was now focusing on the possibility of a Franco-Spanish invasion of Britain. This was a very different scenario from that of late May when the threat to Britain seemed minimal. Now, preventing France from entering the war became a matter of importance and dispute. Walpole and Harrington urged that Haddock be ordered to give up the blockade of Cadiz and sent back into the Mediterranean. This would allow

---

22   BL, Add Ms 32801 (Newcastle Papers – Diplomatic), ff. 80–83, Waldegrave to Newcastle, 15 August 1739 n.s.; f. 75, Newcastle to Waldegrave, 3 August 1739 o.s.

23   Vaucher, *Robert Walpole*, op. cit., 294–295.

24   BL, Add Ms 33004 (Newcastle Papers), f. At Walpole's 26 July 1739.

25   BL, Add Ms 32801 (Newcastle Papers – Diplomatic), f. 52, Newcastle to Waldegrave, 27 July 1739 o.s.

26   BL, Add Ms 32692 (Newcastle Papers), f. 204, Hardwicke to Newcastle, 4 August 1739.

the *Flota* to get in and the French merchants investments would be secure.[27] This was not acceptable to Newcastle as he did not believe Fleury would, in any case, remain neutral. The Brest and Toulon fleets were now reportedly fitting out.[28] On 13 August Hardwicke had an interview with the King to consider action against Spain in the light of French threats. They agreed that any 'revenge' or 'vindictive justice' that Britain carried out against Spain was best done in the West Indies, where direct French interests were not immediately threatened.[29] Tension continued to be high, but on 16 August news arrived from Paris that the Buenos Aires ships had got safely into Santander, on the Northern coast of Spain which temporarily calmed the situation.[30] At the end of August news arrived that Cambis would arrive shortly in Britain to demand an audience with the King and to present French grievances. For Fleury it was another twist in his threat and retreat strategy.[31] It was interpreted differently in London. Newcastle appears to have begun to see the pattern emerging. He wrote to Hardwicke on 26 August that Cambis' representations 'cannot in anyone's opinion be hearkened to. I take it both France and Spain wish for an accommodation but that it must be upon their terms, which will be destruction to us'. 'The Cardinal fears his joining with Spain will produce a general war and that makes them so averse to it but if we don't accept what Cambis has to propose it looks as if the Cardinal would at last take part against us'. In Newcastle's opinion the crisis had come. 'Let us put our Fleets upon action some where, or all will be called a farce and we shall be said to have delayed Vernon that the Azogues might escape'.[32] This time Hardwicke agreed. Perhaps influenced by a visit to the fleet at Portsmouth, he wrote to Newcastle that the fleet must do something, 'you know

---

27   BL, Add Ms 35406 (Hardwicke Papers), f. 136, Newcastle to Hardwicke, 11 August 1739.

28   Ibid., f. 138, Newcastle to Hardwicke, 12 August 1739.

29   BL, Add Ms, 32692 (Newcastle Papers), f. 235, Hardwicke to Newcastle, 13 August 1739.

30   TNA, SP78/221 (State Papers – France), ff. 104–110, Waldegrave to Newcastle, 20 August 1739 n.s.

31   Vaucher, *Robert Walpole*, op. cit., 295.

32   BL, Add Ms, 35406, (Hardwicke Papers), f. 140, Newcastle to Hardwicke, 26 August 1739. *Azogues* were naval vessels detailed to take mercury to Mexico for the refining of silver ore. They returned with bullion. The British correspondence relating to the Buenos Aires ships refers to them as *azogues*, but it is more likely that the were *registros*, ships licensed to travel to the ports like Buenos Aires, which were distant from the treasure fleets' routes.

my notion is in the West Indies and as they have no winter snow, the season of the year makes that the more proper'.[33]

Cambis' memorial on the seizure of French vessels was considered on 3 September. The envoy was reassured that French ships would not be stopped and justice was promised for those made prizes. The time had come to call Fleury's bluff – either he would use the question of an insult to French honour to join Spain or his fear of sparking a general war would force him to back off.[34] Fleury continued his old tactics. He denied the intention to join Spain, but used the threat to warn the Dutch that if they joined the British France would be forced to join Spain.[35] To an extent the power of the French threat had been broken. Fleury was going to hang back from the brink. On 29 September The ministry were assured by the First Lord of the Admiralty, Sir Charles Wager, that the 25 ships of 60 guns or more that were in good repair at home were more than adequate in the short term to deal with both Spain and France.[36] The plans that had been laid over the summer could now be put into action.

Mobilisation: The Fleet in Peacetime

On 6 June, Admiral Sir John Norris was appointed commander-in-chief of the Fleet.[37] Orders were sent to make all preparations to commit hostilities against Spain. Particular care must be taken to defend Britain's most vulnerable positions – the infant colony of Georgia and South Carolina, which abutted Spanish Florida.[38] This was going to be a naval war. The state of the fleet and the ability of the administration to bring the navy quickly into effective service were vital. On paper the navy was immensely powerful.[39]

Since 1677 British warships had been 'rated' according to their establishment of guns. It was a convenient way of classifying both resource needs and

---

33   BL, Add Ms 32692 (Newcastle Papers), f. 256, Hardwicke to Newcastle, 26 August 1739.

34   TNA, SP 78/221 (State Papers – France), f. 181, Newcastle to Waldegrave, 4 September 1739.

35   Ibid., f. 200, Waldegrave to Newcastle, 16 October 1739.

36   BL, Add Ms, 28132 (Journal of Sir John Norris), f. 29 September 1739.

37   BL, Add Ms 28132, f. 6 June 1739.

38   TNA, SP44/225, f. 4, Newcastle to the Admiralty, 8 June 1739.

39   This table is taken from TNA, Adm8/23.

the purpose of the ship. Over time the number of guns, their weight, the dimensions of the ships altered in response to design or financial imperatives, but by 1719 both guns and ship dimensions had been broadly settled in the 'establishments'.[40] Minor changes and some experimentation took place in the decades following 1714, but generally, the ship design and armament reflected the accumulated wisdom as it stood at the end of the War of Spanish Succession.

The first and second rates were the large three-decked warships carrying between 90 and 100 guns, intended as the floating fortresses of the line of battle. These ships were considered too large and expensive to send on cruising operations. They acted as squadron flagships, but as there had been no major battle at sea since 1718 they were generally kept in reserve for major fleet action in home waters. In 1739 they were mostly 'in ordinary', stripped down and kept water-tight at Chatham and Portsmouth. The third rates consisted of the largest two-deck warships. The 80s and 70s were the backbone of the fleet. Large enough to stand in the line, they were also reasonably effective cruisers. The fourth rates consisted of 60- and 50-gun ships. The 60s like the third rates could stand in the line of battle effectively, but by 1739 the role of the 50 was becoming difficult to determine. The establishments dictated the size of the guns on each rate of ship, in order to blend the sailing qualities of the ship with the weight of the ordnance. This meant that although the 50 carried only 10 fewer guns than the 60, she threw only about 72 per cent of the weight of metal in a broadside, which was crucial in the quick-fire close-range engagements of the line. During the 1720s and 1730s the 50 was being up-gunned or replaced by the 60, but by 1739 the significant firepower difference remained. While formally the 50 remained a line of battle ship until 1756, it was generally used as a powerful cruiser.[41] The Fifth rate 40-gun ship had evolved at the beginning of the century as a purpose-built, two-deck cruiser, powerful enough to take on French privateers and frigates. The smallest rated ship, the Sixth rate 20-gun,

---

40 For details of this evolution, see Lavery, *The Ship of the Line*, op. cit.

41 For the development of the 50, see R. Winfield, *The 50-Gun Ship*, London, 1997. Although they could form part of the line in a squadron, contemporary calculations for line of battle often excluded them. For this reason, in this work, calculations of ship numbers or strength have not included 50s. The 50 has been classified as a 'cruiser' rather than a ship of the 'line'. A new establishment of guns in 1733 up-gunned the main gun deck battery of the 50 from 18 lb to 24 lb cannon. This would have closed the gap with the 60, but it was not implemented until a revised ship design became available after 1745.

was the workhorse small station and reconnaissance ship. Like the 50s, these ships were upgunned as a result of the war.[42] The smallest ships on the navy's list ranged from the six royal yachts usually moored in the Thames, to sloops on various stations and to three-bomb ketches usually moored at Woolwich, near the Board of Ordnance depot (Table 2.1).

The Royal Navy was by far the largest in the world, but not all ships were available for service. Some vessels were awaiting rebuilding. The *Royal Anne* (100) had been broken up at Chatham in 1727 and was waiting a rebuilding that never happened. The *Prince* (90), also at Chatham was never rebuilt. Others, like the *Northumberland* (70) and *Devonshire* (80), both at Woolwich, were broken up or hulked, rather than rebuilt. Those that were rebuilt could be out of service for years. The *Monmouth* (70) and *Revenge* (70) at Deptford would take over two years to complete. Rather more fortunate was the *Prince Frederick* (70), which had been on the slip at Deptford since October 1736 and was being constructed substantially from the timbers of the *Expedition* (70). This ship would be ready by the end of the winter. Others were in 'great repair'. This involved the substantial dismantling of the ship and its rebuild. The *Cornwall* (80) at Chatham would not be ready until the middle of 1741. Ships on the slips when hostilities began had to be completed. Two 50s, the *Dartmouth* at Woolwich and the *Woolwich* at Deptford, had been ordered in 1736, but were not completed until the spring of 1741.

In the summer of 1739 the largest single force on station was Admiral Haddock's command in the Mediterranean. With his flag on the *Somerset* (80), another 80, three 70s, three 60s, two 50s, a 40, and five 20s, he had a force that balanced concentrated firepower with cruising capability. Haddock certainly needed such a force. It would be in these waters that the Spanish threat to British trade would be the most immediate and consistent. Haddock's responsibilities ran from Gibraltar to the Levant, from Barbary to Italy. He had Gibraltar and Port Mahon to protect against sorties by the Spanish ships from Cadiz or Cartagena. The French squadron at Toulon also posed a threat which could not entirely be assessed. It was not to be long before the war began to take its toll upon Haddock's health.

In the West Indies, Commodore Charles Brown flew his flag on the *Hampton Court* (70). He had a 60 and a 50 with him, but the majority of

---

42   R. Gardiner (ed.), *The Line of Battle: The Sailing Warship, 1650–1840*, London, 1992, 32. There was gradual up-gunning of these ships to 44s during the course of the war. Likewise, the 20s were up-gunned to 24 and 30 guns during the war.

Table 2.1 Disposition of the Royal Navy, August 1739

Rate	Guns	Crew	Home	Guard	Ord.	Med	W.I.	N.Am	Transit	Total
First	100	850			7					7
Second	90	750			15					15
Third	80	600			11	2				13
Third	70	480		6	14	3	1			24
Fourth	60	400	3	3	18	3	1		1	29
Fourth	50	300	7	1	16	2	1		1	28
Fifth	40	250	1		6	1	3	2	1	19
Sixth	20	130	5		1	5	4	4		19
Others	Various		16		5	2	2	2	2	29
Total			32	10	93	18	12	8	5	181

his command was the smaller 40s and 20s. The *Anglesea* (40) patrolled the Leewards with a 20 and a sloop. The *Roebuck* (40) was at Barbados and a 20, the *Spence*, off the Bahamas. In North America, the *Hector* (40) was the largest station vessel at Virginia, supported by the *Wolf* sloop. Two 20s were stationed in South Carolina, with two more in New York and Boston.

In home waters, the ships in commission were split between the guardships and those on service. The guardships were the line of battleships kept ready for service. Three 70s lay at Chatham, three more at Portsmouth. At Plymouth there were three 60s, and a 50 was at Sheerness. Vessels on service were predominantly smaller for coastal cruising. The *Augusta* (60) headed two 50s at Spithead. The *Jersey* (60) and the *Pembroke* (60) did the same at Plymouth and the Downs, respectively.

From this peace time footing, the fleet moved to war. The speed and effectiveness of this move would depend on a number of factors, the first of which was the royal dockyards and the merchant yards.

Mobilisation: The Dockyards

British naval dockyards were supervised by the Navy Board, which was itself responsible to the Admiralty. They had developed over the preceding two centuries in response to the immediate demands of the navy. They were not just building facilities. They carried out major repairs to the fleet as well as a general maintenance for squadrons using the port.[43] The earliest yards were in the Thames, at Deptford and Woolwich. They had been created to meet the needs of the fleet covering the Thames/Channel area. Deptford had two small dry docks that could take 40s, but nothing larger. The continuous silting of the Thames made further development of the yard problematic. In contrast, Deptford was ideally placed to receive a secure stream of supplies from the prosperous London markets, and had good access to the main pool of maritime labour in the Thames. In 1739 Deptford was still the third largest employer of the six royal yards, but it main function had evolved into fitting out rather than repair and building. Woolwich was about six miles further down the Thames. It did not suffer so much from silting and with its two dry docks it could build and repair

---

43   The following descriptions are largely based on D. Baugh, *British Naval Administration in the Age of Walpole* Princeton, 1965; J. Coad, *The Royal Dockyards, 1690–1815: Architecture and Engineering Works of the Sailing Navy*, Aldershot, 1989; J. Coad, *Historic Architecture of the Royal Navy*, London, 1983.

ships up to 90 guns and was particularly well placed to fit out the bomb vessels from the Board of Ordnance yard nearby.

Chatham, on the Medway, developed to confront the Dutch threat in the seventeenth century. It had been eclipsed by Portsmouth as an operational base as a result of the wars against France. It was seriously affected by river silting, but could still provide maintenance facilities for the majority of the ships of the line in ordinary. With four dry docks it was a major base for repair work. At the mouth of the Medway lies Sheerness, which had been established in 1665 as a more convenient base for ships operating in the North Sea. The two dry docks could take in anything up to a 60. However, sited among marshes, it was a sickly place. Nevertheless it continued to expand throughout the war to clean and repair the smaller ships of the fleet.

By far the most important dockyard was Portsmouth. An excellent sheltered harbour, a good roadstead at Spithead, good connections to the London and the West Country markets and facing the Channel and Western Approaches, made Portsmouth a vital element in Britain's maritime defence. With four dry docks, a wet dock, plenty of space for development and working, it was an excellent building and repair yard as well as an operational base. After 1713 the buildings were re-arranged, the yard was expanded and new facilities, such as piped water were installed to accelerate watering ships. A reconstruction of the north dock with the ability to receive a first rate was nearing completion in 1739.

To the west lay Plymouth. The wide Catwater provided the security of an ideal cruising base. The yard itself was located across the Hamoaze estuary. Like Portsmouth its grounds and facilities had expanded since 1714. With two dry docks and three building slips it had the capability for building and repair of large ships.

These six yards, but particularly Portsmouth and Plymouth, provided the essential infrastructure for the navy. However, their effectiveness depended on access to large pools of labour, and huge quantities of wood, iron and cordage. The navy was possibly the largest single consumer of iron and employer of civilian labour in this period. Fortunately, the yards had evolved in the context of a thriving maritime economy. The Navy Board and Victualling Board had great experience of contracting with merchants for the supply of materials and the contracting system worked well throughout this period of mobilisation.[44] There was a lack of skilled shipwrights, leading to indus-

44   Bernard Pool, himself a former Director of Navy Contracts, considered the efficiency
     of the contracting system to have been slack in this period. The war improved prac-

Map 1 British dockyards, 1739–1748

trial unrest and culminating in a strike at Portsmouth in 1742. The cumulative effect of the war over a period of years was to strain almost every part of the administrative system. However, when viewed from the perspective of 1739–1740, the yards performed and there were no significant bottlenecks at this stage of the mobilisation process. Besides the royal yards the navy could call upon the services of private yards for the building and repair of smaller ships. The private yards along the Thames and the East Coast of England, particularly, offered capacity for expansion.

While Britain's home defence was secured by a powerful naval infrastructure, the effective exercise of sea-power across any distance demanded facilities overseas. By the end of the War of Spanish Succession in 1713, Britain had two potentially important harbours and anchorages – Gibraltar and Minorca. Despite its position at the mouth of the Mediterranean and its proximity to the major Spanish port of Cadiz, Gibraltar was not developed

---

tices. This is no doubt true, but the system as it existed in 1739–40 worked and it was the strains of later years that forced it to evolve. See B. Pool, *Navy Board Contracts, 1660–1832* London, 1966, 108.

Table 2.2 Distribution of the ships in ordinary

Guns	Deptford	Wool-wich	Chatham	Sheerness	Ports-mouth	Plymouth
100			5		2	
90			10		5	
80	1	2	6		2	1
70	3	3	4		3	1
60		1	2	3	6	6
50	1	2	2	2	4	4
40				1	6	1
20						
Others	1	3			1	

Note: Three ships were in ordinary outside the royal yards. The *Enterprise* (40) was at Liverpool and hulked there in 1740. Two more 40s, the *Dover* and *Feversham* were in the Thames.

as a significant naval yard. The bay was ill positioned to protect ships from southerly gales and the Rock was in practice a front-line fortress. The main naval area was only just outside of direct cannon range from Spanish positions across the isthmus.[45]

The main naval base for the ships operating in the Mediterranean was, therefore, Port Mahon on Minorca. Situated near the head of a huge natural inlet, it was well protected from the elements. The island hinterland provided secure access to food and labour. Work had begun on developing the site soon after it had been captured in 1708. In the first half of the eighteenth century it was uncommon to budget for regular repair and maintenance of large-scale defensive or government buildings in peacetime and by 1739 many of the buildings were in disrepair. Nevertheless, there was a hospital, a mast-house, a mast pond and smithy. The careening wharf provided space for three 90-gun men of war and by 1739, it was capable of maintaining a substantial squadron. However, like all overseas bases, it relied on convoys from Britain for critical supplies. Foodstuffs and some stores could be purchased locally in Italy or on the Barbary coast, but skilled labour and almost all naval stores had to be replenished from Britain.

On the other side of the Atlantic, the West Indies had seen the growth of dockyard facilities during the decades of peace. The major base at this

---

45   Harding, 'A Tale of Two Sieges', op. cit.

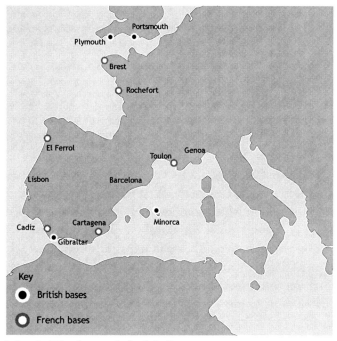

Map 2 Gibraltar and the Mediterranean

time was Port Royal on the south side of Jamaica. Situated at the end of a sand spit enclosing a large bay, it had long been a major place of refuge for merchantmen and warships. Kingston, the main commercial port of the island, lay across the bay. By 1713 Port Royal had not recovered from the disastrous earthquake of 1693, in which part of the town slid into the mud.[46] Hulks had been placed there to enable ships to careen, which were replaced in 1728, but it remained relatively under-developed until 1735. Between 1728 and 1735 more attention had been paid to creating a new base on the north side of the island, at Port Antonio. Cheaper, less prone to earthquake and positioned closer to the French and Spanish sea communications, it was hoped that this would be a better base. However, it proved to be a very unhealthy spot and by 1735 the labour force was directed back to Port Royal. Two new wharves, new storehouses, and watering wharves had been built by 1739. By the time war broke out, the facilities at Port Royal had grown to meet the needs of a powerful squadron.

---

46   G.R. Clark, 'Swallowed Up', *Earth*, iv (1995), 35–41.

To the east, in the Lesser Antilles, there were no major naval facilities until 1728. This was a potential problem as the trade winds and the currents dictated that ships entered the Caribbean in this region and left by the Gulf of Florida. Warships based at Jamaica found it very difficult if not impossible to beat back to the Leeward Islands. In 1728 work began on developing a naval base at English Harbour, Antigua. By 1739 it had a careening wharf and three storehouses to support the small vessels on station there.[47] Like the Mediterranean bases these yards had to be supplied from Britain or from the Northern Colonies.

In the Northern Colonies, there were no royal yards. The Royal Navy relied upon private yards. Unlike the West Indies, there was a thriving ship-building industry upon which to draw, with materials and skilled labour in plentiful supply. Furthermore, the Royal Navy had not, historically, main-tained a strong presence there. The small ships at Boston, New York, Norfolk (Virginia) and Charlestown (South Carolina) could be easily supplied from private maritime resources. Prices were high but a problem would only emerge if large ships of war were to be sent to North America.

Overall, by 1739 Britain had a good network of naval yards stretching from Port Royal to Minorca, but their effectiveness had not been tested in war. If British ambitions and interests were to be met, a great deal would depend on the ability of the domestic naval infrastructure to support the overseas yards. However, Britain's provision was far superior to any of her potential enemies. Neither France nor Spain possessed any dry docks for cleaning large men of war. Their yards were partially dependent on convict and conscript labour. They could not rely on the large pool of local mari-time expertise. For the most part, their access to high quality naval stores was inferior to that of Britain. Brest had to rely on coastal shipping to bring most stores to it. While Spain had some powerful naval facilities in the West Indies, notably Havana and Cartagena de las Indias, France had almost none in the Americas. Louisbourg, built from 1713, to protect the French cod fisheries possessed a fine harbour, but little supporting infrastructure.[48] Britain commenced this war not just with a far larger force of warships than

---

47   Baugh, *British Naval Administration*, op. cit., 352–354; D. Crewe, *Yellow Jack and the Worm: British Naval Administration in the West Indies, 1739–1748*, Liverpool, 1993, 232–233.

48   The best comparative examination of the French and Spanish ports in the Americas is J.R. McNeill, *Atlantic Empires of France and Spain: Louisbourg and Havana, 1700–1763*, Chapel Hill, 1985.

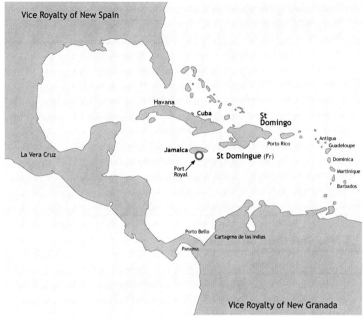

Map 3 The West Indies

the Bourbon powers, but an infrastructure that promised greater robustness, reach and flexibility over a long period.

Mobilisation: The Mobilisation of the Fleet, Summer 1739

The pace of work in the yards is indicated in Tables 2.3 and 2.4. The availability of the line of battle ships grew steadily. While these ships were being prepared, the Navy Board turned its attention to adding new ships to the fleet. The line of battle formed the basis of the fleet, but much of the work load of naval operations fell upon the small fifth and sixth rates and sloops. Unlike the line of battle ships, they could be built fairly rapidly, and in the case of fireships, purchased directly from merchants. Between June and September 13 merchant vessels were purchased to be fitted out as fireships at Woolwich and Deptford. Five of these were ready to be put in commission within the month. In November two more vessels were purchased to become hospital ships. The sixth rates could not be simply converted from merchantmen, but the merchant yards had the capacity to build vessels of this size. Ten vessels of 20 to 24 guns were ordered from shipbuilders, mostly on the Thames, between August and October. These ships came into commission from late spring to early summer of the following year.

Table 2.3 Ships put in commission

Rate	Guns	June	July	August
First	100			
Second	90/80	3	1	2
Third	70/60	14	1	5
Fourth	50	5	3	8
Fifth	40			1
Sixth	20	1		
Other	various	6	6	
Total		24	11	14

Table 2.4 Nominal ships on station

Rate	Guns	June	July	August
First	100			
Second	90/80	3	6	8
Third	70/60	19	11	16
Fourth	50	12	19	17
Fifth	40	3	1	1
Sixth	20	6	3	3
Other		23	24	24
Total		67	64	69

Throughout the mobilisation period, manpower was the critical problem.[49] The Admiralty envisaged the numbers of seamen in pay to double from just over 16,000 to 35,000. An embargo on vessels leaving Britain and a press was approved on 3 June.[50] However, these measures were highly unpopular in the maritime community and on 2 July the embargo on coasters and fishing boats was removed.[51] As September passed, the manning problem remained unresolved. The Cabinet discussed the matter on 21 September. Sir John Norris estimated that of the 40 to

49   For a good overview of the impressment, see N. Rogers, *The Press Gang: Naval Impressment and its Opponents in Georgian Britain*, London, 2007.

50   BL, Add Ms 33004, 3 June 1739. This excluded any vessel employed by the Navy and Victualling Boards and the Customs.

51   BL, Add Ms 32693, f. 104, Admiralty to Newcastle, 2 July 1739.

60 ships available at this time, about 25 were in a good state for immediate employment. This was enough to secure the country even if France joined Spain, but he pointed out that despite the legal powers of impressment, he did not think the magistrates were supporting the naval pressing officers ashore. As there were no legal remedies against recalcitrant justices, other methods of manning had to be considered. Only about one-third of the crew of a ship of the line needed to be able seamen. Another third, 'waisters' could be men of no special maritime skills at all and traditionally soldiers or marines had been put on ships to carry out these functions in times of crisis.[52] However, this plan ran into the opposition of the King, who was unwilling to have his soldiers serve on ships. Thus, as October approached, the administrative system was turning out ships, victuals and stores, but the question of manpower remained unresolved.

Mobilisation: The Army

George II was a soldier and greatly concerned with anything that affected his army. Since early August, George had feared that France would invade Britain once war was declared with Spain.[53] It was this that underpinned his reluctance to put soldiers on the fleet. Unfortunately, his subjects did not share his love of the army. A long history of resistance to large standing armies was deeply entrenched in the British political mind. Even the most modest expansion in the size of the army, whatever the urgency of the situation, could stimulate a political furore. In 1739 the army stood at a nominal 26,891, including all garrisons overseas, which was approximately the figure it had been since 1736.[54] In addition to this there were a nominal 12,000 troops on the Irish Establishment.[55]

---

52 For a general discussion about the level of expertise needed on warships, see S. Willis, 'The High Life: Topmen in the Age of Sail', *Mariner's Mirror*, xc (2004), 152–166; Willis' *Fighting at Sea in the Eighteenth Century: The Art of Sailing Warfare*, Woodbridge, 2008, is an excellent general survey of the art of naval war.

53 BL, Add Ms 35860, f. 136, Newcastle to Hardwicke, 11 August 1739.

54 *Journal of the House of Commons*, xxiii (1737–1739), 223. The size of the army had gradually crept up from about 20,000 in 1723 to a figure averaging 23,000 for most of the next 10 years, with the exceptions of a spike up to 32,000 in 1727 owing to conflict with Spain. It crept up again from 1734, peaking at 34,354 in 1735, during the War of Polish Succession and further tension with Spain. It settled at about 26,000 for the rest of the decade.

55 A. Guy, *Oeconomy and Discipline: Officership and Administration in the British Army,*

The defence of Ireland and the overseas possessions occupied about 25 per cent of the units of the army. In peacetime all regiments were maintained well below their nominal strength. This kept the cost of the army down, while maintaining the regimental infrastructure for rapid expansion. On 3 June the Cabinet agreed to augment the army, by recruiting to fill existing regiments.[56] During the summer when casual, seasonal labour was in high demand, recruiting parties had some difficulty, but when the winter set in and the jobs disappeared, the pickings would be richer. The expanded regiments required more officers and on 24 August an order was despatched for all officers on half pay to report their current address and ages.[57] Despite this, the King was still concerned about the lack of troops in the kingdom and when the Privy Council met to consider a formal declaration of war on Spain on 2 October, it also considered a proposal to hire 6,000 Hessians and 6,000 Danes to reinforce the kingdom, but no decision was made at this point.[58]

As the army gradually expanded in response to the conflict, the new recruits had to be trained. During the peace regiments could not be maintained in a high state of efficiency.[59] Regiments were dispersed across the country and much of a soldier's time was spent marching between postings and living in small detachments. The lack of action or opportunity also reflected in the officer corps, as it gradually aged without developing either skills or experience. For the regiments on overseas service there was no policy of rotation until 1749. Mortality on these stations was high and boredom even worse, so obtaining recruits was even more difficult.

The maintenance of the regiment was the responsibility of the colonel. There was an established regime of the replacement of clothing on a regular basis and it was expected that weapons would be maintained by the troops. Reviews and inspections by officers reporting to the Board of General Officers were the means by which this was carried out. However,

---

1714–63, Manchester, 1985, 9–10. The number was established by the Disbanding Act 1699 and did not vary with an annual vote as it did in Britain.

56   BL, Add Ms 32692, f. 54.

57   TNA, WO26/19, p. 195, 24 August 1739.

58   BL, Add Ms 33004, 2 October 1739.

59   The following paragraphs are based largely upon J.A. Houlding, *Fit for Service: The Training of the British Army 1715–1795*, Oxford, 1981, and Guy, *Oeconomy and Discipline*, op. cit. See also, T. Hayter, *The Army and the Crowd in Mid-Georgian England*, London, 1978.

Table 2.5 Dispostion of the British Army, September 1739

Force	Home	Ire.	Gib.	Min.	L. Is.	NS	NY	WS
Horse Gds (squadrons)	4							
Horse Grenadier Gds (squadrons)	2							
Horse Regts	4	4						
Dragoon Regts	8	6						
Regts of Foot Gds	3							
Foot Regts	20	10	5	5	1	1		
Indep Cos	31						4	4

Notes: Ire. = Ireland; Gib. = Gibraltar; Min. = Minorca; L. Is. = Leeward Islands; NS = Nova Scotia; NY = New York; WS = West Indies.

in practice, this was not be regularly done and the general decline in the material effectiveness of the army is evident from the papers of the Board of Ordnance. The colonel was responsible for the weapons of the regiment. After an initial issue of muskets and accoutrements by the Board of Ordnance, all replacement arms had to be ordered and paid for by the colonels. It was not unusual, therefore, for delays in replacing arms until an emergency occurred. The Master General of the Ordnance, the Duke of Argyle, reported that on 1 January 1739 the Board had 42,121 muskets in stock. Fifteen months later they had issued 28,153, virtually a replacement musket for every soldier in the army.[60] This first mobilisation did not break the Board's ability to supply the needs of the army. The Board bought muskets and gunpowder from private manufacturers.[61] However, by October 1741, the drain on stocks and continuing high level of demand caused some concerns, so warrants were issued to seek supplies of arms and saltpetre from Holland.[62]

---

60 TNA, SP41/36, Argyle to Newcastle, 4 February 1739/40.

61 For part of the work of the Ordnance in this period, see J. West, *Gunpowder, Government and War in the Mid-Eighteenth Century*, Woodbridge, 1991. A good overview of the Ordnance's role in the war machinery of the time is G.W. Morgan, 'The Impact of War on the Administration of the Army, Navy and Ordnance in Britain, 1739–1754', unpublished PhD thesis, University of Leicester, 1977.

62 TNA, SP41/36, unfoliated, 'October' 1741.

Mobilisation: The Board of Ordnance

The Board of Ordnance was an important body, separate from the army and navy. At its head was the master general, who was a member of the Cabinet. The Board was responsible for the provision of all arms and ammunition to the army and the navy. It had to supply all tentage and camp necessaries, barrack bedding, candle and kindling to the army. It was also responsible for all the artillery forces and engineers, fortifications and barracks in Britain, Gibraltar and Minorca. With this level of responsibility the Board's relations with the army and the navy were inevitably difficult. Senior officers complained that they could do nothing to improve fortifications without a warrant from the Board, nor could they even move materials.[63] This division of responsibility grated on officers in both services and it was exacerbated by social and professional factors. Promotion within the artillery and engineers was based on seniority not purchase, which elsewhere was an important part of the promotion system in the army. Specialist mathematical training distinguished the artillery and engineers, whose status was claimed by special or elevated technical expertise, but married to a certain social inferiority. It was a mix that easily affronted the more socially stratified army officer corps.[64] This was especially so as the expertise was not confined purely to artillerymen and engineers. Ambitious or conscientious officers of both the army and navy could obtain at least partial training in these sciences from attending the military schools in Europe.[65] The Board was to face a range of major problems during the course of the war, but this underlying hostility from the other services must be taken into account when assessing the effectiveness of the Ordnance Board and its servants.

Mobilisation: Finance

While the materials for war were being assembled over the summer, another key resource had to be attended to. Since the 1690s the banking system and money market had underpinned the British ability to conduct large-scale,

---

63   TNA, SP41/36, unfoliated, Sabine to Yonge, 4 October 1739.

64   See D.W. Marshall, 'British Military Engineers, 1741–1783: A Study of Organisation, Social Origin and Cartography', unpublished PhD thesis, University of Michigan, 1976.

65   One of the most bitter invectives against these branches, which has clear overtones of social distaste, is the pamphlet *An Account of the Expedition to Cartagena*, London, 1743, by Captain Charles Knowles.

long-term warfare. By 1739 Britain had sophisticated money and stock markets, which like all markets were sensitive to sentiment and rumour. Even in relatively peaceful times, the shifts in market sentiment and speculative behaviour could have dramatic repercussions on these markets. The South Sea Bubble of 1721 had shown just how dangerous that could be.[66] In war time the threat to stability was even greater. Ever since the overthrow of the Stuarts in 1688, the fear of Jacobite revolt haunted the political nation. In any war, the enemy would try to stimulate Jacobite revolt, which could only escalate if there were a threat of invasion to assist it.[67] One of Sir Robert Walpole's great contributions was his work in restructuring the national debt after the South Sea Bubble burst. The cautious fiscal stance he had taken for over 20 years had reduced the debt by a net figure of over £6 million, with a solid sinking fund to continue that process.[68] Any doubts that Britain was capable of undertaking a successful war against Spain or that the war would expose Britain to a Jacobite revolt would have been reflected in these markets.[69] On 14 June 1739 an act was passed authorising the ministry to raise £300,000 in long-term bonds for the prosecution of the war, but it was far less than previous authorisations and the markets were easily capable of absorbing the demand. The issue had no significant impact on the price of government 3 per cent stocks. Other stocks also showed little sensitivity to the rumours and preparations for war, so it seemed the financial structures were sound for the commencement of war.[70]

---

66 The best account of the crisis is J. Carswell, *The South Sea Bubble*, 2nd edn, Stroud, 1993.

67 J. Black, *British Foreign Policy in the Age of Walpole*, Edinburgh, 1985, 139–155; J. Black, 'Jacobitism and Foreign Policy, 1731–5', in E. Cruickshanks and J. Black (eds) *The Jacobite Challenge*, Edinburgh, 1988, 142–160.

68 The best account of the financial situation is, P.G.M. Dickson, *The Financial Revolution in England: A Study of the Development of Public Credit, 1688–1756*, London, 1967. Walpole's fiscal objectives and his sensitivity to the credit market played an important part in his diplomatic objective of maintaining stability in Europe. See J. Black, 'British Neutrality in the War of Polish Succession, 1733–1735, *International History Review*, vii (1986), 345–366.

69 For the institutional economic history view of the relationship between politics, parliament and the money markets, see J. Wells and D. Wills, 'Revolution, Restitution and Debt Repudiation: The Jacobite Threat to England's Institutions and Economic Growth', *Journal of Economic History*, lx (2000), 418–441.

70 Ibid., 207–8. Stock prices can be followed in the pages of the *London Magazine*. See

Over the summer the military and naval resources of Great Britain gradually mobilised. The administrative system which had not been seriously tested for over 25 years was moving smoothly enough. A number of factors had become clearer. The cost and uncertainty of war seemed to pose no great worries to the money markets and exchanges. The Dutch would not support this war. The Portuguese would tolerate British ships using the Tagus, but insisted upon strict neutrality in all other matters. France looked threatening, but by late August the ministers had come to the conclusion that Fleury was bluffing. The best information that the ministry had from Wager was that Spain alone posed no threat to the British Isles or her colonies. The Spanish fleet would remain in harbour either from lack of resources or fear of facing superior British forces at sea. From the early summer plans had been discussed for a major expedition to the West Indies which would be decisive in forcing Spain to come to terms. At this point, the war seemed to present far more opportunities than threats.

The Declaration of War: October 1739

By the beginning of October Vice Admiral Vernon was in the West Indies with orders to take, sink or burn any Spanish vessel he could lay his hands upon, and likewise to seize what Spanish territory he could. Vice Admiral Haddock was under similar orders to do the same in the Mediterranean and to blockade the Spanish warships in to their ports of Cadiz and Cartagena. In Georgia, General Oglethorpe was to move from defending this infant colony to attack the main Spanish settlement of St Augustine in Florida.[71] An expeditionary army in the West Indies was now under consideration. One important question remained: should Britain make a formal declaration of war on Spain?

On the one hand, the sailing of an expeditionary force to the Americas was as good as a declaration of war. To declare war was to eliminate any hope that the defensive alliance with the Dutch could be called upon. It would also give France the pretext to join Spain in consequence of their defensive alliances. Sir John Norris particularly disliked the idea of declaring war during the autumn. British naval forces would not be ready to sail for the West Indies until the spring, so any declaration could be safely delayed until

---

also, D.M. Joslin, 'London Bankers in Wartime, 1739–84' in L.S. Pressnell (ed.), *Studies in the Industrial Revolution*,London, 1960, 156–177

71   BL, Add Ms 28132 (Journal of Sir John Norris), f. 25 September 1739.

then.[72] He felt that the French neutral stance was bound to change in the light of a declaration. Horace Walpole, the ambassador at The Hague, and Hardwicke also saw the negative consequences of the declaration.[73]

Newcastle, on the other hand, saw the declaration as a natural development from the necessity of undertaking hostilities against Spain. The general argument for peace had been lost in the weeks following the failure of the Convention of the Pardo. The public expectations were for vigorous naval or expeditionary action. Although ministers had been worrying about the intentions of France, these worries had not been articulated strongly to the public and with parliament due to meet in November the critical question would be how the preparations for war would be viewed in the House. There were indications that the opposition had not diminished over the summer despite all the preparations in hand. In late September Sir George Champion had been passed over for Lord Mayor of London because of his support for the Convention. It was a lead other corporations followed. *The Craftsman*, an opposition newspaper, praised the London Liverymen who 'began the laudable work which hath been followed by several great trading Towns and Corporations in both parts of the Kingdom'.[74] Indeed the preparations, like the raising of new troops during the parliamentary recess could have made things worse. The sensitivity of members to the King raising soldiers which had not been voted by parliament was notorious. Newcastle wrote to Hardwicke on 30 September that 'The season of the year is undoubtedly an objection, but then it is the same season that warr (sic) was declared in 1718 and though that was after a meeting of parliament <u>I really think now we want a Declaration of War to make the parliament and nation think we are sufficiently in earnest</u> to justify the demand of more troops.'[75] Hardwicke remained unconvinced, but was more receptive after talking to Sir Benjamin Keene, who arrived in London from Madrid on 1 October. He also felt that Keene would do much to convince Walpole. That day, Hardwicke had met with Newcastle, Walpole, Harrington, Lord Islay (Walpole's manager in Scotland), Sir Charles Wager and Sir John Norris at Newcastle's

---

72 Ibid., 2 Octobrer 1739.

73 BL., Ads Ms 35506, (Hardwicke Papers), 14 October 1739, H. Walpole to Hardwicke, 14 October 1739.

74 *The Craftsman*, 8 December 1739. *The Craftsman* had been covering the development of this matter since October.

75 BL, Add Ms 35406 (Hardwicke Papers), f. 156, Newcastle to Hardwicke, 30 September 1739, original emphasis.

office in Whitehall. They agreed that they would advise the King to declare war on Spain. Hardwicke, Walpole and Norris were uncomfortable with the decision, but the others carried the day. The proposal would be put to the Cabinet Council on the 11 October.[76] Newcastle's fear was not a declaration of war, but facing parliament without a clear plan of action, which had still not been agreed. Among others anxiety and uncertainty remained high and on the 11 October the Cabinet Council only agreed to consider a draft declaration of war at a later meeting.[77] On Friday 19 October the draft was considered and accepted and by the time the proclamation was published to the world on Tuesday 23 October the ministers' minds were fully focused on the great expedition upon which they pinned their hopes of a quick and decisive victory.

76   BL, Add Ms 28132 (Journal of Sir John Norris) 2 October 1739.
77   BL, Add Ms 33004 (Newcastle Papers), f. 17, 11 October 1739.

3

The Opening Moves, October 1739– January 1741

The Main Thrust: The West or East Indies?

The declaration of war in October put Britain on a course into the unknown. Never before had Britain plunged into a conflict with a major European power without allies. That the campaign would take place in the late summer and autumn of 1740 against the Spanish colonies in the Caribbean underlay both the expectation of a swift victory and the declaration of war.[1] Over the coming winter and spring the forces had to be assembled and during this time France had to be kept neutral. A great deal was being gambled on an ability to do both.

The Spanish Empire in America was a vast region that stretched from Buenos Aires in the south to St Augustine in Florida to the north. At the heart of the empire were the silver mines in Peru and Mexico and it was the treasure fleets, bringing silver back to Spain that was the main focus of British attention. The *Galeones* and the *Flota* provided the crucial link between Spain and her American colonies. The latest *Galeones* had arrived in Cartagena in 1737 and was awaiting the arrival of silver bullion from Peru to go on to Porto Bello for the fair before returning home. The *Flota* was preparing in Cadiz for its outward journey.[2] However, silver not only came eastward to Spain, but was also sent west, across the Pacific Ocean from Acapulco to Manila, where it was a valuable element in the Spanish trade to China. The *galeon*, which took the silver to Manila was a rich if distant 'Prize of all the Oceans'.[3]

It had long been understood that the vulnerability of the empire lay in these lines of communication from Porto Bello and Vera Cruz to Cadiz and from Manila to Acapulco. The initial plans for deploying ships under Vernon

---

1   BL, Add Ms 32692, f. 256, Hardwicke to Newcastle, 26 August 1739.

2   Walker, *Spanish Politics*, op. cit.

3   Williams, *The Prize of all the Oceans*, op. cit.

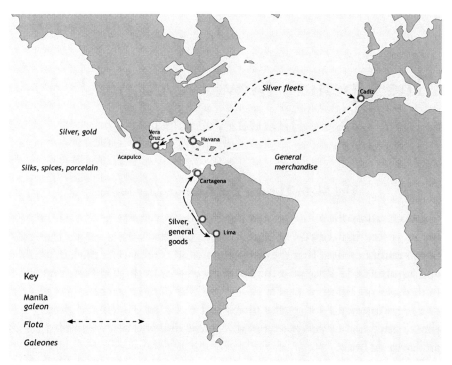

Map 4 Spanish imperial trade routes

and Haddock were to intercept the treasure ships. However, from the British point of view the capture of any outposts near the key trade routes could present a permanent threat to Spain. As early as 3 June, Sir Charles Wager presented a proposal to take Porto Rico as this island lay at the point where Spanish ships traditionally sailed into the Caribbean.[4]

While the general weakness of the Spanish Empire was well understood, the ministry's knowledge of the current situation in the Caribbean was sparse. The British intelligence system of the mid-eighteenth century centred upon the offices of the two secretaries of state. The Duke of Newcastle received the diplomatic correspondence from the courts of southern Europe and the colonies. Harrington, the Secretary of State for the Northern Department, received the correspondence from the northern courts. Both secretaries had an under-secretary and maintained a small staff of clerks. Between them they had access to translators and three decipherers. The letters sent home by British envoys and consuls were a vital

---

4   BL, Add Ms 32993, f. 59, Cabinet Papers, 3 June 1739.

source of information. So was the interception at the Post Office of foreign diplomatic post from London to courts across Europe.[5] Beyond the secretaries, other bodies were receiving intelligence that could be valuable. The Board of Trade was in contact with colonial governors. Not only did they receive reports on relations with foreign colonies and native populations, but, from 1721, took an increasing interest in gathering economic and social information about the colonies themselves.[6] Colonel Martin Bladen, an energetic member of the Board from 1717, held a wealth of information relating to the colonies. The Admiralty also had the potential to gather a great deal of current information by its correspondence with naval officers at sea. Through stopping British and neutral merchantmen, news could be gathered and sent on to London. These official sources of information were extremely important but they relied on a relatively few individuals. If their correspondence was stopped or delayed, gaps rapidly opened in the intelligence picture. Once war had broken out with Spain diplomatic correspondence ceased. The same happened with France in 1744. Consuls or agents in Portugal, Italy and the United Provinces, as well as diplomats from neutral countries kept some information flowing, but the networks of dedicated correspondents were thin.[7] In this situation, the mass of private and commercial correspondence carried to Britain by letter and newspapers, which circulated in the London coffee houses, was an important additional source of intelligence. During the summer of 1743 the ministry was heavily reliant on this unofficial intelligence for the course of events in Germany. Overall, the system was capable of delivering a good supply of reasonable quality intelligence to the ministry. However, the management of this information had problems. The papers were lodged in the secretaries' offices and arranged according to whatever system seemed appropriate to them and their staffs. While letters were laid before the King, the manner in which the secretaries conducted their correspondence or used the intelligence they received very much depended on their own temper. Jealously between secretaries, indolence or a wish

---

5   J.C. Sainty, *Officials of the Secretaries of State, 1660–1782*, London, 1973; K. Ellis, *The Post Office in the Eighteenth Century: A Study in Administrative History*, Oxford, 1958, 60–77.

6   I.K. Steele, *Politics of Colonial Policy: The Board of Trade in Colonial Administration, 1696–1720*, Oxford, 1968; J.A. Henretta, *'Salutary Neglect': Colonial Administration under the Duke of Newcastle*, Princeton, 1972.

7   D.B. Horn, *The British Diplomatic Service, 1689–1789*, Oxford, 1961, 237–283.

to control the channels of communication with overseas correspondents could lead to difficulties in the dissemination and interpretation of information. When a secretary was replaced, new working relationships had to be built, which in 1742–1743 were to have a direct bearing on the conduct of policy. Furthermore, whether the papers even remained in the office on the resignation of a secretary was also a matter of chance.[8]

The result was that when a crisis erupted it took time to gather together information to inform action. In July, Vice Admiral Vernon had been sent out to the West Indies to destroy as much Spanish shipping as he could. He was also told that 'the greatest detriment to the Spaniards', would be to gather intelligence about the ports of the region, and make some judgement about the number of troops it would take to seize somewhere of value.[9] Newcastle gave instructions to his staff to examine the papers lodged in his office and on 2 July he presented their findings to the inner Cabinet. He laid before his colleagues a paper prepared by his predecessor, Lord Townshend, in 1727, proposing attacks on Havana and Porto Rico. Colonel Martin Bladen of the Board of Trade was also present at this meeting. He had a plan to settle Darien, on the isthmus of Panama.[10] From there British ships would pose a permanent threat to windward of Porto Bello. However, it was agreed to defer further discussion until the manning situation had been improved. It was not until 4 September that the matter of an expedition was re-examined. It was agreed to invite Bladen back to explain his Darien scheme the following week. In the meantime, other proposals were placed before the ministers. Wager and Norris were asked to consider a small expedition the Pacific. Wager presented a plan to attack St Augustine.[11] On Monday 10 September, Bladen attended the Cabinet meeting. He believed that 2,000 soldiers would be adequate to attack Darien.[12] Newcastle presented some of the plans that had reached his office from private individuals, but it was soon clear that it was unproductive for such a large and inexpert body to discuss

---

8   M.A. Thomson, *The Secretaries of State, 1681–1782*, Oxford, 1932, 91–104.

9   BL Add Ms 32692, f. 140 Newcastle to Vernon, 'secret instruction', 16 July 1739.

10   BL, Add Ms 33048, f. 454, Heads of Business, 2 July. This paper has been misfiled and applies to 1739, not 1759–1763. For an introduction to Anglo-Spanish conflict in Central America, see T.S. Floyd, *The Anglo-Spanish Struggle for Mosquitia*, New Mexico, 1967.

11   BL Add Ms 33004 (Newcastle Papers – Cabinet), f. 8, 4 September 1739, f. 9, 6 September 1739; Add Ms 28132, (Norris Journal), f. 10 September 1739.

12   BL Add Ms 32694, f. 31, Reasons for making a lodgement on the Isthmus of Darien.

these undigested military proposals.[13] It was agreed that all plans would be referred to Wager and Norris for detailed consideration.

The two admirals met between 17 September and 16 October. They concluded that an attack on St Augustine could be supported with little cost and the orders for this were agreed at the Privy Council on 25 September.[14] In contrast, they thought that a plan to go to the Pacific, to take Chiloe, a large island off the coast Chile, with 1,500 troops would achieve little and take far too long.[15] The Pacific trade could be more easily disrupted by landing 500 troops at Chagres, in the Caribbean and marching them across the isthmus to Panama.[16] Bladen's plan for Darien with 2,000 troops was acceptable, but Havana was the obvious prize in the Caribbean. For this they reckoned that 10,000 troops were needed. The next best objective was Cartagena de las Indias. The French admiral de Pontis had taken that city in 1697 with 3,000 troops and as far as the admirals knew, little had been done to put the place into a better state of defence. They felt, therefore, that a force of about this size could do the same again.[17] On 17 October the admirals reported their findings privately to Walpole. Walpole accepted the attraction of Havana but was sure that the King would not permit such a large number of soldiers to be sent overseas. The 3,000 needed for Cartagena or Darien seemed more probable and Walpole promised he would inform the King, but otherwise keep the proposals secret.[18]

At this point, the most likely objective looked like Cartagena, but this suddenly changed. When Norris arrived at Wager's house on 18 October he was met by Mr James Naish, a merchant who had worked for both the East India Company and the Austrian Ostend Company.[19] Naish proposed an expedition to Manila. He claimed that a single regiment would be enough

---

13   BL Add Ms 32692, f. 290, Extract of the Paper of Observations, undated. Newcastle continued to gather information and opinions, for example from Vernon, ibid., f. 342, Newcastle to Vernon, 28 September 1739.

14   BL Add Ms 28132, f. 25 September 1739.

15   BL, Add Ms 32694, ff. 41–45, Tassell to Walpole, 11 September 1739.

16   Ibid., f. 51, 16 October 1739.

17   Ibid. For de Pontis' attack, see, J.-Y. Nerzic and C. Buchet, *Marins et Flibustiers du Roi-Soleil – Cartagena 1697*, Paris, 2002. Significant improvements had been made in the wake of de Pontis' attack, see P.J. Dousdebes, *Cartagena de Indias: Plaza Fuerte*, Bogata, 1948; J. Marchena Fernández, *La Institucion Militar en Cartagena de Indias, 1700–1870*, Seville, 1982.

18   BL, Add Ms 28132, f. 55, 17 October 1739.

19   For James Nash, see BL, India Office Library, East India Company, B/65 (Court Minutes), f. 365, 1 June 1739.

to capture the city. The capture of this place would shatter the western end of Spain's imperial trade routes. It would open a thriving trade to China and there were rumours of gold deposits on the island of Luzon. A further advantage was that France might remain neutral as she had no legal interests to protect in the South Sea. Wager was very impressed and the admirals agreed to inform Walpole of the plan.

The admirals met Walpole the next day. Walpole said that if they would approve the plan, he would support it. They were to meet the next day with Naish. Overnight Wager developed the project. A naval force of one 60, a 50 and a 40 (with a bomb or mortar) would be adequate. Naish proposed that he be made the King's chief agent on the expedition with Mr Tassell, a South Sea Company director and a friend of Walpole, as deputy commissary. He proposed that the prizes and profits be divided equally between the members of the expedition and the King. Walpole agreed to gauge the King's opinion. Two days later Walpole reported that the King approved and it was agreed that Newcastle should be informed, but that the East India Company, in whose exclusive trading area the Philippines lay, should not be told yet.[20]

The next day, 23 October, as the declaration of war was being proclaimed across London, the admirals attended Newcastle to explain the plan. Newcastle agreed that the plan was practicable, given speed and secrecy, but it did not answer public expectations of a dramatic and decisive blow. Havana had been the main object in his mind. The admirals agreed that if General Wade would go they would find seamen to cover the expedition. However, this operation would require at least 8,000 troops and reinforcements to replace the losses through disease. They pointed out that Cartagena might be taken and held for half that number. There was now a danger of an impasse between Newcastle's preference for a large West Indian operation, which Walpole doubted the King would approve, and the latter's preference for a small-scale operation in Philippines, which Newcastle was convinced the public would never accept. Newcastle and the admirals agreed that there should be a private meeting between Walpole, Newcastle and the potential commander of the expedition, with the admirals in attendance for advice.[21]

This critical meeting took place on the 29 October. Present were Walpole and his brother Horace, Newcastle and his brother Henry Pelham, the Duke of Grafton, Harrington, Wager and Norris. The admirals outlined the plans.

---

20   BL, Add Ms 28132, ff. 57–58, 19–22 October 1739.

21   BL, Add Ms 28132, f. 59, 23 October 1739. See also, BL, Add Ms 32692, f. 156, Newcastle to Hardwick, 30 September 1739.

Havana was the most popular, but in the end, it was accepted 10,000 men could not be raised. Cartagena was then considered and it was agreed that the King might agree to release 4,000 troops. Attention then turned to Manila, which demanded only 1,000, and the plan to take Chiloe, which demanded 1,500 troops. In the end the lack of troops seems to have forced the ministers to accept that the South Sea options were the only viable projects and it was agreed to prepare ships for sailing around Cape Horn to attack the Peruvian coast and Manila.

While resources had dictated this decision, Newcastle and Harrington were unconvinced by its wisdom. Parliament opened on 15 November and immediately pressure grew for decisive action. The declaration of war was greeted solemnly, but calls were made to attack the Spanish Indies.[22] In the days that followed all the debates reinforced the universal assumption that the seat of war would be in the West Indies. Lord Carteret, responding to the motion on the King's speech powerfully reminded the House of the argument that had led to war and the centrality of America; 'The King hath it in his power to make as great a figure as any prince that ever sat on the throne. He hath it in his power to take and hold in America. Nobody would connect with you till they saw you were willing to help yourself.' The French were in no position to help Spain. All Europe would rally to Britain if France disturbed the peace of the continent.

> America is the place where we ought to direct our chief force. There the Spaniards cannot resist us, and there we may do more than make incursions. We may take and hold such places, as we think may be either convenient or useful. It is what Spain cannot hinder; it is what Europe cannot prevent; and by holding the places we take, we add to our own strength, at the same time that we diminish the strength of our enemy.[23]

In the days that followed, debates on encouraging seamen, raising marines and British rights of navigation in American waters, reinforced the universal assumption that the seat of war would be in the West Indies.

Walpole continued to resist this pressure and the dispute with Newcastle continued throughout November.[24] In his office Newcastle discovered a

---

22   Corbett, *Parliamentary History*, op. cit., xi (1739–41), 10–15.

23   Corbett, *Parliamentary History*, op. cit. xi (1739–41), 10–15.

24   BL, Add Ms 32692, f. 450, John (Bishop of Chichester) to Newcastle, 8 November 1739.

proposal dated 1727 in which the Lieutenant Governor of Virginia, Alexander Spotswood proposed to raise a regiment of troops in America. This was reinforced by two similar proposals by Lord Cathcart, an army officer who had ambitions to lead an expedition to the West Indies, and the Governor of Jamaica, Edward Trelawney.[25] On 22 November he presented this to a meeting of ministers. Although the discussion was described as only 'cursory', Newcastle did not let it rest and at a later meeting restated his view that France would not join Spain. The news that Spanish reinforcements had left Ferrol for the West Indies, only added urgency to the situation.

The pressure finally broke Walpole's resistance. On the 5 December Norris reported that Walpole opened a meeting about Manila by stating that 'at the first preparation for it he thought it a proper enterprise, but as it would take up such a strength by sea with the regiment of a thousand men, and that everybody's thoughts were upon an undertaking in the West Indies, he was for giving over the thoughts of sending to the Manila'.[26] An expedition would still go into the South Seas as projected, but to attack the Pacific coast of South America, not to attack Manila. This expedition would go out under the command Captain George Anson.[27] Those attending seem to have been expecting this change, for immediately the shape and size of the West Indian expeditionary force was agreed. Walpole noted that the King would probably agree to send the six new regiments of marines then being raised, along with the regiment of foot, which had been allocated for the Manila operation. The availability of the American troops made the up numbers needed. Norris and Wager emphasised the need to blockade the Spanish coast to prevent more reinforcements being sent. It was agreed that Admiral Balchen should be despatched with 10 ships to cruise off the Spanish coast. Newcastle confirmed that Cromwell's orders to his commanders sent to the West Indies in 1654, which had been located in his office, were an effective precedent for the new expedition. Wager was ordered to prepare six men of war to act as a convoy to this expeditionary force. The precise destination and composition of the force had now to be agreed and the planning moved to a new secret committee consisting of Norris, Wager, Wade, Colonel Lascelles of the Board of Ordnance and the proposed commander of the expedition,

---

25   BL, Add Ms 32692, ff. 544–545, Cathcart to Newcastle, undated.

26   BL, Add Ms 28132, f. 86, 5 December 1739.

27   Ibid., f. 73, 1 November 1739. However, Anson was given permission to return via the Philippines.

Lord Cathcart. The broad outline of the expedition was agreed. It was to depart in the spring for the decisive campaign over the summer.

Losing the Initiative in Europe: the Mediterranean and North Atlantic, October 1739–June 1740

As autumn turned to winter the operational demands of war slackened, but the build up of resources continued. The ministers were satisfied that the war was proceeding according to expectation. The Mediterranean command looked the most daunting. With bases at Minorca and Gibraltar Haddock had to protect those places, defend the trade, intercept Spanish shipping, keep communications open as far Lisbon, lie off Cadiz, gather intelligence and otherwise commit what hostilities he could against the Spaniards.[28] Haddock positioned his main force at Gibraltar and spread his ships out to carry out his duties as best he could. The trade links from Lisbon into the Mediterranean remained largely undisturbed. Reinforcements were arranged from Britain. In late July Sir Chaloner Ogle had been sent to cruise off Cape St Vincent with three 60s in search of the Buenos Aires ships, reported to be returning home.[29] In September he had been reinforced by fire ships in case he was able to attack Spanish ports. In early October the *Newcastle* (50) was ordered to convoy provision ships and a bomb tender to Gibraltar and in November six more 70s under Captain Falkingham of the *Elizabeth* (70) were ordered to convoy victuallers, merchantmen and the storeship *Deptford* to Gibraltar.[30] In return, Haddock was to send home four of his warships.

On 11 September Ogle's force joined Haddock off Cadiz. From London Haddock seemed to be in command of the situation. On the King's birthday, 30 October, news arrived that the *St Joseph*, a rich ship of the Guipuzcoa Company, en route from Caracas to Cadiz, which had been captured by Captain Cooper of the *Chester* (50) had arrived in Portsmouth. It was rumoured to be worth £130,000.[31] Other prizes were thought to be on

28 BL, Egerton Mss 2530, ff. 16–19, Instructions to Haddock, 6 June 1739; TNA, SP 42/86(State Papers Naval), f. 53, Newcastle to Haddock, Most Secret, 6 June 1739.

29 BL, Egerton Mss, 2530, ff. 21–22, Newcastle to Haddock, 31 July 1739. Haddock sent Ogle a further 60 to reinforce him.

30 Ibid., f. 28–29, Newcastle to Haddock, 5 October 1739; ff., 34–35, Newcastle to Haddock, 8 November 1739.

31 TNA, SP 42/86 (State Papers Naval), f. 109, Haddock to Newcastle, 26 September 1739;

their way. Haddock's despatches gave no particular cause for concern. The ministry expected him to remain off Cadiz as long as possible and then keep enough ships at Gibraltar to cover the Rock while he returned to Minorca to repair and re-victual the rest of the squadron.[32]

By the beginning of October Haddock was forced to take most of his squadron into Gibraltar, leaving Ogle with five ships off Cadiz. Gibraltar was not a good natural harbour and did not have the facilities for a large number of ships.[33] This was made worse by the dryness of the season. Watering the squadron was extremely difficult, causing the numbers of sick to rise steeply. Haddock decided that he could not return to Cadiz without repairs, so leaving two ships at Gibraltar, and three more cruising between St Vincent and Cadiz, he took the rest of his squadron to Minorca. He was aware that this exposed Gibraltar and as soon as he possible he sent Captain the Hon. John Byng back to the Rock with two more ships.[34] Over the winter Haddock kept his command split between Gibraltar and Minorca with cruisers off the Spanish coast for intelligence. By 13 January 1740 he was back at Gibraltar with the bulk of his squadron, when Captain Falkingham of the *Elizabeth* (70), the five other 70s and the convoy of victuallers appeared over the horizon after a difficult winter voyage.

Throughout the early weeks of 1740 the ministry had been carefully assessing the news arriving from France. Fear of French intervention had been a major factor behind the Manila plan.[35] Waldegrave still believed Fleury had no intention of going to war.[36] However, he also reported that Fleury had warned him that if Britain was successful in the West Indies, France would have to act.[37] As the weeks passed Waldegrave reported that Spain was trying hard to get the French to threaten the British coast, but that Fleury was deterred from committing himself to war because of the expense.[38] Nevertheless, the French were augmenting their marine compa-

    Add Ms 28132(Norris Journal), f. 71, 31 October 1739.

32   BL, Egerton Mss, 2530, ff. 31–32, Newcastle to Haddock, 7 November 1739.

33   Coad, *The Royal Dockyards*, op. cit., 315–317; Harding, 'A Tale of Two Sieges', op. cit.

34   Ibid., 329–331.

35   BL, Add Ms 19033, f. Wager to Norris, 7 December 1739.

36   TNA, SP 78/221, f. 317, Waldegrave to Newcastle, 23 December 1739 (n.s.)

37   TNA, SP 78/221 (State Papers – France), f. Waldegrave to Newcastle, 23 December 1739 (n.s.) and f. Waldegrave to Newcastle, 28 December 1739 (n.s.).

38   TNA, SP 78/222 (State Papers – France), f. Waldegrave to Newcastle, 24 January 1740 (n.s.), 27 January 1740 (n.s.), 31 January 1740 (n.s.).

nies and news coming from consuls indicated that the Toulon and Brest squadrons were being prepared for sea. Rumours abounded that the defences of Dunkirk were being rebuilt and the French fleet was preparing to escort the *Galeones* home from the West Indies.[39] Fears that the French squadrons might actually sail for the Caribbean came to a head at a meeting of the Cabinet on 24 January 1740. The ministers had to accept that the plans for pressing seamen and the continued embargo were meeting significant resistance, particularly from the East India Company as the time of sailing of those ships to the east approached. The severe winter also meant that demand of coal from the North East was heavy and pressing disrupted that vital trade. Some concessions had to be made. However, the situation was so serious that withdrawing the Mediterranean squadron to Gibraltar was considered. Norris was adamantly opposed as it would mean the loss of Minorca and the Mediterranean trade. He noted the whole British fleet of 50 guns or more should be 120; more than enough to counter the French and Spanish.[40] In the end the ministry settled for a general embargo on all shipping, except colliers, coasters and East Indiamen, until the fleet was manned.[41]

By early February the military situation was ambiguous and worrying. The preparations for the expeditions to the South Sea and the West Indies continued without delays. The Brest and Toulon fleets were preparing for sea. Large Spanish armies were assembled in Catalonia and Galicia, posing, it was thought, a threat to Minorca and Ireland, respectively. Newcastle wrote to Haddock on 6 February informing him of their fears and the need to defend Minorca. As the month progressed, Waldegrave continued to report his belief that Fleury was bluffing.[42] Also there were growing doubts that the Spanish threat to Minorca was credible, and news was also arriving of reinforcements leaving the Basque Country for Havana.[43]

Haddock had a substantial force of 13 line of battle ships at his disposal. He remained at Gibraltar where he continued to send out single vessels on convoy to Lisbon or to gather intelligence. By the end of January he had

---

39 TNA, SP 36/50, f. 49, Hall to Stone, 22 Januaury 1740; SP 78/220 (State Papers – France), f. 334, Newcastle to Waldegrave, 20 December 1739; f. 356, Newcastle to Waldegrave, 27 December 1739.

40 BL, Add Ms 28132 (Norris Journal), f. 136–139, 24 January 1740.

41 Ibid., 31 January 1740.

42 TNA, SP 78/222, f. 114, Waldegrave to Newcastle, 2 March 1740 (n.s.); f. 139, 9 March 1740 (n.s.); f. 156, 12 March 1740 (n.s.).

43 BL, Add Ms 28132, f. 149, 14 February 1740.

heard the rumours of Spanish preparations at Majorca and Barcelona for an attack on Minorca and decided to return to that island, redistributing his forces as follows.[44] On 6 February he wrote to Newcastle explaining his plan and on the 11 February he sailed from the Rock.

At Gibraltar, Ogle's force had suffered badly from winter cruising. Over 28 per cent of his nominal crew strength was sick and incapable of service.[45] Of his ships, only the *Tiger* (50) was capable of getting to sea immediately. Although he was disturbed by information about Spanish preparations at Barcelona as well as new rumours that the Toulon squadron was preparing for sea, the reports from Cadiz suggested all was quiet there. On 4 March the *Assistance* (50) and *Litchfield* (50) arrived from Britain. On the passage they had spoken to a Dutch vessel four days out of Cadiz. The Dutch master told them that 5,000 troops had arrived from Galicia and 15 ships of the line were being prepared for sea. At that point they were still unready to sail, but Ogle despatched those ships back to Cadiz to confirm this news. Two days later the *Falmouth* (50) arrived, carrying Newcastle's despatch of 6 February, warning Haddock of the troops massing at Barcelona and the need to prevent a landing on Minorca. Ogle immediately saw Haddock was under strength for this task and made plans to join his commander. He ordered the *Superb* (70), to join three 50s, the *Tiger*, *Assistance* and *Litchfield*, off Cadiz and prepared the rest of his ships for Minorca.[46] Meanwhile, Haddock had reached Mahon on 27 February. The more he considered the intelligence from Barcelona, the less credible he believed it to be, but before he could do anything, Ogle arrived at Mahon.[47]

Haddock's despatch of 6 February explaining his move to Minorca was received in London on 3 March, but was quickly overtaken by tremendous news from the West Indies. Vernon had captured Porto Bello and Chagres in November 1739 with just five men of war and 280 soldiers. He had destroyed the fortifications and had practically severed the silver route from Peru. The speed of events held out great promise for the larger expedition in preparation.[48] Perhaps the war would be over before France could intervene effectively. On the 25 March the inner cabinet considered their reply

---

44   TNA, SP 42/86, f.167, Disposition of the Squadron, 21 January 1740.

45   Ibid., f. 208, Ogle to Newcastle, 4 March 1740.

46   Ibid., f. 214, Ogle to Newcastle, 7 March 1740.

47   Ibid., f. 212, Haddock to Newcastle, 6 March 1740; f. 241, Haddock to Newcastle, 10 April 1740.

48   Ibid., f. 157, 17 March 1740.

Table 3.1 Distribution of Mediterranean Squadron, February–March 1740

	80s	70s	60s	50s	20s	Others
With Haddock to Mahon to clean and refit	1	1	4	1	1	2
At Mahon				1	2	
With Ogle at Gibraltar	1	2	4	1		3
Cruising		3 (2 to G.B.)			3	
Total	2	3	8	3	6	5

to Vernon. Three fire ships and two bomb vessels had already been sent out under escort of the *Greenwich* (50), but he needed naval stores. It was agreed that two more men of war would convoy out the stores he requested. Walpole also received news that two Buenos Aires ship had left America in December and were expected in Europe soon. Two ships were also preparing in Cadiz to take the new Viceroy of Mexico to La Vera Cruz and two Spanish warships had sailed for America from San Sebastian on 17 February.[49] It was agreed that three warships should be despatched immediately to the northern coast of Spain and that Admiral Balchen should follow as soon as seven more ships were ready in case any of these Spanish vessels should be making for, or passing, Ferrol. Ogle, who was still believed to be at Gibraltar, was ordered to cruise off Cadiz for the same purpose.[50]

Four days later, on the 29 February, Ogle's letter, telling of his decision to follow Haddock, arrived. This was disappointing, but there were still three men of war off Cadiz so the plan to intercept the Buenos Aires ships was not entirely defeated. However, the larger question of the Spanish intentions remained unsolved. Ships had already left Ferrol and the northern Spanish ports for the Americas and news that the Cadiz squadron was preparing to sail had reached London in Ogle's despatch. The expedition at Barcelona was also predicted to be ready within 11 days, and earlier reports indicated France was intending to assist them with warships from Toulon.[51] The Brest

---

49 TNA, SP 78/222, f. 171, Waldegrave to Newcastle, 16 March 1740 (n.s.).

50 Ibid., f. 160, 25 March 1740; TNA, SP42/86 (State Papers – Naval) f. 231, Newcastle to Ogle, 25 March 1740.

51 TNA, SP 78/222, f. 213, Advice from Spain, in Waldegrave to Newcastle, 27 March 1740 (n.s.).

squadron of 18 ships of the line was said to be ready to sail.[52] If the Cadiz squadron sailed it could head eastwards to join forces with ships at Cartagena and Toulon to protect an invasion of Minorca. Equally, it might sail to the West Indies or to Ferrol. After consideration it was the ministry's view that it would steer for the West Indies, so Ogle should be sent back to Cadiz as quickly as possible with whatever ships could be spared.[53]

At Mahon, Haddock was tending to the same conclusion. His latest intelligence suggested that Spain had not yet got together enough troops to attack Minorca. He was more concerned by the rumour that the Cadiz squadron was preparing to join the Ferrol squadron at sea before sailing together to the West Indies.[54] He also ordered Ogle to go back to Cadiz to prevent the union of the Cadiz and Ferrol squadrons.[55]

Ogle sailed on 19 April. Convinced now that the preparations at Majorca were indeed a feint, Haddock immediately prepared three more 60s to reinforce Ogle, leaving himself with just two 80s, a 70, two 60s and a 50 for his line of battle.[56] Haddock's force was now extremely stretched. It was vital that his small ships constantly watched the coasts. He kept a particularly careful watch on Toulon, from where Captain Pocock of the *Aldborough* (20) sent a report of the state of the squadron there. The French had about eight line and three 54s fit for sea – far more firepower than Haddock's remaining ships could muster, but he could not let this delay him careening his foul ships. The two careening wharfs at Mahon had been busy all year cleaning ships in rotation, but in early May, only two ships, his flagship the *Lancaster* (80) and the *Pembroke* (60), were ready for immediate service.[57]

In London rumours of French intentions to join Spain in an invasion of the British Isles mingled with other rumours that Fleury's ministry was about to collapse as the French crown ran out of money.[58] The reports were

52   TNA, SP 78/222, ff. 237–238, Waldegrave to Newcastle, 3 April 1740 (n.s.), ff. 239–240, 4 April 1740 (n.s.).

53   TNA, SP 42/86, f. 233, Newcastle to Haddock, 4 April 1740.

54   Ibid., f. 268, Translation of a letter from Barcelona, 1 April 1740 (n.s.)

55   Ibid., ff. 241–247, Haddock to Newcastle, 10 April 1740; f. 262, Haddock to Ogle, 14 April 1740.

56   Ibid., f. 260, Haddock to Newcastle, 21 April 1740.

57   Ibid., f. 273, Pocock's report from off Toulon 20 March 1740; f. 277, Dispositions of the Ships at Mahon, 7 May 1740.

58   BL, Add Ms 32693, f.199, G. Dawson to Newcastle, 8 April 1740; TNA, SP78/222, f. 178, Waldegrave to Newcastle, 19 March 1740 (n.s.); f. 257, Waldegrave to Newcastle,

so confusing that Waldegrave admitted 'we have such a variety of reports about it, and about what is doing in their other ports, that there is no such thing as knowing what to believe or think of them'.[59] Fleury enjoyed seeing the British confusion. He was delighted that the richly laden Buenos Aires ships finally got into Portuguese and Spanish ports unmolested. 'He seemed to extol the conduct of the Court of Spain in timing their orders for their squadrons to get out of Cadiz and Ferrol, which he does not doubt of their having executed, and he believes the two squadrons are proceeding together to the West Indies.' Waldegrave continued 'it was whispered about Court yesterday that fresh orders were gone to Brest and Toulon to hasten the arming and manning their ships'.[60]

The ambiguity surrounding French intentions seriously concerned the British ministry. On 10 April the inner cabinet met at Newcastle's house. Newcastle reported that eight men of war had sailed from Cadiz. Their destination and purpose were all unknown, but it was agreed that if two men of war escorted the storeships being prepared for Vernon, his squadron would be strong enough to counter the Cadiz ships if they went to the Caribbean.[61] The following day news arrived of 12 French men of war putting to sea. News from Holland now suggested that 12 men of war had left Cadiz and 11 from Ferrol bound for the West Indies. If this were true then the Spaniards would only have four men of war fit for service in Europe and the focus of the war had shifted decisively to the Americas. It was agreed that Ogle, off Cadiz, should be ordered to sail with 10 of his line to join Vernon, or if he found they had gone to Ferrol or towards Britain, he was to follow them there. Haddock would be ordered to Gibraltar and watch Cadiz where the Spaniards were said to be preparing eight more men of war.[62]

Over the next two weeks the ministry waited anxiously for news of the Spanish and French squadrons. At a Cabinet meeting on the 17 April, Newcastle reported confirmation of the sailing of the Cadiz squadron. It was said to be carrying over 5,000 troops, but whether they had gone to America or Ferrol was still unknown. The French were said to have 20 men of war at Brest and Rochefort. If the French joined to the combined Spanish squad-

---

15 April 1740 (n.s.).

59   Ibid., f. 300, Waldegrave to Newcastle, 20 April 1740 (n.s.) (rec. 20 April).

60   Ibid., f. 320, Waldegrave to Newcastle, 4 May 1740 (n.s.) (rec. 29 April).

61   BL, Add Ms 28132, f. 165, 10 April 1740.

62   TNA, SP 42/86, f. 250, Newcastle to Haddock, 18 April 1740 and enclosed advice.

rons at Ferrol they would pose a huge danger to the British Isles. Norris had been frustrated for some months over what he saw as his lack of influence in naval affairs and suggested privately to Walpole that if George II would permit him to take two regiments on the ships, he would undertake to blockade the combined Spanish squadrons in Ferrol, if they were there.[63] In principle this was agreed. Balchen was to be reinforced by six ships, but command was given to Vice Admiral Stewart, rather than Norris.[64]

By the last week of April the junction of the Cadiz and Ferrol squadrons at Ferrol looked increasingly likely. Dutch and French reports now talked of embargos along the Biscay coast and transports being taken up for an expedition to Scotland or Ireland. The decision to send Ogle to the West Indies with 10 line looked increasingly mistaken. Ogle's ships were manned and worked up, but suffering from the wear and tear of months at sea. The ships being prepared at home, on the other hand, could manage a trans-Atlantic crossing better, but no ships were then ready for sea. Balchen, off Ferrol, whose five ships had not yet been reinforced, would have to fall back if the combined Spanish squadrons came out. At a meeting on the 23 it was agreed to suspend Ogle's orders. Ogle was to come home with his 10 ships and 10 other ships would be prepared for the West Indies in due course.[65] However, something went wrong. The orders to prepare the ten ships in Britain were sent to the Admiralty. Orders recalling Ogle had already been despatched overland via Haddock, but it was agreed to stop the ship carrying the same orders by sea, until more information was known.[66] At a Cabinet meeting on 28 April, Newcastle pointed this out to Wager, noting that if Ogle were not stopped, it was possible twenty warships would soon be on their way to the West Indies. Wager, according to Lord Hervey, 'muttered something in answer to this, most of it inarticulately, that it seemed like sounds without words, and where the articulation was plain it seemed words without sense'.[67]

---

63   Ibid., f. 169, 17 April 1740. Wager was junior to Norris, but as First Lord of the Admiralty had a place in cabinet. Norris only attended by special invitation 'as an auxiliary when anything was under deliberation relative to our present maritime war with Spain' (R. Sedgwick, ed., *Memoirs of the Reign of King George II by John Lord Hervey*, 3 vols, London, 1931, vol. iii, 925). This led to his exclusion on other important occasions, but Walpole did not wish to increase the size of the cabinet. See BL, Add Ms 28132, f. 179, 29 April 1740.

64   Ibid, 18 April 1740; TNA, SP42/23, f. 84, Wager to Admiralty, 18 April 1740.

65   Ibid., f. 174, 23 April 1740.

66   TNA, SP45/2, unfoliated, 23 April 1740.

67   Sedgewick, *Memoirs of Lord Hervey*, op. cit., vol. iii, 927.

Even allowing for Hervey's waspish memoir, there does appear to have been a problem. Wager deflected the comment towards the problems of manning. The discussion over recalling Balchen also ended without agreed action. Norris was not at this meeting, but he had noted Wager's lack of attention to detail on earlier occasions. Perhaps Wager was ill, but at least temporarily he seemed unable to provide constructive advice. Nevertheless, on 30 April some re-disposition was agreed. The immediate need was to establish a credible force in the Soundings. Balchen would be recalled with three of his ships, leaving two off Ferrol for early warning. However, it was to be nearly another month before Ogle was to be recalled with his 10 ships.[68]

During the first week of May the balance of information continued to reinforce the impression that preparations were being made at Ferrol to mount an invasion of Britain or Ireland. On 6 May Newcastle again pressed to have Ogle's order to follow the Cadiz squadron to the West Indies countermanded, but it was agreed that it was now too late and that the Ogle would not, in any case, go to the West Indies if the Cadiz squadron was in Ferrol.[69]

The middle two weeks of May bought little comfort to the ministry. 15,000 troops under the Jacobite Duke of Ormonde were said to be ready at Ferrol. The Brest and Toulon squadrons were continuing to arm. The Marquis D'Antin had arrived in Brest to command the 18 ships of that squadron and troops were said to be arriving at Toulon to join the 12 men of war there.[70] Nevertheless, the King was determined to visit Hanover at the end of the month and Walpole felt unable to dissuade him at this dangerous juncture.[71]

On 19 May the King left London for Hanover. Once he was reported to be safely landed in Europe, the Lords Justices of the Regency were formally constituted. They functioned like the Cabinet. They deliberated on public affairs and policy was decided there. While the King was at home, sensitive foreign policy was kept in the hands of his most trusted advisors, the 'inner' cabinet, which met at Walpole's or Newcastle's houses. During his absence, these 'lords he usually consulted on secret affairs' continued to meet to discuss foreign correspondence and manage business before putting it to the wider Regency.[72]

---

68   Ibid., f. 180, 30 April 1740; TNA, SP 42/86, f.279, Newcastle to Ogle, 24 May 1740. For Norris' relations with Wager in these critical days see BL, Add Ms 28132 (Norris Journal), ff. 180–183, 30 April–2 May 1740.

69   Sedgewick, *Memoirs of Lord Hervey*, op. cit., vol. iii, 933.

70   Ibid.

71   Ibid., vol. iii, 934.

72   TNA, SP 43/28, unfoliated, 29 May 1741.

The Regents did not doubt that a significant Spanish expedition was in preparation for the West Indies or Ireland, but the lack of manpower prevented the British from getting many more ships to sea. Manpower was always the key problem when it came to mobilising the fleet. For the average seamen life in the Royal Navy was not so desperately bad and there were plenty of men who would voluntarily enlist on a warship, but never enough. Men had to be taken forcibly from the merchant service, which was not popular with merchants or seamen. Bounties were offered, but the merchant service was more highly paid and usually more certain in the duration of the voyages.[73] During wars there was always the danger of being taken by enemy warships or privateers. However, for the seaman there was the alternative of embarking on a privateer himself. It was dangerous and rewards depended on the success in capturing enemy merchantmen, but for many seamen it was worth the risk.[74] Every measure taken to secure semen for the fleet met with opposition. Embargoes were ordered to prevent merchant ships sailing until enough seamen had been taken up by the Royal Navy. These were highly unpopular as maritime commerce was seasonally dependent and any delays could prevent the profitable conclusion of voyages before winter set in. Embargoes could not be imposed indefinitely and any 'press' could be so disruptive to trade, particularly coasting, fishing and river commerce, that seamen in these trades were often given 'protections' or certificates, exempting them from the press. From time to time other trades had to be protected was well. These restraints meant that other seamen had to be pursued more vigorously. Justices of the peace (JPs) and constables were encouraged to take up seamen who were between voyages or apparently unemployed and given conduct money to get them to a port, but this could meet with opposition from local people. The naval press gang ashore often met resistance and violence.[75] Pressing at sea, in which a tender would intercept homeward bound merchantmen in the approaches or

---

73   Seamen had different life experiences depending on the type of trades in which they were engaged. Perhaps two thirds were employed in coastal trades or fisheries as late as the 1770s. They were used to working in small crews, averaging eight or nine men and were paid by voyage, share or month. A good description of these differences can be found in P. Earle, *Sailors: English Merchant Seamen, 1650–1775*, London, 1998.

74   The best overview of this subject is D.J. Starkey, *British Privateering Enterprise in the Eighteenth Century*, Exeter, 1990. The impact of American Privateering in this war is explored in C.E. Swanson, *Predators and Prizes: American Privateering and Imperial Warfare, 1739–1748*, Columbia, 1991. The impact of war on trade patterns is covered in P. Crowhurst, *The Defence of British Trade, 1689–1815*, Folkstone, 1977.

75   Rogers, *The Press Gang*, op. cit.

Channel and take off a proportion of their crew was far more effective. The injustice of pressing seamen was recognised by all, but there was no other way that could be found to man the ships. A bill to register seamen had failed in parliament in February 1740. France and Spain used a register of seamen, which theoretically enabled them to identify and then demand about one-third of seamen annually for naval service. It was never as effective as expected, but the fact that it was used by those absolutist monarchies ensured that it would never have the support for it to be applied to free-born Englishmen.[76] Without new measures a committee of flag officers which met in January to consider the manning problem were forced back on established practice. Pressing should be more vigorously executed. Protections should be limited. The system of tenders, the ships that were used to accommodate pressed men until they were turned over to a warship, should be reformed to be more efficient. JPs should be instructed to round up straggling seamen and the bounties extended to the 20 April.[77] By May it was clear that this had not produced the manpower required.

The inner cabinet assembled at Newcastle's house on 22 May. Newcastle presented the latest news that Spain had 18 ships of the line in Ferrol. The Lords of the Admiralty were then called in to explain the manning problems. They believed that if 1,000 seamen were turned over from other ships then 17 men of war could be got ready for sea. However, the price would be disabling the rest of the fleet. After they withdrew, Norris presented his plan to use two foot regiments and 1,000 marines to man the fleet.[78] He proposed withdrawing Ogle from Ferrol and putting two clean ships as a forward screen. Balchen would be recalled to re-victual before returning to a position off the Lizard. The King's resistance to putting his soldiers on the ships was well

---

76 Corbett, *Parliamentary History*, op. cit., xi (1739–41), 414–445, 5 February 1740. See also, E.L. Asher, *The Resistance to the Maritime Classes: The Survival of Feudalism in the France of Colbert*, Berkeley, 1960; J.P. Merino Navarro, *La Armada Española en el siglo XVIII*, Madrid, 1981, 83–88.

77 Cobbett, *Parliamentary History*, op cit. xi (1739–1741), 414–435; BL, Add Ms 28132 (Norris Journal), ff. 127–128, 16 Januaury 1740.

78 BL, Add Ms 28132, f. 193, 22 May 1740. The fullest account of this meeting is printed in the *Memoirs of Lord Hervey*, iii, 936–941, but Hervey was mistaken about Newcastle's position regarding orders for Ogle's squadron. Hervey and Newcastle detested each other and Hervey supported Walpole against Newcastle. Hervey claimed that Newcastle wanted Ogle sent to America in response to Lord Carteret's call to 'Look to America'. Certainly, Newcastle did think that the victory would be won in the West Indies, as did most all of the ministers, but he did not want to send Ogle's squadron there. He was as ardent as Walpole in his desire to have Ogle returned to Britain.

known, but this time there was no practical alternative and it was agreed to put this to the King. Newcastle did not wait for approval, but began sending the orders immediately.[79] He ordered the two youngest regiments on the British establishment to be distributed on the ships.[80] These troops would be reserved for ships on home service so they could be landed quickly, while 1,800 more marines were also to be raised to put on ships going on foreign service.[81]

The intention was now for Norris to take the war to the coast of Spain. Perhaps 20 men of war could be manned with the help of the soldiers. This would be the most powerful squadron put to sea in the war. Norris's flagship was the 100 gun *Victory*, which with six 80s, four 70s and a 60, formed his line of battle. The line was supported by three fireships. His orders were 'to endeavour to get what intelligence you can, whether the Spanish ships are still at Ferrol and if you shall find that they are remaining there, you are to cruise on that coast, in order to keep them in, or to intercept and take them, in case they should attempt to come out'. If they had sailed he was to discover their destination and if they were bound for Britain or Ireland, he was to follow them with his whole force. If they had gone to the West Indies or Cadiz he was to detach a force to reinforce Vernon or Haddock respectively. If he met Ogle he was to add those ships to his own force.[82] If he succeeded, Norris would bottle up the Spanish fleet, ending the invasion threat and opening the way for the British West Indian expedition to sail safely to its destination.

While the force was preparing more disturbing news arrived. On 6 June new reports arrived of the Spanish squadrons having sailed for the West Indies,[83] but other reports told of them discharging cargoes of quicksilver and that they had no troops on board, which made it highly unlikely that this was their destination. Over the next few days reports of the sailing continued, but no hint of their destination. There were even rumours that the squadron was back in Ferrol, or that Spain had no money and that their demonstrations were purely to keep the British in suspense.[84] Rumours that

---

79   TNA, SP42/86, f. 279, Newcastle to Ogle, 24 May 1740; SP 42/23, f.123, Newcastle to the Admiralty, 223 May 1740.

80   TNA, SP 43/25, unfoliated, Harrington to Newcastle, 4 June 1740.

81   TNA, SP 43/27, unfoliated, Newcastle to Harrington, 3 June 1740.

82   TNA, SP 42/87, f. 2, Lords Justices to Norris, 19 June 1740.

83   TNA, SP 43/27, unfoliated, Stone to Harrington, 6 June 1740; SP 78/223 (State Papers – France), f. 106, Newcastle to Waldegrave, 10 June 1740.

84   TNA, SP 43/27, unfoliated, Stone to Harrington, 13 June 1740; SP 78/223, f. 74, Waldegrave to Newcastle, 13 June 1740 (n.s.).

the French squadrons were ready for sea and headed for the West Indies also continued to flow in.[85]

As preparations continued during July Norris and Wager were captivated by a plan of a Captain Cole. Cole was a spy who had returned from Ferrol in early June with news about the sailing of the Ferrol squadron. He had discussed an attack on Ferrol with Wager and Norris and initially the discussion had centred on Lord Cathcart's expeditionary army attempting the assault on its way to the West Indies. The Lords Justices rejected the plan as a potential hazard to what they saw as the main objective of the campaign, but, nonetheless, asked the admirals to examine the plan in more detail. Norris was impressed by Cole's account of the weakness of the landward defences of Ferrol and went to Wager and Walpole to try to have Cathcart's army diverted to that place. After all, he reasoned, if the Spanish squadrons were destroyed in Ferrol the war at sea would be over for the foreseeable future and the Spanish empire would be at Britain's mercy. Wager seems to have been convinced, but Walpole rejected the idea. Norris did not give up. On his way to Portsmouth, he stopped off at Newcastle's house, Claremont, in Surrey, to try to convince him of the plan. Newcastle, like his ministerial colleagues recognised the public expectation of success in the Caribbean was too powerful to risk losing the expeditionary force in the hills of Galicia.[86] While the expeditionary army remained in Britain, Cole did not give up. In July he sent his plan to Hardwicke, to convince the Lord Chancellor of its practicality. Hardwicke was impressed by the support given to it by Wager and Norris, but he uncovered a further weakness. Cole insisted that the fleet would have to force its way into the bay, much as Admiral Rooke's force had done at Vigo 1702, but he was not clear if this was possible given the defences at the approaches. As far as the ministers were concerned it was too late in the day to undertake detailed re-examination of priorities. The campaign was reaching a crisis. The West Indian expedition had to sail directly to the Caribbean if it was to achieve the results expected of it.[87] Decisive victory here, while France remained neutral, would have an immediate political result and even more lasting impact on Spain that the loss of her fleet.

During this desperate summer the ministers had little time to reflect on news of another event which had reached London on 3 June. King Frederick

85   TNA, SP 43/25, unfoliated, Harrington to Newcastle, 11 June 1740.
86   BL, Add Ms 28133 (Norris Journal), ff. 13–15, 18–22 June 1740.
87   BL, Add Ms 35406 (Hardwicke Papers), f. 215, Hardwicke to Harrington, 23 July 1740; f. 251, Cole to Hardwicke, 17 July 1740; f. 253, Memo on Cole's Scheme, 23 July 1740.

William II of Prussia had died. He was succeeded by his young son Frederick II. In the hectic and anxious days of June, the ministers considered this turn of events as 'a great advantage', with the new king in Prussia providing new diplomatic opportunities in Europe.[88] Little did they realise that within six months that king would have thrown the entire war into disarray.

Organising the Offensive: January–July 1740

By the end of July the West Indian expedition should be ready to sail. The main expeditionary army was to be made up from three sources; two old battalions on the British establishment, the six new marine regiments approved by Parliament on 27 November 1739, and a body of American troops.[89]

The critical factor that had made the expedition possible was the prospect of raising substantial numbers of Americans. Once the decision to raise the troops had been made, the question had been referred to Colonel Martin Bladen of the Board of Trade.[90] He was initially sceptical both of the potential quality of the troops and their willingness to enlist for a distant expedition under regular command. However, he suggested that the latter problem might be overcome if the soldiers served under local officers, and for the next three months a secret planning committee of Bladen, Wade, Cathcart, Norris and Wager worked to give shape to instructions on these lines.

Like the American Regiment, the marine regiments had to be raised from scratch. A core of about 35 per cent of the rank and file was drawn out of existing battalions and the sergeants were selected from men of the Foot Guards. The field officers and captains were recruited from officers on half pay. Over 60 per cent of the first lieutenants were likewise half-pay officers. The rest of the first lieutenants and the second lieutenants were drawn from gentlemen recommended to the Secretary at War and approved by the King.[91] Recruiting for the rest of the rank and file began as soon as the warrants were signed on 21 December.[92] The extremely harsh winter seems to have aided the recruiting parties as the regiments were complete by the time the trans-

---

88 TNA, SP 43/27, unfoliated, Newcastle to Harrington, 3 June 1740.

89 Cathcart Mss, Lord Cathcart's Diary, 21 November to 12 December 1732; TNA, CO 5/41, f. 46, Cathcart to Newcastle, 7 June 1740.

90 R. Harding, Amphibious Warfare in the Eighteenth Century: The British Expedition to the West Indies, 1740–1742, Woodbridge, 1991, 37.

91 Ibid., 66–70.

92 TNA, WO 26/19, ff. 226–229, Warrants for the draft of soldiers, 21 December 1739.

ports were ready to take them to the rendezvous on the Isle of Wight. These new regiments were not the cream of the army and contemporaries and historians have pointed out that the mistake of sending such raw troops on such a vital operations.[93] However, there were powerful political reasons for sending them. The ministry had to tread a delicate path between the King, who refused to allow his foot regiments to go overseas, and Parliament that expected significant land forces to go the West Indies. The decision to raise marine regiments was an attempt to square the circle. Calling them marines signalled to Parliament that these troops were for sea service. By regimenting them under the War Office they were in practice little different to foot regiments, which would placate the King's desire to expand the army. In practice the choice of the marines probably had little impact on the efficiency of the expeditionary force. Almost all regiments were rapidly recruiting after years of peace and officers were returning to their regiments. Blakeney's foot, which had been allocated to the expedition, had recently come over from Ireland and had to be recruited to strength. Lord Cathcart was so dissatisfied with the state of this regiment that he insisted it be changed for another. Major General Harrison's foot was ordered in its place. The marines, on the other hand, spent weeks on the Isle of Wight training under the command of Brigadier Wentworth and by late June, observers, including Cathcart, the young Duke of Cumberland and Admiral Norris were extremely impressed by their discipline.[94]

Getting the troops to the West Indies demanded major effort on the part of the Navy Board. Transports had to be hired and converted, and precedents had to be broken through if enough vessels were to be found in time. It was usual for expeditions crossing the Atlantic to stop to refresh and water at Madeira or friendly ports in North America. This was not to happen on this occasion. The emphasis was on a speedy arrival of the troops at their objective.[95] Wager realised that this could have a devastating effect on the health of the troops on the cramped transports. Tonnage for transports was hired at a fixed rate of

93   Anon., *An Account of the Expedition to Cartagena*, London, 1740, 55; W. Cobbett, *Parliamentary History*, op. cit. xii, 239; Chesterfield in the debate in the Lords on the Address of Thanks, 4 December 1741; *Common Sense*, 18th July 1741; Richmond, *The Navy in the War*, op. cit, i, 135.

94   BL, Add Ms, 32694, f. 172, Newcastle to Harrington, 18 July 1740; Add Ms 28133, f.19, 7 July 1740; TNA, CO 5/41, f. 46, Cathcart to Newcastle, 7 June 1740; f. 50, Cathcart to Newcastle, 8 July 1740.

95   BL, Add Ms 28132, f. 101, 19 December 1739.

tons per man carried. Transport to Europe was hired at the rate of 1 ton per man. Otherwise, 1.5 tons was permitted. On this occasion there was to be no chance to refresh the men before they landed to engage the enemy. Wager enquired if there was any precedent for increasing the allowance of 1.5 tons per man. The Admiralty then applied directly to the King to authorise an increase to 2 tons per man, which was approved by 12 January. Later amendments to precedent included the provision of fishing gear, awnings, vinegar for washing the decks and pilots to facilitate movement.

The 8,000 troops required 16,000 tons of shipping. Invitations to treat were posted at the Royal Exchange on 2 January 1740. The time of year assisted the Board as large numbers of ships were in the River Thames held up by ice. However the ship owners realised that the Board's demands were huge by the standards of the time and it did not take them long to combine to force the Board to accept improved clauses in their charter parties To the credit of the Board and the ministry they quickly realised how the balance of power had changed. On 12 February they accepted a revised charter party which favoured the ship owners and the ships began to arrive at Deptford for inspection and conversion shortly afterwards. That the revised contract suited the new situation is evident from the fact that it became the model for contracts at least until the 1780s.[96]

The demand for ships was so great that the Navy Board could not insist upon minimum internal dimensions, which it was later to do. Norris had estimated that the whole process of inspection and conversion would take about two months to complete.[97] However the officers of the Deptford Yard had to deal with over seventy vessels and it was not until 12 May that the last of the main group of transports received its certificate. Transports were sent to Leith and Newcastle to pick up two marine regiments that had recruited there, while the rest made their way round to Spithead. By the end of July almost all the transports were there. Bad weather delayed the last few vessels coming around the south coast, but the troops embarked within 12 days of Cathcart's original target date.

Victualling this vast force also caused strain and concern. It represented approximately a 15 per cent increase on the expected contracting requirements. The Board had no difficulty in getting biscuit, oats and pease, but the harvest of 1739 had been poor and food shortages were a feature of 1740.

96   Harding, *Amphibious Warfare*, op. cit., 48–50.

97   BL, Add Ms 28132, f. 113, 31 December 1739.

Other provisions caused more problems. The harsh winter hindered transport and water-powered production. The killing season had ended on 25 December and additional salt beef was not immediately available. Brine froze in the carcasses and meat was prematurely barrelled. The provision of cheese also caused a problem. No delays were experienced at this point, but the effects of the winter were felt in the late summer when large quantities of beef and cheese had to be condemned. There was enough beer on the London market, but if the force was delayed at Spithead, replacing it would be a problem.

Victualling the army in the West Indies was undertaken by John Simpson and John Mason, who held the contract for supplying the Royal Navy at Jamaica. Like the ship owners, Mason and Simpson realised that the escalation of demands posed an opportunity. Food prices were rising as a result of the poor harvest. They refused to contract for their standard price of 8d per man per day. They wanted 9½ d and demanded an advance of £10,000. Like the Navy Board, the Victualling Board realised that precedent had to fall in the face of necessity and accepted this revised contract. Despite the cooperation of the Victualling Board, the contractors faced mounting problems. They had to borrow victuals from the King's stores at Portsmouth if they were to have a chance of meeting their obligations in Jamaica. They ran into problems with shipping because of the general embargo and the acute shortage of seamen during the summer of 1740. In the end, Mason and Simpson successfully got the victuals to Jamaica. However, the strain was evident and was enough for them to give notice that they intended to relinquish their contract. In 1741 the victualling reverted to direct supply by the Victualling Board. While this imposed further short-term stresses on the victualling system, there was never again the near break-down of victualling system that was experienced during 1740.

The final department of state which had to react to the demands of the expedition was the Ordnance Board. The appointment of a chief engineer proved problematic. The King's concern for security at home made it impossible to send the chief engineer, Colonel Armstrong, but he recognised the importance of the expedition and agreed to release the second ranking engineer, Colonel Lascelles. Lascelles himself was not keen to go and demanded a regiment on the Irish establishment as a reward. George II refused this and Lascelles simply refused the commission. With only three weeks to go before the expedition was to depart, a replacement was found in Jonas Moore, who had served as chief engineer at Gibraltar during the siege of 1727. There were 14 engineers on the establishment, of whom 12 were originally intended for the expedition. The news in April that the Ferrol and Cadiz squadrons had joined and an invasion might be in the offing caused that number to be reduced to ten. Five were taken from the establishment and five others from officers who had trained privately as engineers. There was no lack of volunteers to fill these posts or to provide additional men who went out in the expectation of filling the shoes of engineers who died. Although much pamphlet criticism was levelled at these men after the expedition, there is little evidence that their performance was unacceptable. Almost all those who survived continued to serve and rise to high rank.[98]

The artillery was also severely criticised after the return of the expedition, but this also appears groundless. The colonel of the Train, Jonas Watson, was the senior artillery officer in the kingdom. The other officers were also highly experienced men and most of the sergeants, corporals, bombardiers and gunners came from the old Woolwich companies. Only the private soldiers (matrosses) were newly recruited during the winter months. The ordnance stores were carefully calculated and quantities adjusted according to intelligence. This did cause some problems as additional *ad hoc* demands required addition shipping and it was not until 5 September that Cathcart declared he had all the stores he required.[99]

On the whole, like the other parts of the administration, the Ordnance Board responded quickly and effectively to the exceptional demands placed upon it in the first half of 1740. It had originally been expected that the force would sail at the end of July. The despatch from Hanover approving Cathcart's instructions arrived on 8 July.[100] The last details were settled over the week and Cathcart left London on the morning of 15 July for Spithead. As the ministry waited anxiously, news arrived that the army was embarking in the first days of August.[101] It was now important that Norris wrest the initiative back by establishing control of the Channel while the expeditionary force departed into the Atlantic.

Failure to Regain the Initiative: July–October 1740

By early July 1740 the pressures of war had taken their toll on the ministry. Walpole had been overruled in the main thrust of the war, but seemed to

---

98   Harding, *Amphibious Warfare*, op. cit., 60–63.

99   Ibid., 63–66.

100 TNA, SP43/25, unfoliated, Harrington to Newcastle, 2 July 1740.

101 TNA, SP43/27, unfoliated, Newcastle to Harrington, 15 July 1740; BL, Add Ms 32694, f. 385, Richmond to Newcastle, 1 August 1740.

be being proved right about the fragility of the assumptions on which the war was based. French neutrality was proving doubtful. The Spanish navy had proved a far more disruptive and capable force than anyone had anticipated in October 1739.[102] However, the decision to put soldiers and marines on the ships seemed at last to offer the prospect of decisive action to regain the initiative. Norris was preparing for sea to blockade the Spanish fleet in Ferrol. The expedition to the West Indies should be ready to sail by the end of July. If France's neutrality could be maintained during the next few weeks the decisive blow could be struck and balance of advantage shifted to Britain. However, the news from France was not good. Waldegrave warned that the sailing of the expeditionary force would signal a clear break with France. Norris could be alerted, but he could not be diverted from his task of blockading Ferrol.[103]

Norris went aboard his flagship, *Victory* (100), at Portsmouth on 23 June. The anchorage at Spithead was full of merchantmen awaiting convoy. The bulk of his squadron, 12 line and four fireships, were ready. However, some of his seamen had been lent to Balchen's squadron and given the sickness that was known to be on that force, Norris calculated that he could only rely on half of that number being returned. Altogether his force was just over 17 per cent short of complement. Five more line were at Plymouth, another three line, his hospital ship and two 20s were between Deptford and the Nore. Norris estimated that the ships at Plymouth would be about 20 per cent short of complement. He had no information on the state of the ships at Deptford, but anticipated that soldiers would be able to make up the complements.[104]

Norris' asked for two more 20s and two 40s or 50s to ensure he could keep patrols out along the Spanish Biscay coast. The two 20s could be had, but there were no more ships ready for sea, so Norris was ordered to take under his command the *Newcastle* (50) and *Dolphin* (20), which were thought to be cruising off Ferrol.[105] As Norris's squadron lay wind-bound at Spithead, Ogle arrived from Cadiz. His eight ships were short of water and carried at least 20 per cent of the crews sick, but otherwise they were still fit for sea. He

---

102 University of Nottingham, Cumber Mss, NeC 104, Newcastle to Pelham, 21 June 1740; NeC 134, H. Walpole to H. Pelham, 6 June 1740; Sedgewick, *Memoirs of Lord Hervey*, op. cit., iii, 927–940; TNA, SP 78/223, f. 111, Newcastle to Waldegrave, 12 June 1740.

103 TNA, SP 36/51, f. 162, Newcastle to Harrington, 24 June 1740.

104 TNA, SP 42/87, f. 6, Norris to Newcastle, 24 June 1740.

105 Ibid., f. 12, Norris to Newcastle, 28 June 1740; f. 14, Newcastle to Norris, 1 July 1740; f. 28, Newcastle to Norris, 8 July 1740.

was ordered to replace his sick with marines and follow Norris back to sea as soon as possible.[106]

At least Ogle brought some comforting news. There were no ships at Cadiz in a fit state to sail. The five Spanish warships at Cartagena which, it was feared, might have convoyed an invasion force from Majorca and Barcelona to Minorca, had been damaged in a storm and had put back to refit. The Ferrol squadron had put to sea in May to attack Balchen, but had been forced back by bad weather. Scarcity of workmen and materials was now delaying the Spanish refitting. News about Brest was less encouraging. Eighteen ships were said to be fitting out, with at least eight already manned. Norris was ordered to find out more about that force. His main objective was to prevent them linking up with the Spaniards in Ferrol and protecting the West Indian expedition from attack.[107] Norris noted that he could watch Brest with a frigate, and prevent the French and Spanish from linking by his blockade of Ferrol, but he could not prevent the French getting out of Brest and attacking the expeditionary force at sea. The ministry recognised this and confirmed that his first objective was to stop the French and Spanish from uniting. With Ogle's ships they expected him to have 26 line at his disposal by the time he reached Ferrol.

Also crowded into the anchorage of Spithead were the transports for the West Indian expedition, due to sail on 20 July. The protection of the expeditionary force was, for Norris, a secondary objective. It might be possible that he would leave on the same wind as the expeditionary force, in which case he would escort them out into the open ocean, but he was not to delay his departure. Captain Gasgoigne of the *Buckingham* (70), with three 60s, two 50s, a 20, two fireships and a hospital ship provided the expedition's escort. Norris was also ordered to detach Admiral Balchen, who had joined him from Plymouth, with two 80s, a 70 and a 60 to provide an additional escort for 150 leagues out into the ocean before returning to Norris off Ferrol.[108]

There was a short shift in the wind on the 14 July and Norris's force weighed anchor, but the winds quickly shifted back and Norris was compelled to

---

106 Ibid., f. 38, News of the French Fleet.

107 Ibid., f. 41, Newcastle to Norris, (secret), 8 July 1740.

108 Ibid., f. 49, Newcastle to Norris, 10 July 1740; f. 52, Newcastle to Norris, 11 July 1740; f. 56, Norris to Newcastle, 12 July 1740; f. 58, Norris to Newcastle, 12 July 1740; BL, Add Ms, 28133, f. 22, 12 July 1740. The escort plan evolved over the week, partly in response to the King's views, culminating in the instructions to Gascoyne. TNA, SP 42/22 (State Papers- Naval), f. 224, Admiralty to Gascoigne, 24 July 1740.

anchor in Torbay. Penned in by contrary winds and thick weather, Norris could do nothing about news that d'Antin was ready to sail with 17 line of battleships from Brest.

At the beginning of August Cathcart's army was embarked. Newcastle anxiously pressed him to depart. Newcastle's hopes for the campaign were rising. If the expedition got away now it would be too late to stop the British plan. He wrote to Vernon 'Such a strength at sea, and such a Number of land Forces have, I believe, scarce ever been seen together in the West Indies and we have great Reason to hope, that the American levies will exceed the number that was at first thought of'.[109]

Newcastle's optimism was to multiply Norris's difficulties. Just before leaving Spithead Norris had been informed that Spanish privateers had 56 prizes in the Basque port of St Sebastian. He had already asked the Lords Justices for a 20 to keep watch off that port and added that he hoped to avenge these insults. This was interpreted by the Lords Justices as an intention to attack the port, which they quickly approved.[110] The soldiers manning the ships would provide the landing force. Norris was horrified as he meant only to intercept privateers coming out of St Sebastian. Nevertheless, he said he would send a 50 and two 20s to lie off St Sebastian, and asked if he could have two bomb vessels to fire on the town.[111]

Over the next week, while Norris waited on the troops and mortars for his new expedition, the situation began to clarify. A Spanish squadron of perhaps 16 line had gone to the West Indies.[112] On 21 August the Regents met to consider the situation. An invasion was now unlikely. The safety of Cathcart's expeditionary force was paramount and it was agreed to strengthen the convoy. However, overnight, as orders were being prepared, the wind shifted and it was realised that Norris and the expeditionary force might both sail before the despatches could reach them. Rather than risk any further delay, the Regents quickly reassembled and revoked their orders[113]. The same day, 22 August, news reached the Admiralty from Dieppe that thirteen French

109 BL, Add Ms 32694, f. 417, Newcastle to Vernon, 7 August 1740.

110 TNA, SP 42/87, f. 64, Newcastle to Norris, 19 July 1740; f. 66, Norris to Newcastle, 20 July 1740; f. 68, Newcastle to Norris, 22 July 1740.

111 Ibid., f. 79, Norris to Newcastle, 7 Aug 1740; f. 83, Norris to Newcastle, 8 August 1740; f. 87, Newcastle to Norris, 12 August 1740; f. 101, Stone to Norris, 14 August 1740.

112 TNA, SP 78/223 f. 324, Waldegrave to Newcastle, 25 August 1740 (n.s.).

113 They were *the Princess Amelia* (80), *Lyon* (60) and *Grafton* (70). *The Augusta* (60) was added a few days later.

men of war had been sighted at sea.[114] With French and Spanish squadrons now at sea, the ministers stuck to their conviction – the expedition must sail with the existing favourable wind.

Balchen sailed with the expeditionary force from Portsmouth on 23 August, but was very quickly forced back to Spithead by the winds.[115] Then, on 3 September, a despatch from Waldegrave arrived, stating that the Brest and Toulon squadrons were both at sea – 26 French line of battle ships were steering for the West Indies to join the 15 Spanish ships already on their way. Even Waldegrave now accepted that France intended to stop British operations in the West Indies and bring home the treasure ships.[116] Balchen and Cathcart were still battling against the wind to get out of the Channel. There was little choice now but to stop them.

On 5 September the Regents met to review the situation. Virtually the whole of the Spanish and French navies could be on their way to the West Indies. To Newcastle the situation was clear and critical. The French had gone to assist the Spanish in the West Indies. Ships had to be sent after them; 'For if the French and Spaniards get the better of us in the West Indies, we must ever after be at the mercy of France.'[117] However, opinion was divided. Others were not convinced that the Toulon squadron had gone west, but they eventually agreed to an escort of thirteen warships under Ogle. They calculated that the Brest and Ferrol squadrons amounted to 28 line. Ogle's reinforcement would give Vernon 29 ships.[118] Speed was essential and the expedition was ordered to sail as soon as six of the additional ships were ready.

Newcastle was aware that the war might be changing. France might want to confine herself to supporting Spain in the West Indies, but war could spread to Europe and he urged Harrington in Hanover 'to form a kind of grand alliance to oppose the ambitious views of the House of Bourbon. I

---

114 TNA, Adm 1/904, unfoliated, Balchen to Burchett, 22 August 1740.

115 TNA, Adm 1/904, unfoliated, Stewart to Burchett, 24 August 1740; SP 41/12 (War Office), unfoliated, Yonge to Newcastle, 24 August 1740; BL, Add Ms, 32694, f. 495, Newcastle to Harrington, 26 August 1740.

116 TNA, SP 78/223, f. 385, Waldegrave to Newcastle, 11 September 1740 (n..s); BL, Add Ms 35406, f. 294, Chandos to Hardwicke, 3 September 1740. *Richmond Newcastle Correspondence*, 42, Newcastle to Richmond, 4 September 1740; Add Ms 32694, f. 581, Newcastle to Harrington, 5 September 1740.

117 BL, Add Ms 32695, f. 5, Newcastle to Harrington, (private), 6 September 1740.

118 Ibid.; TNA, SP 42/23, f. 325, Stone to the Admiralty, 5 September 1740; SP 36/52, unfoliated, Minutes of the Lords Justices, 5 September 1740.

see the difficulty in forming such a concert, but the necessity of such a one should make us get over all the difficulties that are to be surmounted'.[119] On the 7 September the Portuguese envoy confirmed that the Toulon squadron was indeed headed for the West Indies and the next day, there was a private meeting at Walpole's house. Walpole, Newcastle, Hardwicke, Pelham and Wager were present. They reviewed all the latest intelligence. French intentions were not in doubt. The French ambassador at The Hague had declared to the States General that France would not allow Britain to make any conquests in the West Indies.[120] The Spanish squadron was now thought to consist of 16 line and three frigates. The French squadrons, 20 line and nine frigates: a total of 36 line and 12 frigates. Against this Vernon, reinforced by Ogle, would have 29 line. This was inviting disaster and it was agreed that Norris's squadron at Torbay would be broken up and a force of 29 line and four 50s should be assembled under Ogle at Spithead to escort the expedition.[121] This would give Vernon a superiority of 43 to 36 ships of the line. Manpower was critical, but with so few French and Spanish ships left in home waters the rest of the largest ships were to be laid up in favour of manning the remaining three 70s, two 60s, three 50s and eight 40s then fitting out. That afternoon the proposal was put to a rapidly assembled meeting of the Lords Justices and approved.[122] Orders were sent immediately to prepare the ships for service in the Americas.

The vast bulk of the fleet was now preparing for the West Indies. The Kingdom was exposed and if the combined French and Spanish squadrons met Vernon at sea, before he was reinforced, he would be overwhelmed. However, if he stayed in Port Royal the expeditionary force might be destroyed before it joined him. Hardwicke confessed he could think of little else but these possibilities. Wager seems to have been having growing reservations, and Hardwicke was anxious for the arrival of Norris back in London

---

119 BL, Add Ms 32695, f. 5, Newcastle to Harrington, (private), 6 September 1740.

120 BL, Add Ms 32695, f. 47, Newcastle to Vernon, 12 September 1740

121 TNA, SP 42/87, f. 171, Stone to Norris, 8 September 1740. The convoys of storeships waiting to go to the Mediterranean and West Indies were ordered to proceed under an escort of seven warships.

122 TNA, SP 36/52, unfoliated, Meeting at Walpole's 8 September 1740; Minutes of the Lords Justices, 8 September 1740. Only the Archbishop of Canterbury, the Lord Privy Seal, and Montagu joined the other ministers. The ministers calculated the 54s and 50s as ships of the line on this occasion.

for a different, probably more positive, view of naval events.[123] It was vital that Vernon and Ogle joined as quickly as possible. Ogle was ordered not to delay, even to pick up troops on the Leeward Islands, but to find Vernon.[124] The manpower problem had strained the administration almost to breaking point all summer. Despite every method, including taking 600 marines from Cathcart's expeditionary army, the squadron was still 10 per cent short of men.[125] Turning the seamen over from one ship to another was pursued vigorously, but Wager remained pessimistic.[126] Nevertheless, this would not be allowed to stop Ogle. The sudden demand to prepare so many ships for the Americas temporarily broke the victualling system. Of Ogle's ships 84 per cent were short of victuals by 13 October but he was not to let this stop him, but sail at the first opportunity.

As September passed, and the ships awaited favourable winds, contradictory intelligence continued to flow in.[127] The King was, at last, on his way back to Britain, but now a very different war was developing and tensions within the ministry were becoming more dangerous. For over a year Walpole had been engaged in conducting a war in which he had little faith and at the meeting of the Regency on Tuesday 1 October he was in particularly 'peevish' spirits.[128] Hardwicke watched Walpole's behaviour and understood that a real danger lay in distrust within the ministry. He suggested that:

> this conduct seems to proceed from great embarrass and anxiety of mind; doubtfulness of the event and of the rightness of the measures, having no clear fixed plan, and from a willingness to throw out things, that may hereafter be quoted and made use of as future accidents may turn out. Add to this, that Our Friend's humour on these points differs from day to day, as other incidents arise, agreeable or disagreeable to him.

---

123 BL, Add Ms 32695, f. 56, Hardwicke to Newcastle, 12 September 1740.

124 TNA, SP 42/23, f. 365, Stone to Admiralty, 25 September 1740.

125 TNA, Adm 1/904, unfoliated, Balchen to Burchett, 13 October 1740. The *Lennox, Kent, Falkland* and *Salisbury* were later ordered to remain at home. The Salisbury was later ordered to proceed in place of the *Litchfield*, which was considered too old and small for the operation. The *Grafton* struck rocks on 29 September and was also withdrawn from the escort.

126 BL, Add Ms 32695, f. 156, Wager to Newcastle, 29 September 1740.

127 BL, Add Ms 32695, f. 88 Richmond to Newcastle, 19 September 1740; *Richmond-Newcastle Correspondence*, 45, Richmond to Newcastle, 20 September 1740.

128 BL, Add Ms 35406, f. 237, Newcastle to Hardwicke, 1 October 1740.

What was important at this critical point was 'to avoid its sharpening the mind or running into asperity of speech, or wrangling instead of deliberating'.[129] Attention had now to turn on France. Preliminary discussions with the Dutch for hiring warships were put in hand. An attack on French St Domingue rather than the Spanish empire was suggested as a way of disrupting both Bourbon powers.[130] On 7 October the Lords Justices considered the option of declaring war on France. The past weeks had demonstrated that French neutrality could be as costly and diverting as open war, but Britain was in no condition to undertake such a war. Norris reflected the consensus when he noted to Walpole that the best way of controlling France was to have 80,000 men in Flanders.[131] A naval war would not do. The Dutch and Austrians might now be scared into action and at least part of the old Grand Alliance that had held Louis XIV in check during the War of Spanish Succession might be reactivated.[132] In Hanover, with George II, Harrington considered calling on the Dutch to honour their treaty obligations to assist Britain if she was attacked by France, and hiring troops from Hesse or Denmark.

On 7 October, a private letter from Vernon to Newcastle arrived. Vernon had long opposed a large-scale military expedition to the West Indies. Occupying cities would be fruitless as the soldiers gradually died from yellow fever and Malaria. Instead he argued for a force of 2–3,000 under his command, with which he would open the Spanish ports to trade.[133] In this latest letter, Vernon acknowledged the despatch of the expeditionary army, but objected strongly to the plan to attack Havana. It was too far for good communications with Jamaica and the Spaniards had been alerted. After a reconnaissance, he was much more hopeful of an attack on Cartagena so long as artillery and water was available. Nonetheless, 'I see almost innumerable difficulties in land expeditions in this country.'[134] This was not encouraging and could not be kept from the land commander, Lord Cathcart, who was instructed to do his best to work with Vernon when he reached the West Indies.[135] Vernon's belief in the rapid demise of the expeditionary force made

---

129 BL, Add Ms 32695, f. 184, Hardwicke to Newcastle, 6 October 1740

130 BL, Add Ms 32695, f.178, James Knight to Newcastle, 2 October 1740.

131 BL, Add Ms 28133, f. 110, 22 September 1740.

132 TNA, SP36/53, unfoliated, Minutes of the Lords Justices, 7 October 1740.

133 TNA, SP 42/85, f. 122, Vernon to Newcastle (private), 23 Januaury 1740 (rec. 25 March 1740).

134 Ibid., ff. 289–291, Vernon to Newcastle (private), 25 July 1740.

135 BL, Add Ms 32695, f. 247, Stone to Cathcart, 10 October 1740.

him determined to waste no time. He would sail to Dona Maria Bay at the western end of St Domingue and wait for Ogle and Cathcart. He did not want the army to go to Port Royal, where delays and the punch houses would soon take their toll of the troops. Norris approved Vernon's course of action and Ogle's instructions were amended accordingly.[136]

Ogle had to sail immediately. Once the predominant westerlies of November set in, the chance of the expeditionary force getting away was limited. The fleet assembled out in Spithead by 18 October, and on 26 October, just as faith in Ogle's ability to get his fleet out was beginning to crumble, news arrived in London that, at last, the expeditionary force was moving down the Channel.[137]

They had to evade the Franco-Spanish squadrons, which had several weeks' lead on them, and unite with Vernon. The ministry knew that Vernon did not approve of the expedition, but they trusted Lord Cathcart to find a way to make it work. There were many risks ahead, and the initiative was not yet clearly in British hands, but if it succeeded the objective of the war would be spectacularly achieved and a peace might be made during 1741 that secured the Caribbean trade forever.

Planning for a New War: October–December 1740

Ogle's departure was the culmination of over a year of efforts. At the outset, in September 1739, the war had been founded on the judgement that the decisive maritime blow would be struck while France remained neutral. The realisation that war with France could be imminent changed things. Britain had to win. As Newcastle informed Harrington, 'if the French and Spaniards get the better of us in the West Indies, which they do, if they hinder our Expeditions or the success of them, against the Spaniards, we must ever after be at the mercy of France'. Newcastle believed that the French would try to restrict the war to the West Indies, but if they were defeated there, they would have no choice but to seek redress in Europe. If this happened, Britain was ill prepared and he pressed Harrington to consider new alliances with the Dutch, Austrians, Russians, Prussians and Saxons.[138] The construction of a Grand Alliance was an immense and ambitious undertaking and

---

136 Ibid., f. 261, Hardwicke to Newcastle, 12 October 1740.

137 BL, Add Ms 23695, f. 290, Richmond to Newcastle, 19 October 1740; f. 319, Newcastle to Ogle, 23 October 1740.

138 BL, Add Ms 32695, f. 5, Newcastle to Harrington, (private), 6 September 1740.

once the King arrived home on 13 October, it was essential that diplomatic moves were made swiftly. Money was the key to this, but it would not be easy. Prussia and Austria might be secured by subsidies. However, there were disturbing rumours about the old ally, Austria, negotiating with France, perhaps to ensure the neutrality of the Low Countries.[139] Also, the Austrian court was distracted by the death of the Emperor Charles VI on 9 October 1740. Charles bestowed the Hapsburg dominions on his daughter, Maria Theresa. There were other good claimants to the title and Charles had spent the last 27 years of his reign establishing obligations on the other European powers to support her accession by the so-called Pragmatic Sanction. Early in November Russia had also to be given up as news arrived of the death of the Czarina Anna.[140] By the beginning of December 1740, despite a silence from Vienna, it seemed that Prussia might drawn into an alliance, or at least at a subsidy treaty, and the Dutch might respond favourably to British demands that they augment their forces in the light of the French threat.[141]

Alongside diplomatic initiatives, Britain's own preparations had to be reinforced. Over the year there had been a major mobilisation and redistribution of the fleet. There had been a great many innovative responses to the demands, but real problems had been exposed. The manpower available to the navy had been stretched to its full capacity. Ships at home were left with reduced crews and the victualling service had been stretched, temporarily, beyond its capacity in the autumn of 1740.

The year 1741 was going to demand even more resources and on 7 October the Regents examined this problem. The Admiralty was ordered to provide details of ships unmanned, the number of protections that had been issued and tenders that were on station to received pressed men. They considered measures for manning the fleet and raising more soldiers, including Danes and Hessians. They agreed that the victualling demands of the West Indies necessitated an export prohibition on victuals from Ireland and of corn from England.[142] On 16 October the Admiralty was also asked to assess how

---

139 *Richmond Newcastle Correspondence*, 47–48, Richmond to Newcastle, 2 November 1740.

140 Ibid., 48–49, Richmond to Newcastle, 9 November 1740.

141 *Richmond Newcastle Correspondence*, 50, Newcastle to Richmond, 29 November 1740.

142 TNA, SP 36/53, f. 40, Consideration by the Lords Justices, 7 October 1740. Norris had warned the ministers on 22 September that if France joined Spain, Britain would lose the war. The fleet had to be manned with soldiers and the Dutch and Austrians brought in to assist Britain. See BL, Add Ms 28133, ff. 58–61, 22 September 1740.

private yards might help preparing the warships for sea. Wager was asked to report on arrangements for pressing seamen and it was agreed that a bill should be put before Parliament to encourage seamen to volunteer, fix wages in the merchant service and provide penalties for those enticing seamen out of the navy or concealing them during an embargo.[143]

The Admiralty provided their report on 21 October.[144] The figures in Table 3.2 indicate the estimated number of ships that would be ready and requiring seamen at those dates.

The number of ships available in home waters was encouraging. With 16 line of battle ships in October, this was a comfortable margin of superiority over the four line in Brest. By Christmas the figure could be 24 and by April 31. However, the critical problem remained the seamen. In December 1740 40,761 were needed for the ships in commission. The figure for expanding the fleet suggest that it would require 50 per cent more seamen to man the new ships. Given the experience during 1740 this did not appear to be practicable with existing methods. The sick seamen on the books amounted to 1898, about 19 per cent of the seamen then mustered in home waters. Protections covered another 10,449 seamen, which would come to an end on 14 January.

Another source of manpower was the army. The army had been expanded by augmentation of existing regiments and the six marine regiments from about 26,900 to 40,130 during 1740. It was now agreed to raise seven new regiments of foot and four new marine regiments. The latter were specifically for use on the ships rather than as regimental units. This would take the established land forces to almost 54,000 during 1741.[145] Despite the King's resistance, the necessity of soldiers serving on the fleet had been firmly established during 1740. The main problem was ensuring that the Parliament accepted the new establishment.

---

143 BL, Add Ms 33004, f. 41, Cabinet Council, 16 October 1740.

144 TNA, SP 42/22, f. 411, Account of all the Ships, 21 October 1740. These figures have been compared with Adm 8/21.

145 *Journal of the House of Commons*, xxxiii (1737–1741), 548; TNA, WO 4/36 (Sec at War), f. 254, Arnold to new Colonels. The new regiments were Fowke's, Long's, Houghton's Price's Mordaunt's, De Grangues and Cholmondley's regiments of foot and Cornwall's, Paulet's, Hamner's and Jeffrey's regiments of marines. Commissions were issued in January 1741.

Table 3.2 Ships ready and requiring crew

Rate	October 1740	Christmas 1740	April 1741
First (100)	1	4	4
Second (90)	0	5	7
Third (80–70)	5	5	7
Fourth (60–50)	9	10	11
Fifth (40)	2	4	7
Sixth (20)	5	5	7
Others	13	13	15
Seamen required	8,109	14,359	19,609

The Political Impact, November 1740–February 1741

Parliament had played an important part in both the drift to war and the strategy adopted. During the spring of 1740 the opposition had kept up its assault on the ministry, but failed to make decisive progress. The arrival of news that Vernon had taken Porto Bello gave hopes that great things were happening. The Commons was prepared to reject a merchant petition to end the embargo and in this atmosphere, the attempt by the opposition in the Lords to censure the ministry for not sending enough troops with Vernon misfired badly before the session was closed on 15 April.[146] The elections, which had been on Newcastle's mind in the late summer of 1739, were now only a few months away and it was clear that when Parliament met on 18 November 1740 the conduct of the war would again be the focus of attention.

Over the summer the escape of the Spanish and French squadrons and the delays in despatching the expeditionary force to the West Indies provided important new opportunities to attack the government. The bonfires and celebrations that marked Admiral Vernon's birthday on 12 November gave notice of the popular mood.[147] The King's speech at the opening of Parliament asserted that the expedition had been prepared as quickly as manning the fleet would allow; there was a need for new measures to ensure swift manning of the fleet in future and a bill to prohibit the exportation of foodstuff in the light of the poor harvest. The general tenor of the oppo-

146 Corbett, *Parliamentary History*, op. cit., xi (1737–1741), 583–598. The motion was lost 62:40.

147 *Gentleman's Magazine*, November 1740.

sition attack was that the ministry could not be trusted either to act competently or honestly. The fact that nothing had been achieved in over a year against a weak enemy must either be incompetence or design. The demands for control over grain export and the hints of measures relating to manning the fleet were aimed at expanding the domestic power of the ministry, not its war-fighting capability. The growing threat of French intervention was not an argument for delay but for rapid and decisive action. These were interpretations that could not be justified or refuted without evidence and during the first week of December the opposition made calls for the instructions sent to Vernon and Haddock. Newcastle and Pelham anticipated these calls and were confident they could deflect the attack by asserting the need to keep secret of some of their content - a plan which worked well as the ministerial majorities held up.[148]

The attacks on the augmentation of the army produced the same kind of arguments. The claim by the old soldier and ardent convert to opposition, the Duke of Argyle, that establishing new regiments, rather than simply augmenting existing ones, was a device to increase ministerial patronage though additional military commissions, was defeated. During a similar debate in the Commons the ministry had the better of the professional opinion, being able to call on General George Wade to support their cause. Wade rehearsed the key strategic arguments that the opposition had espoused in the lead up to the war and had since informed war policy. The need to send such large naval forces to the West Indies, 'a thing unknown till now' and the threat of European war, which might force the King to support the new Habsburg monarch, Maria Theresa, were useful additional arguments. The opposition were forced back on general denials of the threats from Spain and France and assertions of tyrannical ambitions of ministers at home. The result was a comfortable majority for the ministry.[149]

As MPs left London in mid-December the ministers could reflect that they had bought themselves time and resources to meet the seemingly inevitable war with France. During 1738/9 the ministry had lost the initiative in Parliament over the Spanish war, but during the autumn of 1740 they seemed to have regained it on the conduct of that war. Despite the delays, the actions of the ministry seemed to reflect the best options under the

---

148 Corbett, *Parliamentary History*, op. cit., xi (1737–1741), 698–894; *Richmond Newcastle Correspondence*, 50, Newcastle to Richmond, 29 November 1740.

149 Ibid., 894–927.

circumstances. However, any hope that they had seen the last of the opposition was illusory. The frustration of the opposition at these defeats made them determined to redouble their efforts in the New Year culminating in a direct assault on Walpole himself.

When Parliament reassembled, the skirmishing was heated. The constant theme was that Parliament could not do its duty without detailed documents, which a corrupt ministry was too afraid to make public. The ministerial response was always that our enemies must be prevented from profiting from this intelligence. Building on the campaign against corruption and treason, the opposition launched its great assault on 13 February 1741. Both Houses were full when, at 1.00 pm the motions were made to remove Walpole from office. Vigorously stated and refuted, there was very little new in the arguments, and no specific charges could be made. Fissures within the opposition appeared immediately and the Tories walked out of the debate. The opposition was crushed in the Commons 290 to 106 and the Lords by 108 to 59.[150]

It had been a tough year, with many failings. However, at sea the ministers could feel that they had enough ships to defend the Channel and Soundings, so long as the seamen could be found in time. In the West Indies they had arranged for a massive expeditionary force and expected decisive results. Small numbers of reinforcements and supplies were said to be leaving Brest, St Andero and Cadiz in December, but, so long as Vernon and Ogle united, nothing that could effectively overturn the British numerical advantage in those waters.[151] In Europe it was early days, but it seemed possible that an anti-French coalition might be constructed. At home the administration had worked well enough. There was a lot to be concerned about, but with some good fortune the decisive blow might be struck and Franco-Spanish counter-attacks contained long enough for a good peace.

In some respects European events seemed to assisting British interests. The Austrian succession was beginning to divert Spanish and French attention. By November Charles Albert, Elector of Bavaria, was pressing his claims and Philip V of Spain had been propelled into the dispute by his wife's ambition for territorial acquisitions in Italy for her son Don Philip. By December there were strong rumours that French ships would join the remaining Spanish

---

150 Coxe, *Memoirs*, iv, 162–185, v, 184–207. Historical Manuscripts Commission: Egmont Diary, iii, 191.

151 TNA, SP 42/23, f. Admiralty to Newcastle, 9 December 1740; BL, Add Ms 32695 (Newcastle Papers) f. 460, Newcastle to Vernon, 4 December 1740.

warships to escort an army to Italy. With 10 ships of the line, Haddock was thought to be strong enough to blockade Cadiz if necessary.[152] George II as King and Elector of Hanover was committed to supporting Maria Theresa, as was Prussia. King Frederick II was seen as important in preserving the peace of the Empire, so it came as a shock early in December to learn that he had invaded Silesia, claiming it as his price for supporting the Pragmatic Sanction against other powers.[153] In early January 1741 letters from Vienna arrived, demanding the support promised to defend the Habsburg domains. On the 15 January the Cabinet agreed that the King would write to Frederick to demand his withdrawal from Silesia and he would employ 12,000 Danes and Hessians as the British contribution to the defence of Austria.[154]

In January 1741, as the British ministers looked back on the shattering defeat of the opposition in Parliament, they still had plenty to think about. They had weathered the political storm so far, but the general election was only a matter of months away. Despite the setbacks, their conduct of the war had given them back the political initiative for the moment. The events of war itself had not entirely met expectations. Vernon's capture of Porto Bello and Chagres had shown that the premise of Spanish weakness in the Indies had some foundation. The major expedition had been organised and despatched to the West Indies. However, the ability to contain the Spanish naval forces had proved far less than expected. French actions had complicated matters tremendously, and it seemed that Britain was sliding, almost inevitably, towards war with France. Whether the expedition would be able to make the decisive conquests expected of it before the French and Spanish fleets could intervene was questionable. Alongside these anxieties, Europe was moving towards another war. What this would mean for the British war against Spain and the largest British expedition ever sent to the West Indies was unknown. There was much to hope for, but as much to fear.

---

152 BL, Add Ms 33004, f. 45, Cabinet Council, 16 December 1740.

153 *Richmond-Newcastle Correspondence*, 47, Richmond to Newcastle, 1 November 1740.

154 BL, Add Ms 28133, f. 75, Cabinet Council at Newcastle's House, 15 January 1741.

4

The Widening War and the Fall of Sir Robert Walpole, January 1741– February 1742

War in Europe January to May 1741

The movement of a major part of the fleet to the West Indies at the end of 1740 was a creditable achievement. However, there were worrying signs. The Admiralty could now count on only 13 ships of the line in home waters. There were very few other 70s or 60s ready to be put into commission and orders were given to commission the 'great ships' of 100 and 90 guns, which were lying in ordinary at Chatham and Portsmouth. These ships were less versatile than the smaller ships of the line and demanded larger numbers of seamen to man them, but they were the only ships available.

Manpower was, as usual, the key to the campaign. Norris estimated that 30 ships were laid up for lack of manpower.[1] The pressing of seamen continued. The tenders sent out into the Channel to intercept merchant ships returning home and take seamen from them continued to bring in some sailors for the navy, but once again more radical solutions to the manpower problem failed to make headway. The Register Bill that Wager had brought before Parliament in February 1740 to establish a register of seamen met with such resistance that Walpole was forced to abandon it during the first reading. However, by the end of the year the manning problem was so serious that Wager was ordered to bring it back to the Commons on 27 January 1741, but after a passionate series of encoun-

---

1 However, it was also estimated that only four ships were fit to receive men in mid-January. See BL, Add Ms 28133, f. 75, 15 January 1741.

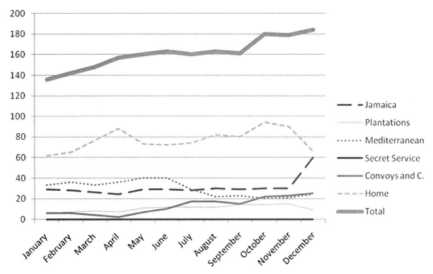

Figure 4.1 Ship dispositons, 1740
Source: TNA, Adm 8/21.

ters, it was dropped again.[2] Once again the ministry was forced back on the old methods. A new press was approved with an end to protections for coasters and colliers and an embargo on outward-bound shipping until the fleet was manned.[3] New bounties for volunteers were approved, but this again proved inadequate, and soldiers were needed to serve on the fleet until new marine regiments could be raised.[4]

There was some relief when Andrew Thompson, Waldegrave's secretary in Paris, was able to re-establish his spies and informants in the French ports.[5] He got the great news that D'Antin was returning to France with his ships devastated by disease. D'Antin had been unable to obtain provisions in the West Indies and forced to return home having drained St Domingue of

2   Corbett, *Parliamentary History*, op. cit. xi (1739–41), 414–345, 5 February 1740; xii (1741–1743), 26–143; BL, EG 2529, f. 121, Thomas Smith to Haddock, 27 February 1741.

3   BL, Add Ms. 28133, f. 75, 15 January 1741; TNA, SP43/3, unfoliated, Whitehall, 16 January 1741.

4   TNA, SP45/3, unfoliated, Whitehall, 18 March 1741. The navy had available for sea in home waters at this time 3 x 100, 6 x 90, 1 x 80, 6 x 70, 2 x 60, 11 x 50 and 11 x 40 gun ships.

5   Ibid., f. 125, Thompson to Newcastle, 18 March 1741 (n.s.). See also, f. 62, Thompson to Newcastle, 20 February 1741 (n.s.).

supplies and achieved nothing. Fleury and Maurepas were furious and now feared that nothing could stop the Spanish West Indies falling into British hands.[6]

The prospect of ending the war with Spain quickly was becoming increasingly important as the crisis in Central Europe grew. On 15 January the Cabinet met at Harrington's house to discuss the Prussian invasion of Silesia. Maria Theresa, Queen of Hungary, had called on Britain to honour its obligation to the Pragmatic Sanction and provide 10,000 troops for the defence of the Habsburg lands. This demand exposed the old fissure in the British body politic – suspicion of the influence of Hanover. It was not in Britain's or Hanover's interest to see the power of Prussia increasing at the expense of Austria. It was also an affront to George II's respect for the institutions of the Holy Roman Empire. Britain would honour her obligations, but the military situation with regard to Spain and France did not permit the despatch of British troops to the Continent. The army at home in the spring of 1741 amounted to about 28,000, including seven new regiments of foot and four regiments of marines that had been approved by Parliament in December 1740 and were in the process of being raised.[7] The King had only reluctantly agreed to send his troops to the West Indies or have them serve on warships. Parliament accepted the need to do this as the purpose was undoubtedly in British interests. It was not obvious that sending troops to Germany were equally in Britain's interest and ministers understood the political difficulty this could create. However, Britain had subsidy treaties with Hesse-Cassel (1727) and Denmark (1734).[8] It was therefore agreed that the King would write to Frederick II requiring him to withdraw or he would put 6,000 Danes and 6,000 Hessians at the disposal of the queen.

6   Ibid., f. 131, Thompson to Newcastle, 24 arch 1741 (n.s.) Rumours of D'Antin's return had filtered through a few days earlier from private letters from the West Indies. See ibid., f. 129, Thompson to Newcastle, 22 March 1741 (n.s.).

7   Corbett, *Parliamentary History*, op. cit., xi (1739–1740), 930–991, 10 December 1740, Debate in the Commons on the Augmentation of the Army. The regiments were raised in the usual manner from December around a core of troops drafted from existing regiments. The seven new colonels of foot were Mordaunt, Houghton, De Grangue, Price, Cholmondley, Fowke and Long. The four marine colonels were Jefferys, Hamner, Pawlett and Cornwall.

8   C. Parry (ed.), *Consolidated Treaty Series*, New York, 1969, vol. 32 (1724–1727), 381–397, Convention between Great Britain and Hesse Cassel, 12 March 1727; vol. 34 (1732–1737), 185–188, Treaty of Alliance and Subsidy between Great Britain and Denmark, 30 September 1734. Under the Hessian convention, 8,000 foot and 4,000 horse were to be provided. The Danish treaty provided for 5,000 foot and 1,000 horse.

In the meantime, the Elector of Bavaria had already launched his claim to the Imperial throne and Spain was sending troops to secure a patrimony for Don Philip in Italy. By the end of January, the Spanish ministers pressed Fleury to act. They argued that this was a great opportunity with Britain disabled by the war.[9] The election of a new emperor was to take place shortly in Frankfurt and by the end of February Thompson reported that France was raising money for Bavaria, and discussing subsidies with Prussia, Russia and Sweden. For additional pressure, 40,000 French troops were to be assembled on the Rhine opposite Frankfurt. Fleury had permitted 40,000 Spanish troops pass through Provence, but so far no agreement had been reached concerning their passage onward through the Kingdom of Piedmont-Sardinia into the Austrian territory of Lombardy.[10] Fleury, who continued to dominate French foreign policy for so long, was as elusive as ever. Nothing could be confirmed, but on the day that Newcastle received this information he wrote to Richmond, 'Our foreign affairs go on, as they did, France rather more taking off the mask every day.'[11] Although worrying, this concentration on the Rhine and Italy might provide Britain with a breathing space to finish the affair in the West Indies. Conversely, if Maria Theresa abandoned the Austrian Netherlands to protect Germany or Italy, a vacuum in Flanders could easily be filled by France – a nightmare that successive British ministers had fought hard to avoid. To prevent this it was important to reconcile Austria and Prussia as quickly as possible. If Maria Theresa would recognise the Prussian annexation of Silesia, perhaps in exchange for a payment from Frederick II, peace might be restored.[12] In the meantime, British influence on Austria would depend on the support provided and it was agreed that Parliament would be asked to grant a vote of credit to support the Austrians.

---

9   Ibid., f. 48, Thompson to Newcastle, 8 February 1741 (n.s.); f. 62, Thompson to Newcastle, 20 February (n.s.).

10   The strategically important territory of Piedmont-Savoy occupied the position between the Alps, France and the Lombardy Plain of Italy. In 1713 the Duke of Piedmont-Savoy had been elevated to the Kingdom of Sicily and in 1720 had exchanged Sicily for Sardinia. Charles Emanuel III was commonly referred to by his royal title of King of Sardinia. The Republic of Genoa occupied the littoral belt between France and Northern Italy.

11   Richmond-Newcastle Correspondence, 57, Newcastle to Richmond, 21 February 1741; TNA, SP 78/225 (State Papers –France), f. 104, Thompson to Newcastle, 1 March 1741 (n.s.). For a detailed narrative of the French move to war, see R. Butler, *Choiseul*, 2 vols, Oxford, 1980, i, 258–275.

12   BL, Add Ms 35407, ff. 7–12, Policy for the Defence of the Low Countries, 3 March 1741.

The supplementary money bill brought the King to Parliament on 8 April. The King's speech was simple. The Queen of Hungary had asked for the 12,000 troops to which she was entitled by treaty and the King had ordered the Danes and Hessians to be ready to march. He now wanted a grant of credit of £300,000 to use for Austria's defence over the summer. This provided the opposition with the opportunity to restate familiar assertions about Walpole's diplomatic ineptitude. This 'deluge of gold', as Chesterfield termed it, would not for be used the support of Austria, but for Hanover or, even worse, to buy the coming elections. However, the ministerial case was strong. It was not contested that the support of Austria was a vital British interest. If Britain and the other guarantors of the Pragmatic Sanction did not assist Maria Theresa, she would be forced into the arms of France. The vote of credit was not a blank cheque. The expenditure on the vote still had to be approved by Parliament in the next session. A division in the Lords was comprehensively defeated and the motion passed the Commons without division.[13] However, it put the ministry on notice. Parliament expected the money to be spent in support of Austria. If this did not happen, questions about the good faith and competence of the ministry and suspicions of Hanoverian influence would re-surface with a vengeance. The need to support Austria emerged more clearly during April. On 11 April news arrived of a Prussian victory over the Austrians in Upper Silesia, at Mollwitz, 11 days earlier.[14] In Paris, the Austrian ambassador, Wasner, was reported to be offering to destroy the fortifications in Luxembourg in an attempt to persuade Fleury to prevent the passage of Spanish troops to Italy.[15]

The King left London on 6 May to spend the summer at his palace of Heerenhausen in Hanover. The Earl of Harrington accompanied him again. Before he left, George had approved of a plan to establish a camp of 10–12,000 troops in the south of England. This was a precautionary move proposed by Newcastle. If the Dutch mobilised in support of the Pragmatic Sanction and the Austrian Netherlands, these troops might be required in Flanders. The King ordered General George Wade, Britain's senior soldier, to

---

13 Corbett, *Parliamentary History*, op. cit., xii (1741–1743), 146–184, 8, 9 and 13 April 1741. For the fragmentation of the opposition on this measure, see, Dobrée, B. (ed.), *The Letters of Philip Dormer Stanhope, 4th Earl of Chesterfield*, 6 vols, London 1932, ii, 448, Chesterfield to Marchmont, 24 April 1741.

14 The campaign can be followed in R. Browning, *The War of Austrian Succession*, Sutton, 1995.

15 TNA, SP 78/225, f. 189, Thompson to Newcastle, 22 April 1741 (n.s.).

command the force should it be sent abroad.[16] Details of the Franco-Spanish agreement were emerging at this time. An army of 80,000 French, 50,000 Spaniards and 15,000 Neapolitans was to campaign in Italy. At a peace, Spain would get back Minorca from Britain, and Parma, Piacenza, and part of Lombardy from Austria. France was to have the *Asiento* and half of Cuba. Spain was to leave France a free hand in Flanders and with the Baltic powers. If Spain agreed France would pay for 25,000 Sardinians to join the army in Italy.[17]

News from Spain remained scanty but there were clearly immediate threats to British interests. Nine Spanish men of war were reported to have left Cadiz for the West Indies with four merchantmen, but 13 more were rigged and ready, preparing to move to Barcelona to convoy more troops to Italy. The three best men of war at Cartagena had reportedly sailed to join the Cadiz squadron.[18] Norris was ordered to take command of the ships at Portsmouth and Spithead.[19] The manning problem was still unresolved and the supply problems noted by Vernon and Haddock were made worse by reports of Spanish privateers hovering off Plymouth. Thompson had confirmed that the Brest and Toulon squadrons were back in their home ports and extensive preparations were in hand. Haddock had to be reinforced, so the Lords Justices agreed to send four more '40s' to join Captain William Martin's small cruising squadron off Cadiz. The Lieutenant Governor of Minorca, Brigadier General Paget was ordered to release 500 troops from his garrison for service on the ships so long as there was no danger to the defences.[20] The one matter of secret business, reserved for the inner cabinet and not given to the Lords Justices, was the draft of a defensive alliance with Russia. This treaty which committed Russia to provide 8,000 troops and Britain to provide 12 line of battle ships if either were attacked by a third power in the future was approved and sent to Harrington in Hanover.[21]

---

16   BL, Add Ms 35407, f. 17, Newcastle to Hardwicke, 1 May 1741.

17   TNA, SP 78/225, f. 239, Thompson to Newcastle, 17 May 1741 (n.s.).; f. 261, Thompson to Newcastle, 20 May 1741 (n.s.).

18   TNA, SP 42/86, f. 366, Haddock to Newcastle, 18 March 1741; BL, Egerton Mss, 2529, ff. 187–192, Sundry Intelligences.

19   BL, Add Ms 28133, f. 79, 15 May 1741.

20   TNA, SP 45/3, unfoliated, Whitehall, 14 May 1741. Martin commanded the *Ipswich* (70) and had with him *Sunderland* (70), *Pembroke* (60) and *Oxford* (50). See BL, Add Ms Egerton, 2529, f. 153, Martin to Haddock, 12 March 1741.

21   Parry, *Consolidated Treaty Series*, op. cit., vol. 36 (1740–1742), 133–154.

West Indies: Victory to Defeat, May to June 1741

On the afternoon of 17 May, Captain William Laws of the *Spence* sloop arrived in London with letters from Vernon and Wentworth. It was news the ministers had been eagerly awaiting. On the 25 March the expeditionary force had captured the outer forts of the lagoons of Cartagena de las Indias. The fleet was now safely anchored in the outer lagoon. The army was healthy and preparing to move into the inner lagoon and towards the city itself. Vernon did not doubt that soon they would be masters of the place. The Spaniards had already burned or sunk their ships to hinder the progress of the army.[22] The fall of the place would give Britain control of the *Galeones* trade route. The excitement is evident in Newcastle's letter to Hardwicke, announcing the news, 'so agreeable to our wishes and so answerable to our expectations. If this is well pursued, I mean there, we must soon be masters of all the West Indies. Many things will be to be done here, supplies of all sorts, and perhaps men to be sent from hence'.[23] Hardwicke summed up the mood in his reply:

> I return you my hearty thanks for your great and joyful news, which so fully answers our hopes and wishes and so strongly justifies the measures which have been taken. I hope it will also be attended with good effects in this part of the World, make Spain break though her dependence upon France and submit to His Majesty's just demands. Your Grace judges right in thinking that the consideration of supplies must immediately be entered upon.

He concluded 'After Cartagena what can stand before you?'[24] Domestically, the political capital of such a victory was not wasted. William Gage wrote to Newcastle that he proposed to 'make a bonfire on Firle Beacon tomorrow night and to give the populace there strong beer to drink the health of Vernon, which I believe will much please our neighbours and manifest with most noise my joy for the good news of our success'.[25]

Laws was interviewed by the Lords Justices on the 19 May. The Regents were divided. Newcastle and Norris were for sending immediate reinforce-

---

22   TNA, SP 42/90, ff. 40–51, Vernon to Newcastle, 1 April 1741.

23   BL Add Ms 35407, f. 19, Newcastle to Hardwicke, 18 May 1741.

24   BL, Add Ms 32697, f. 15, Hardwicke to Newcastle, 19 May 1741.

25   Ibid., f. 27, Gage to Newcastle, 21 May 1741.

ments to Vernon and Wentworth. Newcastle was absolutely clear in his mind:

> I lay it down <u>Cartagena must be kept</u>, at least for the present, if kept it must be properly <u>garrisoned</u> that they say will take up to 2 to 3,000 men which makes Wentworth's army very low. I also lay it down the blow in the West Indies must be followed. The Havana or Vera Cruz attempted, and for that purpose 2 or 3,000 men, must as proposed by Sir John Norris be sent from hence.

Others, including Walpole, were less sure. It was not yet confirmed that Cartagena had fallen. The Brest and Cadiz squadrons were back in home waters. The Ferrol squadron had escaped from Cartagena before the British arrived and was thought by Laws to amount to 18 men of war at Havana. Some or all of these ships might be on their way home. Britain had few ships in home waters ready for sea. Perhaps 16 ships of the line could be put to sea, but of these, six were the large 100 or 90 gun ships. Haddock was stretched in the Mediterranean. He had too few ships to cover Toulon, Cartagena and Cadiz.[26] In these circumstances, to send more forces with escorts across the Atlantic seemed premature. It was agreed that orders would be sent to Vernon not to abandon Cartagena, but the decision on reinforcements was deferred until confirmation of the fall of the city was received.[27]

Over the next few days the pressures pulling the ministry in different directions increased. On 21 May, an order arrived from the King to prepare the regiments encamped for service in Europe. George had decided that the army was to be committed to Germany.[28] During the spring of 1741 British and Hanoverian foreign policy objectives had coincided with regard to Prussia. Both states encouraged Frederick II and Maria Theresa to compound their differences. In early April this coincidence of interest was diverging. Hanoverian policy was aimed at ensuring neutrality in case

---

26 TNA, SP 42/86, ff. 374–375, Haddock to Newcastle, 24 April and 3 May 1741.

27 TNA, SP 45/3, unfoliated, Whitehall, 19 May; BL, Add Ms 28133, f. 81, 19 May 1741; Add Ms 35407, f. 25, Newcastle to Hardwicke, 21 may 1741. Hardwicke was not at the meeting, but he too was cautious, wanting to await confirmation of the fall of Cartagena. See BL, Add Ms 32697, f. 54, Hardwicke to Newcastle, 23 May 1741.

28 TNA, SP 45/3, unfoliated, Whitehall, 21 May 1741. The reference to Germany appears only in Norris's journal, dated 27 May and a letter from Hardwicke to Newcastle dated 23 May.

of a widening war, while Britain was publicly committed to supporting Austria by military action. The incompatibility of those objectives was interpreted by Frederick as bad faith and when George arrived at Herrenhausen he became more concerned for the defence of Hanover and less inhibited about using British resources to that end.[29] This was not fully understood by the ministry in London, but almost certainly caused them some alarm. The army in Germany rather than Flanders smacked unmistakably of Hanoverian rather than British concerns. It would leave only about 15,000 troops in Britain and too few for reinforcements to be sent to the West Indies, where British interests were clearly being pursued.[30] If France intervened, Norris confirmed that there was no squadron ready in home waters.[31] Preparations in Brest and Toulon were said to be for expeditions to the Baltic and Barbary coasts respectively, but Fleury was also said to have warned that he would intervene if the British sent more troops to the West Indies.[32]

At the very point of victory, it seemed that the initiative was about to be lost again. It is to ministry's credit that they saw this danger and acted. On 27 May they agreed that preparations to send 2,000 additional troops to the West Indies must commence. Despite a letter from Harrington, stating that George wanted more information before he issued any additional orders, activity in Britain did not waver as preparations of the West Indian reinforcement continued.[33] Efforts were renewed to get a squadron to sea by ending more protections.[34] A general press was proclaimed on 2 June and bounties offered.[35]

The precise naval threat became clearer over next 10 days. The Toulon squadron was in poor shape and would require a great deal of refitting, but

---

29 For a fuller discussion of Hanoverian-Prussian negotiations, see U. Dann, *Hanover and Great Britain, 1740–1760*, Leicester, 1991, 29–33.

30 TNA, SP 78/225, f. 289, Thompson to Newcastle, 31 May 1741 (n.s.); f. 297, Thompson to Newcastle, 7 June 1741 (n.s.); SP 43/100 (State Papers – Regencies), Harrington to Newcastle, XXX.

31 TNA, SP 42/24, Beauclerk to Newcastle, 27 May 1741

32 TNA, SP 78/225 (State Papers – France), f. 289, Thompson to Newcastle, 31 May 1741 (n.s.); f. 297, Thompson to Newcastle, 7 June 1741 (n.s.).

33 TNA, SP42/24, f. 243, 3 June.

34 BL, Add Ms 28133, f. 27 May 1741.

35 BL Add Ms 28133, f. 83, 2 June 1741; TNA, Adm 106/2179, unfoliated, Navy Board to the Admiralty, 10 June 1741.

preparations were advanced in Brest for an unknown purpose. All Spanish ships capable of sailing had left Cadiz for Ferrol.[36] If the Ferrol squadron was on its way home from the West Indies, then a concentration of force at Ferrol was apparently repeating the Franco-Spanish plan of 1740. Thus, Norris's orders were similar to those he had in 1740.[37] He was to cruise in the mouth of the Channel to intercept the Ferrol squadron from Havana if possible. He was to cruise along the Galician coast and destroy the shipping in San Sebastian and other Biscay ports. He was to keep himself informed of the movements of the Brest squadron. If the Spanish squadrons went to the Mediterranean he was to send ships to reinforce Haddock. If he heard they sailed northwards, he was to follow and attack them.[38] Given the reported state of the Brest squadron, Norris did not think he need be diverted from his main mission against the Spanish coast. He would put a cruiser, the *Ruby* (50) off Ushant to warn the French that his squadron was at sea. They would not know where his squadron was, nor whether he had been joined by Haddock or other ships from the West Indies, making an overwhelming force before the Straits. Thus, he reasoned, the French were unlikely to sail.[39]

However, on 18 June, the same day as Norris received his instructions, Captain Charles Wimbleton of the *Cruiser* sloop arrived in London with devastating news from the West Indies. The expeditionary force had left Cartagena in defeat. The potential political and diplomatic consequences of this were obvious to Newcastle and his priority was to prevent the Lords Justices making a premature decision to defer the reinforcement. Wentworth's letters had been left in Portsmouth, so the ministers had to rely on Vernon's account of events. The admiral blamed the army for the failure of the attack upon the city. Newcastle met Walpole on the 19 June and suggested that one or two more experienced senior officers might replace Wentworth, but 'necessity cannot be withstood; We must, I fear give up America and be for the future, at the Mercy of Spain, if we do not support an operation in the West Indies'.[40] Hardwicke, Newcastle, Walpole and the Earl of Wilmington, met at Walpole's house on the evening of Sunday 22 June

36   TNA, SP 42/86, f. 374, Haddock to Newcastle, 30 April and 3 May 1741; f. 389, Haddock to Stone, undated, (rec. 7 June 1741).

37   TNA, SP 43/100, Minutes on the Spanish News, 11 June 1741.

38   TNA, SP 42/87, ff. 181–183, Lords Justices to Norris, 18 June 1741. Norris' force was to be 12 ships of the line, four 50s, two 20s, four bombs, two fireships and a hospital ship.

39   TNA, SP42/87, f. 205, Norris to Stone, 27 June 1741.

40   BL, Add Ms 35407, f. 29, Newcastle to Hardwicke, 19 June 1741.

to prepare for the Regency meeting. It is significant that Wager, one of the planners of the original expedition, was not present. He was now convinced that expeditionary armies could not produce the results expected. In his despatches, Vernon had argued against large expeditionary forces, which would simply die of disease even if they did capture an enemy port. Wager seems to have accepted that this was the likely fate of any reinforcements and argued against sending them.[41] Among the ministers present at the meeting, speculation as to the cause of the defeat focused firmly on the failings of the army. Nonetheless, They agreed that four battalions could retrieve the situation in the West Indies and that they would recommend two battalions from Britain and two from Ireland with additional marine companies to make up additional numbers.[42]

War in America and Europe: June–September 1741

On the 24 June a letter from Paris announced that France had finally declared its support for the Bavarian imperial candidate and 30–40,000 troops were marching to Augsburg. Other letters confirmed that Austria and Prussia could not reach an understanding over Silesia.[43] While war was confined to Silesia, British ministers had considered whether 'in the desperate situation' Austria could be considered to have brought its troubles upon itself and Britain could, therefore, claim to have done all that was required by providing the Danish and Hessian troops and £300,000.[44] Now, with French troops entering Bavaria, Britain could not afford to consider such a limited liability. The signals from Hanover were very worrying. Harrington was arguing that Austrian obstinacy was preventing a settlement with Prussia. George's offer of a subsidy, as well as Danes and Hessians to defend the western part of the Empire, were embroiling the Electorate with France and he insisted that a neutrality with Prussia was justifiable and desirable. The King also urged the Regents to fix the Great Seal to the treaty with Russia before war broke out, to act as a deterrent to Prussia.[45] The very worst possible scenario was beginning to present itself – defeat in the West Indies and inaction in Europe.

---

41   B. Mc Ranft, *The Vernon Paper*, London, 1958, 242–3, Wager to Vernon, 21 June 1741.

42   TNA, SP 43/100 (State Papers – Regencies), unfoliated, At Walpole's 22 June 1741.

43   TNA, SP 45/3, unfoliated, At Walpole's 24 June 1741

44   BL, Add Ms 35407, f. 41, Queries on Harrington's of 9 June.

45   TNA, SP 43/28, unfoliated, Harrington to Newcastle, 8 June 1741. This was done on 21 June.

The strain on British naval resources was clear. Vernon was sending 10 ships of the line, two cruisers and some fireships and bombs home with the trade ships under the command of Richard Lestock.[46] These ships would not arrive for over a month and could not be added to the line of battle until the autumn. By August three new 44s launched in the spring increased the number of cruisers for convoy and patrol work, and new bomb vessels replaced the ones Vernon was sending home.[47] Until then, Norris had to make do with about 15 line of battle ships. The latest news from Haddock, who was cruising off Cape St Vincent, suggested that the Cadiz squadron had not gone to Ferrol, but was back in its home port. If this squadron united with the three ships of the line at Cartagena, they would have 17 line opposed to 12 under Haddock. No more line of battleships could be found and only four 40s were ordered to join Haddock.[48]

In London the West Indian expedition still dominated attention, but events in Central Europe were beginning to intrude more ominously into ministerial calculations.[49] On 18 July, Newcastle, Devonshire and Andrew Stone, Secretary to the Lords Justices, met Walpole. Walpole had received a private letter from the King. Although Walpole did not show it to the others, he discussed its contents. The King was concerned that the plans of the spring and summer had failed. The Allies had not rallied around Austria. Prussia and France would attack Hanover if George continued to aid Maria Theresa. He wanted £50,000 from the Austrian subsidy to support Hanover and hinted that he would seek a neutrality for the Electorate. Walpole wanted to reverse the decision to reinforce the West Indies and accede to the King's request. Newcastle reacted furiously and a warm exchange followed. Newcastle denied that the situation in Europe had changed. 'I stated and lamented the Hanover influence, which brought so many misfortunes upon us.'[50] He knew the arguments in Parliament about the Austrian subsidy, the reassurances that had been given, and the reaction that there would be when this alteration became public knowledge, particularly if the West Indian expedition was abandoned as a consequence. He urged renewing negotiations with Austria and Saxony. Russia was now an ally and the Dutch were

---

46   TNA, SP42/90, ff. 137–150, Vernon to Newcastle, 30 May 1741.

47   TNA, SP 43/100, unfoliated, Newcastle to Harrington, 14 July 1741.

48   TNA, SP 42/86, f. 389, Haddock to Stone; f. 395, Newcastle to Haddock, 20 June 1741; f. 346, Haddock to Newcastle, 31 May 1741.

49   BL, Add Ms 32697, f. 310, Newcastle to Harrington, 14 July 1741.

50   BL, Add Ms 35407, f. 44, Newcastle to Hardwicke, 19 July 1741.

preparing 12,000 troops. He acknowledged Walpole's concern for Hanover, but queried whether the 12,000 troops assembling at Colchester could be sent to the Electorate without dishonouring 'the solemn engagement to the cause of Europe and Hungary'. Certainly any idea of British neutrality would be 'a fatal compliment to His Majesty'.[51]

It was agreed to defer a decision until tempers had calmed. The West Indian reinforcement became all the more urgent after the arrival of more despatches on 23 July. The army was extremely weak and no agreement could be reached between Vernon and the Wentworth on the next operation.[52] If reinforcements did not arrive soon the army would be useless. Eventually, it was accepted that the West Indian reinforcement would continue, and, in order to prevent a Hanoverian neutrality, the 12,000 troops assembling under Wade would have to go to Hanover. However, no other assistance could be given, except continuing pressure on the Dutch to support them.[53]

In August, as final orders were sent to embark the West Indian reinforcements from Fort William and Cork and new credit arrangements were agreed with the victuallers of the expedition, news from France confirmed what had long been rumoured, that the Brest and Toulon squadrons were to sail to Barcelona to join the Spanish squadron convoying Spanish troops to Italy.[54] An army of 48,000 under Marshal Maillebois was said to be on the march to the Rhine to threaten Hanover. There could be little doubt now that the French were moving rapidly towards a war in Europe.[55]

Norris was by this time at sea, cruising between Ferrol and Vigo, so it would take a long time for any change in orders to reach him. Three more 90-gun ships, *Neptune*, *Barfleur* and *Sandwich*, fitting out at Chatham, were ordered to join Norris. This would give Norris a line of battle of 17, including three 100s and six 90s. He was in all cases to send on one 90 and two 70s to join Haddock. If he found that the Brest squadron had passed by him on its

51   BL, Add Ms 35407, f. 53, Newcastle to Hardwicke, 20 July 1741.

52   *Richmond-Newcastle Correspondence*, 67, Newcastle to Richmond, 25 July 1741; 68, Stone to Richmond, 28 July 1741.

53   TNA, SP 43/100, unfoliated, Newcastle to Harrington, 30 July 1741.

54   TNA, SP 45/3, unfoliated, At Walpole's 4 August 1741; Whitehall, 6 August 1741. Wade suggested General Tyrawly should supersede Wentworth, but this was not done in the end. The reinforcements for Blakeney's regiment (Blakeney was already in the West Indies as Quarter Master General of the expedition), Guise's regiment and 700 drafts from regiments in Scotland; SP 43/101, unfoliated, Newcastle to Harrington, 7 August 1741.

55   TNA, SP 43/101, unfoliated, Newcastle to Thompson, 13 August 1741 (most secret).

way to the Mediterranean, he was to follow them and take command of his own and Haddock's squadrons.[56] In this case there would be no ships of the line left in home waters.

This exposure, coupled with rising tensions in Europe, worried the Regents when they meet on 13 August. Walpole took Wilmington and Newcastle aside, urging them to get Hardwicke to return to London immediately as 'in all probability these next letters would decide the fate of Europe'. The question of delaying the reinforcement was raised again, but Newcastle deflected it. They agreed that 11 more ships should be ordered home from the West Indies. Newcastle was now seriously concerned that Walpole was privately encouraging Harrington in Hanover to support a neutrality. He noted that none of the advice that had been sent from London regarding the Hessians, Danes, Russians, Saxons and Dutch had been acted upon; 'I think they are almost sick of asking our advice and we shall grow sick of giving it. Don't you suspect a certain private letter has had some influence?'[57] 'It is very easy for my Lord Harrington to act and talk agreeably to the King in Hanover; but we must think how we can serve the King in Parliament and defend there what is done elsewhere ... it will be a sad story when it shall appear that a regard for Hanover alone has stop't our armies, promoted and countenanced Neutralities and occasioned universal inaction.'[58]

The very next day, 14 August, a further letter from Harrington confirmed all Newcastle's fears. The King approved General Tyrawly as a replacement for Wentworth, and was pleased by the preparations to send the 12,000 troops to Europe, but, it was now too late and the King intended to hire Saxons instead .He expected Parliament to pay for them as they cost less than the British troops. Newcastle was staggered: 'Was there ever such a letter or such a proposal? So inconsistent and so little becoming an English minister. The troops are laid aside ... If you would send the troops why not send the money? The motives and ends are very different.' On the one hand the King was said to be canvassing the Queen of Hungary's enemies for neutrality and on the other raising troops for the defence of Hanover 'when support of the Queen is neither intended or thought of'. Even more extraordinary was that the Austrian minister in Britain had been asked to apply for a quarter of the £300,000

---

56   TNA, SP 42/87, f. 211, Stone to Norris, 7 August 1741. The letter missed him at sea and was returned.

57   BL, Add Ms 35407, f. 66. Newcastle to Hardwicke, 15 August 1741.

58   BL, Add Ms 35407, f. 66, Newcastle to Hardwicke, 15 August 1741.

subsidy to pay for Hanoverian auxiliaries. The futility of these proceedings was alarming. The troops and subsidy were specifically approved by Parliament for the support of Austria. Hanover was not in imminent danger as a result of its support of Austria and could not legitimately make use of the money.[59]

Newcastle stalled a reply until Hardwicke arrived back in London for a private meeting of ministers. A further letter from Hanover pressed for confirmation that Parliament would pay £10,000 per month for the Hanoverian forces.[60] The ministers stood firm and informed Harrington that Parliament could only pay if Hanover were attacked because of the King's action in support for Austria[61].

At home all that remained were three ships of the line, the *Sandwich* (90) and *Neptune* (90) at the Nore and the *Barfleur* (90) fitting out at Chatham, supported by a handful of 50s.[62] Fortunately, Norris arrived back from Biscay with his squadron on 22 August and news arrived on 31 August that Admiral Lestock had been sighted in the Channel with ten 80s from the West Indies. Wager was pessimistic that they would be ready before the spring.[63] Nevertheless, Norris and Wager agreed that they must stop the Ferrol, Cadiz and Brest squadrons passing the Straits to join with the Toulon and Cartagena squadrons. They also wanted to intercept the Havana squadron rumoured to be returning home. As far as they knew Haddock was still at Gibraltar. The admirals recommended that four more line of battle ships ought to be sent to reinforce him. He should then have 20 in his line of battle – enough to keep a substantial force cruising off Cape St Mary until October. At home a force of 16 line should be prepared at Spithead under Norris, ready to intercept the Havana squadron, reinforce Haddock or prevent the Brest squadron from sailing as necessary.[64]

59   BL, Add Ms 32407, ff. 74–77, Newcastle to Hardwicke, 19 August 1741.

60   TNA, SP 43/28, 24 August 1741, Harrington to Newcastle, 19 August 1741.

61   BL, Add Ms 32697, f. 452, Consideration on Lord Harrington's letters, 25 August 1741; TNA, SP43/100, unfoliated, Newcastle to Harrington, 28 August 1741 (private).

62   TNA, Adm 8/20 August 1741.

63   TNA, SP 43/101, unfoliated, 31 August 1741. The *Princess Amelia*, had escorted the plantations trade to North America and was expected to be following Lestock. By early September there were at Spithead three 100s, six 90s, one 80, seven 70s, one 60. For Wager's opinion, see TNA, SP 43/101, unfoliated, Newcastle to Harrington, 4 September 1741.

64   TNA, SP 42/86, f. 411, Paper by Sir John Norris, 1 September 1741.

The reinforcements for the West Indies had been assembling steadily. Three regiments of foot and 700 drafts were ready to depart.[65] Lestock brought despatches that announced Vernon's and Wentworth's intentions to attack Cuba. He also brought with him the officers of the four youngest marine regiments whose rank and file had been drafted into the four elder regiments as reinforcements. However, the good news was that the sickness seemed to have abated.[66] By mid-September the ministers could count on having just about enough resources in place to conduct the Caribbean offensive and challenge any Franco-Spanish force at sea. On 10 September Norris received orders to take his squadron to cruise off Finisterre for the Spanish ships returning from Havana. If the Brest squadron came out and sailed up the Channel he was to come north to destroy it. If, more likely, it sailed south to Cadiz he was to follow them and join Haddock to prevent it linking up with Spanish squadrons.[67]

Hanoverian Neutrality, September–October 1741

However, the most serious problem was that of Austria and Hanover. French forces were advancing into southern Germany and another army approaching Hanover. The archive at Bremen was ordered onto Royal Navy ships in the Weser.[68] If Fleury died it was believed that war would erupt immediately and the Brest squadron would be sent to support the Prussians and Swedes in the Baltic. The Queen of Hungary was in a desperate position 'abandoned for the sake of the Electorate'. Bavarian forces had been advancing along the Danube since mid-July. Sweden, prompted by France, declared war on Russia on 4 August (n.s.) making it impossible for Russia to come to Austria's assistance. On 4 August the French army of 15,000 crossed the Rhine for Bavaria. On 11 September Franco-Bavarian forces were in Linz, about 100 miles from Vienna. Although the British ministry did not know it, the division of the Habsburg inheritance was agreed between Bavaria and Saxony at Nymphenburg on 8 September. What was obvious was that a French dominated coalition appeared on the verge of dictating a peace to Europe.

---

65   *Richmond-Newcastle Correspondence*, p. 70, Richmond to Newcastle, 19 August 1741.
66   BL, Add Ms 354407, f. 83, Stone to Hardwicke, 1 September 1741. Among the sick officers who returned home was Colonel Edward Wolfe, father of James Wolfe.
67   TNA, SP 42/86, f. 222, Instructions to Norris, 10 September 1741.
68   TNA, SP 43/101 (State Papers – Regencies), unfoliated, Newcastle to Harrington, 8 September 1741.

The strain was clearly telling on Newcastle. He was convinced that Hanoverian jealousy of Prussia thwarted all British attempts to bring about
a reconciliation of Prussia and Austria. The King appeared to ignore the
British ministry. Whatever the consequences in Parliament, the recent weeks
had severely damaged the ministers' relations with the King and whatever
the situation in the closet, an enquiry in Parliament seemed unavoidable.
Twelve thousand Hessians and Danes in British pay were being used to
defend Hanover, while nothing was done to rescue the Queen of Hungary.[69]
Rumours of a neutrality between Hanover and the Franco-Bavarian forces
arrived from the Hague on 12 September. Newcastle wrote to Hardwicke 'I
am greatly at a loss to know what countenance to hold upon this Rumour,
in the midst of the Reproach of my friends and the taunts of my enemies. In
short the piece of news has raised as great a consternation here as the Separation of the Troops in 1712'.[70]

Over the next weeks Maillebois' army was said to be within three weeks'
march of the Hanoverian frontier. With Vienna under threat, Sir Thomas
Robinson reported the intention of the Habsburg court to retire to Buda.
The Danes, upon whom George had relied, had to be coaxed to cross the
Elbe to the Hanoverian camp. The Saxons eventually refused to join the
Hanoverians and joined the Franco-Bavarian allies instead.[71] The Russian
envoy in London, Sherbatov, had good and bad news. The Russians had
defeated a Swedish army in Finland, but he had rumours of a French plan to
invade Scotland or Ireland before the end of the month.[72]

The West Indian reinforcements finally left England on 9 October and at
the end of the month despatches from Vernon and Wentworth confirmed
that they had gone to Cuba. All that could be done now was to wait for
news. Norris had been struggling for a while to get his squadron manned,
provisioned and out to sea. His initial orders were to return before winter,
which in practice meant being back in Britain before the end of October

---

69   BL, Add Ms 35407, ff. 89–95, Newcastle to Hardwicke 9 September 1741 (very secret).

70   Ibid., f. 98, Newcastle to Hardwicke, 12 September 1741. The separation was a reference
      to the British troops under the Duke of Ormonde marching away from the allied army in
      Flanders in June 1712 as a result of a Franco-British agreement for a temporary armistice.
      It was the culmination of Tory ministry's separate peace negotiations which effectively
      ended the War of Spanish Succession, but the desertion of the allies burned deeply into
      Whig consciences. See G.M. Trevelyan, *England under Queen Anne*, 3 vols, London,
      1934, iii (*The Peace and the Protestant Succession*), 218–219.

71   *Richmond-Newcastle Correspondence*, p. 74, Stone to Richmond, 17 September 1741

72   TNA, SP 45/3, Whitehall, 15 September 1741.

and on 22 September he was ordered to remain at Spithead until further notice.[73] Just two days later intelligence from Faro confirmed the arrival of the Havana squadron at the Canaries. Four large ships were also said to be returning to Spain from Caracas. Still more news (admittedly contradicted) told of the Brest fleet putting to sea, heading for Cadiz. Norris was ordered to sea immediately to intercept the Havana squadron and send a cruiser to seek out intelligence of the French. He was to man his ships from any vessels in Portsmouth and he was told to ignore the order to return by winter.[74] Norris objected that his squadron was ill suited for a mid-winter cruise and he could not carry adequate provisions to remain off the Spanish coast that long. The Admiralty accepted the impracticality of their orders. Norris was ordered to return home when he thought necessary, but leave cruisers out. The four additional ships for Haddock were to sail independently with the convoy of provision and supply ships.[75] Norris finally got his ships to sea on the morning of 11 October and cruised off the Biscay coast of Spain, arriving back on 6 November, having encountered nothing.

Three days later, on 9 November, devastating news arrived from France. On 23 October 14,000 Spanish troops had left Barcelona under escort of the small Cartagena squadron. The ministers met for an urgent meeting at Walpole's house. Wager told them that two 90s and three 70s from Norris' command could be provisioned within a week and depart for the Mediterranean. They would sail under the command of Commodore Richard Lestock. Haddock, watching Cadiz, had clearly been wrong-footed and the ministry misled by his reports. His move to Gibraltar was based on intelligence that the preparations in Barcelona were not far advanced. It was now impossible to stop the Spanish forces landing in Italy, but he must now get to Barcelona to stop the 15 battalions, artillery and ammunition that were still there. Haddock's position was fraught with danger. If Haddock moved east, the Cadiz squadron could come out. The Toulon squadron was now thought to be cruising off Barbary – an excellent position from which to unite with the Cadiz squadron to the west of Haddock before following him to Barcelona. All the ministers could do was to instruct Haddock to be governed by events. Standing orders required him to follow, destroy or blockade the

---

73   TNA, SP 43/101, unfoliated, Newcastle to Harrington, 18 September 1741.

74   TNA, SP 42/87, f. 230, Stone to Norris, 22 September 1741; f. 238, Stone to Norris, 25 September 1741; f. 240, Extract of Trevor to Newcastle, 29 September 1741 (n.s.).

75   Ibid, f. 250, Stone to Norris, 29 September 1741. Captain Cornwall of the *Marlborough* (90), took the *Bedford* (70), *Essex* (70) and *Elizabeth* (70) to join Haddock.

Spanish squadrons. If possible he was to destroy the Toulon squadron. It was assumed that the Cadiz and Toulon squadrons would still attempt to unite at Cadiz, so it seemed most likely that his main force should concentrate at this point, while he sent a smaller force to Barcelona to seek out the transports and destroy them.

While Lestock lay wind-bound at Spithead for the next two weeks, news arrived that the Cadiz squadron of 16 men of war had sailed on 4 November. The ships were said to be in poor condition and crewed largely by inexperienced landsmen, but they were, most likely, headed for Barcelona and would link up with the Toulon squadron on the way. Haddock's failure to intercept them meant that he must leave Gibraltar immediately and head for Barcelona to seek out and destroy the combined Franco-Spanish squadrons and the second embarkation bound for Italy.[76] It was a bad situation – a British squadron was sailing away from its reinforcements in pursuit of a Franco-Spanish squadron, possibly twice its size .

The inability of the fleet to get out of Torbay, Norris's futile cruise and Haddock's failure to intercept the Spanish forces going to Italy were seized upon by the opposition press as evidence of ministerial incompetence or, worse still, corruption and treason. However, the strain of events that autumn was not confined to naval affairs. Walpole had not been well for some weeks and was by this time extremely ill.[77] The Hanoverian neutrality was awaited with trepidation. Contradictory rumours flooded the country during September. Newcastle was convinced that a neutrality between Hanover and France had been concluded and part of the price would be that Britain made peace with Spain and ceased aiding Austria. He believed 'the general language' of the political nation was that British interests had been sacrificed and that Britain must be disassociated from the neutrality immediately.[78] Even before news of an agreement between Hanover and France reached London in early October, Newcastle knew he could not support a Hanoverian neutrality in Parliament.[79] His brother re-assured him that 'A partiality to Hanover in general is what all men of business have found great obstruction from ever since this family has been upon the throne', but to

76   BL, Add Ms EG 2539, f. 239, Newcastle to Haddock, 11 November 1741; f. 250, Newcastle to Haddock, 26 November 1741.

77   Devonshire Mss, 245.9, Edward Walpole to Devonshire, 6 October 1741.

78   BL, Add Ms 35407, f. 109, Newcastle to Hardwicke, 18 Sept 1741; f. 113, Newcastle to Hardwicke, 26 September 1741.

79   BL, Add Ms 35407, f. 89–95, Newcastle to Hardwicke, 9 September 1741 (most secret).

resign at such a time would expose the King and appear as opportunist as Pulteney and Carteret.[80]

Furthermore, there was some very good news from Europe. Austria and Prussia had finally come to an accommodation. Maria Theresa had conceded that Frederick should have Lower Silesia so the Austrians could concentrate their forces on Bohemia where the Franco-Bavarian army was continuing its advance.[81] Hanover was now safe from French and Prussian attack and might even be able to send the 12,000 Danes and Hessians hired by Britain to join the Austrian forces in Bohemia, as originally intended.[82]

Nonetheless, the overall Austrian position remained desperate. The Saxons had joined the coalition to divide the Austrian empire and the Franco-Bavarian army captured Prague in November. The Spanish army in Italy was on the march, which compelled the Austrians to divide their forces once again.

The End of the Walpole Ministry, October 1741–February 1742

The King arrived back in London in mid-October. As anticipated, he blamed his ministers for the failure of his plans to support Austria. The general election of that summer was over and the new Parliament would meet in December. It was going to be difficult to manage. Newcastle, who had an acute sense of parliamentary sentiment, estimated that their majority had fallen from about 42 to just 14.[83] Walpole's health had recovered, but he had been ground down by the events of the summer and was not up to leading the ministry in this difficult period.[84] Newcastle began dreaming of hopelessly optimistic scenarios for 1742. France was the great danger, but her finances were exhausted and her West Indian commerce disrupted. A treaty between Britain, Austria, Prussia and the United Provinces could bring an army of 21,000 into Flanders to threaten France. Another Hanoverian–Austrian–Prussian army could be formed to act against the Saxons and Bavarians in Bohemia.[85]

---

80   BL, Add Ms 32698, f. 114, Pelham to Newcastle, 8 October 1741. Hanover and France signed a protocol for neutrality at Neustadt on 12 Oct ns. Although known in outline in London, details were not given to British ministers until after George returned from Hanover. See Dann, *Hanover and Great Britain*, op. cit., 39.

81   The Convention of Kleinschnellendorf was signed on 9 October (n.s.). It was to be kept secret from France and with a British representative, Lord Hyndford, present as a witness.

82   TNA, SP 43/101, unfoliated, Newcastle to Harrington, 13 October 1741.

83   J.B. Owen, *The Rise of the Pelhams*, London, 1957, 5.

84   Egmont Papers, p. 229.

85   BL, Add Ms 35407, f. Newcastle to Hardwicke, 1 November 1741.

However, over the summer, the opposition, buoyed by electoral successes was more united than the ministry had hoped. There were bound to be challenges to election results, which would be settled by a Committee of Privileges. The membership of this committee would be determined in a few weeks and the outcome of this would determine the outcome of those challenges. The debate around the King's Speech could set the tone for those decisions. As Newcastle had feared, the events of the summer provided the opposition with all the ammunition it needed. Parliament opened on 1 December. The opposition responded to the King's Speech on 4 December with a crushing series of indictments. Austria was essential for the preservation of the liberties of Europe, but was now almost extinguished as a power. This was, according to Carteret, no more than the logical outcome of policies pursued by Walpole since 1721. Preparations had been made to defend Austria, but nothing had been done. The 12,000 troops had, instead, been diverted to protect Hanover, which was still completely untouched by the chaos of war. Sir John Shippen pointed out that despite the provisions of Act of Settlement, British money was spent to defend that Electorate without parliamentary approval.

Even more destructive, Carteret asserted in the Lords, was the failure to employ the troops and money voted. It gave grounds for all Britain's allies to distrust her actions in the future. Unable to create an alliance, Austria would fall. The Dutch would follow and all their trade would be taken over by France and 'it cannot be denied that our commerce will quickly be at an end. We shall then lose the dominion of the sea, and all our distant colonies and settlements and be shut up in our own island, where the continuance of our liberties can be determined only by the resolution with which we have to defend them'.[86]

The diplomatic failures were compounded by a naval policy, which was, in the view of the opposition, the mainspring of the catastrophe. The failure of the West Indian expedition had been predicted by the Duke of Argyle. Troops 'newly raised, placed under the direction of officers not less ignorant than themselves' and an inexperienced general committed the expedition to disaster.[87] There was, in the opposition view, little doubt that this was the intended outcome. Haddock's behaviour was even more remarkable. The Royal Navy was twice the size of the Franco-Spanish squad-

---

86   Cobbett, *Parliamentary History*, op. cit., xii (1741–3), 255.

87   Ibid., 272.

4

rons and should have been irresistible. Yet, Lord Halifax noted, British admirals were 'dancing about the sea like the master of a packet boat (Norris) and another (Haddock) keeping his station to let loose Spain upon Hungary'.[88] Before, in 1726–1727, Admiral Hosier, had been ordered to stand by and not attack Spanish possessions. It was hard to explain this inaction except to conclude that the same restraints were at work. Haddock had allowed the Spanish squadrons to escape to the West Indies in 1740. He had not acted to prevent the Spanish expedition leaving Barcelona in October. Vernon had not been reinforced in time to capitalise on the capture of Porto Bello and Norris had not reinforced Haddock in 1741. In the meantime 300 ships and 3000 sailors had fallen victim to privateers. Only one admiral, Vernon, appeared to be active. The opposition did not impute this to cowardice or incompetence on the part of the admirals, but to direct instructions from London. Hanoverian neutrality had been bought at the price of Austrian possessions in Italy.

The ministerial response was extremely weak. In both Houses, they struggled unsuccessfully to confine the debate to the technicalities of a vote of thanks to the crown, but were forced to address the foreign policy issues. Their tactic was to concede the broad proposition of the current danger, but to reject the detailed analysis of cause and effect. They accepted that the House of Bourbon 'is arrived at a very dangerous and formidable extent' and that 'the House of Austria cannot fall without exposing all those who have hitherto been supported by its alliance, to the utmost danger'. The King had done all he could. He expected others to join Austria, but the negotiations had proved unexpectedly slow. Harrington reaffirmed that the Hanoverian neutrality had no direct implications for British policy. The French promises of plunder from the Austrian inheritance had proved more enticing to potential allies than the King's appeals to honour. Nonetheless, the Hanoverian response had forced Prussia to divert 35,000 men from Silesia, blunting any further attack on that province. Austria had only herself to blame for the Saxon defection, by raising that Elector to the Kingdom of Poland. Russia, Austria and Prussia were now united to oppose the French. Nothing was needed for success but the resolve of the princes in opposition to France.

At sea, the war was not going as badly as claimed. British losses were as high as those of Spain, but from a much larger merchant marine. If the defeat at Cartagena was blameable there could be an enquiry. As to Haddock, he was handicapped by facing three potentially hostile squadrons (Brest, Toulon and Cadiz). Reinforcements had been sent, but, Newcastle declared, the ministry was mystified as to why Haddock was not at Barcelona.

The opposition had astutely played on key assumptions of foreign policy. The defence of Austria, which was vital to British interests, had been neglected and future alliances imperilled. The navy, whose power and importance in any war against Spain and France was unquestioned, had been neutralised. The cause of both was at best spectacular incompetence, but more likely corrupt councils in favour of Hanover and even France. The ministry could not deny the outcomes – defeat in the Caribbean, Austria in peril, Hanover secure and the navy ill-positioned in the Mediterranean. They knew the asserted causes to be false, but were ill placed to dispute them. They could not create a convincing alternative explanation. They did not know why the Cartagena expedition had failed. They did not know why Haddock was not at Barcelona. They had no control over the King's policy in Hanover and could not explain why their desire to bring Prussia to an accommodation with Austria or their negotiations with the Dutch, Saxons, Danes and Russians were so slow. They had information and views on all these issues, but they could not be constructed into a convincing explanation of events. Although the address of thanks passed the Lords easily enough, a clause in the Commons address, thanking the King for the conduct of the war against Spain, was given up without a vote.[89]

As the Commons turned to settling the election petitions, the weakness of the ministry became ever more apparent. The key vote was for the Chairman of the Elections and Privileges Committee. In a very full house, Walpole's candidate lost by four votes (242–238).[90] From now on the handling of disputed elections was moving out of the government's control. How far the votes of independent members were swayed by the debates of 4 December is impossible to tell. The political ground was shifting, and men who did not want to be associated with a minority administration were deserting. However, for other independents, it was a critical time in foreign affairs. The competence and honesty of the ministry was questioned and, perhaps wrongly, associated with Walpole himself. Apart from calculations of personal advantage there were good reasons to think the ministry had come to the end of its life.

---

89   Ibid., 226–262
90   Ibid., 322. Egmont Diary, 232.

The Christmas recess ended on 19 January and the attacks resumed on the conduct of the war. Debates in the Lords on a motion for Haddock's instructions and in the Commons for a select committee to examine the conduct of the war as a whole were launched the new year with a flurry of parliamentary excitement. The latter debate on 21 January attracted the fullest house for years and was vigorously contested. In a wide ranging debate, Walpole's grasp of foreign policy astounded his audience, but he managed to win the issue by only three votes (253–250). The narrowness of the majority was a sure sign that the game was almost up. A final attempt at the end of the month to reconcile the King with his son, the Prince of Wales, might have shored up the government, but it came to nothing. The loss of the Chippenham election petition convinced Walpole that he must go. On 3 February 1742 Walpole resigned and Parliament was adjourned. The public waited to see who his successor would be.

The war provided the opposition with plausible grounds to attack Walpole. It provided the reason for independents, who were wedded to the constitutional theory of parliamentary powers, to withdraw their support of the King's ministry. This began the shift that saw the Treasury men absent themselves from the government's ranks. While war was undeniably the province of the King, its conduct put his ministry on the back foot. As in the 1730s, debates were based upon shared systemic assumptions. Austria was the bedrock of the essential alliance system. The Royal Navy was invincible at sea. Hanover had to be prevented from being a drain upon, and diversion from, legitimate policy. Failures were not owing to fundamental systemic weakness, but to the personal incompetence of ministers and officers. In 1741 Austria was not supported, the Royal Navy had failed, Hanover had diverted policy. Ministers had to be to blame.

Like all systems dependent upon confidence, the slide in parliamentary support became unstoppable after a tipping point. In 1739 the slide had been stopped by conceding to war. In February 1741 the attempt to unseat Walpole was not accompanied by any real sense of crisis. The general attack on Walpole offered nothing that had not been said before. By 21 January 1742 the ministry had to acknowledge the crisis was real and had no coherent explanation of how it was to be resolved. With the debate on the Select Committee the tipping point had probably passed. Walpole was a consummate parliamentary tactician. Tired and ill, he fought to the end. If he could have bought off the Prince of Wales and divided the opposition, conceivably, he might have survived, but they held together, the slide continued and with nothing left, the end came quickly.

5

Shifting Focus, the Growth of the Continental Commitment, February– December 1742

Naval Capability, Ministerial Reconstruction and the Admiralty, February–March 1742

As MPs left Parliament on 3 February 1742 they knew the political scene had shifted decisively and the war had been an important context for Walpole's fall. The overall result of the maritime war to date was inconclusive but this was, by common consensus, the fault of ministers and army officers. At the beginning of 1740 Spain had a very limited capability. During 1741 the naval balance of power had shifted towards Spain. However, France, even as a neutral, had significantly multiplied that shift of power and forced the redistribution of the British fleet into the Caribbean and Mediterranean. Lack of manpower was hindering deployments and the fleet was now geographically stretched. This was not noticed by the political public at this point and few doubted the capability of the navy, still less the practicability of the whole West Indian plan. Only the First Lord of the Admiralty, Sir Charles Wager, seems to have realised, by June 1741, that the ambitions for the reinforcements were, by then, unrealistic.[1] Newcastle who dominated the ministry may have understood this, but was clear that the public assumption of success in the Caribbean was so powerful that it was vital to maintain the effort even with the limited resources available. The Spanish threat to Gibraltar and Minorca had been widened to the Italian coastline and it was difficult for Haddock to cover all these points. His numerical disadvantage compared to the Franco-Spanish squadrons had to be eliminated and towards the end of January 1742, four more ships of the line (an

---

1 Ranft, *The Vernon Papers*, op. cit., 243–3, Wager to Vernon, 21 June 1741.

80, 70 and two 60s) were sent to reinforce him. Manpower deficiencies for his enlarged squadron could only be met from the garrison of Port Mahon.[2] From being primarily an offensive force in 1739/1740, with a focus on the Caribbean, the Royal Navy had, by the end of 1741, been forced to move to a more defensive posture with a Mediterranean focus and it was unclear how the maritime war could be developed to deliver the decisive blow against Spain in 1742.

The other aspect of the war at sea, the war against trade, had been equally disappointing. Spanish trade had largely been driven from the sea, or into neutral bottoms, during 1740, giving little incentive to privateers. The monthly activity rate of British privateers remained very low between 1739 and April 1744. There was greater activity in the Americas, where colonial privateers preyed upon local Spanish traffic. However, British trade was far more extensive and attacked by Spanish privateers on both sides of the Atlantic. The net balance of prizes was about even, and although the overall impact was far greater on Spanish commerce, this was not recognised in Parliament.[3]

The final element of the war against Spain, was Georgia. The new colony, which had been settled since 1737, did not play a major part in thinking during the war. Although supported by a parliamentary grant, it was a private project of the Georgia Company. It was hardly capable of defending itself, let alone contributing to the defeat of Spain. A promising expedition under James Oglethorpe, to San Augustine, the most northerly city in Spanish America, had miscarried in 1740 and the Georgian colonists were forced to remain on the defensive throughout 1741.

The reconstruction of the ministry took place over two months. Newcastle and the Old Corps Whigs thought that their days in office were numbered,

---

2   BL, Egerton Ms, f. 270, Newcastle to Haddock, 21 January 1742.

3   Starkey, *British Privateering*, op. cit., 298–299; C.E. Swanson, *Predators and Prizes; American Privateering and Imperial Warfare, 1739–1748*, Columbia, 1991, 122–123; Corbett, *Parliamentary History*, op.cit., xii (1741–1743), 223 et seq. Debate in the Lords on the Address of Thanks, 4 December 1741. Chesterfield jibed that the capture of British ships was so common that the King of Spain now placed an import tax on the captured goods as if it was an item of regular trade. The better method of conducting the war was claimed to be a standing squadron in the Soundings as Lord Berkeley had instituted in 1706 (ibid., 227). On the whole, the value of exports, which had fallen by nearly 20 per cent between 1737 and 1740, showed an upturn of about 10 per cent during 1741 and the rise continued until war with France broke out in February 1744, but this did not register in the political debate. See E.B. Schumpeter, *English Overseas Trade Statistics, 1697–1808*, Oxford, 1960, 15.

but even before Walpole resigned, it was clear that the opposition was united only by a fear that Walpole would continue to rule after his resignation.[4] The appointment of the Earl of Wilmington, the King's 'favourite nonentity' as First Lord of the Treasury on 11 February, gave hopes to some of the opposition that there would be a clear out of Walpole's friends, but it rapidly became apparent that this would not happen. Walpole, now created Earl of Orford, retained favour at court and Wilmington was not inclined to pursue him or his friends.[5] Some prominent opposition members were brought in. Most important were Lord Carteret, who accepted the position of secretary of state for the Northern Department in place of Harrington, who was made Lord President of the Council, and William Pulteney, who was initially satisfied with a peerage as Earl of Bath. They represented their move to government as part of a gradual process of bringing Walpole's opponents into the ministry, but this was furiously rejected by those opponents, such as the adherents of the Prince Wales, who had helped topple Walpole and yet were left out.[6] The negotiations for positions continued into March, and the struggle for the Admiralty saw the final settlement emerge.

Sir Charles Wager had lost confidence in the West Indian policy during the summer of 1741.[7] In January he had asked George II for permission to resign, but the King had refused. Nevertheless, with Walpole's resignation, Wager could not stay and his resignation was accepted on 11 February. Plans for the Admiralty had already been made. On 4 February, Newcastle and Hardwicke met with Carteret and Pulteney, where they hammered out the principal posts of the new administration. Carteret's nephew, Daniel Finch, eighth Earl of Winchelsea, was to be First Lord of the Admiralty.[8] This appointment was both controversial and damaging. The Admiralty was an office of state and a prize of political power, but the post of First Lord

---

4   The best contemporary account of the political manoeuvres around the reconstruction of the ministry is the diary of the Earl of Egmont. See Historical Manuscripts Commission Egmont Diary, op. cit., iii, passim. The best modern account is still Owen, *Pelhams*, op. cit., London, 1957.

5   Egmont Diary, op. cit., iii, 248.

6   For the reaction of the Prince of Wales, see R. Harris, 'A Leicester House Political Diary, 1742–3', *Camden Miscellany*, xliv (1992), 375–411. See also the diary of William Hay, in S. Taylor and C. Jones (eds), *Tory and Whig: The Parliamentary Papers of Edward Harley, 3rd Earl of Oxford and William Hay, M.P. for Seaford, 1716–1753*, Woodbridge, 1998, 176–179.

7   Ranft, *The Vernon Papers*, op. cit., 243–3, Wager to Vernon, 21 June 1741.

8   Owen, *Pelhams*, op. cit., 96.

had been held by a senior flag officer since October 1714. Winchelsea had no firsthand experience of the sea service, nor administration. His father, the Earl of Nottingham, had considerable experience of maritime and naval affairs, but had died in 1730, and it is unknown if any of this knowledge was passed on to his son. For the business of the board, Winchelsea was dependent for advice on other members with naval service. Pulteney, Winchelsea's main ally, had expected that there would be a simple solution. He hoped that the Admiral of the Fleet, Sir John Norris, would join the board under the political command of his social superior, Winchelsea. However, Norris believed that Carteret and Pulteney had earlier hinted that they wanted him as First Lord. Professionally, he believed he had the right to lead the board and refused to serve in a subordinate position.[9]

In the first division of Admiralty Board posts, a respected man of experience was found in John Cockburne. Cockburne, an adherent of the Duke of Argyle, had served on the Board from 1717 to 1732. He had expected to be appointed as First Lord on the retirement of Lord Torrington, so resigned when Wager was promoted over him. So far as naval experience was concerned, the only officer approved was Lord Grannard, also a supporter of Argyle. In mid-February, Argyle was a key figure. Whereas Carteret and Pulteney had abandoned the opposition, Argyle continued to carry weight in the Patriot ranks as a proponent of a broad bottomed administration that would not allow Walpole to hide behind the curtain. Serious negotiations continued and by 17 February it looked as if Pulteney had negotiated a settlement in which Argyle, the Prince of Wales and the Tories were satisfied. They had been promised a change in measures and had got some of their men into office. Argyle would also regain his old office of master general of the Ordnance, and have the senior command of the army.

However, the Admiralty Board remained a problem. Winchelsea recognised the weakness of his own position and insisted the post of First Lord be offered to the Duke of Montagu, who had been turned out of the post of master general of the Ordnance on Argyle's return. Montagu was more interested in a post in the royal household than an important office of government business and turned it down.[10] Why the King was so set against Norris as First Lord is a mystery. The new ministry had one further opportunity to reverse that decision. Admiral Haddock was clearly ailing and had to be

9   BL, Add Ms 28132, ff. 121–124.
10   BL, Add Ms 28133, f. 122, 3 March 1742; Add Ms 32699, f. 66, Montagu to Newcastle, 17 February 1742.

replaced. Norris was the obvious successor and Carteret asked him to go to the Mediterranean. Norris agreed on condition that he was made First Lord. Newcastle placed the request before the King, and on 4 March Norris had a private audience. Perhaps it was Norris's own temper that wrecked his chances. The King asked for time to consider Norris's request, but the old admiral retorted that if it required time he preferred to resign. Given George's own temperament and what he had to endure with the loss of Walpole, it was probably an understatement to describe Norris's ultimatum as 'a procedure condemned as too cavalier'.[11] The King refused and Norris tendered his resignation.

There was no further discussion over the post of First Lord and a list of commissioners was put before the King for his approval on 8 March. However, Sir John Cotton, a Tory, and Lord Grannard, who had refused to serve in the West Indies in 1739, were *persona non grata* to the King. Eventually, the King accepted a revised list, including two of Pulteney's friends, Lord Limerick and Samuel Waller, but they insisted that more of their friends be brought into the ministry. The King, who had probably had his fill of ultimata, reacted furiously and rejected the commission.[12] With Argyle and Pulteney repulsed, the new negotiations presented further opportunities to Newcastle's friends in the Old Corps, the Prince of Wales' Leicester House faction and to increase naval representation on the board.[13] The Prince's friend, Lord Archibald Hamilton, was not only a naval officer, but had been a member of the board between 1729 and 1738. Admiral Philip Cavendish, the illegitimate son of the Duke of Devonshire, was a solid member of the Old Corps. On 14 March 1742 Winchelsea and his new commissioners kissed hands and the new commission commenced on 19 March.

The wholesale removal of the Old Corps had not happened and Walpole remained in favour at court.[14] However, the changes were dramatic. In five weeks, the naval brains that had directed the war since October 1739 had

---

11   Egmont Mss, iii, 259.

12   Egmont Mss, iii, 260.

13   The political tension during these days was intense and the balance of power between the Old Corps and the various opposition groups ambiguous. Argyle's position had collapsed when he resigned over the defeat of a vote for a secret committee to investigate Walpole's activities on 9 March. This was certainly not the end of the opposition or confusion as the secret committee was approved when it returned to the House on 23 March.

14   J. Oates, 'Sir Robert Walpole after his Fall from Power, 1742–1745', *History*, xci (2006), 218–230.

Table 5.1 The Commissioners of the Admiralty, 1738–1743 (listing service in RN, years on the Admiralty Board and political connection)

	1st Lord						
1741–1742	Sir Charles Wager RN + 24 years	Sir Thomas Frankland 12 years	Lord H. Powlett RN +9 years	John Campbell 6 years	Lord Vere Beauclerk RN + 4 years	Lord Glenorchy 7 months	Edward Thompson 7 Months
February–March 1742 (proposed Board) (see Owen, p. 100)	Winchelsea	John Cockburne 15 years (1717–1732) Country Whig (Argyle friend)	Lord Limerick (Bedford Interest, Pulteney friend)	Lord Granard RN (Argyle friend)	Edmund Waller (Pulteney friend)	John Chetwynd (Gower friend)	Sir John Hynd Cotton (Tory)
March 1742 Dec 1743	Winchelsea	John Cockburne 15 years (1717–1732) Country Whig Argyle friend	Lord Archibald Hamilton RN 9 Years (1729–1738) (Leicester House)	Lord Baltimore (Leicester House)	Philip Cavendish RN (Old Corps)	George Lee (Leicester House)	John Trevor (Old Corps)

Table 5.2 Flag officers, January 1742

Admiral of the Fleet	Sir John Norris	London
Admiral of the White	Sir Charles Wager	London
Admiral of the Blue	Philip Cavendish	Portsmouth
Vice Ad of the Red	John Balchen	Plymouth
Vice Ad of the White	Vacant after death of Stewart, 13 Aug 1740	Vacant
Vice Ad of the Blue	Edward Vernon	West Indies
Rear Ad of the Red	Nicholas Haddock	Sick in the Mediterranean
Rear Ad of the White	Vacant	Vacant
Rear Ad of the Blue	Sir Chaloner Ogle	West Indies

been removed from the scene. The formal management and presentation of the naval war now lay in the hands of a man who had no experience of naval warfare. The help he could expect from Cockburne, Hamilton and Cavendish hardly compensated for the loss of 54 years of aggregated experience of the board's work, and the only experience of managing the war effort at sea. The balance of power between the Admiralty, the Navy and Victualling Boards shifted in favour of the last two, whose membership remained unchanged and whose command over their work was, as yet, unchallenged. Equally important was the relationship with the navy. Wager and Norris had been professional heads of the navy since the early 1730s. No one was in a position to take up that role. Cavendish, while third in flag rank, and on the board, had had no connection with naval policy to date and had not served at sea during this war. Balchen had been at sea, but was disconnected from naval decision-making.

The inclusion of Lord Carteret as Secretary of State for the Northern Department was also important. Formally, policy did not change and Carteret carried out his role exactly as would be expected. However, the way in which Carteret related to his ministerial colleagues introduced an entirely new dynamic into British war-making. In the final years of Walpole's ministry, Newcastle had dominated policy. His strength did not come from a particular closeness to the King .Indeed, Newcastle was painfully aware that his policy preferences ran counter to those of George. Rather, his strength lay in his deep knowledge of parliamentary opinion and the intricacies of the Spanish problem. He understood as well as anyone and better than most how to mould policy to the political and diplomatic circumstances of the time. The way he did this was to pay close attention to information from political and diplomatic sources. He shared information and views with friends, particularly with Lord Hardwicke and Henry Pelham, and built up a common understanding of the issues and policies. Carteret was a very different personality. He was an excellent parliamentary orator, but never encouraged close working associations. In opposition and in government he stood aloof from his colleagues.[15] His tendency to self-sufficiency was supported by a fluency in languages, crucially, for the King, German. He had a good knowledge of American affairs and, as ambassador in Sweden 1719 to 1720, had some ministerial experience to call upon. Carteret was not a man to put a premium on detailed communications with colleagues. Seeking advice or sharing views was not his strong point. In a ministry used to this, and with his perceived Hanoverian bias, Carteret's relations with his colleagues were not going to be smooth.

The New Ministry and the Military Situation, March–May 1742

While the British ministry had been locked in a struggle for reconstruction, a remarkable transformation had taken place in Austrian fortunes. The Austrian position looked desperate in January 1742, as Charles Albert, Elector of Bavaria, was elected Holy Roman Emperor at the Imperial Diet at Frankfurt.

Three months later the situation had entirely altered. Marshal Khevenhuller, the defender of Vienna, assembled an army which drove into Bavaria, ravaging the south of the country before occupying Munich and the whole of the Electorate by the end of February. The Austrian position in Italy stabilised as the Spanish armies, slowed down by terrain and desertion, found progress towards Parma tougher than anticipated. Sardinia, encouraged by this loss of momentum and having wrung further concessions out of the Austrians, agreed to a defensive convention and sent troops to Parma. France gave approval for another Spanish army to march through Provence towards Sardinia, but it was blocked by strong Sardinian forces east of Nice. By mid-March the new

---

15 Carteret has not got a satisfactory modern biography. However, his personality may be reflected in his surviving personal papers in the British Library. Much of the collection consists of copies of official documents. Very little remains of his personal views, preferences and prejudices. The biography by A. Ballantyne, *The Life of Lord Carteret*, London, 1887, is a sympathetic portrayal of an urbane, charming and cultured aristocrat. Basil Williams' comparative biographies of Carteret and Newcastle, *Carteret and Newcastle: A Contrast in Contemporaries*, Cambridge, 1943, is more critical and balanced, but the symmetry of Newcastle as a worldly success riddled with 'ridiculous idiosyncrasies' compared to Carteret's 'great man manqué' probably does not do either of them complete justice.

Emperor was an exile at Frankfurt and the Franco-Bavarian army in Bohemia was bottled up in Prague. Prussia, whose invasion of Silesia in December 1740, had started the war, had been bought off by Austria in October 1741 by accepting Prussian occupation of Lower Silesia (Convention of Klein Schellendorf). However, Frederick had not ceased to meddle in order to keep Austria embroiled with France, Bavaria and Saxony. In February 1742, Prussian forces marched into Moravia, but soon became bogged down by peasant resistance and by April the Prussians began a retreat into Silesia.

British policy was unchanged, but its prospects were now infinitely brighter. Britain would continue to support Austria with subsidies and the fleet in the Mediterranean. Troops would also be sent to defend Austrian Flanders. There were now three diplomatic priorities. Flanders and Italy had to be stabilised by persuading the Dutch to join the Anglo-Austrian army in Flanders and brokering an Austro-Sardinian alliance. France had to be ejected from Germany and Bohemia by ending the Hanoverian neutrality and arranging an Austro-Prussian peace. The war with Spain had completely changed. The Spanish attack on Italy made any peace with Spain dependent upon securing a satisfactory Austro-Spanish settlement as well as satisfaction in the Caribbean. The way to peace no longer lay in the West Indies, but in Europe and the route was far more complex. It lay in decisions made in Vienna, Turin and Berlin as much as London, Madrid and Paris. Carteret's appointment occurred at the very time that this shift in the locus of diplomatic weight became evident and when the chances of Britain influencing those decisions seemed to be rising. The rising importance of central Europe to resolving the war increased the formal importance of the Secretary of State for the Northern Department and proportionately reduced Newcastle's direct access to the most critical information. The way Carteret conducted his business with his ministerial colleagues would have a major influence both on the political stability of the ministry and the conduct of the war.

The Royal Navy in the Mediterranean, 1742

Haddock had left Gibraltar with eight line, eight cruisers and some fireships in pursuit of the Cadiz squadron of 17 sail (10 line and 7 others). On 17 December he had sighted the Spaniards and prepared for action. About an hour later as they drew closer, he saw another squadron of 11 ships moving from under the land to join the Spanish. It was the Toulon squadron. Haddock saw that he could be surrounded and called a council of war. They resolved to fall back on Port Mahon gather up the ships there and then follow the Franco-Spanish force. He acknowledged 'We lost a fine opportunity to engage the enemy singly and chose to preserve the squadron rather than risk it against the combined squadrons as their union was inevitable.' He hoped the King would approve this decision.[16] The King was seriously concerned that Haddock had let the Cadiz squadron get out, but was satisfied Haddock had done his best under the circumstance and that this manoeuvre by the French confirmed their hostile intentions in the Mediterranean. Although the majority of the Spanish fleet was now in the Mediterranean, the reinforcement sent out under Lestock should restore his superiority and the instructions to assist the Queen of Hungary were restated.[17]

While Haddock waited at Mahon, the second landing, covered by the combined Franco-Spanish squadrons, took place at Spezia on 31 January 1742. Lestock arrived at Port Mahon on 27 January 1742, but weather and sickness had taken its toll. The *Neptune* came in under a jury rig. About one-third of the crews were sick and over 5 per cent had died on the journey.[18] Two more ships arrived in late February. Orders were sent to the Lieutenant Governor of Minorca and Gibraltar to provide Haddock with another 500 or 600 soldiers and every assistance in procuring seamen.[19]

Before the squadron was ready for sea news arrived that the Franco-Spanish squadron had gone to Toulon. It was important to stop any further reinforcement of the Spanish forces in Italy, and on 29 March, Lestock was ordered to sea with the whole squadron to patrol between Marseilles and Villa Franca. To do this, Lestock reduced the complements of all his ships and completely unmanned the two most decayed 50s.[20] Fortunately, the victualling convoy arrived at Mahon before the squadron sailed. The squadron sailed on the 12 April and arrived off Toulon on the 17 April. Lestock was able to patrol inshore and see the enemy squadrons clearly. He heard that the French squadron was now largely unmanned. The Spanish ships were mostly in the roads, but four line and two cruisers were not there. The two largest Spanish ships, the *Real* (114) and the *Sta Isabella* (80) were in the harbour, so it was

---

16   TNA, SP 42/86, f. 452, Haddock to Newcastle, 9 December 1741.

17   Ibid., f. 463, Undated draft to Haddock, f. 469, Undated draft to Haddock; BL, Egerton Ms 2529, f. 270, Newcastle to Haddock, 21 January 1742.

18   Ibid., f. 493, Haddock to Newcastle, 1 February 1742.

19   Ibid., f. 475, Draft to Col. O'Farrell; f. 477, draft to Major Gen. Hargrave, undated; f. 485, Newcastle to O'Farrell, 21 January1 1742; f. 487, Newcastle to Hargrave, 21 January 1742.

20   Ibid., f. 509, Lestock to Newcastle, 25 April 1742.

unlikely this squadron would be ready to sail soon. Lestock sent cruisers out along the coast as far as Barcelona to intercept any Spanish reinforcements or supply ships. However, a Spanish army of 13,000 under Don Philip had marched overland to Antibes/Nice area, either to march into Savoy/Pied-mont or take the sea route to join the Duke of Montemar in Parma. The King of Sardinia had taken care to block the land routes from Provence into Savoy. Lestock's squadron, now well provisioned and manned effectively, cut the sea routes. Spanish ships with provisions were blockaded in Antibes. If they got out, the only safe haven for them on the Italian coast was at Orbetello, so Lestock placed two cruisers between Corsica, Elba and the Italian coast.[21] Contacts were established with the consuls in Italy, and with the British ministers at the courts of Turin and Tuscany. The basic communi-cations and support for cooperation between the Royal Navy, the Austrians and Sardinians were in place by the end of May.[22]

In London it was clear that Haddock was too ill to continue, but as Norris had refused to serve, there was no senior flag officer to replace him. The immediate solution was to promote new junior flag officers, and Richard Lestock, who had been sent out with reinforcements in December, was promoted Rear Admiral of the White on 12 March.[23] This still posed a problem. Lestock was the most junior admiral on the establishment, but, potentially, had command of the largest and the most important squadron. The ministry had to look further afield. One source of experienced officers was the Navy Board Commissioners. Captain Thomas Matthews had left the sea service in 1736 and had been resident commissioner at Chatham since then. He had served well in that role and retained the friendship of serving naval officers, but he had forfeited his seniority for a secure billet ashore. The circumstances in which he came to be approached to command in the Mediterranean are unclear, but the desperation of the ministry to secure an experienced officer is probable. On 7 April 1742 Mathews was restored to his seniority and advanced to Vice Admiral of the Red; in effect third ranking serving officer in the navy, just behind Balchen and well ahead of Vernon.

Mathews was to follow the instructions that had been given to Haddock. He was to treat any power that acted in support of Spain as an enemy, but

---

21   Ibid., f. 519, Lestock to Newcastle, 1 May 1742; f. 521, Lestock to Newcastle, 8 May 1742.

22   Ibid. f. 525, Lestock to Newcastle, 22 May 1742.

23   TNA, Adm 6/16, f. 28.

Table 5.3 Flag officers, 7 April 1742

Admiral of the Fleet	Sir John Norris	Resigned
Admiral of the White	Sir Charles Wager	Resigned
Admiral of the Blue	Philip Cavendish	Admiralty Board
Vice Ad of the Red	John Balchen	Plymouth
	Thomas Mathews	Bound for Mediterranean
Vice Ad of the White	Edward Vernon	West Indies
Vice Ad of the Blue	Nicholas Haddock	Sick in Mediterranean
Rear Ad of the Red	Sir Chaloner Ogle	West Indies
Rear Ad of the White	Richard Lestock	Mediterranean
Rear Ad of the Blue	Vacant	Vacant

with regard to detail, he was left free to act as he saw fit. He was to inform the Austrian commander in Italy that he would act with him against French and Spanish attacks. Haddock had authority to threaten Naples, and a bomb vessel would be sent if this was what Mathews decided to do. Otherwise, he was to protect the trade in the region.[24] By the end of April Mathews was at sea, with two 90-gun ships and expecting at least three more 60s to follow him.[25] This would give him a line of battle of 26 ships against the combined Bourbon squadron's 25. The shifting balance of British naval force in the early summer of 1742 is evident in Figure 5.1.

However, Mathews' appointment exposed the weakness of the new naval/political structure. Mathews had no sea-going experience in this war, nor any significant contact with Norris and Wager, but he was not slow to exploit his new rank. After reviewing the papers he was given, he estimated that the squadron was 2,000 men short of complement (about 15 per cent in total). The new Admiralty Board knew they could not find the men from Britain and had suggested that soldiers from the Gibraltar garrison be embarked to fill the gaps.[26] Mathews was not satisfied, and warned Newcastle that; 'tis not possible for an officer to do the service his majesty may reasonably expect from him except that he is properly supported. I am greatly apprehensive from what I know of the Condition of his majesty's squadron now in the Mediterranean

---

24   TNA, SP42/93, f. 8, Newcastle to Mathews, 7 April 1742.

25   TNA, Adm 1/4111, unfoliated, Newcastle to Admiralty, 2 April 1742; SP42/93 (State Papers Naval), f. 16, Mathews to Newcastle, 25 April 1742.

26   TNA, SP 42/25, f. 106, Admiralty to Newcastle, 20 March 1742.

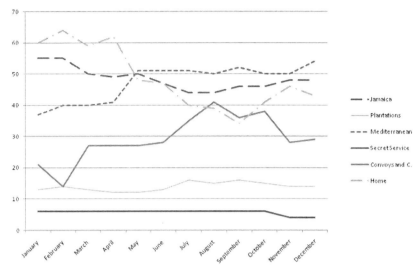

Figure 5.1 Dispositions of Royal Navy warships, 1742

and the very few ships at present designed to reinforce it that I shall not be able to answer his majesty's expectation'.[27]

Without any experienced naval officers to advice them, the ministry felt compelled to accept the opinions and demands of their new Mediterranean commander. What Mathews wanted, Winchelsea was ordered to provide, but the Admiralty was not equipped to deal with those demands. Commanders overseas usually received their instructions from, and corresponded directly with, the secretary of state on matters of strategy, reserving matters of administration and squadron management for their letters to the Admiralty. While the First Lord, like Wager, was a member of the inner cabinet, he saw the letters from the commanders and agreed the Secretary of State's responses. Winchelsea did not attend these meetings and had no records in his office. He and his colleagues were in the dark about the situation on all stations and had to trawl the office for up-to-date information. They could find an account of the number of ships in the Mediterranean, but they had very little else to work with. The board concluded that, together with the ships ordered to follow Mathews, the new Commander would have at least 21 line, 16 cruisers and six smaller ships. To the best of their knowledge, there were 14 Spanish line and three frigates at Toulon. The French squadron there consisted of 11 line and four cruisers. They concluded:

---

27   TNA, SP42/93, f. 2, Mathews to Newcastle, 23 March 1742.

If the number of the opposite ships do not exceed this account, we hope that the strength of His Majesty's squadron is not inferior to their united force; but as we have no intelligence of what is doing in the Ports of France and Spain, nor what services are required to be performed by His Majesty's Instructions to Vice Admiral Mathews, it is impossible for us to judge what will be sufficient strength to enable him to execute what is expected from him and must therefore submit the same to His Majesty's Pleasure.[28]

They could estimate the impact the movement of ships to the Mediterranean would have on the demand for seamen. On the home station there remained only three 100s, three 90s and an 80. Six more ships of the line had arrived back from the West Indies, but were in various states of refit. The only way to get more ships manned for the Mediterranean was to lay up the first rates and 90 gun ships, thus leaving the home station without any ships of the line in a state of readiness.

During the summer of 1741 it had been important to keep hopes alive of a significant victory in the West Indies. By the end of June 1742 news had filtered back that an attack with the reinforcements on Panama had failed and sickness had once again ravaged the expeditionary force.[29] With a campaign in Europe starting and almost no ships of the line available in Britain, there was no question of sending more troops or ships. The defeat was difficult to understand and the tone of Newcastle's letters suggests that the King and ministers placed more of the blame for the failure on Wentworth than Vernon. On 3 August Newcastle wrote to Vernon and Wentworth, ordering them to return home. Ogle would be left at Jamaica with eight line and thirteen cruisers; a strong enough force to be superior to the remaining Spanish ships. Wentworth was to leave enough marines to complete Ogle's ships and the independent companies on Jamaica. They were given permission to attack San Augustine, Florida, on the return journey. Ogle was warned that war with France was possible. He was to defend British islands and trade, intercept Spanish trade and prepare for operations to disrupt French trade. All thoughts of territorial expeditions were at an end.[30]

---

28   TNA, SP 42/25, f. 130, Admiralty to Newcastle, 1 April 1742.

29   *Richmond-Newcastle Correspondence*, 84, Stone to Richmond, 1 July 1742.

30   BL Add Ms 32699, f. 350, Newcastle to Wentworth, 3 August 1742; f. 359, Newcastle to Vernon, 3 August 1742, f. 365, Newcastle to Ogle, 3 August 1742, f. 368, Newcastle to Ogle, 3 August 1742.

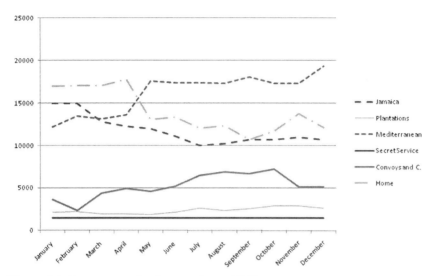

Figure 5.2 Seamen required on stations, 1742

With the end of the Caribbean campaign, the focus of naval attention settled on the Mediterranean. The war was now understood by both government and opposition to be against French power in Europe. Austria was in grave danger and had to be preserved to counter-balance Bourbon power. The King was the leading ruler in Europe to pledge unequivocal support. A British army in Flanders and the squadron in the Mediterranean were vital symbols of British support of Austria and the 'Liberties of Europe'. If France were forced to terms, Spain would follow. This consensus would gradually change during the autumn, but for the moment the Mediterranean squadron had a powerful role to play in European diplomacy, and Mathews' demands had to be satisfied. On 20 July Newcastle, on Mathews' advice, ordered the Board to prepare eight ships to reinforce the Mediterranean squadron, upon which Mathews promised to send eight of his foul ships home. The Admiralty Board, unable to comply, replied that two more line, going out with stores, would have to suffice.

Mathew's demand of sloops was equally problematic. While the Brest squadron looked quiescent, the principal problem on the home station was privateers. An attempt in Parliament to revive the act of 1708 to provide cruisers to protect trade was defeated, but the Admiralty directed a substantial cruising effort in the summer months, employing 41 vessels, just over half the ships in Britain, on that duty in August. In this context, the ministry's unquestioning support of Mathews' demand for more sloops was worrying.

There were none in British waters that were not out on convoy and cruising duty. The Board replied to Newcastle that:

> We are not less distressed ourselves in that particular, though new sloops are constantly building and we purchase all the Spanish privateers taken by our cruisers, which are fit for His Majesty's service. But there are so many stations which require such vessels to curb the insolence of the small privateers and Row Boats of the Enemy, which at this time infest all the parts of Our Channell (sic) and shelter themselves in the Ports of France and our Trading Towns are so intimidated thereby, as to call upon us every day for convoys to their trade to Hamburgh, Flanders and France, which would otherwise be totally at a stand, that we must think these services of such consequence as to deserve our utmost attention and yet we are so strained to supply them, that we actually employ at this time three of the new bomb vessels cruising with their mortars on board; a very unusual thing, but occasioned by our not knowing His Majesty's pleasure whether we might convert them into sloops for this summer's service.[31]

They advised instead that Mathews buy or hire local vessels called xebecks, which Haddock had done.

By this time Haddock had begun his journey home. On 7 May he was at Gibraltar, when Mathews arrived. He was too ill to talk with Mathews, but the latter got his first news of the disposition of the squadron.[32] Mathews hurried on to Mahon and by 22 May was off Toulon, where the fleet began to assemble around him and he moved the main force eastwards to Villa Franca. While the situation in the Western Mediterranean was far better than it had been at the end of 1741, it was far from perfect. The defences of Villa Franca were so poor that Mathews landed swivel guns and powder to support them. He asked Newcastle to arrange for eight more men of war to be sent to him so that he could return his eight most foul ships.[33]

Mathews could not entirely stop small vessels coasting from Barcelona to Marseilles or Toulon, so the build up of Spanish material in Provence was continuing.[34] French and Spanish provision ships were getting into

31   TNA, SP 42/25, f. 299, Admty to Newcastle, 22 July 1742.
32   TNA, SP 42/91, f. 20, Mathews to Newcastle, 8 May 1742.
33   Ibid., f. 34, Mathews to Newcastle, 6 June 1742.
34   Ibid., f. 62, Mathews to Newcastle, 7 June 1742.

Toulon. Intelligence from Toulon also suggested that the 14 Spanish line were poorly armed and badly hit by sickness. The 12 French line had only two months provisions aboard and about one-third of their crews.[35] The arrival of Mathews' main force off Toulon on 3 July caused some panic. The Spanish ships were hauled further up the bay out of range of any bombardment.[36] Still, Mathews was not confident about his position as sickness was growing. He would have to divide his squadron at some point in order to clean, re-supply and refit at Mahon – 'this will be making a voluntary present of so many ships without the probability of preventing it'. His concern is reflected in a concluding statement 'I tell you this to let you know so you cannot question me after'.[37] Five more ships would enable him to have a continuous programme of cleaning.

Many of his smaller ships were patrolling or convoying on the long routes from Lisbon to the Levant.[38] His agreement with the Austrian and Sardinian representatives also increased his demands for sloops and bomb ships. Mathews would further support the land defences at Villa Franca if necessary with gunners and marines. He would station himself off the mouth of the Var River, where he had an excellent view of any approach by the Spanish forces.[39]

Mathews' direct support for the campaign in Italy was provided by Captain Lee of the *Pembroke* (60), who cruised in the Adriatic with the *Warwick* (60) and the *Winchelsea* (24), intercepting supplies and artillery coming from Naples to the Spanish army via Ancona or Rimini.[40] The detachment of Naples from the anti-Habsburg coalition was an objective laid out in Mathews instructions. In late July the arrival of three more bomb ketches, enabled Mathews to send Captain William Martin to 'lay the said city in ashes' unless the King of the Two Sicilies withdrew his army from the Spanish forces in Northern Italy.[41] It was a textbook operation. Martin arrived in the Bay of Naples on the evening of 8 August, anchoring within a cable's length of the batteries. Within 24 hours he

---

35   Ibid., f. 78, Paper 2: Relation de l'homme qui est alle a Toulon.

36   Ibid., f. 88, Mathews to Newcastle, 25 July 1742.

37   Ibid., f. 90.

38   Ibid., f. 237, Disposition of the Fleet under My Command, 17 September 1742.

39   Ibid., f. 76, Points settled by Vice Mathews ...

40   Ibid., f. 101, Lee to Mathews, 16 July 1742.

41   Ibid., f. 109, Mathews to Martin, 25 July 1742.

had confirmation that the King had ordered his army to separate from the Spaniards.[42]

In the meantime Mathews heard that Don Philip and the Spanish army in Provence were on the move. Seamen were being sent to Toulon and some ships there were preparing for sea.[43] Lestock was left off the Isles de Hyères, east of Toulon, to watch that port with eleven line and a fireship, while Mathews took four line to Villa Franca to support the Austro-Sardinian forces. The behaviour of the Genoese authorities was also giving concern. They were encouraging desertion from the Sardinian army and building a magazine, rumoured to be for the use of the Spanish forces. Martin's bomb vessels were again useful. He insisted that he be shown the magazine or he would burn the town. The town council rapidly complied with his request to destroy the magazines.[44] However, Mathews soon heard the Spanish army was not intending to strike out along the coast, but had marched north to invade Savoy.[45]

Mathews returned to Hyères to join Lestock as more rumours arrived of the Franco-Spanish squadrons being prepared for sea. Rumours also suggested that the Brest squadron was on its way to Toulon.[46] Although the weather was expected to deteriorate Mathews decided he had to winter in the bay as if the Spanish forces suddenly moved down to Antibes they were only six hours sail (with a fair wind) from Genoa and then into Italy. He was sure he could blockade the Spanish force in Toulon with only half his force, but if the French joined, he needed his whole squadron to face them. With this intention he again requested more clean ships (a 70 or 60 with two 50s) and more seamen.

The Admiralty's apparent parsimony disgusted Mathews, particularly their response to his request for small ships. The local vessels could not keep station in the winter gales and it was a short journey for the Spanish from Antibes to Genoa. The Neapolitan army was rumoured to be rejoining the Spanish forces and France could join the war against the Austro-Sardinians at any moment, entirely tipping the balance of naval power. His squadron was already badly in need of stores and refit. He did not expect to survive

---

42   Ibid., f. 163, Martin to Mathews, 10 August 1742.

43   Ibid., f. 155, Mathews to Newcastle, 16 Aug 1742.

44   Ibid., f. 205, Martin to Mathews, 1 September 1742

45   Ibid., f. 175, Mathews to Newcastle, 30 August 1742. The best account of the campaign is still, H.S. Wilkinson, *The Defence of Piedmont, 1742–1748: A Prelude to Napoleon*, Oxford, 1927, 57–73.

46   TNA, SP 42/91, f. 195, Mathews to Newcastle, 17 September 1742.

the winter without loss, while the Spanish squadron was at ease in Toulon and free to come out whenever it wished.[47] Sustaining his squadron in the shelter of the Hyères islands was essential, but this required French permission for wooding and watering. If refused, he would have to water by force or retire and with that Italy would lay open and he would be in no position to prevent the Brest squadron entering Toulon, if it should be on its way.[48] He was now sending regular, detailed reports of the decay of his ships and twice more he renewed his demands for more small vessels.[49]

During 1742, the navy was achieving what was intended. Austria and Sardinia were getting effective help for their campaigns, ranging from gunners, artillery, intelligence, blockade of enemy sea routes to the removal of Naples from the enemy ranks. Newcastle, assured Mathews that the ministry would continue to order the Admiralty to supply the stores and seamen that Mathews requested.[50] Newcastle did, however, try to get Mathews to understand the situation. The Admiralty would replace ships that he sent home and would send out more stores as soon as possible.[51] Despite these reassurances, it was still unclear if the effort required to maintain long-term control of the western basin of the Mediterranean was beyond the logistical power of the Royal Navy.

The Changing Political Context of the War, June–December 1742

While the Admiralty struggled with the orders to expand the Mediterranean squadron, the new ministry had enough political strength to control the House of Commons. Nevertheless, opposition unity had been shattered, but not destroyed. Men who had come into the ministry, the so-called 'New Whigs', could not or would not abandon all matters of principled opposition. Hardwicke had foreseen that the Commons was now governed by a new 'Sett of young men' and it would be a troublesome session.[52] However,

---

47   Ibid., f. 272, Condition and Disposition of HM Ships in the Mediterranean, 24 October 1742; f. 340, Condition and Disposition of HM Ships in the Mediterranean, 22 December 1742.

48   Ibid., f. 288, Mathews to Newcastle, 8 November 1742.

49   Ibid., f. 338, letter from Marseilles to Mathews, 28 Dec 1742 (n.s.).

50   TNA, Adm 1/411, unfoliated, Newcastle to the Admty, 13 October 1742.

51   TNA, SP 42/91, f. 240, Newcastle to Mathews, 30 September 1742; SP 42/93, f. 19, Newcastle to Mathews, 18 January 1743.

52   BL, Add Ms 32699, f. 209, Hardwicke to Newcastle, 6 May 1742.

the Pelhams were highly experienced parliamentary managers and they handled the situation as they had done in the late 1730s, giving ground, explicitly endorsing opponents' principles, but disputing their conclusions. Thus, they convinced enough MPs to support the war policies. By the judicious admission of New Whigs and even a senior Tory (Lord Gower), they took the heat out the disappointments felt by initial settlement in March.[53] On some points of supposed principle there was no sacrifice at all. Indeed, the deeply held view that Walpole had sacrificed British interests to France and Hanover actually played to the advantage of the ministry. Men like the Earl of Stair, who had long charged Walpole with pro-French sympathies, was now attached to the ministry and proclaiming publicly its new anti-French complexion. Carteret was equally happy to allow the impression of a significantly new anti-French, anti-Hanoverian position to mature in the public mind. He boldly reassured Stair in June that, now, 'No French counsel can operate here'.[54] He reassured Robert Trevor, at the Hague 'That he stakes his whole on keeping the El(ector) an Englishman'.[55] Nor was this entirely rhetorical. By April, Carteret, more than anyone in the ministry, had been instrumental in convincing the King that the Hanoverian neutrality had to be terminated.[56]

The dangers for the future lay in two areas. The first was within the ministry itself. The way Walpole's administration did business, by private meetings of ministers and selected officers, had broken down. Under Winchelsea the Admiralty as an office was not only deprived of the most experienced naval advice, but it was deprived of information that emerged from the close discussions of the inner cabinet. Carteret's inclusion had signalled to some of Walpole's most staunch opponents that there would be a new 'English' policy, and his influence with the King initially promised much.[57] However, his distance from his colleagues was keenly felt by Newcastle and probably by others. This distance may have contributed to a significant shift in Carteret's relationship with the King. Emerging from his source of strength in the opposition, he started out pressing an 'English' policy on the monarch, but,

53   BL, Add Ms 35363, f. 3, P. Yorke to J. Yorke, 17 June 1742.

54   BL, Add Ms 35459, f. 2, Stair to Carteret, 13 April 1742; J.M. Graham (ed.), *Annals of the Viscount and the First and Second Earls of Stair*, 2 vols, Edinburgh, 1875, vol. 1, 286, Carteret to Stair, 8 June 1742 (hereafter *Stair Annals*).

55   HMC, Trevor Mss, 82, Weston to Trevor, 19 March 1742.

56   Dann, *Hanover and* Britain, op. cit., 43–47. The neutrality was terminated in May 1742.

57   BL, Add Ms 3540, f. 242, Newcastle to Hardwicke, 8 August 1742.

with the collapse of his credit within the opposition and his distance from his ministerial colleagues, he was very soon forced to rely entirely on the King, whose favour was ensured by supporting an overtly pro-Hanoverian policy and attempting to foist it on parliament.

The second danger lay in the Mediterranean. Mathews was in a very powerful position, not just because he was commander of the Mediterranean squadron, but because there was almost no professional opinion in London that could counter-balance his demands with the needs of the wider war. From the first, Mathews' letters displayed a worrying tendency to shift responsibility from himself to the administration. With regard to reinforcements, he warned that 'in my humble opinion the fate of Italy will be determined, before I can reasonably expect them'.[58] The political consequences of failing to meet his demands were clear and the Admiralty was ordered to keep Mathews well supplied with sloops and small vessels sufficient for his purposes.[59] The consequences of this decision only became apparent over years, but the signs were there. In January 1741, Haddock's command consisted of 19 warships. By December that had risen to 31 and by June 1742, Mathews commanded 51 warships, a rise of nearly 270 per cent. The number of seamen nominally required on station rose from 5057 January 1741 to 17356 in June 1742, a rise of over 340 per cent. The strains this would impose on the local and British naval infrastructure would be critical.

The War in Flanders 1742: Dunkirk or the Rhine?

In the first weeks of the new ministry, Carteret easily fitted himself into existing policy. Parliamentary support was assured for measures to support Austria.[60] An army of 16,000 troops would be sent to Flanders, as had been intended in 1741. The need to replace them by bringing over 4,000 troops from the Irish establishment met some opposition on the usual formula that it was the Royal Navy that defended Britain, but there was no dispute over the need to send the army to Flanders.[61] The new political settlement had led to the appointment of a new commander for that army. Wade was to stay

---

58   TNA, SP42/93 (State Papers – Naval), f. 72, Mathews to Newcastle, 24 June 1742.

59   TNA, Adm 1/4111, unfoliated, Newcastle to the Admiralty, 20 July 1742.

60   HMC, Egmont Diary, op. cit., iii, 263, 23 March 1742. On the day that the Old Corps lost the motion to set up a committee to investigate the actions of Walpole's ministry, the motion for supporting the Queen of Hungary was passed without division.

61   Cobbett, *Parliamentary History*, op. cit., xii (1741–1743), 611–626, 29 April 1742.

in Britain. The Earl of Stair, a veteran soldier and diplomat, but also long standing member of the Patriot opposition, was appointed. Stair had been proposed as commander of the West Indian expedition in 1740, but the King had vetoed that appointment. With Walpole gone, both the King and Stair were willing to accept the challenge.[62] Stair was ordered to The Hague to press the Dutch to join a Pragmatic, or Confederate, Army, before going on to Flanders to join the army in the field.[63]

As the first battalions arrived at Ostend on 6 May, Stair became convinced that, even without the Dutch, the existing British and Austrian forces could have an important and immediate impact on the outcome of the war. If the Austrians left a covering army to keep the Franco-Bavarians bottled up in Prague, Prince Charles of Lorraine (brother in law to Queen Maria Theresa) could bring the main Austrian army to the Rhine. The Pragmatic Army could march down the Rhine to join him. This would, in Stair's view, compel all the princes of the Empire to declare their neutrality or adhere to the Queen of Hungary. The possibility of the Allies wintering in Alsace would also force Maillebois to quit Westphalia, thus ending any threat to Hanover or the eastern United Provinces.

During the spring and early summer of 1742 Stair's arguments, entreaties and occasional sarcasm left the Dutch unmoved. The Prussian victory over the Austrians in Bohemia at Chotusitz on 6 May made the Dutch more anxious that their eastern borders were exposed to French and Prussian pressures, and by mid May Stair was losing hope of getting any help from the United Provinces.[64] Instead, Stair was looking at an Austro-British attack on northern France.

In June news of a renewed Austro-Prussian peace (Treaty of Breslau, 11 June 1742 [n.s.]), guaranteed by George II, revived hopes that the allies could concentrate their force on the Franco-Bavarian armies in Germany. On 22 June the United Provinces agreed to mobilise an army of 50 battalions and 50 squadrons.[65] Stair thought this would make an allied force large

---

62   BL, Add Ms 35459, f. 2, Stair to Carteret, 13 April 1742.

63   National Library of Scotland, GD 135/41/26, George II to Stair, 23 March 1742. TNA, SP 87/89 (Military – Low Countries), f. 1. Instructions to Field Marshal Earl of Stair, 23 March 1742 and succeeding secret instructions.

64   TNA, SP 87/8, f. 163, Stair to Carteret, 24 May 1742 (n.s.).; f. 212, Stair to Carteret, 30 May 1742 (n.s.).

65   TNA, SP 87/9, f. 33, Stair to Carteret, 3 July 1742 (n.s.). The definitive treaty was signed in Berlin on 28 July (n.s.).

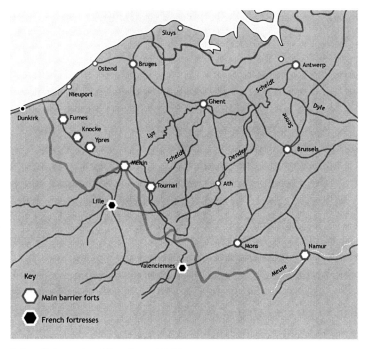

Map 5 Austrian Flanders, 1742

enough to force Louis XV to terms. He was given further grounds for optimism in early July. Maillebois was on the march south-west from Westphalia to relieve Marshal Belleisle who was besieged in Prague. Stair saw a
great opportunity. With the French army besieged in Prague, another held
in check in Bavaria by Khevenhuller and Maillebois' army the other side of
the Bohmer Wald in Bohemia, France would have no major field army west
of the Rhine. The Austro-British forces would be free to invade Northern
France, or Alsace Lorraine at will.[66]

In London, this proposal looked promising. George II had received a great
deal of the credit for brokering the Treaty of Breslau and acting as its guar-
antor.[67] Now he could cut an even grander figure on the international stage.
By bringing the Hanoverian and Hessian troops to the Rhine to join the
British and Austrian armies, a major force could be created.[68] This force
could either move into France or cross the Rhine to join Prince Charles'

---

66   Ibid., f. 82, Stair to Carteret, 17 July 1742 (n.s.).

67   BL, Add Ms 35354, f. 5, Hardwicke to J. Yorke, 21 June 1742.

68   TNA, SP 87/9, f. 136, Carteret to Stair, 20 July 1742.

Austrian army to trap Maillebois. It was a project great enough for the King himself to come to command the army. However, it was contingent upon the Cabinet agreeing to take the Hanoverians and Hessians into British pay. It was potentially a controversial step, but on 30 July the Cabinet agreed to do this without waiting until Parliament approved it.[69] Some 53,000 allied troops could soon be in Flanders and if the Dutch joined, an army of over 80,000 would be there before the end of the campaigning season.[70]

While these preparations were underway, Stair was reviewing the possible lines of advance for the Pragmatic Army and his eyes were now fixed on Dunkirk.[71] The French were reinforcing the works around the port and building an armed camp, but with no field army in Flanders, Stair believed that the French could not prevent its capture. During August he became convinced of an even more ambitious plan 'which I think cannot fail to decide the war'. Britain entirely commanded the waters from the Western Approaches to the North Sea and 'the advantage of being masters of the sea; when that advantage is rightly used, it must evidently put Great Britain into a situation, to get the better of France entirely in a few months, there [sic] trade is ruined and there [sic] whole coast is put under contribution and as things stand at present, Brest it self may be taken with all the ease imaginable, and the whole marine of France destroyed at one Blow'.[72]

The Austrians initially wanted to unite the Pragmatic Army on the Meuse or Rhine to be ready to move into Germany at the first opportunity, but they lacked the money to provision the planned march. The Austrian commanders in Flanders, Field Marshal the Duke of Arenberg and Field Marshal von Niepperg, were attracted to Stair's alternative as it had the added advantage of putting the British, rather than Austrian, troops, in danger. Together they framed an overall plan of campaign. Instead of marching Austrian troops out of Flanders, more should be sent to replace the British forces that advanced into France. Saxons or Danes could replace the Austrians taken out of Germany. The British army would march rapidly on Paris, capturing magazines as it advanced. Using these as supplies, the army would march down the Seine to Le Havre de Grace, which Stair believed could be taken without difficulty. Once there, the army could establish winter quarters, living off the richest

---

69 BL Add Ms 33004, f. 55, Cabinet Council, 30 July 1742. According to Carteret it had been informally agreed at least 10 days prior to this.

70 TNA, SP 87/9, f. 214, Carteret to Stair, 3 August 1742.

71 Ibid., f. 174, Stair to Carteret, 3 Aug 1742 (n.s.).

72 TNA, SP87/10, f. 8, Stair to Carteret, 1 September 1742 (n.s.).

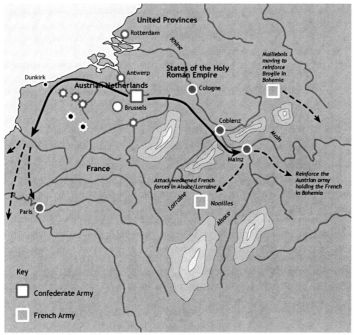

Map 6 Stair's options, 1742–1743

areas of France. Additional troops (British or Danish) could be brought in by sea. The French garrisons in the Low Countries were partly militia and, in any case, could not be gathered together in a hurry. Their armies on the eastern frontier and Germany would take months to return. The navy could supply any material required directly from Britain. Stair thought this prospect would be intolerable to Louis XV and he would hastily come to terms.[73] As Stair claimed, at a single blow, George II could bring peace to Europe.

This audacious plan (received on 23 August) was immediately handed over to General Wade and the chief engineer, Colonel Thomas Lascelles, for consideration. Both dismissed it as impracticable. Lascelles and General Ligonier were despatched to The Hague to convince Stair of this. Stair was furious and on the same day as his interview with the officers made preparations to return to London to argue his case.[74] Reaching London on 28 August, his unexpected arrival caused an immediate stir, and Newcastle was hurriedly recalled from his house in Sussex.[75] Details of the meeting

73   Ibid., f. 13, Memoire 1 September 1742 (n.s.); f. 35, Stair to Carteret, 3 Sept 1742 (n.s.).

74   Ibid., f. 50, Lascelles to Carteret, 7 September 1742 (n.s.).

75   *Richmond-Newcastle Correspondence*, 88, Newcastle to Richmond, 28 August 1742,

with Newcastle, Carteret and others, have not survived. Wade and Lascelles argued that the army had too little heavy artillery to make any successful siege. Wade also believed that the army was too unseasoned to conduct a winter campaign.[76] Hints in Stair's correspondence suggest that the King was not entirely against the Dunkirk or Paris plans, but eventually came down in support of the Rhine plan.[77] Stair delayed his return in the hope of Wade changing his mind and his anger was hardly abated when he arrived back in The Hague, damning Wade for his 'imaginary terrors' and the lost opportunities.[78] He continued to press the case for an invasion of Northern France; 'When the King is once master of Paris, and the whole wealth of France, not only diverted, but flowing into the Treasuries of their enemies, I can have no notion of how French army's [sic] can either be pay'd or recruited'.[79] Nonetheless, he and his Austrian colleagues continued planning for the move of the army eastward. By the end of September everyone was aware that the campaigning season was coming to a close. If the army was not to winter in Normandy, then it had to move into winter quarters on the Rhine ready for operations early in the spring of 1743.[80]

Rising Controversy: The Hanoverian Troops and the Revival of Opposition, September–December 1742

When the parliamentary session had ended on 15 July there had been some satisfaction that although the opposition continued to rage at the ministers, especially the New Whigs, the stability of the ministry and, particularly, the conduct of the war had not been seriously challenged.[81] Defeating French ambitions and protecting the Queen of Hungary were objectives declared by opposition and ministry alike. However, when the decision was made in the third week of July to unite a large Anglo-Hanoverian-Hessian army in Flanders in British pay, before informing Parliament, Carteret knew that this

---

BL, Add Ms 35396, f. 52, Birch to P. Yorke, 2 September 1742.

76   BL, Add Ms 32699, f. 400, Hardwicke to Newcastle, 10 September 1742.

77   TNA, SP87/10, f.127, Stair to Carteret, 12 October 1742 (n.s.).

78   TNA, SP87/10, f. 67, Stair to Carteret, 17 September 1742 (n.s.). Ligonier, at The Hague, possibly influenced by the high level of support from the Austrian generals and Dutch opinion, was in favour of the plan; ibid., f. 78, Ligonier to Carteret, 19 September 1742 (n.s.).

79   Ibid., 116, Stair to Carteret, 2 October 1742 (n.s.).

80   Ibid, f. 164, Project (undated); f. 168, Stair to Carteret, 1 November 1742 (n.s.).

81   BL Add Ms 35363, f. 9, P. Yorke to J. Yorke, 17 August 1742.

was a dangerous provocation. He was comforted by the fact that Stair, whose standing with the opposition was still high, fully supported the project and it was approved by the Duke of Argyle.[82]

Abroad, the siege of Prague had been given up, and the Dutch still had not joined the Pragmatic Army in Flanders.[83] Yet by the end of September, the overall balance looked promising. The neutrality of the King of the Two Sicilies, enforced by Captain Martin's squadron, was applauded as a reassertion of British sea power reminiscent of the days of Cromwell.[84] Both the Emperor and Spain seemed to be distancing themselves from France. Although Prince Charles had given up the siege of Prague and moved his army west to face Maillebois, the city remained blockaded. During the last two weeks of September, London waited for news of a battle that might decide the fate of the French in Bohemia. Reflecting on the situation, the Reverend Thomas Birch, thought that 'the conduct of the new ministry is so generally approved of that I believe Lord Hervey in the one house and Mr Dodington, Sir John H. Cotton and Sir W.W. Wynne in the other will not have any considerable support in the opposition expected from there since the Nation will for the future not much concern themselves in the struggles of particular men for place and power'.[85]

What had escaped Birch's notice was that the news the Hanoverian troops were to be paid by the British Treasury had tapped into the deeply held fear that British policy was being directed in the interest of Hanover. Initially, it was expected that the new ministry had reversed Walpole's Hanoverian tendencies, but this one act seemed to prove that the 'Hanover Rudder' was still steering the ship of state. The news that Britain would pay for Hanoverian troops, was a rich field for pamphleteers. The tone was set by Earl of Chesterfield, whose pamphlet, *The Case of the Hanover Forces*, published anonymously ran into eight editions in a few months.[86] As in 1739, electors in the City of London sent instructions to their MPs, condemning the measure. By end of October few could miss the rising tension and clamour. Parliament was due to meet on 16 November. For ministerial managers the issue of the Hanover troops became the baseline for their calculations of

82   Stair Papers, vol. 1, 287, Carteret to Stair, 27 July 1742; BL, Add Ms 35407(Hardwicke Papers), f. 242, Newcastle to Hardwicke, 8 August 1742 (private).

83   BL, Add Ms 35396, f. 52, Birch to P. Yorke, 2 September 1742.

84   BL, Add Ms 35396, f. 57, Birch to P. Yorke, 9 September 1742.

85   Ibid., f. 69, Birch to P. Yorke, 30 September 1742.

86   Harris, *A Patriot Press*, op. cit., 129.

potential support.[87] The danger was also apparent in the behaviour of some ministers. On 11 November a Cabinet Council was called to settle the King's Speech for the opening of Parliament, in which the Hanoverian troops would feature prominently. Lord Gower, the only Tory who had been taken in, and Lord Cobham, refused to come to a Cabinet Council until they had talked to their friends on the issue.[88] London was full of MPs as the day approached for Parliament to meet, in expectation of a major test of strength.

Parliament opened on 16 November with a determined attack in the Commons on the address of thanks. The ministry won the day with a majority of 109 in a house of over 400. In the Lords, Birch had been right; there was no appetite for confrontation and Newcastle anticipated no real business until after Christmas.[89] The opposition were badly wrong-footed on 6 December with the debate on supply for the army, which included maintaining the troops in Flanders. The danger from France, the defence of the Queen of Hungary and winning the war against Spain, were objectives shared throughout a large part of the House, which could not be effectively contradicted by the opposition. The opposition claimed that it was in every-one's interest to defend Austria, so action should not be carried out alone. Austria should be forced to come to terms with Prussia, but while France was bogged down in Germany, Britain had nothing to fear from her. Money not troops should be sent to the Queen. None of these propositions, except the last, was denied by the ministry, but they had little trouble in pointing out that none of them resolved the real present danger of French domination of Europe. As Newcastle pointed out to Richmond 'last year Sir Robert Walpole was to be hanged for not carrying on the war with vigour in defence of the K. of Austria, and this year, we are to undergo the same fate, for having acted in support of the Q. of Hungary and in pursuance of the Addresses of both houses of Parliament'.[90] The motion in support of the army in Flanders was passed by a majority of 120.

However, the question of paying the Hanoverians remained. On 10 December the matter came before Parliament. The ministry understood the opposition arguments and carefully opened the debate to defuse their

---

87   BL, Add Ms 51390, f. 69, Fox to Hanbury Williams, 13 October 1742. In the event they under-estimated the opposition by 15 votes. See Ibid, f. 89, Fox to Hanbury Williams, no date, but probably 16 November 1742.

88   *Richmond-Newcastle Correspondence*, 91, Newcastle to Richmond, 11 November 1742.

89   BL, Add Ms 35363, f. 5, P. Yorke to J. Yorke, 3 December 1742.

90   *Richmond Newcastle Correspondence*, 94, Newcastle to Richmond, 6 December 1742.

strength. The hiring of the Hanoverian troops was not to benefit Hanover, but was essential for the defence of Austria. The money would not be spent in Hanover. The Hanoverians were the first troops that Britain could get, and they would be unquestionably loyal to the Elector/King (unlike other German auxiliary troops). They were the best troops that could be had and it was better to expose Hanoverians than British subjects to the trials of war. This policy was consistent with countering the real French threat.

So far, Prussia had been bought off and the Sardinians had been brought into the alliance, aided by the Royal Navy, but the Flanders campaign was essential to encourage the Dutch and divert French troops from the Italian theatre. Opposition hints that the King simply wanted Britain to pay for his electoral troops while there was danger in Europe were false. He could have defended himself far better by joining the anti-Austrian confederacy. The Dutch were moving towards joining the allies, but to claim, as the opposition did, that Britain should not act without Dutch support was to subordinate British policy to the States General. This last appeal to the sovereignty of British policy was reinforced by three other claims. First, that the House was honour bound to support the measure because by their address of March 1742 they had promised to support the King in whatever measures he thought necessary for the defence of Britain. Second, that the language of division between Briton and Hanoverian was bordering on treason, or even Jacobite in its intent. Third, that the opposition seemed to be demanding a new doctrine in which Britain was to have no interest in the affairs of Europe, which, given the French threat, was nonsense.[91]

The opposition relied heavily on the general assertion that policy was directed in the interests of Hanover, and that the policy would not work. Britain could not preserve Austria alone. Sending an army to support Austria would only encourage the Queen of Hungary not to come to terms with Prussia and force the Emperor to rely more heavily upon France. The Hanoverians, being loyal subjects of the Holy Roman Empire, could not fight the Emperor and so would be useless, Money was far more useful to Austria than Hanoverian troops. The war should focus on Spain. The Royal Navy could destroy Spanish power and the French as well. Colonial conquests would divert the profits of the West Indies to Britain for the duration of the war. The more difficult dimension to this debate for both sides was the claim that anti-Hanoverianism was bordering on treason. Opposition speakers

---

91   The following paragraphs are based on, Corbett, *Parliamentary History of England*, op. cit., xii (1741–17443), 833–1057.

were certainly aware of this in the early parts of this debate, as emphasis was put on the right to discuss this matter. However, William Pitt caused a sensation with his invective against Hanover. Condemning the ministry as 'weak and pernicious', he claimed that Britain had no need to engage on the continent at all. Others had not done so and at the very least, Hanover should engage in support of the Queen of Hungary, in its own right; 'it is all too apparent, that this powerful and formidable kingdom, is considered only as a province to a despicable electorate; and that in consequence of a scheme formed long ago, and invariably pursued, these troops are hired only to drain this unhappy nation of its money'. Ever since the Hanoverian dynasty had ascended the throne, policy had been characterised by a 'ridiculous, ungrateful and perfidious partiality'.[92]

As a parliamentary performance it drew great attention, bringing into the house the sort of rhetoric that was common in pamphlets. Pitt was both vigorously condemned and supported for just this, but he did not add significantly to the arguments about the role of the Hanoverian troops in the Pragmatic Army in Flanders.[93] As Lord Perceval pointed out later in the debate, if Austria was to be supported it had to be done with all the power available and the Hanoverians contributed to that power. Essentially, the opposition case rested on supporting Austria only with money in the face of an immediate French threat, which was a step most MPs were not prepared to take and the motion to pay for the Hanoverians was passed by a majority of 67 (260–193). The violence of the debate encouraged the opposition to renew the attack on the estimates in the Lords, but the balance of this argument, which took place on 1 February 1743, was unchanged.[94] The motion was defeated 90 to 35[95].

As the new campaigning season approached, the pamphlet and press war against Hanoverian troops showed no sign of letting up. The governmental press machinery had been neglected in the wake of Walpole's fall from office and made an ineffectual response.[96] However, unlike the press campaign against Spanish depredations in 1738–1739, the anti-Hanoverian rhetoric could not easily be turned into plausible alternative policies. Inside Parlia-

92   Ibid., 1035.

93   BL, Add Ms 35363, f. 19, P. Yorke to J. Yorke, 14 December 1742.

94   *Richmond-Newcastle Correspondence*, 96, Newcastle to Richmond, 18 December 1742.

95   Corbett, *Parliamentary History*, op. cit., xii (1741–1743), 1058–1180.

96   Harris, *A Patriot Press*, op. cit., 34–38.

ment, the opposition had not been able to make a consistent or coherent case for another approach to the present crisis. Anti-Hanoverianism was a powerful tool, but in the wake of Walpole's fall the unity of the opposition had been shattered by defections and their grasp of the political agenda had been loosened by events in the war. The newly structured ministry was seen as powerfully anti-French. The Royal Navy was percived as working successfully in the Mediterranean to support Austria and Sardinia. The army in Flanders did have a plausible role in thwarting French ambitions. In contrast the opposition case was incoherent. Some argued that France could not be fought effectively. Others argued that pressuring Austria to come to terms would break the Franco-Bavarian alliance and restore the balance of power at the expense of France. Others insisted that Austria could be best supported with money. Still others thought that Austria should not be supported as it ran counter to the wishes of the generality of the German princes. The opposition could unite only around a general antipathy to Hanoverian domination of British policy, but could not articulate a policy for controlling France.

Nonetheless, the debates from November to February had made a difference. As Chesterfield noted, the debate in the Lords had placed the ministry on notice that they were again suspected of neglecting British interests in order to buy favour in the closet. Given the intensity of popular anti-Hanoverian rhetoric, it was a threat that was not taken lightly. Equally significant, was that the opposition targets had been, principally, the New Whigs, who had joined the Old Corps. The Pelhams understood the importance of working with the assumptions of the political nation and presenting policies in a manner that was both consistent with those assumptions and clearly addressed the demands of the current situation. Carteret understood the latter, but was less concerned about the former. With a lofty approach to his colleagues and parliament he was running serious risks.

6

The Continental Commitment, January 1743–February 1744

Throughout the first half of 1743, the vigorous press and pamphlet campaign against Hanoverian influence continued, but the parliamentary turmoil died down. Looking back over the period after Parliament rose on 21 April, Sir Benjamin Keene observed, 'We had a very easy session under Mr Pelham. Pitt is the only opposition. Dodington is sleepy. Waller, who collects matters is called their Commissary of Stores. These are the chiefs that enter against us, so terror does not come from without.' A far greater problem, Keene observed, was the difficulty of getting agreement within the ministry where no individual or group was clearly dominant.[1]

Part of the reason for this quietness was the progress of the war. Prague finally surrendered to the Austrians on 13 December and the remains of the French army driven back into Bavaria. Sickness was raging within the French army and it was rumoured that it was falling back towards the Rhine.[2] The United Provinces seemed close mobilising 20,000 troops.[3]

The news from France was equally encouraging. Ten ships of the line and four frigates were said to be arming in Brest, but probably only for their own coastal defence.[4] However, the agent supplying information from Brest was arrested shortly after this report and nothing more was heard from this port despite the best efforts of the British resident in Paris, Andrew Thompson.[5] Fleury tried to put a defiant face on events, but the general reports

---

1   *Keene Correspondence*, 51–2, Keene to Castries, 10 May 1743.

2   BL, Add Ms 57036, f. 54, Robinson to Weston, 23 January 1743 (n.s.). Butler, *Choiseul*, op. cit., i, 359–373.

3   BL, Add Ms 22536, f. 1, Carteret to Newcastle, 6 May 1743.

4   TNA, SP 78/227(State Papers – France), f.399, Thompson to Newcastle, 14 October 1742 (n.s.).

5   TNA, SP 78/228 (State Papers – France) f. Thompson to Newcastle, 12 January 1743

were of confusion and depression at the French court. By the beginning of December 1742 Fleury was ill and had been desperately seeking peace since the late autumn, initiating secret discussions, which were discovered and only served to destroy the confidence of Prussia and Bavaria in the integrity of French declarations.

On 18 January 1743 Fleury died.[6] One of the great statesmen of the age had gone. For years he had managed to keep French policy a mystery to the British and it was no clearer how it would now unfold. The war party, to which Fleury had cunningly presented himself as a counter balance, led by Marshal Belleisle had suffered with the humiliation of the retreat from Prague. Reports continued that Bavaria would be abandoned and the army withdrawn to defend Lorraine and Northern France. Later it was reported that Louis, now seemingly in sole charge of policy, would try to shore up the position in Bavaria, which was even more promising for the allies, as it trapped a substantial part of the French field armies in an increasingly precarious situation.[7] With the Pragmatic Army advancing into Bavaria from the north-west and the Austrians pouring in from the east, it looked like the Franco-Bavarian armies might be crushed.[8] By the end of February, Maillebois' army was on the move towards the upper Danube, where the Franco-Bavarian army under Marshal Broglie and the Emperor Charles VII was being pressed by an Austrian force under General Count Maximilian Browne. By early April the probability of that the French would try to remain anchored in Bavaria was reinforced by information that Maurice, Comte de Saxe, one of the most active and famous officers in the service of France, had been made a marshal and was to take command of the French army there.[9] The news from Flanders was also good. Stair was preparing to move his head quarters to Aix-la-Chapelle as the Pragmatic Army moved eastwards towards its final winter quarters.[10] The opportunity for George II to play a decisive role in bringing this war to a glorious conclusion at the head of the Pragmatic Army looked even better than in the late summer of 1742.

(n.s.). He was hanged in October.

6   P.R. Campbell, *Power and Politics in Old Regime France, 1720–1745*, London, 1996, 173–175.

7   TNA, SP 78/228, f. 25, Thompson to Newcastle, 13 February 1743 (n.s.); f. 38, Thompson to Newcastle, 27 February 1743 (n.s.).

8   BL, Add Ms 57306, f. 181, Robinson to Weston 3 April 1743 (n.s.).

9   BL, Add Ms 57306 (Weston Papers), f. 181, Robinson to Weston 3 April 1743 (n.s.).

10   BL, Add Ms 57036, f. 68, Robert Daniel to Weston, 25 February 1743.

The war against Spain had slipped into the background. After the recall of Vernon on 5 August 1742, the campaign in the West Indies was kept alive by sending Commodore Charles Knowles back to the Leeward Islands with instructions to attack the ports of La Guaira and Caracas, in hopes of devastating the trade of the Spanish Guipuzcoa Company.[11] News was still awaited of this operation, and events in the Mediterranean were far more pressing. In early January Vernon and Wentworth arrived back in London. Vernon typically stole a march on the general by putting into Bristol while Wentworth toiled up Channel to Portsmouth. Vernon arrived in a confident mood, prepared to defend himself and damn Wentworth. His arrival in London was attended by bonfires and the City presented him with the Freedom in a gold box. Vernon knew that he, unlike Wentworth, as a member of parliament, would have ample opportunity to put his case.[12] He claimed he would confidently face an enquiry, but would not push for it as Wentworth would inevitably suffer. If anyone could put fire into the case for a British maritime war, then it was Vernon and he did not waste time.[13] His careful manipulation of information about the Caribbean campaign, his huge popularity in the country and the gap that existed at the professional head of the navy potentially gave him great influence. His meeting with ministers was cordial, but he did not spare them his views on the conduct of the war. The next week he had an audience with the King for half an hour, 'to whom he had said that his majesty's security lay in being master of the sea, and that when he ceased to be so, his land army could not preserve him, at which words, he said the King gathered himself up and seemed not pleased, answering that soldiers were necessary. I was resolved, said the Admiral, to take that opportunity of letting the King know what no ministry will tell him, for they flatter the King in his passions'.[14] The new Admiralty under Winchelsea was now facing pressure from senior flag officers and captains.

---

11   J.C.M. Oglesby, 'The British Attack on the Caracas Coast, 1743', *Mariner's Mirror*, lviii (1972), 27–40.

12   Vernon's popularity was enormous at this time. He was put up for five seats in the General Election of 1741 and elected to three of them. He chose to sit for Ipwich. R. Harding, 'Edward Vernon' in P. Le Fevre and R. Harding (eds), *Precursors of Nelson: British Admirals of the Eighteenth Century*, London, 2000, 170–171. See also S.M. Sommers, *Parliamentary Politics of a County and a Town: General Elections in Suffolk and Ipswich in the Eighteenth Century*, London, 2002, 20–22.

13   K. Wilson, 'Empire, Trade and Popular Politics in Mid-Hanoverian Britain: The Case of Admiral Vernon', *Past and Present*, cxxi (1988), 74–109.

14   Egmont Diary, op. cit., iii, 270 (15 January), 280 (21 January).

Men like Mathews, Vernon and Knowles, experienced in command and
without a clear professional head to whom to defer, did not feel they needed
to deal with the Admiralty cautiously. Vernon offered advice to Newcastle,
but it did not lead to an invitation to take up a new command.[15] Despite
intense popularity and lobbying on his behalf by Knowles and his brother,
James Vernon, doubts about Vernon's ability began to arise once Wentworth
and Governor Trelawney of Jamaica reported their frustrations more fully.

Throughout 1742, despite British pressure, Austria resisted Sardinian
conditions for an alliance, which prevented a definitive treaty for the defence
of Italy.[16] The Spanish army under Don Philip in Provence could not break
into Italy along the coast, so in mid-winter he had switched his line of attack
northward into Savoy, forcing the Sardinians to withdrawn from the duchy.
The King of Sardinia, whose support of the Austrian cause was purely pragmatic, might easily be induced to switch sides if the balance of force swung
much further against his current alliance. From the British point of view, a
definitive Austrian-Sardinian treaty was an essential objective for the coming
year.

As the year opened, the ministers knew that the war had changed. The
defeat of Spain now depended on the defeat of France. France had to be
defeated in Europe and this was not a job that the Royal Navy could achieve.
Nevertheless, they flattered themselves that the King's influence over Maria
Theresa, the Pragmatic Army in Germany and the power of the Royal Navy
in the Mediterranean would have a decisive impact on events. What neither
they nor the opposition understood was that other powers did not share
their view of the threat and road to peace. British views centred restraining
French power in Europe. Both ministry and opposition were dismayed at
Austrian refusals to accept Prussian terms early in 1742. Both pressed plans
for a pacification of Europe on the basis of Austrian compensation for the
loss of Silesia and some Italian lands by the incorporation of Bavaria in the
Habsburg inheritance. The Emperor Charles VII would be compensated by
cession of Lorraine and Alsace by France. It was an elegant proposition. It
preserved Austria as a central European power. It pushed France back behind
a barrier guarded by the Emperor himself, and acknowledged the new powers
of Prussia in the east and Sardinia in Italy. However, it totally ignored the
wounded pride of Habsburg and Wittelsbachs, who could never accept the

---

15 BL, Add Ms 32700 (Newcastle Papers), f. 23, Vernon to Newcastle, 5 February 1743.

16 See R. Lodge, *Studies in Eighteenth Century Diplomacy, 1740–1748*, London, 1930,
   49–52.

loss of traditional patrimonial lands. The British ministers were well aware of Maria Theresa's resentment at British pressure, and of Prussian anxiety that Austria would again turn on Silesia, but they were convinced that British sea and financial power held the key to forcing all of them to come into a general plan whose prime objective was to curb the power of France.

The Financial Position

One of the claims made by the opposition was that Britain could not afford the expense of the war on land. Although contemporaries did not have public income and expenditure figures at hand, the rising expenditure and fairly static income were known from parliamentary estimates.[17] After years of stability and a falling national debt, the gap between income and expenditure was steadily rising (Figure 6.1).

In contrast, confidence in the financial stability of the government remained high and its ability to raise loans was unimpaired. Unlike the commercial capital market, subscription of government debt was dominated by a small group of wealthy financiers. Their judgement was that not only was such investment safe, but it was capable of turning a profit. A loan of £800,000 issued in June 1742 was fully subscribed. A new loan of £1.8 million issued on 22 March 1743 was also fully subscribed and the market price of government 3 per cent stock remained stable during this period.[18] On the whole, therefore, the government could feel that the financial situation would support another campaign.

The Pragmatic Army and the Battle of Dettingen, April–June 1743

The fate of the campaign rested ultimately on the ability of the Pragmatic Army to march into Bavaria and inflict a decisive defeat upon the Franco-Bavarian forces. The winter march to the Rhine was gruelling and there were already said to be 6,000 sick among the British troops (37 per cent

---

17   The exact manner in which military expenditure added to the public debt was not always obvious to contemporaries because of a traditional practice of under-reporting the estimates of the army and the navy and then converting the navy debt to the national debt. See H. Roseveare, *The Treasury, The Evolution of a British Institution*, London, 1969, 93; C. Wilkinson, *The British Navy and the State in the Eighteenth Century*, Woodbridge, 2004, 39–50.

18   Dickson, *Financial Revolution*, op. cit., 216, 286–289.

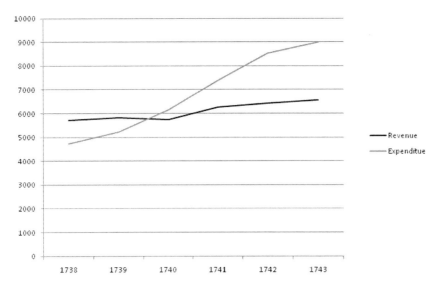

Figure 6.1 Revenue and expenditure, 1738–1743 (£000s)
Source: Mitchell and Deane, op. cit., 387, 390.

of the army).[19] Nevertheless, Stair reported his army to be in good spirits
and ready for an early start to the new campaign. The leading elements
of the army crossed the Rhine at Mulheim (Hanoverians) and Coblenz
(Austrians and British) in early April, but the cold and wintry spring
delayed its march along the east bank of the Rhine. The leading units
arrived at Mainz by the beginning of May but the rear of the army was
still not across the Rhine.[20] Stair believed that Noailles' army in Lorraine
was too weak to hinder the Pragmatic Army's advance into Bavaria and
he intended to advance over the Maine near Frankfurt to destroy Broglie's
army.

On 2 May George II arrived in Holland on his way to join the Army.
First, he went to Hanover, while Carteret stopped at The Hague to hurry
the Dutch into committing troops to the Pragmatic Army. Carteret was
pleased with what he found; 'You can hardly imagine the happy change
in this country since October last.' No opposition was expected in any
of the states to the augmentation of the army. On the 10 May the States

19   On the scepticism in the army see the letters of Joseph Yorke, BL, Add Ms 35363. On the
     sickness see, ibid., f. 73, Birch to P. Yorke, 5 October 1742.
20   TNA, SP 87/11, f. 184, Carteret to Stair, 29 March 1743.

General approved the augmentation under Prince Maurice of Nassau. The troops were to assemble between Maastricht and Namur to cover the rear of the Pragmatic Army.[21]

The rest of May continued to bring in good news. The Austrian army in Bavaria, under Khevenhuller and Browne, pushed the Franco-Bavarian army before it. An attempt to hold the Austrians on the right banks of the Iser and Danube failed after the French were defeated at Deckendorf (Deggersdorf 27 May 1743 [n.s.]). The Franco-Bavarian alliance was in complete disarray. Broglie wanted to fall back towards the Necker and Rhine. Charles VII, who had only returned to Munich in March, was again forced to flee as his capital fell to the Austrians in early June.[22] The Bavarian general Seckendorf was rumoured to be dying and there was no one who could replace him. The princes of the empire were also deserting the Emperor and declaring neutrality. The imperial garrison at Braunau surrendered towards the end of the month, opening the supply routes from Upper Austria to Munich. The situation of Bavaria looked hopeless. Charles turned to Prince William of Hesse to persuade George II to mediate his cause with Austria. Noailles' army in Lorraine seemed in confusion. Initially he seemed ready to pose a threat to the right flank and rear of the Pragmatic Army if it advanced into Bavaria, then surprise rumours reached London that Noailles intended to split his army by detaching 10–20,000 across the Rhine to link up with Broglie around Donauworth.[23]

The Anglo-Danish marriage treaty between the Prince of Denmark and the King's daughter, Princess Louisa, was coming to a successful conclusion.[24] The Russo-Swedish war seemed on the verge of ending in Russia's favour, at last releasing Russian forces to support Austria. Sardinia looked like keeping to its Austrian alliance. After recent attempts to stir up the princes of the Empire against the Pragmatic forces, Prussia appeared to have slipped back into quiet neutrality. Carteret declared that with all these circumstances, the King 'will make the Greatest figure that has been of late'.[25]

---

21   BL Add Ms 32700, f. 11, Carteret to Newcastle, 10 May 1743.

22   The reports of this campaign can be found in Carteret's despatches to London. A concise account can be found in C. Duffy, *The Wild Goose and the Eagle*, London, 1964, 71–85.

23   BL Add Ms 35407, f. 194, Stone to Hardwicke, 26 May 1743.

24   TNA, SP 45/4, unfoliated, Carteret to Newcastle, 9 June 1743 (n.s.).

25   BL, Add Ms 32700, f. 138, Carteret to Newcastle, 30 May 1743 (most secret and particular).

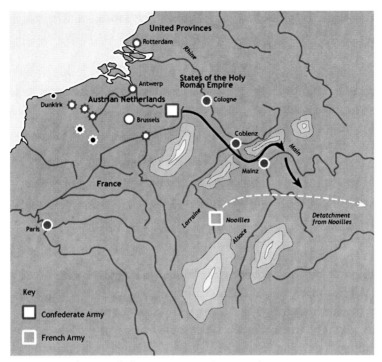

Map 7 Stair's intended interception, May 1743

Stair wanted to move immediately to intercept the detachment that Noailles was sending to Broglie. In London and Hanover they felt that Noailles was luring Stair into spreading his army so Noailles could attack him piecemeal.[26] The Austrian commanders were also cautious.[27] A probe by General Ligonier across the Maine in early June found a French army advancing north with substantial supporting artillery.[28] The Pragmatic Army continued to advance along the Maine as far forward as Aschaffenburg while George II hurried to join it. He arrived at Aschaffenburg on 8 June (o.s.), where he gave orders for the army to halt and wait for the Hessian and Hanoverian divisions, still at Hanau, to come up.

26   BL, Add Ms 32700, f. 132, Hardwicke to Newcastle, 21 May 1743; Add Ms 35396, f. 93, P. Yorke to T. Birch, 27 May 1743.

27   BL, Add Ms 32700, f. 173, Newcastle to Carteret, 31 May 1743; Add Ms 22536, f. 41, Extract of Baron Taxheim to Neipperg, 28 May 1743 (n.s.); f. 43, Carteret to Newcastle, 5 June 1743 (n.s.).

28   BL, Add Ms 35396, f. 103, Birch to P. Yorke, 11 June 1743.

By this time, Noailles had closed in on the south, or left, bank of the Maine. His right wing was camped about three miles from Aschaffenburg, and the left wing had occupied Seligenstadt, down river from the main camp of the Pragmatic Army, where he threw a bridge of boats across to occupy the right bank behind the allies. Noailles now lay along the Maine, occupying and overlooking the allied line of communication on the right bank from Aschaffenburg back to Hanau and Frankfurt. With poor supply, the allied troops started plundering villages and churches, causing the peasantry to flee with their livestock and possessions.[29] A supply line could be opened up to Hesse in the north, but this would take time, and hopes that Hessian troops would get provisions through from Hanau to Aschaffenburg was soon dashed.[30]

On the morning of 15 June George ordered a retreat back down the Maine. The army marched on the 16 June. Noailles had placed his artillery along the left bank covering the route the Pragmatic Army had to take. As the Allies moved out of Aschaffenburg, Noailles sent his own troops to occupy the town, cutting the Allies off from any retreat northward. He also sent his nephew, the Duke de Grammont, across the Maine at Seligenstadt, taking a position at the village of Dettingen, to block the route to Hanau. The Pragmatic Army was now trapped between two French forces. The battle was a race between Grammont, anxious to catch the allies in the flank while they faced the artillery across the river, and the allied generals as they struggled to change front. It was narrowly won by the allies, largely due to Ligonier and his piecemeal cavalry charges which bought enough time for the infantry to reorganise for a general advance.[31] The prime of the French cavalry was devastated at the battle and the allied army broke free to unite with the Hessians at Hanau.

A defeat at Dettingen might have been catastrophic, but victory had less strategic impact. A decisive victory from which peace could be dictated had not been won in Germany. This was not understood in Britain. There, the news of Dettingen was greeted with great celebration. There was public rejoicing like that which had greeted the news of Vernon's capture of Porto

---

29   BL Add Ms 32700, f. 201, Carteret to Newcastle, 23 June 1743 (n.s.).

30   Ibid.

31   BL Add Ms 35407, f. 212, Account of Dettingen by Lt Gen Ligonier; BL Add Ms 32700, f. 225, Harcourt to Newcastle, 30 June 1743 (n.s.). A translated French account can be found in the Royal Archives, Cumberland Papers, Box 1, 219, De Montibert, 17 July 1743 (n.s.).

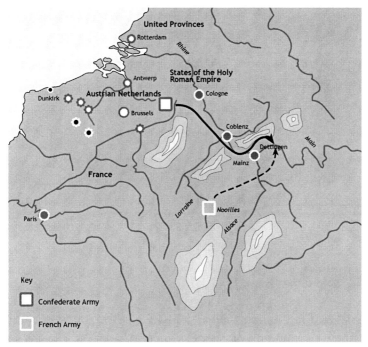

Map 8 The March towards Dettingen, 1743

Bello, windows were smashed and bonfires lit up the night, this time stoked by the railings of Hanover Square. The King had won a mighty victory over the French. The army had performed well and the King had gained credit which no anti-Hanoverian propaganda could diminish and now great consequences were expected.[32] Newcastle wrote to Carteret that 'This victory makes us all masters of everything and it is our own fault if we do not make good use of it.' Expectations were now running high.

The Admiralty and the War at Sea, January–September 1743

During 1743 the pressure on the Admiralty remained unchanged. There was some movement between the West Indies and North America and a slow rise in ships under Mathews' command, but no major movement of forces (Figure 6.2).

---

32   BL Add Ms 35396, f. 111, T.Birch to P. Yorke, 25 June 1743; Add Ms 32770, Newcastle to Carteret, 24 June 1743.

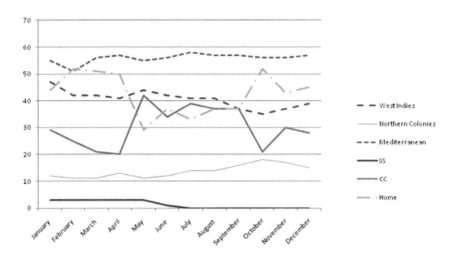

Figure 6.2 Ship dispositions, 1743

Complaints from neutrals about seizures of their shipping continued.[33] In the Americas rumours of Spanish forces massing at Havana to attack Georgia and South Carolina were worrying, but unconfirmed.

The movement of large naval forces overseas placed considerable strain on local resources.[34] The main problem was, as always, manning the ships. The pressure was particularly acute in the Mediterranean, but even in North America, where the number of warships was small, resistance to pressing for seamen on the eastern seaboard was increasing. High wages and a thriving economy made service in the Royal Navy unattractive.[35] Ships arrived there undermanned and sickness reduced their numbers further.[36] The Admiralty had urged colonial governors to arrest deserters and obtain recruits, as threats of legal action by merchants made captains reluctant to press.[37]

During this period, the weak connection between the Admiralty and

---

33   For the development of law and practice observed at sea, see R. Pares, *Blockade and Neutral Rights, 1739–1763*, Oxford,1938.

34   TNA, Adm 1/4112, unfoliated, Stone to the Admty, 1 June 1743.

35   TNA, Adm 1/4112, Stone to the Admty, 7 June 1743.

36   TNA, SP 42/26, f. 38, Admty to Newcastle, 5 April 1743; f. 54, Admty to Newcastle, 8 April 1743.

37   TNA, SP 42/26 f. 24, Admty to Newcastle, 15 March 1743.

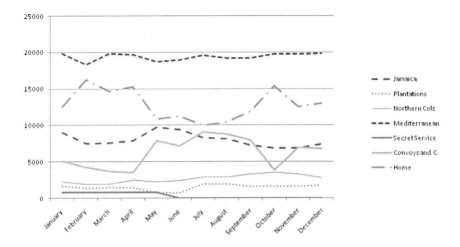

Figure 6.3 Seamen required on stations, 1743

the ministry was obvious. It was two months after Vernon's return and eight months after the original order, before the board was formally told that Ogle had superseded Vernon in the West Indies.[38] The board was also dangerously isolated from the profession. Wager died on 23 May and Cavendish died 14 June. Norris was consulted, but would barely cooperate with the Admiralty. Vernon was resentful at his failure to receive another command, which he attributed to Winchelsea's personal antipathy towards him. In early June the Admiralty received a request from Mathews to resign his commission. He intended to leave the squadron under Lestock's command in order to recover his health at Villa Franca. He was probably ill before he left England, but in the thirty weeks he had been on board his flagship he had developed a severe bowel disorder, kidney stones and swollen legs. In early June he suffered a fit which left him incapable for forty-eight hours. His worries were compounded by what he saw as the neglect by the Admiralty. He resented the fact that rather than send the ships he requested, the Admiralty had responded only by promising to send what they could. Mathews informed Newcastle that 'I believe the Admiralty ignore my complaints ... because I am not under their imme-

---

38   TNA, Adm 1/4112, unfoliated, Newcastle to the Admty, 2 March 1743.

Table 6.1 Ships on the home station, June-August 1743

	Line	Line	50s	50s	44s	44s	20s	20s
	Service	Fitting	Service	Fitting	Service	Fitting	Service	Fitting
June	5	9	0	3	0	1	2	3
July	5	7	0	0	1	0	3	4
August	5	7	1	2	0	1	1	2

diate command in regard to my military operations.'[39] This was not true. The Admiralty was used to commanders on station corresponding directly with the Secretary of State for the Southern Department. More likely, the reason for their response can be found in Table 6.1. It shows the available ships on the home station from 1 June to 1 August 1743. This suggests that there were few ships available, but despite Newcastle's reassurances Mathews remained convinced of deliberate Admiralty obstruction.

By mid-June rumours reached Mathews that the Brest squadron was on its way to join the Combined Squadron at Toulon and that the army under Don Philip would attack Nice to open their way to Italy. Leaving Lestock in Hyères with the main squadron and orders to prevent the Brest squadron getting into Toulon, Mathews took six line, a bomb vessel and two fireships eastwards to Nice and Genoa.[40]

During July Mathews' health continued to deteriorate.[41] Violent pains wracked his body and impaired his memory. He felt burdened particularly by the instructions to co-ordinate operations with the King of Sardinia and frustrated by the failure of the British minister at Turin, Arthur Villettes, to get him an audience with the King.[42] He anticipated that the French and Spanish squadrons would soon sortie from Toulon to cover Don Philip's attack on Nice. The latest intelligence from Lestock was that eight line and two frigates were coming from Brest. To make matters worse, Lestock was laid low by gout and was reportedly slipping into a paralytic disorder.

---

39   TNA, SP 42/93, f. 155, Mathews to Newcastle, 22 May 1743; f. 159, Mathews to Newcastle, 13 June 1743 (quotation); f. 162, Mathews to Carteret, 4 June 1743, with enclosures.

40   Ibid., f. 209, Mathews to Lestock, 23 June 1743.

41   TNA, SP 45/4, unfoliated, 7 June 1743; SP 42/93 (State Papers – Naval), f.188, Newcastle to Mathews, 17 June 1746. They did permit him to go ashore to recover, but to be ready to return to the squadron at the earliest notice.

42   TNA, SP 42/93, f. 257, Mathews to Newcastle, 17 July 1743.

Mathews returned to Hyères to resume command of the main squadron.[43] At this point Mathews believed that a Franco-Spanish attack by land and sea was in the offing and his orders to protect and defend Sardinia obliged him to engage French ships.[44] He cancelled orders to send four of his most decayed ships home, complaining that the Admiralty had failed to send out clean ships.[45]

In London Mathews' request to resign was refused, but his despatches were received with growing annoyance by the Admiralty. The Secretary to the Admiralty Board, Thomas Corbett, prepared a reply which was sent on 22 August. Corbett rejected Mathews' 'disagreeable repetition of complaints', pointing out that the squadron he now commanded was bigger than he said he needed while in London, while the Spanish squadron in the Mediterranean was smaller. Ships had gone out to join him and more would follow. If Mathews would let them know exactly when he would be sending back the foul ships, they would best know when to sent out the replacements and protect the trade. In frustration, the board pointed out to the Lords Justices that Mathews now had under his command half of all the seamen voted by Parliament and sent copies of their correspondence and lists of the ships with Mathews.[46] Mathews continued to refuse to send home the four ships and warned Newcastle that 'I have so many irons in the fire I cannot help fearing His Majesty's flag will suffer a rebuke.'[47]

By early October Mathews was very ill and angry.[48] Corbett's letter only incensed him further. It contained 'such gross expressions, tho' they do not directly call me a Coward, they boarded so close on it's heels that I confess it is past my understanding to separate them'. He hoped all commanders in chief would learn from this for 'Somebody must be the first that finds Rock or Shoal, I have been that unfortunate person by whom they will avoid such strong innuendos of Cowardice'.[49] The news of the Lords Justices' refusal to

---

43 Ibid., f. 273, Mathews to Newcastle, 2 August 1743. The report of a paralytic disorder proved wrong. Lestock was suffering from severe gout.

44 Ibid., f. 286, Extract Mathews to Villettes, 25 July 1743 (o.s.). Villettes, at Turin, did not fully agree.

45 Ibid., f. 316, Mathews to Newcastle, 15 September 1743.

46 Ibid., f. 307, Extract of Corbett to Mathews, 1 August 1743; f. 313, Admty to the Lords Justices, 22 August 1743.

47 Ibid., f. 316, Mathews to Newcastle, 15 September 1743.

48 Ibid., f. 351, Mathews to Newcastle, 11 October 1743.

49 Ibid., f. 353, Mathews to Newcastle, 30 October 1743.

accept his resignation also came as a terrible disappointment to him.[50] In the mean time, intelligence from France was again becoming scarce. Thompson's informer at Brest had been arrested and hanged. Mathew's two informers at Toulon had been discovered and fled to Villa Franca.[51]

In early June a despatch from Commodore Knowles in the West Indies, confirming the repulse of his attacks on La Guaira and Caracas, arrived in London.[52] His and other reports indicated that both attacks had foundered, at least in part, through ill-discipline. La Guaira was attacked first, but the Spaniards had been alerted. A day spend bombarding the forts (19 February 1743) was destructive on both sides but indecisive, so after resting and making repairs Knowles intended to send boats in to burn the ships in the harbour the following morning. All went well initially, but then a lieutenant from the *Suffolk* 'out of an avaricious temper' decided to cut out a 24-gun ship that he had boarded. This alerted the defenders and the fire from the forts forced the boats back.[53]

The expeditionary force moved along the coast to Porto Cabello, but poor discipline and difficult winds delayed his arrival until 14 April. The entrance to the bay was extremely narrow and Knowles decided to make a landing to attack the forts defending each side of the entrance. The night landing (22 April 1743) was successful, but the parties of soldiers fired on each other in the confusion and fled back to the boats. An attempt to cannonade the forts was made on 24, but failed to open the way into the bay. At 9.00 pm, with tears running down his cheeks, Knowles ordered the squadron to withdraw.[54]

Whether indiscipline or lack of security was the critical factor is difficult to tell, but it again raised questions about command in the navy.[55] Knowles had a great deal of credit when he had returned from the West Indies in 1741, but he was by now, better known as the author of a violently anti-army pamphlet, *An Account of the Expedition to Cartagena*, which had been circulating in manuscript since the end of 1741. It had

50   Ibid., f. 392, Mathews to Newcastle, 23 November 1743.

51   TNA, SP 42/93, f. 392, Mathews to Newcastle, 23 November 1743.

52   Royal Archives, Cumberland Papers, Box 1, 198, Capt Ed. Pratten from Curacoa, 18 March 1742/3; 204, Copy of Mr R. Pratten's letter, 7 May 1743 from Porto Rico; TNA, Adm 1/2006, unfoliated, Knowles to Corbett, 18 March 1742/3

53   TNA, SP 42/26, f. 125, Knowles to Corbett, 18 March 1742/3.

54   Royal Archive, Cumberland Papers, Box 1, f. 204, Copy of Mr R. Pratten's letter, 7 May 1743 from Porto Rico.

55   BL, Add Ms 32700, f. 148, Hardwicke to Newcastle, 27 May 1743.

been published in the spring of 1743, in the wake of the anti-Hanover controversy, and it fitted neatly into the narrative of ministerial corruption and army incompetence which contrasted to the Patriotism of Edward Vernon and a maritime war.[56] The pamphlet was then in its third printing and not yet received any rebuttal from the army or ministry. According to Thomas Birch, this 'increased the ferment of popular ill humour'.[57] Knowles' failure seems to have taken some of the heat out of the situation. Again, naval power had not achieved what was expected and on this occasion the navy carried the blame. Knowles' letters contained furious denunciations of several of his officers. He wanted his third lieutenant, Benjamin Ferrand, tried by court martial for trying to cut out the ship at La Guaira, but Ferrand was killed at Porto Cabello before this could take place. He had denounced the captains who retired to Curacao for repairs despite his orders and he had dismissed Captain Thomas Gregory of the *Norwich* (50) for failing to respond to orders at Porto Cabello.[58] In sum, the story neither reflected well on the performance of the navy nor on the effectiveness of naval power.

After nearly three years of war with Spain in the Caribbean, the only conquest was the little island of Roatan in the Gulf of Honduras. The American troops who formed the garrison were unimpressed by this service and mutinied.[59] The commander on the island, Major Caulfield, considered them unfit for the service and although the fortifications were strong, there was little prospect of immediate economic development. Nevertheless, Governor Trelawney of Jamaica and Ogle thought it could be held and developed and on 9 June 1743 the Lords Justices approved a proposal to hold on to the island. Given the timing of the decision, two days after confirmation of the failure of Knowles' expedition, it must be suspected that this decision was taken as much for political as economic reasons.[60]

---

56   *Gentleman's Magazine*, April 1743, p. 207.

57   BL, Add Ms 35396, f.107, Birch to P. Yorke, 18 June 1743.

58   Gregory was sent home and court marshalled. On 17 September 1743 he was dismissed from the service. He was reinstated in November 1745 without seniority on the recommendation of Admiral Vernon.

59   *Gentleman's Magazine*, May 1743, p. 273; TNA, CO 5/42, f. 290, Caulfield to Wentworth (?), 19 March 1742/3; CO 136/57 (Sec of State – Jamaica), f. 273, Trelawney to Stone, October 1742.

60   TNA, SP 45/4, unfoliated, 9 June 1743.

Table 6.2 Flag officers, 9 August 1743

Admiral of the Fleet	Sir John Norris	In retirement
Admiral of the White	Sir John Balchen	Home station
Admiral of the Blue	Thomas Mathews	Mediterranean
Vice Admiral of the Red	Edward Vernon	In retirement
Vice Admiral of the White	Nicholas Haddock	In retirement/ill
Vice Admiral of the Blue	Sir Chaloner Ogle	West Indies
Rear Admiral of the Red	Richard Lestock	Mediterranean
Rear Admiral of the White	James Stewart	Home
Rear Admiral of the Blue	Sir Charles Hardy	Home

Source : TNA, Adm 6/13.

As the autumn approached, the Admiralty could not look back on the season as a great success. The war in the Caribbean was stalemated. The ships available at home for service were limited, but they had sent out the reinforcements, stores and victuals to Mathews. They knew that Mathews could not clean and refit such a large force at Port Mahon, and they could not send many more clean ships out to him until they were sure he was returning his foul vessels. He would not send the foul ships home until he knew others were coming. The Admiralty knew both Mathews and Lestock were ill. They also knew that Mathews had no respect for Lestock.

Mathews had offered to resign, but the Lords Justices and the Admiralty had little room for manoeuvre. After the deaths of Wager and Cavendish, the King approved the new list of flag officers on 9 August 1743. It stretched out the existing flag appointments, but did not provide new blood. With Norris refusing to serve, Balchen had to remain on the home station. Mathews was the next most senior officer and had the largest operational command. Haddock and Ogle were not available to take over that command and Vernon was distrusted. Lestock was very junior for such an important command as the Mediterranean, but had at least significant experience in the West Indies and the Mediterranean. Stewart and Hardy had neither (Table 6.2).

The Treaty of Worms: A Diplomatic Opportunity or Disaster?, May–September 1743

Although the naval war was stalemated by mid-summer 1743, matters in Europe looked promising. The French army was out of Bavaria and for all intents and purposes the Franco-Bavarian alliance looked dead. The princes of the Empire, including the King of Prussia, were in a state of anxious neutrality. It looked possible that the Emperor and the Queen of Hungary could be brought together on the basis of a new barrier erected in Lorraine and the Rhineland. In Italy, an Austrian-Sardinian treaty would return the *status quo ante bellum* with the exception of the territories that Austria had promised cede to Sardinia. At this point, Carteret in the field with the King, and the ministers in London and Hanover, were all speaking the same language.[61] In Carteret's view events were 'highly tending to our wishes for a general peace'.[62] There were still dangers. Particularly, Bavarian attempts, through Prince William of Hesse, to settle unilaterally with Austria had to be resisted if France was to be forced to accept a general peace.[63]

By mid-July Noailles and Broglie were west of the Rhine at Worms. This left Charles VII no option but to declare Bavaria neutral (25 June [n.s.]) and two days later he agreed an armistice with Austria at Niederschöenfeld. Bavaria would remain under Austrian administration pending a peace, but the remnants of the Imperial Army would be allowed to remain in being for the Emperor's protection.[64] The Pragmatic Army meanwhile had fallen back to Hanau and the Austrian army under Prince Charles, which had been pushing the French along the Danube, was moving to the Necker. In London, where news of a decisive follow-up to Dettingen was eagerly expected, this movement was baffling. Also some worrying changes in Carteret's behaviour were noted. Prince William of Hesse was still urging Carteret to settle the peace of Germany. Instead of rejecting the proposals, Carteret agreed to examine them. Carteret had always believed that the essential point was to bring the Emperor into the allied camp. The essence of the proposal was that the Emperor should be given a subsidy by Britain (£300,000) until a final peace settlement, satisfactory to the Emperor, was made. This infuriated Newcastle and the other ministers of the inner circle, who rejected the plan out of hand. Potentially, it shifted the whole basis of the war. Britain and Holland would be in a war against France to gain a settlement for the Emperor, while the Queen of Hungary could choose whether or not to engage as auxiliary.[65] The Dutch

---

61   BL, Add Ms 22536, f. 57, Newcastle to Carteret, 3 June 1743.

62   BL, Add Ms 22536, f. 29 Carteret to Newcastle, 2 June 1743 (n.s.)

63   BL, Add Ms 32700, f. 122, Newcastle to Carteret, 13 May 1743; Add Ms 22536, f. 11, Carteret to Newcastle, 7 May 1743.

64   Browning, *Austrian Succession*, op. cit., 136. Although never formally ratified either by the Emperor or Maria Theresa, the armistice was maintained.

65   BL, Add Ms 34507, f. 235, Newcastle to Carteret, 16 July 1743.

were unlikely to accept the proposal. The House of Commons was unlikely to support any more subsidy treaties. It made no reference to the refortification of Dunkirk. When Carteret received the reaction, he rapidly dropped the plan, but the apparent opening of negotiations contrary to agreed policy soured his relations with the ministers in London.[66]

Another issue raising its head was Sardinia. The Austro-Sardinian convention of Turin in February 1742 was never much more than a half-hearted agreement. For the next 18 months British ministers saw Sardinia as vital to the Austrian position in Italy. However, King Charles Emmanuel had no compunction about maintaining his right to join either an Austrian or Bourbon alliance as his situation demanded. Partly because of this, British ministers had been particularly sensitive to Sardinian demands, much to the disgust of Austria, at whose expense Sardinian financial or territorial claims had to be met. Despite many setbacks, the general terms for territorial redistribution in northern Italy had been agreed by early June 1743, and Carteret wanted full powers to negotiate a final Anglo-Austro-Sardinian alliance.[67] However, after Dettingen, the Austrians proposed that Charles VII might be given Naples in exchange for surrendering Bavaria and the Upper Palatinate. Sardinia could be compensated by the island of Sicily, in which Charles Emanuel had already shown great interest. Any Austrian territory in Lombardy surrendered to Sardinia would be conditional on Austria keeping Bavaria. Carteret recognised that this proposal, which would exile the Emperor to southern Italy, and greatly strengthen Hapsburg power in Germany, would not only dangerously provoke Prussia but enrage the German princes who had elected the Emperor. By early September Carteret convinced the Austrian envoy, Wasner, that Sardinia would join the Bourbons if the Austrians did not accept the transfer of Piacenza, (the final territorial sticking point). Wasner was empowered to sign and did so on the 2 September (o.s.) as a final resort. By this Treaty of Worms, Britain agreed to maintain a powerful squadron in the Mediterranean in support of the Austro-Sardinian forces and to provide Sardinia with a subsidy of £200,000 per annum while the war lasted. The only additional concession Maria Theresa was able to wring out of Carteret was an additional clause to pay the £300,000 subsidy as long as the war and the need demanded.[68]

---

66   For a fuller discussion, see R. Lodge, 'The So-Called Treaty of Hanau of 1743', *English Historical Review*, xxxviii (1923), 384–407.

67   BL, Add Ms 22536, f. 81, Carteret to Newcastle, 25 June 1743 (n.s.).

68   For a description of the negotiations, see R. Lodge, 'The Treaty of Worms', *English*

By early October 1743, George II stood at the head of an army poised to attack France. Germany was free of French forces and an Austrian army was on the upper Rhine. In Italy, the Austro-Sardinian army, supported by the Royal Navy, seemed likely to contain the Bourbon invasion from the north and could attack Bourbon possessions throughout the peninsula. It was, as one historian has noted, the time when 'the grand design was virtually realised and Bourbon Europe virtually isolated'.[69] However, to contemporaries in Britain the situation did not look so satisfactory. Great things had been expected after the victory at Dettingen. Yet the campaigning season had slipped by without action in northern Europe. The French had been allowed to consolidate their forces in Alsace, Lorraine and Flanders. The Austrians were on the Rhine, but their purpose was unknown. Newcastle was convinced that Hanoverian considerations were at the root of it and that Carteret had encouraged the King in this. Instead of following up the withdrawal of Noailles and linking up with the Austrians in Germany George had withdrawn to the Rhine, fearing that Prussia would invade Hanover if the allies united in Germany.[70]

The continental campaign had failed to deliver what was expected, but war at sea was not offering much greater prospects. The Mediterranean squadron was holding its own, but not capable of acting decisively against an enemy that remained in port. In the West Indies the situation was at best stalemate. A few weeks later it became evident that the war was changing. France and Spain were infuriated by Sardinian acceptance of the Treaty of Worms. Spain declared war on Sardinia in September, and in October, on the signing of a Franco-Spanish offensive alliance (Treaty of Fontainebleau, 25 October 1743 [n.s.]), France declared war on Sardinia. France was now committed to supporting the war aims of Spain, including included those aims against Britain.

The Political Impact of the War: September 1743–February 1744

When Carteret left England in May the ministers seemed to be agreed on the outline of policy – to the defeat of the Franco-Bavarian forces in Germany,

---

Historical Review, xlv (1929), 220–255. For the treaty see, Parry, *Treaty Series*, op. cit., New York, xxxvii (1742–1746), 183–207.

69   Browning, *Austrian Succession*, op. cit., 148.

70   BL, Add Ms 32701, f. 198, Newcastle to Hardwicke, 24 October 1743.

leading to the imposition of a favourable general peace.[71] Carteret had always displayed a lack of sensitivity in consulting his ministerial colleagues, but events were to make this natural inclination particularly dangerous. In accompanying the army, he travelled without the usual complement of clerks and decipherers, who were left in Hanover, so he was unable to deal with business as speedily as usual. At the same time the volume of business was rising.[72] He took on direct negotiations with representatives who came to the King's headquarters, including those whose courts lay geographically in the domain of the Southern Secretary, Newcastle. Carteret's despatches to London were initially reasonably frequent and informative, but rapidly tailed off in quality and quantity. Carteret justified his lack of detail and private intelligence by claiming that he was in the theatre of war and communications with the Channel coast were under threat from the French. While true, Carteret's letters were so barren that by July, Newcastle and his colleagues found that even the normal publication of the *Gazette* was endangered for lack of official news and they were forced to rely upon private correspondents to keep themselves informed of events in Europe.[73] Almost as soon as news of Dettingen came through, suspicions that Carteret was playing his own game began to rise. His account of the battle, received on 23 June, was understandably brief and immediately led to requests for details.[74] Private letters rapidly spread though out the country, but nothing came from Carteret. Carteret next wrote on 1 July (n.s.).[75] This letter contained anecdotes of the battle, but still lacked details of losses. Newcastle explained to Carteret that: 'You can be no stranger to the situation we must be in here at present and the figure your humble servants make being totally unacquainted either with the schemes for carrying on the war or the steps that may be taken for bringing about a Peace. Whatever the first may be, we most heartily and sincerely wish success to them. As to the latter if there are any negotiations of that kind on foot as seems probable from appearances till we know what they are and with whom, it is impossible to say anything of them.'[76]

---

71   BL, Add Ms 32700, f. 122, Newcastle to Carteret, 13 May 1743.

72   BL, Add Ms 22536, f. 15, Carteret to Newcastle, 21 May 1743 (n.s.).

73   BL, Add Ms 32700, f. 338, Newcastle to Hartford, 29 July 1743.

74   TNA, SP 45/4, unfoliated, Lord's Justices 23rd June 1743; BL, Add Ms 32700 (Newcastle Papers), f. 244, Newcastle to Carteret, 24 June 1743.

75   BL, Add Ms 22536, f. 87, Carteret to Newcastle, 1 July 1743 (n.s.). For private correspondence, see *London Daily Post*, 16 July, 21 July and 25 July 1743.

76   BL, Add Ms 32700, f. 278, Newcastle to Carteret, 5 July 1743.

This stirred up fears that Carteret was using his position close to the King to reinforce his own political influence and, closely associated with this, that he would use German politics to strengthen his position. Despite continuing parliamentary support for Hanover, the issue was still hugely divisive, and the pamphlet and press campaign was still in progress. The policy was precariously balanced. Both the King's concern for Hanover and public suspicion of the Electorate were powerful political forces. The policy that saw the defeat of France in Germany as a first step towards a general peace in which British interests in Europe and the Americas were served, was one that could be accepted by the King and the political nation. Any deviation from policy, or silences, were immediately suspect.

Suspicions of Carteret's intentions were further intensified by the death of the First Lord of the Treasury, the Earl of Wilmington, on 2 July. Wilmington was the compromise official head of the ministry agreed at Walpole's resignation. Before Carteret left for Europe, he had agreed that in the event of Wilmington's death, Henry Pelham, Newcastle's brother, should have the place.[77] After Newcastle informed Carteret of Wilmington's death he had expected to receive the King's approval of Pelham's appointment almost by return. Instead, there was an ominous silence. Newcastle began to suspect that Carteret was manoeuvring to get Winchelsea transferred to the Treasury. The Duke of Richmond, one of Newcastle's trusted correspondents, who was with the army, did not believe this. He reassured Newcastle that Carteret was embarrassed by an earlier promise to support the Earl of Bath for the post, but would not push the matter. Richmond's faith in Carteret's integrity was shaken when he later heard that Carteret had, indeed, put Bath's name forward.[78] Richmond had to agree that if Pelham did not force the issue, a large number of MPs would withdraw their support from the Old Corps.[79] Newcastle was convinced that Carteret was now making his bid to reshape the ministry.

Eventually, Carteret admitted that he had recommended Bath, but the King had agreed to Pelham's appointment.[80] Carteret still did not understand Newcastle's need for 'confidential communication'. He dismissed the negotiations with the Emperor and explained that he sent good news, but did not

---

77 *Richmond-Newcastle Correspondence*, 118, Newcastle to Richmond, 12 August 1743.

78 BL, Add Ms 32700, f. 183 Richmond to Newcastle, 12 August, 1743.

79 *Richmond-Newcastle Correspondence*, 114, Richmond to Newcastle, 27 July 1743 (n.s.).

80 BL, Add Ms 32701, f. 29, Carteret to Newcastle, 27 August 1743.

bother London with bad news, which would only give them pain and about which they could do nothing. The only other substantial negotiation being conducted was the attempt to get an Austro-Sardinian agreement, which, Carteret claimed, was being done on the basis of plans laid before Carteret had even come into office. Besides this, both Carteret and the King had been ill for over two weeks and he would never agree to correspond on military details. Newcastle was unimpressed, but delighted by Pelham's appointment, which he saw as a victory over his rival. The damage done to relations between the Old Corps and Carteret was substantial. Immediately, moves were made to find a new set of allies to support the Old Corps and to find someone who could get as close to the King as Carteret himself. On 22 July, the Duke of Bedford was invited to attend a meeting to consider the possibility of a French invasion. Bedford was one of leading members of the opposition, who, with Lord Cobham and his 'Boy Patriots', who included William Pitt, had sustained the attack upon the alleged pro-Hanoverian policies of the ministry.[81] Richard Temple, Lord Cobham, was an old soldier whose career had been terminated by Walpole for opposing the Excise Scheme in 1733. Cobham's intense dislike of Walpole was the basis of him raising a political grouping from his nephews in the Grenville and Lyttleton families.[82] On the fall of Walpole Cobham was restored to favour and give the rank of field marshal, but nothing was provided for his 'Cubs'. Nothing more is known of this meeting, but it suggests that the ministers were looking to create a counter-balance to Carteret's supposed Hanoverianism. On 22 August, Newcastle and some close friends, including the Duke of Devonshire, met to discuss this situation. They resolved to bring back into their group Carteret's predecessor, Lord Harrington, who was popular with the King and an ideal counter to Carteret.[83]

It was not just Carteret's poor communication that undermined confidence in London. The conduct of the war itself was causing concern. Carteret's tentative negotiations with the Emperor in July not only ran counter to policy agreed in London and potentially shifted the entire focus of the war on to the Maritime Powers, but also seemed to justify the opposition mantra that the war was being fought in the interest of Hanover. The sole objec-

---

81   BL, Add Ms 32700, f. 321, Hardwicke to Newcastle, 23 July 1743.

82   J. Beckett, *The Rise and Fall of the Grenvilles: Dukes of Buckingham and Chandos, 1710 to 1921*, Manchester, 1994, 16–26. See also L.M.Wiggins, *The Faction of Cousins: A Political Account of the Grenvilles, 1733–1763*, New Haven, 1958.

83   BL, Add Ms 35407, f. 249, Newcastle to Hardwicke, 22nd Aug 1743.

tive of Carteret's plan, Newcastle noted to Richmond, is 'To appear a good German'. 'German politics, German measures and (what perhaps is near as bad as either) German Manners.'[84] It coincided with worrying events in Germany. The King's preference for his Hanoverian household servants and military aides was so strong that it could not be ignored by those attending the King. The Duke of Richmond resigned his post of Master of Horse and Lieutenant Colonel John Mordaunt resigned as equerry. The story of partiality spread through the army like wild fire. Rumour had it that at Dettingen the King had put himself at the head of his Hanoverian troops alone. This was contested and not generally believed at the head quarters, but other events, such as the King's decision to wear the yellow sash of the Hanoverian army rather than the red British general officer's sash was festering with the British troops. According to Richmond 'there is not a general nor a common soldier in the whole army that is not in some degree discontented, but it is too true and it is with the most deep concern that I say it. Pray burn the letter.[85] This was not helped by a rumour spread by one of the official messengers that the Horse Guards had not done their duty at Dettingen. Although this was soon proved false, it was another example of rumours undermining confidence both within the army and the political nation.[86] The withdrawal of the French across the Rhine and the allies advance to that river had raised expectations of an invasion of Alsace. For weeks nothing happened, and rumours began to circulate of disputes within the command. The Austrians were against advancing into Alsace and threatening to break the alliance over Carteret's negotiations with the Emperor. The British and Hessians were at odds with the Hanoverian commanders and Stair was threatening to resign.[87]

Finally, as the army began to move up the Rhine to Worms and Prince Charles' Austrian force approached Freiburg, an invasion of Alsace looked like opening a new phase in the war. Trevor wrote to Stair from The Hague 'All our eyes and hearts are on the Rhine to hear Prince Charles and you have crossed the Rubicon.'[88] Even Carteret and the King were convinced that France would soon abandon her role as auxiliary to Bavaria and engage openly against the Maritime Powers. Orders were sent to make all preparations to seize French

84   BL, Add Ms 32700, f. 314, Newcastle to Orford, 22 July 1743.

85   Ibid., f. 264, Richmond to Newcastle, 20 July 1743 (n.s.).

86   Ibid., f. 327, Newcastle to Richmond, 26 July 1743 (private).

87   BL, Add Ms 32701 (Newcastle Papers), f. 45, Richmond to Newcastle, 31 August 1743.

88   Scottish Record Office, (SRO) Stair Muniments, GD135/141/27, f.74, Trevor to Stair, 23/8/1743.

commerce.[89] Yet Carteret insisted that if pressed at the Rhine the French would panic and peace could be made from a position of strength.

From September tension was mounting in Britain as prospects of an open war with France increased. New pamphlets and graphic prints appeared reflecting on British subservience to Hanover[90]. Britain appeared to be invading France to secure territory for the Emperor in exchange for his loss of Bavaria.[91]

In the Mediterranean Mathews had intercepted packages indicating a Franco-Jacobite plan to invade Britain[92]. At home the alliance of Old Corps and New Whigs was beginning to crumble. Bath, angry that he had not become First Lord of the Treasury, threatened to withdraw from the Regency. To the Old Corps this was good news. It proved to MPs that, despite Carteret's closeness to the monarch, the Old Corps carried the greatest weight with the King. Bath's anger was aimed as much at his old ally Carteret as the Pelhams, thus dividing them and diminishing Carteret's power within the ministry. It also gave some pleasure to Bath's old friends, such as Bedford and Cobham, whom he had abandoned and left in opposition. Observers in the ministry and opposition saw that the time might be approaching when a new set of political alliances had to be negotiated.[93]

On 4 September confirmation arrived in London of Stair's resignation. He felt ignored and sidelined by the King and suffered other marks of contempt in front of the whole army. Once the French had reinforced Alsace and Lorraine his recommendation was to shift the focus of the campaign back to Flanders, but nothing had been done and he felt he could go on no longer.[94] Newcastle and Hardwicke both saw that this could bring on the crisis. All the letters from Germany suggested that Stair had a point[95]. Hardwicke wrote that political opinion was not willing to accept the 'present awkward

89   TNA, SP 43/34, f. 145, Carteret to Newcastle, 12 August 1743; BL, Add Ms 32701, f. 35, Newcastle to Ogle, 15 August 1743.
90   BL, Add Ms 35396, f. 121, Birch to P. Yorke, 16 July 1743; *The Hanover Horse and British Lion*.
91   BL, Add Ms 32700, f.314, Newcastle to Orford, 22 July 1743.
92   BL, Add Ms 35407, f. 252, Stone to Hardwicke, 3 September 1743.
93   Ibid., f. 95, Bishop of Salisbury to Newcastle, 4 September `1743; Bedford Correspondence, i, 14, Gower to Bedford, 21 November1743.
94   S(cottish) R(ecord) O(ffice), Stair Muniments, GB135/141/27, unfoliated. Memorial of Lord Stair, 4 September 1743 (n.s.). This is a nineteenth century copy
95   BL, Add Ms 35407, f. 259, Newcastle to Hardwicke, 6 September 1743.

disposition of command'. I see by a letter which my son received today that it is already the subject of a joke and Ridicule. No other vehicle can make all this go down but another victory and God grant we may have it <u>within an Empire</u> before the campaign is over'. Political survival depended on keeping the Old Corps together by Newcastle's preferred method of confidence building; 'Activity and frequent consultations.'[96]

By 11 September Stair's resignation was the talk of London. Tories and Jacobites proclaimed that he was the only officer fit to command the combined army. As if to support this claim, the campaign on the Rhine seemed to be floundering. The Austrian attempt to cross the river stalled. On the same day, details of the proposed Anglo-Austro-Sardinian Treaty of Worms arrived. Although eagerly anticipated, Newcastle was disturbed by it. Under the treaty the Sardinians were promised specific lands in northern Italy. Austria, on the other hand, was promised nothing specific from the treaty. Instead, the Austrian ambassador, Wasner, had managed to convince Carteret that the Britain should continue subsidise Austria until the best possible compensation had been gained by Maria Theresa in exchange for her concessions to Prussia and Sardinia.[97] Although Carteret congratulated himself that no specific guarantee had been given, Britain seemed committed to continue the subsidy until Austria was satisfied the war had run its course. Worse, Carteret also wanted the Lords Justices to ratify the treaty. Formally, the King would do this, but by insisting the Lords Justices declare their ratification, Carteret was implicating them in the treaty. The Lords Justices had had no hand in the negotiations nor were they invited to discuss the clauses. They were simply to endorse the treaty and if it led to a general war to obtain lands for Maria Theresa, they would be held as culpable as Carteret. For Newcastle, it was Carteret's inept and insouciant disregard for agreed policy in opening secret negotiations with the Emperor that had undermined Austrian confidence in Britain and led to their insistence on the subsidy. By accepting it Carteret was again carelessly committing Britain to follow Austrian policy into new wars for compensation. Newcastle realised that nothing could be done at this stage, but it undermined any remaining confidence Newcastle had in Carteret.[98]

---

96   BL, Add Ms 32701, f.103, Hardwicke to Newcastle, 8 September 1743, original emphasis.

97   BL, Add Ms 35407, 262, Act de Declaration Separée.; f. 265, Newcastle to Hardwicke, 13 September 1743

98   Ibid.; BL, Add Ms 32701, f.111, Newcastle to Orford, 16 September 1743.

As the autumn approached the Pragmatic Army began to move up the Rhine to Spier, closer to the Austrians under Prince Charles. Dutch forces were arriving. Noailles fell back from Spier in order to concentrate the army opposite Prince Charles, but few now thought that there would be any action this year. Relations between the allies were not good at any level. Sickness was also rising with the army. The British army had lost about 5,000 men, over 40% of the force during the course of the campaign.[99] The King was soon to leave the army for Hanover and it was unclear what would be done next.[100]

By the second week of October the campaign was over and it had not ended well. Relations between the British and Hanoverian armies were terrible. Stair had delayed his return to England, but Lord Orford (Robert Walpole) pointed out that his arrival would be the 'foundations of renewing and aggravating the odious distinction of English and Hanover'. If this occurred, it would only drive the King closer to Carteret. Fortunately, Stair decided to stay at The Hague until the King returned to London and it was a welcome relief to the ministry that he had parted from the King on good terms.[101] The protracted negotiations with Lord Cobham and the Boy Patriots had progressed to the point of under-standing their conditions for joining a ministry. However, Orford warned, that if they raised the cry against Hanover, there was little hope of bringing them in 'for he and his wild youth must cease to make Hanover their darling topick (sic) of familiarity'.[102]

The key question was how to fight the war in 1744? Upon this turned the fate of the ministry and the future of the war. Over the summer the vigorous anti-Hanoverian press campaign had been fuelled by news from Europe. British officers returning home had various tales of slights and dishonour heaped upon them by their Hanoverian allies. Senior officers besides Stair had resigned their posts. When Parliament met there would be calls to remove the Hanoverians from British pay. However, the King and Carteret would insist, with some justice, that the Hanoverians were essential to policy. To remove either the 22,000 Hanoverians or the 16,000 British troops from the Pragmatic Army would be a disaster[103]. The Dutch, who had only just agreed to contribute 20,000 to the

---

99   BL, Add Ms 35407, f. 273, Newcastle to Hardwicke, 1 October 1743.

100 BL, Add Ms 35356, f. 164, P. Yorke to T. Birch, 4 October 1743.

101 BL, Add Ms 32701, f. 125, Drummond to Newcastle, 3 October 1743 (n.s.). Stair was permitted to keep his regiment and government.

102 BL, Add Ms 32701, f. 148, Orford to Newcastle, 4 October 1743.

103 Sixteen thousand Hanoverians were in British pay, but 6,000 additional troops were available paid directly by the Electorate.

Army, would retract. The Austrians would see that the British would not earnestly assist them gaining compensation for their losses. The Sardinians would see in the collapsing alliance serious danger and immediately negotiate with the French and Spanish. The old fear revived that, *in extremis*, the Austrians would abandon Flanders to the French to preserve their core interests in Germany and Italy, and an essential British interest would be lost to France. Peace would have to be made with the French in control of Flanders. Without any counter-advantage, the war with Spain would also end in ignominy.

The alternative, proposed by the Cobham, was to confine the European commitment to subsidies to other German princes. Prussians or Saxons were reputedly better soldiers. They could campaign with the Austrians in Alsace or Lorraine and they would win from France the compensation for the Emperor or Austria. Britain would pay for a continental war that would humble France and reward its allies. For Newcastle the choice was difficult. He recounted the dilemma at length in a letter to his friend Hardwicke on 24 October. At the core of Newcastle's view was that Carteret simply could not be trusted. Although it was unanimous ministerial policy to hire the Hanoverian troops in August 1742, Carteret was now parading the policy as uniquely his own. His uncritical championing of the King's views, regardless of other ministers' opinions, was both militarily dangerous and destructive to the ministry. Carteret had supported the Hanoverian refusal to march into Germany over the winter of 1742/3. His negotiations with Sardinia and Austria had produced proposals that were open-ended and dangerous. All this had raised a furore about Hanoverianism and made the Old Corps' supporters doubt the influence of their leaders in the closet, tending to break the solidarity between them. It also raised questions about how the war could be carried on. For Newcastle, Carteret's *'management'* was the dominant problem.[104]

Two weeks later his views had crystallised a solution. Meetings with Carteret early in November, convinced Newcastle that he could not carry on with Carteret. He believed that the war, as negotiated by Carteret, was unwinnable. It had always been understood that French territory would provide compensation in settling the quarrel between the Emperor and Austria. An invasion of northern or eastern France was now inevitable and with that an open war with France. Perhaps, strongly influenced by the Duke of Richmond, who was fully persuaded that the British and Hanoverian armies could never serve effectively together, Newcastle was sure the Prag-

104 BL, Add Ms 32701, f. 202, Newcastle to Hardwicke, 24 October 1743.

matic Army would fragment, leaving Flanders exposed. He now accepted Cobham's view that British forces should be withdrawn and a new army of German troops subsidised to fight for Austrian compensation.

The Old Corps had to break with Carteret and his war policy. If they clung to it and it succeeded Carteret would reap the praise and the Old Corps would fragment. If, as Newcastle believed, it failed, they would be blamed as much as Carteret and unable to form a new government or war policy.[105] However, the Old Corps was not unanimous in this view. Richmond, and to a more limited extent, Hardwicke, agreed with Newcastle, but the majority were inclined to follow a more moderate line espoused by Newcastle's brother, Henry Pelham. They recognised that Carteret's power lay in the King's approval of the policy. If they went along with it there was a chance of retaining their influence in the closet and, with that, retain Old Corps solidarity in the Commons. With this solidarity, and a reasonably coherent case of the war policy, winning any debates in Parliament was entirely possible. Now back from the heady atmosphere of Hanover and the campaign, Carteret would soon realise he needed the Old Corps as much as they needed him.

However, the coherence of the war policy rested on two assumptions. First, that the British and Hanoverians would serve together and that, on the back of this unity, pressure could be applied to the Dutch to join the Pragmatic Army early in the new campaign. Second, that the articles of the Treaty of Worms could be clarified to ensure British commitments were limited. The first of these assumptions could only be tested by events in the new year. The second proved immediately problematic. The treaty was discussed by the Cabinet Council on 24 November where they split broadly down party lines. The majority (Old Corps) rejected the treaty, which Carteret, and his three colleagues (Bolton, Tweeddale and Winchelsea) approved.[106] The King remained silent and it seems that with Henry Pelham guiding the meeting along a middle path, it was agreed to propose amendments. Over the next few days, Pelham was successful, and with minor amendments the seal was put on the treaty on 3 December.[107]

---

105 Ibid., f. 238, Newcastle to Hardwicke, 7 November 1743; Add Ms 35407, f. 295, Newcastle to Hardwicke, 11 November 1743.

106 TNA, SP45/4, unfoliated, 24 November 1743; Egmont Diary, iii, 276, 27 November 1743. Argyle, without explanation, rejected the treaty.

107 Britain was, by implication in article 10 of the treaty, committed to provide the money for

Newcastle was hurt by his brother's growing ascendancy over policy, and, pleading gout, stayed away from Parliament on 1 December.[108] In the Lords the session started quietly, without a division on the King's Speech. However, the next two weeks in the Commons were filled with long and violent arguments over the behaviour and payment of the Hanoverian troops. William Pitt's condemnation of the Hanoverians and Carteret drew praise from the House as well as a reprimand from the Speaker. The debate on the King's Speech ranged widely over policy since 1741, full of assertion and contradiction based upon extrapolating cause or effect from known events. Despite the violence of anti-Hanoverian feeling, the opposition could not make an solid *prima facie* case that the policy was contrary to British interests. It was easy for the ministerial speakers to assert the contrary; the army had caused the collapse of the French position in Germany; it had prevented the French from reinforcing the Spaniards in Italy; it had defeated the French party at The Hague and brought about Dutch participation, and the Treaty of Worms had secured Sardinian participation on the side of the allies. None of these assertions were provable, but they were more plausible than any assertions to the contrary. The result was a ministerial majority of 129.[109]

A few days later, the ministry was surprised by a renewed attack in both Houses on the continued employment of the Hanoverian troops. Great efforts were again made to demonstrate that the war in Flanders could not be won as the French had been allowed time to concentrate a larger force around their heavily defended frontier areas. Still, the debate was conducted by both sides with generally unsupported invective. On 6 December, in the Commons, Carteret was condemned as that 'infamous minister '(Pitt) or that 'unpopular and detested minister' (Barrington). The Hanoverian troops were condemned as cowardly, even treacherous. On the ministerial side, the stories of Anglo-Hanoverian disputes were dismissed as fabrications or, at worst, just infractions of discipline. It was not possible to see how the war was to be fought without the Hanoverians. Only Admiral Vernon, now sitting as MP for Ipswich, seems to have raised the possibility of a renewed colonial or maritime campaign,

---

the purchase of Finale from Genoa.

108 BL, Add Ms Add Ms 35407, f. 295, Newcastle to Hardwicke, 11 November 1743; Pelham's role was further strengthened by his appointment his appointment as Chancellor of the Exchequer on 8 December.

109 Corbett, *Parliamentary History*, op. cit., xiii (1743–1746), 100–230.

but judging from the lack of reporting of this speech, he was ineffective.[110] The ministry's majority was cut to 50 (231–181), but the ministers felt that they had endured the '*most critical and delicate part of the session*', and they could rely on a majority from now on.[111] The same arguments were deployed in the Lords on 9 December, with the same results. A half-hearted motion in the Commons on 15 December to petition the King not to enter into any more foreign treaties was decisively defeated by 77 votes (132–209).

As the new year began, it seemed Pelham had been right. Backing Carteret and the Hanoverian troops had consolidated the Old Corps vote in the Commons. However, the decision had destroyed the negotiations with Cobham and the opposition Whigs for the moment. In protest, Cobham resigned his commission in the Horse Grenadier Guards and Lord Gower, his close supporter in the ministry, resigned as Lord Privy Seal on 8 December. In the re-shuffle, Pelham strengthened his own position by becoming Chancellor of the Exchequer as well as First Lord of the Treasury.[112] Newcastle, still sore, considered resigning, but was dissuaded by Richmond, who pleaded with him to remain in office to counter Carteret, '*who I think is drawing our Master and Country into destruction*'.[113] Politically, Carteret looked triumphant. Newcastle, Pelham and the Old Corps would follow his lead. They were committed to a renewed war in Flanders or eastern France in search of a peace that would satisfy Maria Theresa. The British force there was to be expanded to 21,000. The prospects were not particularly encouraging. The opposition was right - the campaign depended on the allies working wholeheartedly and effectively together against a well defended French border. A new commander in chief had to be found and a new campaign plan agreed.

---

110 Ibid., 232–381. The majority in the Lords was 35 (71–36). The lack of success in the naval war to date left the opposition in difficulty to explain how the war could be won. They could assert that the continental campaign would not work as the allies were too weak to wrest Lorraine from France. Such attacks had proved ineffective during the War of Spanish Succession, leaving only heavy debt. While the naval campaigns had disappointed, they asserted that privateers on either side could cut the 'nerves of war' by disrupting trade, but they could add little to the arguments that had been rehearsed since 1739. See *The Craftsman*, 3rd September 1743.

111 BL, Add Ms 35337 (Journal of P. Yorke), f. 14.

112 *Egmont Diary*, iii, 278; BL, Add Ms 32701, f. 302, Cobham to Newcastle, 9 December 1743.

113 *Richmond-Newcastle Correspondence*, 300, Richmond to Newcastle, 8ht December-ember 1743; 310, Richmond to Newcastle, 11 Decemberember 1743.

The opposition mounted another attack on the annual estimates on 11 January 1744.[114] The arguments were the same and the result was much the same, being lost by a majority of 112 (277–165). When the motion to hire the Hanoverian troops for another year was brought forward on the 18 January, the House was crowded. The debate continued over two days, with the same abuse, assertion and counter-assertion. That the Anglo-Hanoverian disputes of 1743 had made a deep impression was clear, but there was no clear articulation of an alternative policy that did not include a powerful Pragmatic Army. The ministerial majority held in the Commons at 45 (271–226) and in the Lords at 45 (86–41). On 1 February the subsidy treaty with Sardinia (£200,000 p.a.) passed the Commons successfully by 37 (167–125).[115]

By the beginning of February the outlines of policy for 1744 were in place. Funds to support the Pragmatic Army in Flanders had been granted and the subsidies to Austria and Sardinia were approved. The objective was to bring France to terms by an invasion. Open war with France was accepted as inevitable. Once France came to terms, Spain would follow. The main offensive role of the Royal Navy was still to support the Austro-Sardinian forces in Italy by providing supply and transport, while blockading the Spanish/Neapolitan armies.

---

114 Russell, J. (ed.), *Correspondence of John Fourth Duke of Bedford*, 3 vols, London 1842, i, 18, Sandwich to Bedford, 10 January 1743/4. Despite this, the opposition was not united. Neither Pitt nor Lyttleton would participate in the attack.

115 BL, Add Ms 35337, ff. 21–46.

7

War with France and Crisis of the Worms Policy, February 1744– December 1744

The Naval–Military Balance, January 1744

During the winter of 1743/4, while the political battles still raged in Parliament, arrangements for the coming campaign were proceeding. Open war with France was now expected. France was a far more dangerous enemy than Spain and there was already evidence that the French were fostering a Jacobite rebellion.[1] So far the Royal Navy had not achieved what was expected of it in the offensive war against Spain, but it was still seen as the principal and reliable safeguard against invasion. Anxiety about invasion and rebellion was rising, but with faith in the navy still intact, the offensive against France could be undertaken in Europe. Six new foot regiments were to be raised and the army in Flanders was being reinforced to 20 British battalions and 29 squadrons. Recruits for the regiments already in Flanders were on their way to Ostend by early February.[2] The senior commander of the Pragmatic Army had still to be decided. Although Stair continued to advise on military matters, it was no longer possible for him to work with the Austrian and Hanoverian general officers. The King's second son, William Augustus, Duke of Cumberland, had been considered. He was only 23-years-old and a major general, but he had proved his bravery at Dettingen where he had been wounded in the leg. Promoted to lieutenant general after the action, it was thought that he might command the army if he were advised by other senior allied generals.[3] In the end, the matter remained unresolved.

---

1   BL, Add Ms 35407, f. 252, Stone to Hardwicke, 3 September 1743.

2   TNA, SP44/225(State Papers – Military), unfoliated, Newcastle to the Admiralty, 11 January 1744; Admiralty to Newcastle, 13 January 1744.

3   R. Whitworth, *William Augustus, Duke of Cumberland*, London, 1992.

Success now depended on a number factors. First and foremost was money. The fiscal system continued to prove extremely robust. Expenditure had risen steadily during 1743 and, despite an increase of almost £2.5 million in the national debt, there appears to have been no pressure on credit. The 3 per cent interest rate on government bonds held as the small number of large-scale investors in public debt remained confident. Pelham estimated that a further £1.8 million would have to be borrowed during 1744. The credit was not a problem, but it took longer than anticipated to agree the tax revenues to be assigned to it.[4]

The second vital factor was the speed and effectiveness of the mobilisation of the field army. Intelligence suggested the French army in the north was now concentrated west of the Meuse and that about 60 battalions and 83 squadrons would be put into the field, with another 53 militia battalions garrisoning the frontier fortresses. This would be the first campaign since 1712 in which the Dutch would participate fully. Nevertheless, the allies could only hope to put 61 battalions and 132 squadrons in the field. If they were to have any hope of making significant conquests in Flanders or Alsace the allies had to be first into the field.[5] Much depended on their ability not just to get their armies into the field, but to mobilise wagons and horses to support an advance beyond the magazines. During the campaign in 1743, it was decided that in order to move fast against the French in Germany the army would not develop a logistical infrastructure by constructing forward magazines to support the march.[6] This almost led to catastrophe before Dettingen when Noailles succeeded in cutting the supply routes westward back to Mainz and blocked the Pragmatic Army's potential supply route eastward to Hesse. It was determined that this would not happen again. Despite the delays and difficulties, the magazines would be built up before any move into France.

Outside Flanders there were major uncertainties. If Spain was to be drawn into a general peace, pressure had to be exerted effectively in Italy, but the signs were not good. In response to the Treaty of Worms the French had

---

4   BL, Add. Ms 35337, f. 50, Limerick's motion, 20 February 1744.

5   Royal Archive (RA) Windsor, Cumberland Papers, Box1/ 243, French Troops in Flanders, February 1744.

6   Ibid., 242, Letter from Stair 30 January 1744. For Carteret's role in this see, Coxe, *Pelham*, op. cit., i, 149. This contrasted markedly with Marlborough's careful planning for magazines to support his march to the Danube in 1704. See D. Chandler, *Marlborough as Military Commander*, London, 1973, 128–132.

concluded an offensive alliance with Spain against Sardinia. Maria Theresa was pushing her allies hard for a campaign against Naples, and making demands that were plainly unrealistic to the ministers in London.[7] It seemed that for the immediate future the Italian theatre had to be maintained on a defensive posture. The other uncertainty was Prussia. Frederick did not want to see the Emperor humiliated. If France looked like making a peace which abandoned the Emperor and raised Austrian power in Germany it was unclear how Frederick would react. All these factors suggested that the campaign in 1744 would open with fewer prospects for success than it had done 12 months before.

Invasion: The Crisis of February 1744 and the Political Collapse of the Admiralty

At the beginning of January 1744, the naval balance appeared broadly unaltered since mid-summer. Since the end of 1742, when the British spy in Brest had been arrested, intelligence relied largely on news from passing ships. Andrew Thompson, in Paris, made occasional reports of accelerating naval preparations, but without details.[8] Throughout 1743 it was assumed that although the French had over 30 ships in Brest, they were only capable of putting about 10 ships of the line to sea.[9] Nevertheless, by the end of 1743, it was expected that war with France would soon become general and the war at sea would intensify. The number of cruisers covering Ostend and Calais had been increased in the autumn. In November two ships of the line, the *Monmouth* (70) and *Medway* (60), were sent out to join the *Alderney* (20) watching Brest. The *Phoenix* (20) and *Drake* (20) joined the cruising force during December as the *Alderney* moved down to Lisbon.

Over the previous six months the number of ships of the line in home waters fluctuated between 12 and 20, although the number fit and ready for sea remained significantly lower (Table 7.1). By December 1743 there were seven active flag officers (if Vernon's enforced unemployment is counted as inactive). On 7 December four new officers were appointed, three of whom were active.[10]

---

7   *Richmond-Newcastle Correspondence*, 132–133, Newcastle to Richmond, 16 January 1744.
8   TNA, SP 78/228, f. 274, Thompson to Newcastle, 14 August 1743 (n.s.).
9   BL, Add Ms 28133, f. 129, 25 April 1743.
10 Clinton had been governor of New York since 1741, but, a relative of the Duke of Newcastle, was permitted to maintain his seniority on the flag list.

Table 7.1 Ships of the Line at home and fit for service, Aug 1743–Feb 1744

	August	Sept	Oct	Nov	Dec	Jan	Feb
Line	12	16	20	16	17	15	18
Fit for Service	5	5	6	5	8	9	13

Source : TNA, Adm8/23 and Adm8/24.

Table 7.2 Flag ranks (new posts in italics), 7 December 1743

Admiral of the Fleet	Sir John Norris	Britain
Admiral of the White	Sir John Balchen	Britain
Admiral of the Blue	Thomas Mathews	Mediterranean
Vice Admiral of the Red	Edward Vernon	Unemployed
	Nicholas Haddock	In retirement/ill
Vice Admiral of the White	*Sir Chaloner Ogle*	West Indies
	Richard Lestock	Mediterranean
Vice Admiral of the Blue	*Sir Charles Hardy*	Britain
	James Stewart	Britain
	William Martin	Britain
Rear Admiral of the Red	*Thomas Davers*	Britain
	Hon George Clinton	Governor of New York
Rear Admiral of the White	*William Rowley*	Mediterranean
Rear Admiral of the Blue	*William Martin*	Britain

Source: TNA, Adm 6/16.

The balance seemed about right. The two senior admirals were in Britain. The Mediterranean was served by an admiral, vice admiral and rear admiral. The reduced West Indies squadron had a senior vice admiral. Three vice admirals and two rear admirals were also available for service in home waters (Table 7.2).

Throughout 1743, the Admiralty continued to try to supply Mathews with the ships he demanded. Mathews insisted that he needed 31 ships of the line to be sure of matching the combined Franco-Spanish fleet at Toulon. Over the autumn, three 80s and two 70s had left Britain for the Mediterranean and a month later, two more line, the *Duke* (90) and the *Cornwall* (80) were under orders to proceed there. However, disturbing reports from the cruisers off Brest were reaching the Admiralty. Captain Broderick of the *Phoenix* (20) had first reported that the Brest squadron had seventeen line and four frigates ready to sail. Four more line would soon be ready to join them. The

Admiralty immediately alerted Newcastle to this, with a request for the King to review his instructions to send additional ships to the Mediterranean.[11]

Over the next two weeks, urgent preparations continued and the number of ships fit for service at Spithead rose to 13 by 1 February. On 30 January the Board had received reports from its two other cruisers, *Dolphin* (20) and *Drake* (20), confirming Broderick's report. Eighteen line and four frigates had moved into Brest Roads. The same day, Broderick himself put into Plymouth with even more devastating news. By 9.00 pm on the night of 1 February this news was in the hands of the Admiralty, and the Cabinet met in urgent session the next morning. Six days previously, on 26 January, Broderick had been watching the Brest roads. On that day, 21 French warships had sailed, taking a southerly course. Broderick kept them in sight all night and followed them the next day as they altered course to the north-west and then north-east, towards the British Isles. As they reversed course, Broderick, originally astern, was now ahead of them. At 7.00 pm, 16 leagues off Ushant, in snowy, squally weather, Broderick decided to break contact and rush to Plymouth.[12]

On the morning of the 2 February, the full Cabinet assembled, with Admiral Norris in attendance. They were faced with clear reports that a large French fleet was heading towards Britain. Where this squadron was destined and for what purpose was unknown, but the major possibilities had to be covered. An alert was sent to the Lord Lieutenant of Ireland and to Sir John Cope, the commander-in-chief in Scotland. Norris had been recalled to take command of the ships at Spithead. His anger and contempt for the present Board of Admiralty were unabated and he came with an ultimatum. He would take complete command of all ships in home water and, like commanders on a foreign station, he would correspond directly with the secretary of state for the Southern Department. With the First Lord, Winchelsea, in attendance, these terms were agreed.[13] Instructions for Norris were immediately drawn up and signed that afternoon. He would go to Portsmouth and take command of all

---

11   TNA, SP42/27, f. 12, Admty to Newcastle, 17 January 1744. The figures for the strength at home have been deduced from Adm 8/24.

12   Ibid, f. 30, Admty to Newcastle, 30 January 1744; f. 32, Capt Geary (*Dolphin*) to Corbett, 21 January 1744; f. 34, Capt Lord Thomas Bertie (*Drake*) to Corbett, 28 January 1744; f. 36, Capt Broderick to Corbett, 30 January 1744.

13   TNA, SP45/5, unfoliated, Cabinet Council, 2 February 1744; SP44/225, unpaginated, Newcastle to the Admty, 2 February 1744; SP42/87, f. 264, George II to Norris, 2 February 1744. Norris's *carte blanche* was noted by correspondents writing from London to Paris. See, Colin, 133, letter to d'Argenson, 24 February 1744 (n.s.).

the ships there. He was to get intelligence of the French squadron and if it were headed for any part of the British Isles he was to follow it as soon as he had sufficient ships, in order to destroy it.[14]

The reason for this shift in established command practice can only be inferred. Professional hostility towards the Admiralty Board was well known and probably taken very seriously by ministers. Winchelsea himself had always been diffident about his competence. Certainly, the Old Corps had no reason to defend the Board. Whether Winchelsea's Board performed as badly as historical opinion has generally claimed, is open to question, but there is no doubt that this meeting and decision was symbolic of the Board's political and professional collapse. The same afternoon the Cabinet met again to consider the wider implications of the news. All officers on leave were to be ordered to their posts. Reports of Jacobite agents infiltrating into Britain had been received from Paris, and an alert was sent to the Dover and Harwich packets.[15] The Treasury was to alert their customs officers around the coast to keep a watch on the horizon. Although a voyage towards the Channel looked most likely, it was possible that the French might be heading for the Mediterranean. Mathews was informed that Norris was sailing to defend the British Isles and trade, but reassured that if the Brest squadron were heading for the Mediterranean, Norris would not follow. Instead, a reinforcement would be sent out under a junior admiral, so preserving Mathews' command in the Mediterranean.[16]

When Norris reached Portsmouth he was pleased to find that all the ships in the Spithead were ready to sail. There were 12 ships of the line ready with three more ready in Portsmouth.[17] The next day he was joined by two 70s from the Nore, and daily expected another from Plymouth, bringing his total force, including the *Preston* (50), to 19. Norris was confident that he had enough ships to deal with the Brest squadron, but he knew from

14   TNA, SP 45/5, unfoliated, 2 February 1744; SP42/87(State Papers-Naval), f. 264, George II to Norris, 2 February 1744.

15   TNA, SP 45/5, unfoliated, 2 February 1744.

16   TNA, SP 45/5, unfoliated, 2 February 1744. Orders were sent to Dublin and the Isle of Man, to send pilots to join Norris' squadron in case he should have to pursue the French into those waters. See, SP42/87, f. 268, Norris' Memorial, 3 February 1744. The French force was commanded by Lieutenant General, the Comte de Roquefeuil.

17   TNA, SP42/87, f. 270, Norris to Newcastle, 6 February 1744; f. 272, List of Ships at Spithead.

a report by Captain Geary of the *Dolphin* (20) that the French were also making preparations in L'Orient. The same could be happening at Rochefort. If these forces united, Norris was under no illusion that he would have a desperate fight on his hands.[18] As soon as the three ships in harbour were ready and manned he intended to sail.

Suddenly, intelligence of the French squadron dried up. On the 7 February it seemed likely that the French squadron was hovering in the Chops of the Channel to prevent any further reinforcement reaching Mathews.[19] However, the next day, news arrived of an embargo on all vessels from Dunkirk and the arrival of seamen from Calais. A report that four more men of war had left Brest was received on the 9 February, and that 20 warships from Brest were expected at Dunkirk.[20] Still, there was no firm news of the French squadron.

Out in the stormy Atlantic, the French squadron under Lieutenant General Comte de Roquefeuil was labouring towards the Channel. Even before news of his departure had reached England, three of his ships were forced by storm damage to return to Brest. The operation was part of a serious invasion plan that had been organised and begun without the British even being aware of it. Over the previous months an expeditionary force of about 9,600 troops had assembled around Dunkirk. The plan had been made in conjunction with Jacobites, who promised a rising as soon as the French army landed. The Pretender's son, Prince Charles Edward Stuart, had arrived in France and Jacobite agents on both sides of the Channel were busy making preparations.[21] The British had noticed the build-up of troops around the Dunkirk, but had assumed that this was a defensive move to protect it from British attack. In command of the invasion force was the celebrated Comte de Saxe. Not only was he one of France's most successful commanders, but a Lutheran protestant, who, the Jacobites hoped, would reconcile the British to a foreign army imposing a new regime. Roquefeuil's task was to draw off the British battle fleet to the west or to blockade it in Spithead, while he detached four line under chef d'escadre, Mon. de Barrailh, to cover the movement of Saxe's army from Dunkirk to the Thames estuary.[22]

---

18   Ibid., f. 277, Norris to Newcastle, 7 February 1744.

19   TNA, SP42/87, f. 275, Newcastle to Norris, 7 February 1744.

20   Ibid., f. 291, W. Boys to Norris, 8 February 1744.

21   A good narrative of the Jacobite activities can be found in E. Cruickshanks, *Political Untouchables: The Tories and the '45*, Edinburgh, 1979, 52–65.

22   The best account of the expedition is still, J. Colin, *Louis XV et les Jacobites: Le Project*

The British knew little of this, but waited for two more anxious days, until, on 11 February, news came from Dover and Deal that French warships had been sighted off the back of the Goodwin Sands. In the long wintry nights, they had slipped past Spithead without being seen. The French intentions were now much clearer. A battle squadron would not come into the Channel just to intercept trade and supplies to the Mediterranean. The Cabinet met with Wade on the morning of the 12 February. The Admiralty was ordered to remove all buoys in the Thames. An embargo on the movement of all ships and boats on the east coast was ordered. Renewed orders were despatched to march all regiments to London. Any marines left in Rochester were ordered to join the garrisons at Tilbury or Sheerness. The dockyard workforce was to be prepared to defend Sheerness. In London a complete battalion of Guards was put into the Tower and the militia was to be called out. The Lord Lieutenant of Ireland was ordered to divert the drafts of troops intended for Flanders to Bristol. All the troops at Bristol were ordered to march on London. Likewise, the drafts from the horse regiments in Ireland were to be landed at Chester and march on London from there. The Commander-in-Chief in Scotland, Sir John Cope, was ordered to prepare to move troops south from Berwick.[23]

On 12 February other, conflicting, reports arrived. One, from Dartmouth, claimed that 16 French men of war had been seen off Start Point on the 10 February. Another that 17 warships had been seen off the Goodwin Sands on the 11 February. Norris was still at Spithead. He believed that the Brest squadron would not dare pass to the east of him. Once to east of Spithead, the French would be trapped in the Channel with no refuge for their large ships. In London, however, another opinion had taken shape. On the evening of the 11 February Newcastle received a ciphered account from his French spy, Bussy, explaining the complete invasion plan. 'All reasoning about the Brest squadron are now over, for last night, there came a certain account that they are all come to Dunkirk Road, where there has been an embargo for some Days on all ships.'[24] By 3.00 am on 12 February the letter had been deciphered and Newcastle had the King's order to Norris to sail immediately for the Downs. Newcastle gave no hint of his source to colleagues. The information was presented directly by the King as intel-

de *Débarquement en Angleterre de 1743–1744*, Paris, 1901.

23   TNA, SP45/5, unfoliated, 12 Feb 1744.

24   *Richmond-Newcastle Correspondence*, 135, Newcastle to Richmond, 12 February 1744. See also Cruickshanks, *Political Untouchables*, op. cit., 57–58.

ligence from Dunkirk gathered from Deal and Dover when it was discussed in the Cabinet Council on 14 February.[25]

The Dutch were requested to honour their obligation to send troops if Britain were attacked. The Earl of Stair was given command of the army in England. The guard was doubled in London.[26] The critical issue was Norris. 'If Norris can get time enough, to put himself, between Dunkirk and us, all is safe, but if our heavy arsed sailor does not come up, till after the French squadron is got into ye River, God knows what will become of this affair.' 'My Dear Duke, things are in great Crisis, tho' most people are more easy than I am. Can Sr J.N. sail with the wind, SSW, I have wrote to Him as pressing as possible.'[27]

The public had, so far, been largely unaware of the imminent threat, but it did not take long for the news to spread. On 14 February the Cabinet agreed that Parliament had to be informed of the invasion plan. The King spoke to both Houses on 15 February. There was little debate in the Lords before a loyal address was passed. However, in the Commons the opposition struck at the ministry's weakness – the Admiralty. They claimed that: 'There had been a visible neglect and slowness in our naval affairs and a want of intelligence as to the designs and motions of the enemy.' It was moved 'that we would enter upon an immediate enquiry into the Conduct of the Marine and the times of the fitting out and sailing of the Brest squadron'.[28] Most speakers, including Pitt, had to rely upon history, drawing parallels with the Dutch invasion of 1688 and the feared French invasion of 1690. Vernon, conversely, could speak with professional confidence and was in his element. He 'attacked the Admiralty with his usual virulence, complained that he had often foretold of the French superiority at sea, had not been regarded, till they were seen riding triumphant in our Channel and scattering terror on our coast'. He went on to denounce the folly of sending Norris up to the Downs, asserting, like Norris, that no French fleet would have dared pass up the Channel with the British fleet at Spithead. Vernon did not realise, or point out, that the decision had nothing to do with the Admiralty and in the

25   TNA, SP45/5, unfoliated, 14 February 1745; SP42/87, f. 311, Newcastle to Norris, 12 February 1744. Once again a measure of inference is demanded on this matter. The French discovered the ciphered note, but it is not referred to in British records. However, that the information received on the night of 11 February was considered by Newcastle and the King as more reliable that the usual conflicting reports from mariners, is suggested by Newcastle sending a letter to Norris at 3.00 am the next morning with the King's order to sail, while the matter was not discussed in cabinet council until two days later.

26   BL, Add Ms 35337, f. 46, 13 February 1744.

27   *Richmond-Newcastle Correspondence*, 135, Newcastle to Richmond, 12 February 1744.

28   Corbett, *Parliamentary History*, op. cit., xiii, 645–646.

crisis of the moment the message of loyalty prevailed. All the City members, except the veteran opponent, Gilbert Heathcote, rallied to the court and motion failed by a majority of 165. Nevertheless, the credibility of the Admiralty and naval policy was further compromised.[29]

The next few days seemed to reinforce the impression of confusion. Norris took his squadron of 18 ships of the line out of Spithead on 14 February and arrived at the Downs on 17 February. The same day, Newcastle received information from Southampton, that 18 French men of war had been seen seven leagues off the Needles.[30] If this were true, Norris had beat Rocquefeuil to Dunkirk and if Bussy were right, the Brest squadron was advancing straight into Norris. However, if Norris was right, and Rocquefeuil had no plans of going east, St Helens lay exposed to attack. Norris remained unconvinced of the invasion threat. He was under orders to destroy the invasion flotilla known to be massing at Dunkirk and the Brest squadron, on the assumption that they were together. In reality, Norris lay at the Downs, with his topmasts and yards struck in violent weather, between the two. Norris knew he must do something. He called a council of war, consisting of Vice Admirals Hardy, Martin and Medley. They agreed that they had to act, but that they could not split the squadron to attack both the Brest fleet and Dunkirk. They would do one or the other. For Norris the main threat came from the Brest squadron, which might even be covering an invasion from Normandy, as had been planned in 1690, but he knew the king and ministers were focused upon Dunkirk. He insisted on receiving a direct order from the King as to the course he was to take.[31] The response arrived the next day – he was to destroy the Dunkirk embarkations and then turn his attention to the Brest squadron.[32]

Norris now had clear instructions and sent Captain Philip Durrell to reconnoitre Dunkirk, while the main squadron remained at anchor in stormy weather. On the evening of 22 February Norris gave the order to unmoor, but the next morning, before the fleet could stand away for Dunkirk, the weather worsened and the pilots refused to take the ships to sea. During the evening of 22 February and throughout the next day, Norris received reports that the Brest squadron was closer than he thought. It had passed

29   BL, Add Ms 35337, 15 February 1744; Devonshire Mss, 260.26, Hartington to Devonshire, 16 February 1744.

30   TNA, SP42/87, f. 333, Account of James Young.

31   Ibid., f. 346, Norris to Newcastle, 19 February 1744.

32   Ibid., f. 335, Newcastle to Norris, 20 February 1744

Brighthelmstone (Brighton) and Rocquefeuil was coming to Dunkirk.[33] On 23 February Norris re-assembled his council and they decided to move the squadron off Dunkirk. If Rocquefeuil was intending to support an invasion, he would have to defeat Norris. Simultaneously, Norris would be blockading the invasion forces.[34] The next day, 24 February, Norris received a letter from Newcastle informing him that the Brest squadron was at anchor off Dungeness. With north west winds, and assisted by an ebb tide, Norris believed he could fall upon them and destroy them before the invasion forces could be assembled. On the morning of 24 February the squadron was on the move down the Channel, but as it approached Dover the winds shifted. Despite the contrary wind, Norris used the ebb tide to creep closer to the French, but when the flood set in he was forced to bring his squadron to anchor about eight miles to the east of the French squadron. There the two fleets lay during the evening and into the night. By 8.00 pm the wind had shifted north-easterly and, if the Brest squadron did not break off and run before the wind, a battle looked certain the next day.

By 1.00 am on the 25 February the wind had strengthened to a violent storm. Neither fleet could manoeuvre in those seas. Ships were being dragged from their anchors and cables parted. Visibility was poor throughout the day and it was not until the next day (26 February), when the storm had subsided, that Norris was able to survey the situation. The Brest squadron had gone from Dungeness. The *Anglesea* (50), which had lost its anchor early on the morning of the 25 drove past Dungeness, and noted the French were no longer there, suggesting that they had borne away out to the safety of the open sea during the early hours of 25 February. By 1 March Norris and his squadron were firmly established back at the Downs. There was now little prospect of Saxe risking the venture and although it was not known in London for some weeks, the order to abandon the operation had been sent out on 26 February.

From his anchorage, Norris was not only commanding his squadron, but giving orders to all ships in home waters. The Admiralty retained power to order the movement of transports, storeships and victuallers, but had no power to give orders to any warships, nor the power to demand ships from Norris.[35] All this correspondence had to go through Newcastle to Norris.

---

33   Ibid., f. 337, Norris to Newcastle, 19 February 1744; f. 364, Norris to Newcastle, 23 February 1744.

34   Ibid.

35   TNA, SP42/27, f. 83, Admty to Newcastle, 23 February 1743; f. 87, Admty to Newcastle, 24 February 1743; f. ?, Admty to Newcastle, 28 February 1743; SP45/5, 28 February 1745.

The system worked, but it was slow. The East India Company had sent a request for their usual convoy to St Helena for its outward-bound trade. There were essential convoys of victuallers and storeships that were awaiting escorts to the Mediterranean. The Dutch did responded positively to the British demand for troops required under the defensive treaty and troops were assembling at Ostend to come to Britain. They needed a convoy. Money and victuals were urgently required for Gibraltar, which could only be sent under the protection of a man of war.

While all was his responsibility, Norris' priority was the invasion forces at Dunkirk, and he did not know what ships were available at Spithead for other duties. Most of his squadron had suffered some damage during the storms in the Channel and he did not need such a large force to oppose the Dunkirk flotilla. So he decided to use the large first and second rates to escort the convoys waiting to leave the Channel. He ordered three of his more badly damaged ships, the *Duke* (90), *Princess Royal* (90) and *Prince Frederick* (70) to return to Spithead under Sir Charles Hardy to gather the escort together.[36]

With the Brest squadron now well to the west, it was possible that Rocquefeuil was on his way to the Mediterranean. On 6 March news came from Paris of a battle in the Mediterranean. The Toulon squadron had sailed with the Spanish fleet and met Admiral Mathews at sea. A furious battle had followed, but reports of the outcome were ambiguous. It was said that the Spanish fought well and the French had tried to assist them, but that the current situation was that the Toulon squadron was at Alicante, while the Spanish ships had found refuge in other ports along that coast.[37] It was

---

36 Ibid., f. 370, Norris to Newcastle, 26 February 1744.; f. 390, Norris to Newcastle, 5 March 1744. The French reported, incorrectly, that *the Prince Frederick* had collided with another ship in the storm and had been lost with all hands. This has subsequently become part of the accepted story. See Cruckshanks, *The Political Untouchables*, op. cit., 63; C. Duffy, *The 45: Bonnie Prince Charlie and the Untold Story of the Jacobite Rising*, London, 2003, 43. Roquefeuil had news of Norris's movement towards him on the morning of the 24 February and had already decided to return to Brest under cover of night. The French squadron started its move at about 9.00 pm as the storm was rising. Although scattered by the storm, nine ships were back in Brest by the afternoon of the 27 February. The rest came in over the following days. See Colin, *Louis XV et les Jaco-bites*, op. cit., 86–87. The order to suspend the operation was sent on 27 February (Colin, 159–160). British estimates of French losses at Dunkirk were wildly optimistic. One account put French losses as 1200 troops. (See Devonshire Mss, 260. 434, Hartington to Devonshire, 13 March 1744.) Eleven transports ran ashore, but almost all the soldiers were saved (Colin, 147–152, 172).

37 Woburn Archive, Bedford Mss, ix, f. 48, Sandwich to Bedford, 6 March 1744; Devonshire Mss, 260.42, Hartington to Devonshire, 6 March 1744.

196 THE EMERGENCE OF BRITAIN'S GLOBAL NAVAL SUPREMACY

unclear if the French planed to unite with the Brest squadron to destroy Mathews in the Mediterranean, or destroy Norris to re-open the way to invasion.[38] The immediate threat was the Brest squadron in the Western Approaches and on the 6 March Norris was ordered to send more of his great ships to join the convoy escort under Hardy. Hardy was also to sweep the Normandy and Brittany coasts for news of the Brest squadron.

Norris remained with the smaller ships off Dunkirk and prepared plans to destroy the embarkations there.[39] However, the winds were too strong and contrary.[40] As the days passed, rumours of the battle in the Mediterranean continued to arrive in London, but nothing was heard from Mathews. Plans continued to be developed in case the Toulon and Spanish squadrons were coming north.[41]

By 16 March Thompson in Paris reported that war would be declared within days at Versailles. Although confirmation was needed, there was no delay in sending a warning to Mathews. The strong north-easterly winds continued to keep Norris pinned in the Downs with his yards and topmasts struck. From this spot, Norris heard that four warships (presumably those of Mon Barrailh) had left Dunkirk and were sailing before the wind down the Channel. To Norris this was the sign that the French had abandoned the invasion attempt and he immediately requested leave to retire; 'I have served the Crown longer as an Admiral than any man ever did' and he had never wanted to serve with the present Admiralty. With open war almost certain, George asked him to defer his retirement for a few days.[42] There was growing anger in the City over the delays to convoys caused by Norris' command of all ships in home waters. Possibly encouraged by merchant support, the Admiralty Board presented a memorial to the King pointing out the unprecedented loss of power and the problems that occurred when all decisions had to come from Norris in the Downs.[43]

---

38   BL, Add Ms, 32702, f. 179, Thomas Cole to Newcastle, 8 March 1744.

39   TNA, SP 42/87, f. 398, Newcastle to Norris, 5 March 1744; f. 402, Newcastle to Norris, 6 March 1744; f. 408, Newcastle to Norris, 10 March 1744.

40   Ibid., f. 412, Norris to Newcastle, 12 March 1744.

41   SP 45/5, unfoliated, Cabinet Council, 15 March 1744; SP 42/94 (State Papers-Naval), f. 147, Newcastle to Mathews, 16 March 1744.

42   TNA, SP 42/87, f. 414, Norris to Newcastle, 18 March 1744; f. 416, Newcastle to Norris, 21 March 1744.

43   TNA, SP 42/27, f. 141, Admty to Newcastle, 17 March 1744; f. 147, Memorial to George II, 17 March 1744; f. 153, Admty to Newcastle, 21 March 1744. Devonshire Mss, 260.45,

On the evening of Tuesday 20 March, Mathews' despatch finally arrived in London with the packets from Turin. It confirmed the disappointing rumours of the previous few days. Despite claims that the French had failed to support the Spaniards and the serious damage inflicted on some Spanish ships, the key message was the Mathews had not captured or destroyed a single ship of the Combined Fleet. Mathews' squadron was short of naval stores before the battle and was now badly damaged in rigging and masts. The Combined Fleet was to the westward of Mathews, possibly to rendezvous with the Brest squadron. Worse, was the reported behaviour of Mathews' second in command, Lestock. Lestock had commanded the rear division, which, by the morning of the battle lagged five miles astern so that they were unable to come into action until too late. This was the beginning of a major political crisis for the navy, but for the moment, the King's approved of Lestock's suspension pending an enquiry.[44]

Confirmation of Louis XV's declaration of war arrived on 21 March. The performance of the navy was now a problem. A French squadron had come uncomfortably close to covering an invasion. Norris and Mathews continued their open and deep hostility to the Admiralty, echoed loudly by Vernon in the House of Commons. The convoy arrangements had proved unsatisfactory both to the City and the government. The performance of the Mediterranean squadron had disappointed. The reasons why all this happened was not clear to contemporaries. Neither the evidence nor a method of enquiry was immediately available to ministers to quell escalating disquiet.[45] On 28 March the Cabinet Council met to consider the position. For the moment the pressure was relieved. The latest news of the Brest squadron was that it was back in its home port in a shattered condition.[46] It was unlikely to be going to the Mediterranean or coming back to the Channel. The Dunkirk preparations seemed to be laid aside. Norris could be allowed to come ashore and the traditional communication and command patterns restored.[47]

Hartington to Devonshire, 22 March 1744. Over the following week a number of petitions from merchants reached Newcastle' office requesting that the Admiralty powers be restored. See TNA, SP 45/5, unfoliated, 28 March 1744.

44   TNA, SP 42/94, f. 155, Newcastle to Mathews, 24 March 1744.

45   BL, Add Ms 35337, f. 21 March 1744.

46   BL, Add Ms 32702, f. 252, John Pye to Stone 24 March 1744.

47   TNA, SP 45/5, unfoliated, Cabinet Council, 28 March 1744; SP 42/87 (State Papers – Naval), f. 420, Newcastle to Norris 29 March 1744; SP 44/225, unfoliated, Newcastle to

Fighting a War Against France: Threats and Opportunities, March–August 1744

Just a month later, France declared war on Austria. The European war that had started in Silesia and Bohemia had evolved into a conflict in the west. Confidence in victory was not as high as a year earlier, but the ministry was broadly reconciled to the Treaty of Worms as the best way of conducting this war. The war could only be ended successfully by forcing France to cede lands in Alsace and Lorraine to the Emperor. The Pragmatic Army, now more commonly called the Confederate Army, was assembling in Flanders to pressure the French northern frontier. The Austrian field marshal, Count Traun, had an army of 80,000 Austrians on the Upper Rhine ready to invade Alsace. The Austro-Sardinian army held Don Philip's army back in Provence, while another Austrian army was holding back a Spanish/ Neapolitan army under the Duke of Montemar at Rimini. Throughout the Mediterranean, the Royal Navy was holding the ring, preventing the Franco-Spanish forces from using sea communications to reinforce or move their armies.

Command of the Confederate Army had to be decided. In early 1743 George II had thought of himself as the saviour of European liberties, prepared to lead the Pragmatic Army in a decisive campaign in Bavaria. A year later, the experience of that campaign and the invasion scare had dramatically changed his view; 'the king himself said he would not sacrifice any more of his subjects a king making which had had such ill success already'.[48] The only officer with the experience and social standing who could fill this role was Prince Charles of Lorraine, brother in law to the Queen of Hungary, Maria Theresa. In January Prince Charles had married Maria Theresa' sister and they had been appointed co-governors of the Austrian Netherlands. However, the Queen was unwilling to let him take military command in Flanders as she wanted him to command in what she saw as the decisive theatre – Alsace. To her, Flanders was a sideshow that could look after itself. While Prince Charles remained at Brussels, he imposed his authority in command, but when he returned to Germany, command devolved on the newly promoted Field Marshal

---

the Admty, 29 March 1744; SP 45/5, unfoliated, Cabinet Council, 28 March 1744. It is not clear whether the Cabinet was claiming that the Admiralty's powers had never been curtailed, which is not true, or whether the Admiralty's powers had been restored, which is true. Perhaps the phrasing was deliberately ambiguous.

48   Devonshire Mss, 260.32, Hartington to Devonshire, 4 February 1744.

George Wade, whose master, George II, was paying for most of the troops in this army.[49]

The British and Dutch were committed to Flanders, but Austrian indifference, Dutch hesitancy, and British distraction meant that nothing much was done to prepare the Confederate Army for an early start to the campaign. There was no money in the Pay Office, no contracts had been signed and no agreements had been made between the allies on their relative financial contributions. The British regiments were almost ready, but few recruits had reached them over the winter and they were very weak. The Hanoverians were complete and ready, but no orders had been sent for them to assemble in Flanders. Far fewer Austrian troops turned up than were promised, and those that did looked, 'in good measure composed of deserters'.[50] The Hessians, who had provided an important contingent to the Pragmatic Army during 1743, had been drawn into a neutrality with Prussia and the Emperor by French diplomacy and thus been removed from the potential force.[51]

Meanwhile, intelligence suggested that 80,000 French troops were assembling. A council of war at Brussels, held on 17 April, concluded that the allies would only be able to field 55,000 troops. It was agreed that the army take up an offensive posture on the frontier, but had to assemble further back around Aalst. This may have been prudent, but had destructive side effects. The army could not lie in close support of the Barrier Towns. This meant that the garrisons could not provide additional horse and foot for the field army or sustenance from the town magazines, and there was the danger of losing the towns to the French. The Dutch protested vigorously, their generals arguing that the allied infantry was of superior quality and could halt any French advance rapidly. The States General sent a new minister to London, Boetslaer, to convince the King that the army should assemble closer to the frontier.

By mid-May Wade confessed that he was doubtful that the allies would be able to stop the French overrunning Flanders. Rumours spread that King Louis XV was at Lille and the French army was on the move. A large contigent (40,000) of French troops were reported moving from Lille to Menin, with another

---

49   Royal Archive, Windsor, Cumberland Papers, Microfilm Box 1/248, George II to Wade, 1 March 1744. Wade was promoted Field Marshal in December 1743.

50   TNA, SP87/14, f. 55, Wade to Carteret, 4 April 1744.

51   This Recess of Frankfurt was signed on 22 May 1744 (n.s.). See Browning, *Austrian Succession*, op. cit., 169–170.

corps of 10,000 moving to cover them by masking the Scheldt. Rather than attacking, the Austrians and Dutch wanted to move the main army eastwards to Mons. From there they could protect Mons and might threaten Valenciennes. The British and Hanoverians objected, pointing out that they risked leaving the French a free hand to sweep through maritime Flanders, occupying Ostend, Bruges and Ghent. Audenarde could not hold out for more than 12 days and the road to Antwerp would be open. After a heated discussion, the decision to assemble around Ghent was carried by a single vote.[52]

Clearly, a decisive defeat was unlikely to be inflicted upon France in Flanders. Although this was an important element in the strategy emerging from the Treaty of Worms, Carteret seemed curiously unconcerned. It was Newcastle and his Old Corps colleagues who were determined to shake the Dutch into action. A second corps of 20,000 Dutch troops might make all the difference to a Flanders campaign. However, the Dutch had seen the anti-Hanoverian press and parliamentary campaign in Britain and were not convinced that the King was committed to the alliance so much as to Hanover. They wanted the return of the 6,000 troops they had sent to Britain during the invasion scare. Stair, Commander-in-Chief of all forces in England, wanted to use them to resurrect his plan to land on the Normandy coast as a diversion. In the end it was agreed to abandon these landings of the understanding that the Dutch battalions went to join the field army.[53]

As these negotiations proceeded the French army was advancing. Almost from the beginning of the campaign, French cavalry screens disrupted the post from Wade's headquarters to Ostend and news from Flanders in London dried up until duplicates began to arrive from the long journey via The Hague and Williamstadt.[54] On 23 May (o.s.) Menin capitulated and the army under Louis and Noailles advanced to lay siege to Ypres, while Saxe moved directly up the River Lys to Courtrai. By 7 June the seriousness of the French advance was known in London. If these towns fell, Ghent and Ostend lay open to French attack.

The King hesitated about his planned summer trip to Hanover and it seemed, at last, the Dutch would have to act if they were to save their Barrier.

---

52 TNA, SP87/14, f. 104, Wade to Carteret, 16 May 1744 (n.s.); f. 109, Wade to Carteret, 19 May 1744 (n.s.).

53 BL, Add Ms 35408, f. 13, Paper delivered to Boetslaer, 21 May 1744; f. 9, Newcastle to Hardwicke, 17 May 1744. See also, Richmond Newcastle Correspondence, 138, Newcastle to Richmond, 17 May 1744.

54 TNA, SP 87/14, f. 116, Carteret to Wade, 25 May 1744.

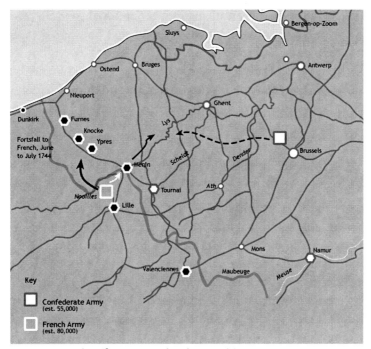

Map 9 French offensive in Flanders,1744

To Henry Pelham's exasperation, the Dutch envoy, Boetslaer, made a final attempt to get the British to continue to pay the 6,000 Dutch troops as auxiliaries after they returned from Britain to Flanders, but it was evident the Dutch could not avoid direct involvement in the war. It was agreed that the Dutch should send an envoy to France with peace proposals, on the condition that if they were not accepted the United Provinces would declare war on France. Such peace feelers were bound to raise the suspicions of Austria and Sardinia, but Robert Trevor, the envoy at The Hague, was convinced that once this was done and the peace proposals rejected, the Dutch would come into the campaign wholeheartedly and the second Dutch corps would move to Flanders.[55]

In Flanders, the three commanders (Wade, Prince Maurice of Nassau and Field Marshal the Duke of Arenberg) prepared to meet the expected next move from Noailles. In quick succession, Ypres (25 June), Knocke (28 June) and Furnes (1 July) fell to the French. The Barrier looked close to collapse and the way open for the French to advance on Ostend and Ghent.

55   HMC, *Trevor Mss*, 98, H. Pelham to R. Trevor, 12 June 1744; BL, Add Ms 35408 (Hardwicke Papers), f. 23, Stone to Hardwicke, 16 June 1744.

Although the Dutch had been stirred into action, Wade had no news of the promised second Dutch corps. Wade claimed that he wanted to cross the Scheldt as soon as he had received news of the siege of Ypres, but the Arenberg refused to move, fearing to expose Brussels to a rapid French switch of direction. Now it was too late as news arrived that additional battalions were reinforcing Saxe's force covering the river.[56] By the end of June it looked as if maritime Flanders would soon be in French hands.

The War at Sea and the First Breach in Political Faith in the Navy, May–July 1744

For the navy the early months of 1744 had brought only bad news. The brush with invasion, the apparent removal of any authority from the Admiralty, the disappointing battle off Toulon, the failure to provide timely convoys, the public knowledge of Mathews' acrimonious correspondence with the Admiralty, bewildering news of disobedience in the face of the enemy by Admiral Lestock were taking their toll on confidence. On 16 April the navy came under direct attack in the Commons. The session was coming to a close and the opposition, whose focus of attack had been on Hanover, was not inclined to see the navy's performance as a politically significant issue. It was, after all, their long standing contention that the Royal Navy could win a war against Spain, if not France. However, two naval officers saw their opportunity and struck. Lord Grannard, an old officer who had been superseded after his refusal to serve in the West Indies led the demand for a committee of enquiry to examine the 'miscarriages' of the navy over the last two years, but it was Edward Vernon, still basking in public popularity, who was the main assailant. With his usual storming invective he laid into Winchelsea. Winchelsea, he claimed, knew nothing of naval affairs, never listened to advice and alienated the naval officers on his board. Vernon's old friend, the late Admiral Philip Cavendish, found that 'the only way of showing his dislike to the absurd and ridiculous orders which were issued was to refuse to sign them and a worthy colleague of his did likewise'. He widened the attack to the Surveyor of the Navy, Sir Jacob Ackworth, blaming him for having 'altered the proportions of the ships for the worst, building them slighter and less serviceable than they used to be'.[57]

---

56   TNA, SP 87/14, f. 142, Wade to Carteret, 2 July 1744 (n.s.); f. 183, Wade to Carteret, 6 July 1744 (n.s.).

57   BL, Add Ms 35337, f. 73, 16 April 1744. The interpretation of events rests very heavily

The ministry was taken by surprise and the defence fell upon Winchelsea's friends, the New Whigs. They had no hesitation shifting blame upon their Old Corps colleagues in the ministry. During the invasion threat, the fleet had put to sea promptly and with enough force to meet the French. As to the anything else 'the military orders came from the Secretaries of State and for the execution of those orders the Commanders who received them were answerable'. The same was true In the Mediterranean. Ackworth was defended by reference to the late First Lord, the Earl of Torrington's high opinion of him. These were not convincing responses; at best it only shifted responsibility for the miscarriages to others in the ministry, but both the opposition and ministry seemed rather taken aback. The ministers conceded that the matter should be considered by a Committee of the Whole House, but neither side wished to press the matter in the remaining few weeks of the session. The performance of the navy was a concern, but not a political issue with deep ideological roots, unlike the size of the army or the influence of Hanover. The debate faltered and ministers conceded on a vote (225–201) that the matter be considered by a Committee of the Whole House, but let the matter die quietly with the close of the session on 12 May. However, the admirals' attack had made an impression and shaken relations between the Admiralty and the Old Corps, which reached a new low.

Before the debate in the Commons, the Admiralty had been ordered to provide advice on the disposition of the fleet across the oceans. The Admiralty took this opportunity to put Mathews' complaints into context. He had more ships than the Franco-Spanish forces at Toulon and had not complained that he was in any danger. Since then two 80s, a 70 and a 50 had reinforced him. 'We mention these passages only to show, that if His Majesty's arms had not the expected success in the Action with the Enemy, it was not owing to any distress from hence.' The victuallers and storeships would soon be with him. His refusal to send ships home was placing a great strain on the manpower of the navy. His forces already employed over 23,042 seamen. If the reinforcements were sent out that number would rise to 32,122. Mathews himself had argued that some of his ships had been out in those waters for so long, that they were urgently in need of returning home before for repair before the decay was too excessive. With the Franco-Spanish forces at Barcelona and Cartagena and their intentions

on this parliamentary journal by Philip Yorke.

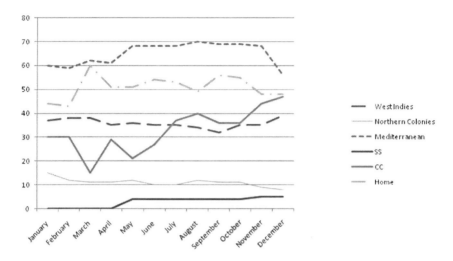

Figure 7.1 Ship dispositions, 1744
Source: TNA, Adm 8/24.

unknown, it was impossible to send Mathews more ships until others came back in Britain. The stresses imposed by maintaining the Mediterranean squadron at this level was hamstringing the re-disposition of the fleet.[58]

Newcastle could not argue with this, but was not happy that the Admiralty merely listed the problems, and provided no advice. He sent the King's order for them to provide advice and by return the advice arrived – the King must send peremptory orders for Mathews to send some of his ships home.[59] Newcastle was pleased that four ships of the line, a sloop, bomb and fireship could be sent to Mathews, but refused to allow the Admiralty to push the responsibility for issuing orders concerning ship dispositions on to his shoulders and instructed the Admiralty to order Mathews to send half of his ships to be replaced home immediately and half when the reinforcement arrived.[60]

The insistence that the Admiralty play its part in advising the King and Cabinet was reinforced a few days later when they were ordered to advise on how to proceed against Lestock 'according to the Laws and Rules and Practices of the Navy'. Lestock was not a prisoner, but had been sent home

---

58   TNA, Adm 1/4113, unfoliated, Newcastle to the Admiralty, 12 April 1744; SP42/27 (State Papers – Naval), f. 187, Admty to Newcastle, 8 May 1744.

59   TNA, Adm 1/4113, unfoliated, Newcastle to the Admiralty, 16 May 1744; SP42/27 (State Papers – Naval), f. 211, Admty to Newcastle, 17 May 1744.

60   TNA, Adm 1/4113, unfoliated, Newcastle to the Admty, 23 May 1744.

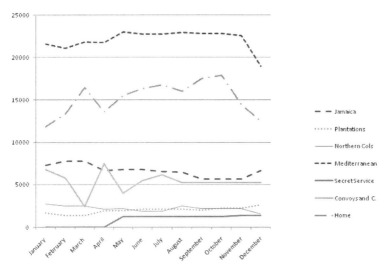

Figure 7.2 Seamen required on station, 1744
Source: TNA, Adm 8/24.

to await the King's pleasure regarding his conduct at Toulon. He had arrived in England on 27 May and, although detained by quarantine, lost no time in applying for permission to print all the relevant correspondence for the public.[61] Vernon had already demonstrated that there was a ready market for this type of publication by his pamphlet war with the army following his return from the West Indies. As he was not charged with any specific misconduct it was difficult to see how to proceed, but the Admiralty wanted him ordered back to the Mediterranean to face a court martial there, rather than bring all the evidence to London.[62] There matters rested until details of any charges arrived from Mathews.[63]

There was some good news. The vital convoy of victuallers for the Mediterranean had reached Lisbon safely, although the same despatch brought information of the Spanish squadron at Cartagena arming. On the 15 June some exceptionally exciting news reached London. Commodore George Anson, who had commanded the expedition sent to the Pacific in September 1740 had arrived at Spithead. Only the *Centurion* (60) had survived from the small force, but she was loaded with treasure from the captured Manila

61   Ibid., unfoliated, Lestock to Newcastle, 1 June 1744.
62   TNA, SP42/27 (State Papers – Naval), f. 227, Admty to Newcastle, 6 June 1744.
63   TNA, Adm 1/4113 (Admty Papers), unfoliated, Newcastle to the Admty, 14 August 1744.

Galleon, *Nuestra Senora de Cavadonga*. The rumours were that his plunder was worth at least £500,000.[64] This was not the news that heralded the collapse of Spain, still less anything to influence France, but it was, at least, confirmation that the fleet could achieve what was expected of it. Horace Walpole dismissed the parade of the treasure through London as 'trumpery' at a high cost, but it was undoubtedly a triumph of navigation and leadership of the highest standard. The rewards seemed to support the idea that successful war at sea could be crowned with unparalleled riches. Amid the anxiety regarding the navy, Anson stood out as a model officer, untainted by the vicissitudes of four years of war. It was a fortuitous time as the new promotions and slight expansion of flag ranks were confirmed on three days later, on 19 June and Anson received the rank of Rear Admiral of the Blue (Table 7.3).

This round of promotions was the opportunity to replace Mathews. While Lestock had been Mathews' second in command he was reluctant to hand over to a man he considered more of an invalid than himself, but with Lestock gone and William Rowley assuming the role, Mathews renewed his pleas to retire.[65] No suspicion for the failure at Toulon had fallen upon Mathews, but the effectiveness of his squadron declined rapidly after the battle. He was unable to prevent the French squadron returning unmolested to Toulon in early April and seemed unable to prevent its departure again in May.[66] This was undoubtedly partly owing to the growing problem of victualling such a large squadron. Individual victuallers got through, but Mathews was forced to stretch the squadron to obtain fresh provisions in Italy in order to preserve his stock of salt victuals. The fall of Villa Franca to the French in April cut him off from a good supply of victuals close to the anchorage in Hyères Road, forcing him to range further for provisions. Mathews decided to concentrate his available force on the coast of Italy from Vado Bay to Leghorn. It protected his most important source of supply, Leghorn, and fulfilled his principal mission of supporting the Austro-Sardinian forces in the peninsula. However, he had too few forces to cover the Franco-Spanish squadrons at Toulon and the Spanish ports. Although he had some cruisers out, he was unable to prevent Spanish and French squadrons ranging across

64   BL, Add Ms 35408, f. 23, Stone to Hardwicke, 16 June 1744. The best modern narrative of the expedition is Williams, *The Prize*, op. cit.

65   TNA, SP 42/95, f. 1, Mathews to Newcastle, 5 May 1744.

66   TNA, SP 42/94, f. 205, Lingen to Mathews, 3 April 1744.

Table 7.3 Flag officers (new flag ranks in italics), 19 June 1744

Admiral of the Fleet	Sir John Norris	In retirement
Admiral of the White	Sir John Balchen	Britain
	Thomas Mathews	Mediterranean
Admiral of the Blue	*Nicholas Haddock*	In retirement/ill
	Sir Chaloner Ogle	West Indies
Vice Admiral of the Red	Edward Vernon	Britain/unemployed
	James Stewart	Britain
	Sir Charles Hardy	Britain
Vice Admiral of the White	*Thomas Davers*	Britain
	Hon George Clinton	Governor of New York
Vice Admiral of the Blue	*William Rowley*	Mediterranean
	William Martin	Britain
Rear Admiral of the Red	Richard Lestock	Suspended
Rear Admiral of the White	*Henry Medley*	Britain
Rear Admiral of the Blue	*George Anson*[a]	Britain
	Issac Townsend	Britain

Source : TNA, Adm 6/16.

Note: [a]Anson resigned this commission on 24 June as the Admiralty refused to confirm the promotion of his first lieutenant, Piercy Brett, as post captain, which Anson had made while on the circumnavigation. He was restored to the flag list in the next promotions in April 1745.

the western Mediterranean.[67] On 28 June he was sent permission to resign his command to William Rowley, who had been newly promoted to Vice Admiral of the Blue.

The reason for the Spanish squadron stirring in Cartagena became apparent a few days later. A despatch from Ogle at Jamaica informed Newcastle that Admiral Torres at Havana was about to depart for Spain with the treasure fleet. On the heels of Anson's success, the prospect of capturing this fleet was intoxicating and Newcastle ordered the Admiralty to prepare a squadron for sea. At this point, the crippling impact of the feud between Mathews and the Admiralty, and the insistence on reinforcing the Mediterranean became apparent. The Admiralty's report of the ships currently in home waters, fit and manned is given in Table 7.4.

67   TNA, SP 42/95, f. 206, Mathews to Newcastle, 11 August 1744.

Table 7.4 Ships in home waters fit for service, summer 1744

100	90	80	70	60	50
1	2	1	4 + 1 cruising off Cape Clear	4 + 1 cruising off Cape Clear	2 cruising off Shetland 2 cruising off Flanders

If the planned reinforcement for the Mediterranean departed, this would leave only four 70s and four 60s immediately available at home.[68] Despite orders, sent by the Admiralty on 25 May, Mathews still refused to send any ships home until he had them careened and refitted at Mahon for the voyage.[69]

All the tasks of the Channel and Eastern Atlantic had to be carried out by a few 70s and 60s. If the Brest fleet came out to meet Torres, there would be no hope of success against the treasure fleet. Worse still, the Brest squadron could cruise for the victuallers and storeships, sheltering at Lisbon, awaiting a convoy from Mathews to go on to Mahon. The ministry agreed that the reinforcement to the Mediterranean had to be suspended and Mathews had to be told that he must send ships home immediately. Balchen was ordered to take command of 13 men of war assembling to escort the trade and convoys clear of the French coast and, if possible, stop the Brest fleet from sailing.[70] He would be joined by 10 Dutch men of war, which the States General had promised.

Balchen did not want to wait for the Dutch, who were straggling into Spithead, as news arrived that the Brest squadron of 13 men of war had sailed sometime before the 11 July.[71] Although news was scanty over the next weeks, there was no doubt that the mouth of the Straits was where the critical action was likely to take place. From Lisbon, Captain Henry Osborn reported that three French squadrons were cruising for his convoy around Cape St Vincent and the others were heading for the Mediterranean. Eleven Spanish ships were cruising close to Cartagena. Balchen was ordered to Lisbon to escort the convoy to Gibraltar, where it was hoped they would meet a force sent by Mathews to take them on to Mahon.[72]

---

68 TNA, SP 42/27, f. 284, Admty to Newcastle, 7 July 1744.

69 TNA, SP 42/95, f. 71, Newcastle to Mathews, 25 May 1744; f. 77, Mathews to Newcastle, 6–17 June 1744 (o.s.).

70 TNA, SP 42/27, f. 381, Instructions to Balchen, 14 July 1744.

71 Ibid., f. 386, Admty to Balchen, 23 July 1744.

72 Ibid., f. 392, Admty to Balchen, 24 August 1744

By late August the British had lost the initiative in the waters of Western Europe. The Brest squadron was at sea somewhere around Cape St Vincent. Another six line, with a storeship, were somewhere near the Straits, perhaps heading for Cartagena with naval stores. Another 20 French and Spanish ships of the line were said to be ready in Toulon.[73] Balchen was at sea with 12 line and seven Dutch warships, cruising down to Lisbon. Osborn was at Lisbon with the precious convoy of victuallers and storeships, with three line, two 50s and one 44. Rowley was concentrated at Leghorn, supporting the Sardinians. More ships were preparing at Portsmouth to reinforce Balchen and the West Indies. All was not lost, but the prospects of another dramatic blow against Spain had evaporated.

The Collapse of the Ministry, July–September 1744

The crumbling confidence in the naval war reopened fissures within the ministry. Friction between Newcastle and Winchelsea rumbled on throughout the summer. Relations with Carteret were even worse. Newcastle had only reluctantly accepted the policy implicit in the Treaty of Worms. Henry Pelham and others of the Old Corps had at least embraced it during the winter, but like his brother, Pelham saw that for the policy to have any hope of success it had to be pursued vigorously by all the allies and that the Dutch were key to effective offensive action in Flanders. By the end of May Pelham was increasingly concerned not only at Dutch reluctance, but the rapidity with which allies were looking to their own regional concerns. The Austrians were concentrating their main army in Bavaria. Any hope that Prince Charles would lead the Confederate Army in Flanders or that additional Austrian battalions would be released for the field army there had gone. Pelham wrote to Trevor that if Holland did not engage wholeheartedly, 'I am apprehensive we should have Electoral difficulties to deal with in the Cabinet and an utter impossibility of supporting in Parliament what in private an honest man might think just and necessary to undertake. The expense this country is now at, is immense, and if no fruit is found from it this year, nor expecting reaping the next, who can promise for success in another session of Parliament.'[74]

The Electoral problem emerged almost immediately. The King showed a worrying lack of concern for the Flanders campaign and was prevaricating

---

73   TNA, SP 42/96, f. 6, Rowley to Newcastle, 28 August 1744.
74   HMS Trevor Mss, p. 97, Pelham to Trevor, 29 May 1744.

as to whether to go to Hanover for the summer. In the view of the Old Corps, nothing could be worse, but their objections met with such open royal resentment on Friday 8 June that it shattered Newcastle's confidence. Most of all, Newcastle was devastated by Carteret's failure to support his objections to the King's journey. In a letter to his brother two days later he summed up the impossibility of a working relationship with Carteret. 'This opinion chiefly arose from the Nature of the Man; who never will have any fixed Scheme of acting, lives upon events and has such a contempt for Every Body else, that He will not so much as vouchsafe to communicate His thoughts to those with whom He Acts whoever they are.' His failure to support Newcastle's objection to the King going to Hanover showed that 'His chief view, in all He does and proposes to do is, making Court to the King, by mixing with, or preferring Hanover Considerations to all others. By this method he secures the Closet, whether the Schemes succeed or not.'

This fairly reflected Newcastle's long-held view of Carteret. His inability to communicate with his colleagues and his apparent indifference to the logic of his own policy exasperated Newcastle. One of the key demands of the Dutch for entry into the war was that Prince Charles send 15–20,000 Austrians to Flanders from Germany. This had been accepted by Carteret and the King, but now both seemed indifferent to the fact that nothing would make the Austrians detach such a number from their army in Germany. Newcastle now feared the worst. Carteret seemed determined to retain favour 'by measures of war calculated chiefly for the service of Hanover, or Ld Harrington, by a renewal of His Hanover Neutrality, which upon this principle that the last was made would equally ruin, distress and confound this country'. It now seemed likely that the King would go to Hanover and there, under the influence of his German advisors, would renew the Hanover neutrality. Newcastle knew that when Parliament met they would face a storm of resentment, much like that which had proved irresistible in 1739 and realised that unlike Walpole, Carteret would not swim with the tide.

Newcastle decided to resign, 'Content that my past help lay aside overran (by) the Treaty of Worms, calculated (as Mr Sharpe said) for the Meridian of Germany.' The only way 'we might hope to get the better of Lord Carteret upon the only solid Foot, viz That of pursuing this War or making a peace if practical upon an English principle, in opposition to those who would make both instruments of Gaining power to themselves by a contrary behaviour'. He would not resign immediately, but 'confine myself singly to the Business of the Southern Province, which is singly now confined to the Court of Turin, never on any account to promote any meeting of the King's servants; to come however when it is desired by others and give my opinion <u>pro re nata</u> to go into the King's closet as seldom as possible and to avoid being there with Lord Carteret whenever I can'. He would never explain his conduct to the King, nor join a ministry if Carteret was removed until 'this Hanover Complaisance is no longer to influence all our conduct, there is the sore' . 'There is the grievance; This preserved the peace; This made the war and what is worse makes it not War; and war and peace with this is destructive to this country.' However, if the King went abroad, 'Things are then brought to a precision.'[75]

Newcastle was not alone in his concern. In late June, Newcastle, Pelham, Hardwicke and Harrington agreed that the King must not leave Britain. The weak force in Flanders gave little hope for effective action there. The failure of the allies to raise troops meant that the King was forced to send four more British regiments to Flanders, leaving Britain dangerously short of troops at home. Even if the King intended to go to command the Confederate Army, it would appear absurd while the Dutch were negotiating with France and the French poised to sweep through maritime Flanders. They agreed to put all these points to the King and that if he did leave Britain they would not consent to join the Regency. Newcastle would argue the case first, to be followed by his colleagues if necessary.

On Friday 22 June Newcastle had an audience with the King. George listened, but argued that troops could be easily returned to Britain if needed and asserted that Newcastle's opposition was just a cover for his hostility to Carteret. Newcastle required no cover; 'I did not spare my master one jot. I told him my opposition to Lord C was not his going to ye War, but His not carrying it on, his Having no scheme, no plan, no concert with the Dutch, or Plan to bring them into, yt H(is) M(ajest)y would see, C would run, as hastily into a Peace as he had done into a War.'[76] Dorset attended the King on the same day with the same arguments. On the following Monday Hardwicke attended for his audience, but before he was admitted Carteret had had a private meeting with the King and George announced he would not be leaving Britain. The King claimed he had changed his mind as a result of a letter from Major General Reid at Ostend, informing him of the weakness of that port and the presence of 400–500 transports assembled at Dunkirk. With invasion still a threat and links between Britain and Flanders insecure, he would not leave, but he made no secret of his resentment.[77]

---

75   BL, Add Ms 32703, f. 108, Newcastle to Pelham, 10 June 1744, original emphasis.
76   *Richmond-Newcastle Correspondence*, 141, Newcastle to Richmond, 23 June 1744.
77   BL, Add Ms 32703, f. 156, Hardwicke to Newcastle, 24 June 1744.

From the perspective of the Old Corps, the worst nightmare had been avoided, but there was still uncertainty as to how the war was to be brought to a successful conclusion. Relations with Carteret and the New Whigs were now so poor that they barely formed a working coalition. Suddenly, on the morning of 29 June the whole scene was transformed. Prince Charles' army had crossed the Rhine. The French forces under Prince Conti on the upper Rhine were cut off and the whole of Alsace lay exposed to the Austrians. Within days, Noailles took the main army in Flanders towards the Moselle, leaving Saxe with just a covering force on the left bank of the Scheldt. More good news followed from St Petersburg, announcing the fall of the French faction at the Russian court. Russia was now more likely to act as a restraint on Prussia, while the Austrians finished the job in Alsace.[78]

The ministry agreed that it was now vital that the Confederate Army moved quickly against Saxe.[79] The reinforcements from Britain and Holland had joined the army and, finally, the allied generals agreed it was safe to move, but without any objective other than to close in on Saxe.[80] In London, Stair urged the King to adopt his plan for 1742 – a direct advance on Paris then establishing the army at the mouth of the Seine for supply and support from Britain. Although Wade had rejected the plan in 1742, George ordered the Field Marshal to reconsider.[81]

The ministry's return to this daring plan, may have been influenced by other news of 'infinite consequence' that reached London on 16 July. An express from the British Envoy Extraordinary in Berlin, the Earl of Hyndford, announced that King Frederick II had declared his support for the Emperor against Maria Theresa. Prince Charles' campaign in Bavaria had forced Charles VII to flee Munich again and placed almost the whole Electorate under Austrian control. Frederick was concerned that if Maria Theresa finished with the Emperor and France, it would not be long before she turned her attention to Prussia and, in a pre-emptive strike, he intended to march through Saxony to invade Bohemia. Frederick had requested permission from the Saxons for free passage and it was not clear how the Elector of Saxony would respond. That evening ministers met to consider whether to offer assistance to Saxony. The King was fervently in favour of sending

---

78 *Richmond-Newcastle Correspondence*, 142, Newcastle to Richmond, 30 June 1744.

79 TNA, SP87/14, f. 228, Carteret to Wade, 13 July 1744.

80 Ibid., f. 257, Wade to Carteret, 30 July 1744.

81 Ibid., f. 262, Carteret to Wade, 31 July 1744; f. 266, Stair's Memorial.

money to Saxony, but British involvement in Europe was already deep. The campaign in Europe only made sense if the allies could field forces adequate to defeat France. Prince Charles' invasion of Alsace shifted the balance of force in Flanders and a glimmer of hope appeared. If the Prussian threat led the Austrians to withdraw back across the Rhine all that would all change. Without more commitment from the allies, particularly the Dutch, what good would aid to Saxony do? It was agreed to do nothing until they knew the Dutch intentions.[82]

From Wade's perspective, the allies had to do one of two things. They must either defeat Saxe's field army or they must be able to lay siege to the French held towns. By defeating Saxe, Northern France would lay open to the Confederate Army and French towns could be taken at leisure. If Saxe could only be held in check, then smaller forces would need siege artillery to reduce towns quickly. Over July and August it became apparent that they could do neither. Saxe refused to be tempted out of his entrenched position on the Lys between Menin and Courtrai, and the allies could not assemble a siege train to besiege towns. The Dutch refused to commit themselves to providing the financial support to bring the siege train from Ostend, nor would they allow large vessels up the Scheldt to bring the guns and equipment to Antwerp.[83] Ultimately, all the Confederate Army could do was take up a position threatening Picardy and hope that Saxe would be tempted to give battle.

During the first part of August, the King was in low spirits. The situation at sea unstable, the campaign in Flanders stalled and a Prussian invasion of Saxony imminent, He could not induce his ministers to agree to subsidise Saxony. Henry Pelham had a long audience with him on the position. He agreed that the Dutch remained critical to any policy. Whatever was done had to appear a 'British' measure. If the Dutch refused to act wholeheartedly in Flanders and failed to join Britain in supporting Saxony, how could the ministry claim that British interests were more fundamentally exposed in these theatres? The King and his ministers were agreed – the Dutch had to be forced into action.[84] One way to encourage the Dutch was to prove that the Confederate Army was capable of decisive action and this was why Wade

---

82 *Richmond-Newcastle Correspondence*, 147, Stone to Richmond, 17 July 1744. See also, Add Ms 32703, f. 258, Hardwicke to Newcastle, 'Sunday Night' (probably 3 August 1744).

83 TNA, SP87/14, f. 236, Wade to Carteret, 25 July 1744 (n.s.).

84 BL, Add Ms 35408, f. 33, Newcastle to Hardwicke, 8 August 1744.

was ordered to reconsider Stair's plan to advance on Paris.[85] The generals in Flanders again rejected the plan, and the ministers reluctantly had to accept that they could not force the matter. A plan to besiege Maubeuge was also impossible without Dutch assistance. Hardwicke noted that 'I own I see such a spirit of Confusion, Contradiction and Irresolution in the Army that I am full of melancholy apprehensions least the campaign should wear out without anything material being even attempted.'[86]

In late August news arrived that Prince Charles had re-crossed the Rhine to counter the Prussians. It was the end of any hope of an effective campaign in Flanders and defending the Worms policy in Parliament was now going to be extremely tricky. It was not helped by the King, who seemed pleased that the balance of power in Central Germany was being redressed by Austrian action.[87] The only good news was that the main French army had elected to follow Prince Charles across the Rhine, which relieved pressure on Flanders for the rest of the year. Henry Pelham, considering the financial requirements, noted that 'nothing can induce the parliament to go on with these great expenses except that they see before hand, some well concerted plan, in which the Dutch are equally concerned with ourselves and by which even the Queen of Hungary shall be obliged to consider the interests of her allies'.[88] If the Dutch could not be brought into the war, then Pelham argued that Britain should agree with France a neutrality for the Low Countries and withdraw her army. The same message was sent secretly by Newcastle to Robert Trevor at The Hague. Austria must be supported out of 'honour and interest', but it was understood that the necessary measures:

> would meet with such clogs as might in the end entirely defeat them and experience has convinced me that the misfortunes and disappointments we have met with, are rather owing to the manner in which vigorous measures, viz the war, had been carried on, or rather not carried on, than to the measure itself. To speak plainly – Too great attention to Electoral considerations has been in my opinion the cause of most of our difficulties.

For six months they had tried to get the Dutch to join the fight as full allies.

---

85   TNA, SP 87/15, Carteret to Wade, 14 August 1744.
86   BL, Add Ms 32703, f. 270, Hardwicke to Newcastle, 16 August 1744.
87   BL, Add Ms 35408, f. 41, Newcastle to Hardwicke, 28 August 1744.
88   BL, Add Ms 32703, f. 283, H. Pelham to Newcastle, 'Saturday Night'.

Plate 1 Robert Walpole, 1st Earl of Orford, by John Faber Jr, after Sir Godfrey
Kneller, Bt mezzotint, 1733. © National Portrait Gallery, London.

Plate 2 Thomas Pelham-Holles, 1st Duke of Newcastle-under-Lyne, by James Macardell, after William Hoare, mezzotint, mid-18th century. © National Portrait Gallery, London.

Plate 3 John Carteret, 2nd Earl Granville, by and published by Thomas Major, after Dominicus van der Smissen, line engraving, published 12 September 1757. © National Portrait Gallery, London.

Plate 4 King George II, by Simon François Ravenet, after David Morier, line engraving, 1743 or after. © National Portrait Gallery, London.

The Hon: George Wade Esq
Lieutenant General and Commander in Chief
of all His Maj Forces, Castles, Forts and Barracks in North Britain, &c.

Plate 5 George Wade, by and published by John Faber Jr, after Johan van Diest mezzotint, published 1736. © National Portrait Gallery, London

Plate 6 William Augustus, Duke of Cumberland, by Gerhard Bockman, published by John Bowles, mezzotint, published circa 1750–1775. © National Portrait Gallery, London.

Plate 7 Edward Vernon, by Arthur N. Sanders, after Thomas Gainsborough
mezzotint, 1860s–1890s (circa 1753). © National Portrait Gallery, London.

GEORGE ANSON ESQ. COMMANDER IN CHIEF OF THE
LATE EXPEDITION TO THE SOUTH SEAS.

Plate 8 George Anson, 1st Baron Anson, by Charles Grignion, after and published by Arthur Pond, line engraving, published 1744. © National Portrait Gallery, London.

The King had tried to convince the Dutch of his enthusiasm for the fight, but to no avail and now it was time 'if we cannot make war together, that we should endeavour to make the best peace together we can'.[89] The Worms policy had failed and another way had to be found to put a satisfactory end to the war with France and Spain.[90] More importantly, the King had to be convinced that this was necessary. He continued to behave with regard to his Hanoverian forces so as to rouse suspicion at home and abroad. In October, he wanted his Hanoverians separated from the Confederate Army to winter in Westphalia.[91] His eyes appeared to be more focused on the Austro-Prussian campaign in Bohemia than the war in Flanders. The campaign itself petered out with recriminations among the allied generals, and even Wade, who was extremely ill, removed the British forces from close winter quarters with his allies.[92] The time was approaching 'to remove the cause and the Author of all these misfortunes'.[93]

On the evening of 18 September 1744, Hardwicke, Newcastle, Henry Pelham, Dorset and Grafton met and agreed the policy that must be pressed upon the King. Prussia must be taken out of the war by conciliation and the Dutch must fully engage in common cause with the allies. Within two days Hardwicke had drawn up a detailed memorandum explaining the necessity of these points, but did not press matters immediately as other critical events again intruded. On the night of 21 September news arrived that the Brest squadron, which was thought to be near the Straits, had been sighted at the mouth of the Channel. The transports were still at Dunkirk, and another invasion attempt looked possible. All captains at home were ordered to go to Portsmouth, from where Vice Admiral Thomas Davers was ordered to sail immediately with as many ships as he could muster.[94] As the days passed, it became apparent that the ships were more probably the returning East or West Indies trade coming to France in convoy.[95] Tension eased, but the shock was enough to force the ministry to think again about naval defence. Davers had been preparing to sail for the West Indies. He was ordered to sail with

89   HMC, Trevor Mss, p. 100, Newcastle to Trevor, 28 September 1744.

90   BL, Add Ms 35408, f. 49, Stone to Hardwicke, 6 September 1744.

91   *Richmond-Newcastle Correspondence*, p. 153, Newcastle to Richmond, 6 October 1744.

92   Ibid., p. 155, Stone to Richmond, 18 October 1744.

93   BL, Add Ms 32703, f. 307, Newcastle to Hardwicke, 14 September 1744.

94   TNA, SP 44/226, unfoliated, Newcastle to the Admty, 22 September1744.

95   Ibid., f. 428, Admty to Newcastle, 25 September 1744.

four ships of the line, only when 12 warships were ready for home defence. It was now ordered 'that the said number of twelve men of war of 50 guns and upwards, should be constantly kept for the Channel service and a flag officer should be appointed to take command of the said ships'.[96] Although they were not necessarily to be kept as a standing squadron, but deployed as required for home defence and trade protection, it was an important step towards a permanent force in the Channel.

With the Flanders campaign effectively over by early October and the fears of the Brest squadron at least temporarily laid aside, it was time for the Old Corps to strike, before Parliament met. On 1 November Newcastle presented Hardwicke's memorandum to the King. Two days later he and Pelham had an audience at which Carteret, now Lord Granville, since the death of his mother, was present. Despite ill humour, the King conceded that these policies were necessary and was willing to order Granville to execute them and incorporate them in the King's Speech on the opening of the new session of Parliament. For the war to be continued it had to be 'popular' and money had to be raised. The key popular measure was to insist upon a Dutch declaration of war. The army in Flanders had to be reorganised, with proportions of forces and funds agreed in advance. Granville seemed to prevaricate.[97] His continued indifference to his cabinet colleagues was, to them, staggering. In the following days, Granville was unwilling to discuss the details of the King's Speech and expected Pelham to prepare the Treasury for a new campaign without letting him know how the campaign was to be conducted.[98] On 9 November, Hardwicke renewed the attack in the Kings' Closet on Granville and his conduct of the war. The expected resistance from George II did not materialise. He agreed with the policy. He accepted that the loss of Granville would mean the defection of the followers of Bath and the Prince of Wales, but his only substantive objection was to remind Hardwicke of the British desertion of the allies in 1712. He would not countenance that disgrace being attributed to him.[99] Newcastle was jubilant 'By what the king said to your lordship, and by lord Granville's looks afterwards, I should fancy the thing is over.'[100]

---

96   Ibid., f. 17, Newcastle to the Admty, 27 Sept 1744; TNA, Adm 1/4114 (Admty Papers), unfoliated, Newcastle to the Admty, 5 October 1744.

97   Coxe, *Pelham*, op. cit., i, 185–187.

98   BL Add Ms 32703 f. 407, Stone to Richmond, 4 November 1744.

99   *Richmond-Newcastle Correspondence*, 158, Newcastle to Richmond, 10 November 1744; BL, Add Ms 35408, f. 90, Newcastle to Hardwicke, 16 November 1744.

100 Coxe, *Pelham*, op. cit., i, 187, Newcastle to Hardwicke, 10 November 1744; *Richmond-*

The Pelhams had been given control of the King's Speech, but George was not prepared to let Granville go. The King knew he might have to accept a speech that would implicitly condemn Granville's conduct of the war.[101] The Pelhams knew that the King and Granville would do all they could to retain the latter in post. In the end all the plans foundered on parliamentary arithmetic. The Pelhams had already ensured that they could call upon the anti-Granville Whigs in Parliament. The largest group, associated with the Duke of Bedford, were willing to join the Old Corps on condition of Granville's dismissal and the more vigorous measures in Flanders that formed the basis of the Pelham's approach to the war. They would more than compensate for the loss of the connections of Bath and the Prince of Wales. The King tried to induce parts of the opposition to join Granville, but without any real hope of success. He tried to split the Old Corps by enticing Harrington to join Granville and by enlisting Lord Orford (Robert Walpole) to mediate a compromise. Harrington was unmoved and Orford avoided giving any hint of support for Granville.[102] Granville's attempts to coalesce with part of the opposition were also futile. Newcastle realised that the speech was the 'touchstone'. It was the statement that would determine the attitude of the King and the opposition.[103] It had to be carefully crafted to ensure that it included a general statement that the King would not desert his allies, but that those allies must prosecute the war in Flanders with more vigour.[104] On 23 November, with the speech ready and his options exhausted, George II agreed to let Granville resign the next day, handing the seals of his office over to Harrington. As Henry Pelham noted to Robert Trevor, it would make no difference to the general measures for carrying on the war, but 'bring to a greater precision both the objects of the war and the means of carrying it on'.

As winter hardened its grip on Europe, there was some good news to reflect upon. In Bohemia Prague had fallen to the Prussians in September, but after a terrible campaign, Frederick was forced to abandon the city and fall back into Silesia in December. The Franco-Spanish forces that had threatened to overrun Piedmont during the summer had been skilfully halted in September and then forced to withdraw back across the mountains. A few

---

Newcastle Correspondence, 158, Newcastle to Richmond, 10 November 1744.

101 BL, Add Ms 35408, f. 90, Newcastle to Hardwicke, 16 November 1744.

102 Ibid.; Coxe, *Pelham*, op. cit., i, 189.

103 Ibid.

104 HMC *Trevor Mss*, p. 108, H. Pelham to Trevor, 27 November 1744.

days after the departure of the Franco-Spanish army snow closed the passes. Nevertheless, if Britain was going to emerge from the war successfully, it would take a great deal more than defensive campaigns in Bohemia and Piedmont. Anson's return to Spithead in June had reminded the public of the vast wealth of the Spanish Empire, but the navy had lost its dominant position. It maintained an effective presence in the Mediterranean, but had lost its grip on Toulon and the Spanish ports. The navy had been dangerously exposed in the Channel in February and September. After the French declaration of war, privateering increased both in Europe and the Americas. Trade was disrupted, losses steadily increased and insurance rates in the City rose to 20 per cent.[105] At this stage there was no evidence that this war on trade was going to have a decisive impact on the outcome of the war as a whole. The vital supply line to the Mediterranean had been threatened. Balchen's expedition to Lisbon had secured the vital supply convoys, but on his way back to England in October he and the entire crew of the *Victory* (100) were lost in a storm in the Channel.[106]

There were suggestions that an operation might be mounted from the West Indies against Louisbourg under Commodore Peter Warren, but this was a local initiative.[107] It was only in Flanders that ministers could conceive of inflicting the decisive defeat upon France. While France was dominant in Western Europe the prospect of Spain submitting to British pressure was slim. The Low Countries seemed to offer the only way to a good peace, but the new campaign would have to be well funded, well organised and in the field early to retake the initiative there.

---

105 BL, Add Ms 35351, f. 49, Hardwicke to P. Yorke, 13 October 1744. See also Starkey, *British Privateering*, op. cit., 122–129,137; Swanson, *Predators and Prizes*, op. cit., 148–9, C.E. Fayle, 'Economic Pressure in the War of 1739–48, *Journal of the Royal United Services Institution*, 1923, 434–446.

106 Traditionally thought to have been wrecked on the Casquets near the Channel Islands, the remains of the *Victory* were found in 2008 located over 100 kilometres away to the west of those rocks. See S. Kingsley, 'Balchin's Victory : The World's Mightiest Warship Discovered', *Current World Archaeology*, 34(2009), 26–35. I am indebted to Mr Jeremy Toynbee for this reference.

107 TNA, Adm 1.4154, unfoliated, Newcastle to Admty, 7 November 1744.

8

Rebellion and the End of the Flanders Policy, January–December 1745

The New Ministry and the Preparations of the New Campaign in Flanders

Although George had lost Granville he was far from reconciled to the situation. Harrington, who replaced Granville, was an old friend, and entirely acceptable, but the King had great reservations about the 'New Allies' with whom the Pelhams had created the new 'Broad-Bottomed Administration'.[1] The Duke of Bedford had long opposed both Walpole and Granville. His constant opposition and landed influence, made him a centre of gravity for other opposition groups such as Viscount Cobham and his 'Cubs' and the Prince of Wales' Leicester House grouping. Bedford's father in law, Lord Gower, a prominent Tory, also gave him links to this large, but excluded group.[2]

The Pelhams knew that these groups had to be accommodated and by 17 December the main changes had been agreed.[3] The most significant changes were at the Admiralty. Winchelsea had to go. Bedford claimed this office for himself and insisted that the Earl of Sandwich be second Lord.[4] This meant that the loyal Old Corps Whig, John Cockburne, had to be sacrificed. Lord

---

1 For a fuller examination of the negotiations, see Owen, *Pelhams*, op. cit., 231–250.

2 For an overview of the Bedford connection, see, J. Haas, 'The Rise of the Bedfords, 1741–1757: A Study in the Politics of the Reign of George II', unpublished PhD thesis, University of Illinois, 1960.

3 *Richmond-Newcastle Correspondence*, p. 160, Newcastle to Richmond, 8 December 1744.

4 For Sandwich's career, see N.A.M. Rodger, *The Insatiable Earl: A Life of John Montagu, 4th Earl of Sandwich*, London, 1993.

Table 8.1 Admiralty commissions

26 December 1744	27 December 1744
Earl of Winchelsea	Duke of Bedford
John Cockburne	Earl of Sandwich
Lord Archibald Hamilton	Lord Archibald Hamilton
Charles Lord Baltimore	Lord Vere Beauclerk
George Lee	Charles Lord Baltimore
Rear Admiral Charles Hardy (d. 27 November 1744)	George Anson
John Phillipson	George Grenville

Archibald Hamilton, an adherent to Leicester House, retained his post. Lord Baltimore, another Leicester House man, had to cede precedence to Lord Vere Beauclerk, the naval officer and Old Corps Whig, who returned to the Admiralty, possibly to counter the loss of Cockburne. Rear Admiral Charles Hardy had been appointed by Winchelsea after Admiral Cavendish's death in July 1743, had himself died on 27 November 1744. He was replaced with Captain George Anson. Anson was the naval hero of the moment, but he was also politically well connected. His family home was at Shugborough, Staffordshire, where he was neighbour to Lord Gower the prominent Tory and father-in-law of Bedford.[5] Although firm Whigs, the Ansons were well established in this strongly Tory county society. Phillipson, the most junior member, had to go in favour of George Grenville, a leading and ambitious member of Cobham's 'Cubs' (Table 8.1)

The political balance was broadly maintained with an almost straight replacement of the Granville–Bath connection with that of Bedford–Cobham, but the professional balance was enhanced with the inclusion of Beauclerk and Anson.

There were few other changes.[6] The King accepted another long-standing opponent of Walpole, the Earl of Chesterfield, as Lord Lieutenant of Ireland and envoy to Holland. This last role was very important. The basis of the new political alliance was a more vigorous campaign in Flanders, which meant the Dutch had to be made to commit themselves. Chesterfield could be

---

5   W.V. Anson, *The Life of Lord Anson*, London, 1912, N.A.M. Rodger, 'George, Lord Anson', in P. Le Fevre and R. Harding (eds) *Precursors of Nelson: British Admirals of the Eighteenth Century*, London, 2000, 177–199.

6   Owen, *Pelhams*, op. cit., 245–248.

trusted to insist upon this. On the whole the Pelhams were delighted by their new allies, although Newcastle was not convinced that the agreement would hold. He was unsettled by the continued sullenness of the King. George had accepted the ministerial changes as necessary to maintain popular support of the war, but he made no secret that he considered that he had been forced against his will into these measures. If this did not change, long-term public confidence in the ministry was bound to decay.[7] Another uncertainty was the reaction of William Pitt. The new 'Broad Bottom' administration, as the name suggests, was not a unified block, but a loose connection of groups, whose strength lay not in its own unity, but by its inclusion of almost all significant interests that could effectively co-ordinate opposition to it.[8] Pitt, one of the most able speakers in the Commons, had connected himself to Cobham's 'Cubs', but had been refused even minor office by the King. In revenge or frustration, his rhetorical and theatrical brilliance could easily be employed against the ministry and be extremely damaging. All Newcastle could do was urge Pitt to be patient.[9]

The first months of the Broad Bottom were difficult. The King made no attempt to exclude Granville from his counsels. Chesterfield pressed Newcastle to put it to an open trial of strength; 'Your Grace says, and very truly, that the King's servants must be his ministers exclusive of all others, or they cannot remain his servants.'[10] Newcastle rejected the idea, but on 9 April, matters came to a head. The King accused the Pelhams of deceiving him over command in the army and concessions to the Tories. He threatened 'to strike a strong stroke', which Henry Pelham invited him to do. The King fell silent, but Pelham did not believe he had heard the last of the matter and prepared to resign.[11] Nothing came of it, but with the King intending

---

7   P. Yorke, *Life of Lord Hardwicke*, 380, Narrative; BL, Add Ms 32704, f. 3, Hardwicke to Newcastle, 5 March 1745.

8   BL, Add Ms 35408, f.114, Hardwicke to Newcastle, 5 March 1745.

9   Pitt's patience at this point has been variously attributed to an imminent expectation of inheritance from the Duchess of Marlborough, who would not countenance him taking office, illness and a recognition that he had to spend time rebuilding his relationship with the King, who detested him for his violent opposition to support for Hanover. Owen, *Pelhams*, op. cit., 248–9; Tunstall, *William Pitt*, op. cit., 72–74. See also, M. Peters, *Pitt and Popularity: The Patriot Minister and London Opinion during the Seven Years War*, Oxford, 1980.

10   R. Lodge, *Private Correspondence of Chesterfield and Newcastle, 1744–1746*, London, 1930, 21–2, Chesterfield to Newcastle, 10 March 1745.

11   P. Yorke (ed.) *Life and Correspondence of Philip Yorke, Earl of Hardwicke*, 3 vols,

to spend the summer in Hanover, it was clear that control of policy would remain a problem if Granville attended the King.[12]

In terms of policy, the political alliance was held together by the expectation that the war would be carried on with vigour in Flanders. Parliament had opened on 27 November. The key division would be on the estimates for the army in Flanders, which it was proposed to increase from 21,000 to 28,000. This debate took place on 23rd January 1745. There was no effective opposition and the proposed subsidies for the year passed without serious difficulty on 18 February. The Austrian subsidy was raised from £300,000 to £500,000. Other subsidies consisted of £200,000 for Sardinia, £24,299 for Cologne, £8,260 for Mainz, and £100,000 on account for expenses in Flanders. Some opposition persisted, but Newcastle reported to Chesterfield, that 'Our Parliamentary affairs go swimmingly.'[13] Henry Pelham seems to have captured the sense of the House; 'it seemed the general wish that we should strain every nerve, and collect our whole strength to act offensively the next campaign'.[14] He was delighted that despite popular views of Dutch inaction there was evidence that they were, at last, stirring. If the French continued to concentrate their forces in Germany a confederate army in Flanders might large enough to achieve decisive results. If the French concentrated in Flanders it would release Austrian forces to re-cross the Upper Rhine into Alsace again. Either way, this plan could force France to an acceptable peace.[15]

Suddenly, on 26 January news reached London that the Emperor Charles VII had died. The war in Europe had started on the death of the previous Emperor and the death of Charles offered an opportunity to resolve it. Prussia and France had lost the cover for their actions against the Hapsburgs. Almost immediately, Prussian diplomats were putting out feelers in London for an accommodation with Austria. The French court was said to be willing to open negotiations.[16] However, achieving a settlement in Germany was not going to be easy and there were different views on whether Britain

---

Cambridge, 1913, 385, Minutes, 9 April 1745.

12   BL, Add Ms 32704, f. 155, Newcastle to Cumberland, 12 April 1745.

13   BL, Add Ms 32704, f. 24, Newcastle to Chesterfield, 22 January 1745; Lodge, *Private Correspondence*, 17, Newcastle to Chesterfield, 22 February 1744.

14   Corbett, *Parliamentary History*, op. cit., 1175–1176.

15   Ibid., 1175–1176

16   BL, Add Ms 35408, ff. 120–123, Newcastle to Hardwicke, 26 January 1745; Yorke, *Hardwicke*, op. cit., 391, Bolingbroke to Hardwicke, 10 March 1745; Lodge, *Private Correspondence*, op. cit., 8–9. Newcastle to Chesterfield, 8 February 1745.

should support an Austrian or Saxon candidate for the imperial crown. If Maria Theresa's husband, Prince Francis Stephen, Duke of Lorraine, were elected, it would put a strong anti-French power again at the head of the Empire. Saxony, Bavaria and Prussia would have to be bought off by Austria, who might be willing to concede lands with the imperial dignity back in Hapsburg hands. Other news hinted that, with the Prussians penned back in Silesia, the Austrians were again ready to march an army across the Rhine. The Hessians seemed prepared to rejoin the Confederate Army and the Princes of the Empire willing to unite to eject the French from Bavaria. A weaker, Saxon candidate, in contrast, might make peace with France and Prussia easier.[17]

Throughout February the Saxon position was unclear. On the one hand the court at Dresden signalled its willingness to give its electoral vote to Maria Theresa's husband.[18] At the same time, Saxon ministers were manoeuvring for the maximum concessions. The Austrians were unmoved and by the end of the month, it looked like Saxony would hold out for the imperial title, with the support of Prussia and Bavaria. British policy was threatened. To continue to support Austria might alienate Prussia, Saxony, Bavaria and even Russia. With the most significant German powers hostile, peace with France would be even more difficult. Newcastle hoped that Maria Theresa would accept Elector Augustus of Saxony (who was also King of Poland) as emperor, with her husband anointed his successor as King of the Romans.[19] Secret Prussian advances, offering to end the French alliance and vote for the Duke of Lorraine, if Frederick's possession of Silesia were confirmed, were seized on to urge Austria to settle with Prussia. This could bring in the votes of Bavaria and Hesse and thus release troops for the re-conquest of Naples, but the Austrians continued to drag their feet.[20] By late March, news from The Hague hinted that if the Austrians did not concede the imperial title to Saxony, the Dutch might withdraw from the war. The potential coalition of the Bourbons, Prussia, Bavaria, Saxony, and Cologne, against Austria and the Maritime Powers was too strong to make decisive headway in the campaign.[21] For the next month, while prepara-

---

17   BL, Add Ms 35408 (Hardwicke Papers), f. 120, Newcastle to Hardwicke, 26 March 1745.

18   Lodge, *Private Correspondence*, op. cit., 8, Newcastle to Chesterfield, 8 February 1745.

19   Ibid., 15, Newcastle to Chesterfield, 22 February 1745.

20   Ibid., 30, Chesterfield to Newcastle, 22 March 1745.

21   Ibid., 34–35, Chesterfield to Newcastle, 30 March 1745 (n.s.).

tions continued, matters hung in the balance. The Prussian offer was turned down and the prospects looked bleak, until the announcement of an Austro-Bavarian settlement. With Bavaria occupied and ravaged by the war, Maximilian III Joseph, the seventeen year old successor to Charles as Elector of Bavaria, was soon convinced that further war to pursue the imperial crown or Hapsburg territory was hopeless. After a decent interval, in the spring of 1745, he concluded a settlement (Treaty of Fussen, 22 April 1745 [n.s.]), which exchanged Austrian evacuation of Bavaria for the renunciation of all Bavarian claims to the Hapsburg succession.[22]

However, there was no prospect of a general settlement before the next campaigning season opened, so it was vital that it got off to an early start. Newcastle still hoped to revive the Grand Alliance against France of 1689 and 1702, but Chesterfield was clear that he was negotiating only for temporary military expedients, not a 'plan of general alliance and operation'.[23] The Dutch had made clear that they would make peace at the end of the year, so this had to be the great effort. Britain was committed to providing 40,000 troops for Flanders. The 28,000 British troops were about the maximum force that the British could sustain with provisions in their area. Twelve thousand more would be hired from elsewhere and deployed separately. Four thousand Hanoverians were already in British pay in Flanders, which left a shortfall of 8,000. These were to be provided by adding additional troops to existing Austria regiments, for which Britain paid. It was a quick method of increasing the size of the Confederate Army, but raised serious questions of verification which were to bedevil Anglo-Austrian relations until the end of the war. It was expected that the troops could be raised within three months.[24] Investigations were also set on foot to see if troops could be hired from Denmark, Hesse or Munster.[25]

The Dutch agreed to mobilise 60,000. However, they were ambiguous about the number that would actually join the field army. If the army assembled quickly and took up a position close to the French border, they would release a larger portion for the field army than if the army took up camp

---

22 Ibid., 49, Newcastle to Chesterfield, 23 April 1745; Browning, *The War of Austrian Succession*, op. cit., 196–197, 203–204.

23 Lodge, *Private Correspondence*, op. cit., 42–3, Chesterfield to Newcastle, 13 April 1745 (n.s.).

24 TNA, SP 87/16, f. 57, Ligonier to Harrington, 12 February 1745 n.s.

25 Ibid., f. 62, Ligonier to Harrington, 9 February 1745 (n.s.).

close to the Dutch borders.[26] Hanover would provide 23,000, although they would not necessarily join the Confederate Army. Instead, they would concentrate on the middle-lower Rhine to cooperate with the Austrian army. The Austrian army in Western Europe was over 32,000 strong, but the contingent in Flanders was limited to 6,000, exclusive of the troops paid for Britain. The rest were in garrisons through the eastern counties and Luxembourg, or had moved to the Rhine over the winter.[27] It was clear, therefore, that the field army was going to be much smaller than its paper strength. The French were rumoured to be putting into Flanders 100 battalions and 160 squadrons in the spring. Ligonier doubted that the allied army would amount to 73 battalions and 78 squadrons.[28]

It was vital to expand the field army. The Dutch were holding back a *corps de reserve* of about 20,000 in the Netherlands, capable of moving either to Flanders or Westphalia, and the British pressed for their release to Flanders. The Dutch countered by demanding that the King demonstrate his commitment to Flanders by sending the Hanoverian troops back to the Confederate Army. However, George retained ambitious, dangerous thoughts of invading Prussian territory, with which he teased Pelham, and refused to change the existing disposition of the Hanoverian forces on the Rhine.[29] Chesterfield urged the King to compromise. If the King would release three more regiments from England he felt sure the Dutch would reciprocate.[30] Eventually, the King agreed to release two regiments.[31] By late April the field army assembling around Brussels was still dangerously weak, but at least growing.[32]

During this period the question of command was finally settled. It was agreed that the Duke of Cumberland would have supreme command. The 71 year old Austrian Field Marshal Lothar von Kőnigsegg and the Dutch commander, the Prince of Waldeck were to be his advisors.[33] The other

26 Lodge, *Private Correspondence*, op. cit., p. 17–18, Chesterfield to Newcastle, 9 March 1745 (n.s.).
27 TNA, SP 87/16, f. 83, Memoire, Austrian Troops established in the Netherlands.
28 TNA, SP 87/16, f. 43, Allied Troops in the Low Countries, March 1745 n.s.; BL, Add Ms 32704 (Newcastle Papers), f. 157 Newcastle to Cumberland, 12 April 1745.
29 BL, Add Ms 32704, f. 72, Stone to Newcastle, 19 March 1744.
30 TNA, SP 87/16, f. 102, Cumberland to Harrington, 7 April 1745 n.s.
31 BL, Add Ms 32704, f.158, Newcastle to Cumberland, 12 April 1745.
32 TNA, SP 87/16, f. 137, Cumberland to Harrington, 23 April 1745 n.s.
33 BL, Add Ms 32704, f. 72, Stone to Newcastle, 19 March 1744.

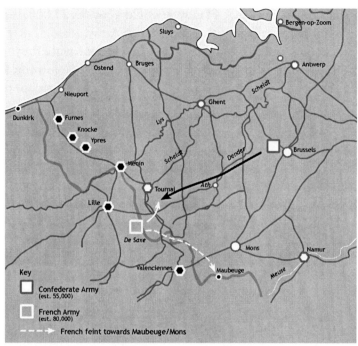

Map 10 Moves towards Fontenoy, May 1745

matter of importance was the artillery, particularly the siege train. This expensive and cumbersome equipment was vital for successful operations in Flanders. The Dutch could provide all the artillery requirements, but baulked at footing the bill. After weeks of negotiation Chesterfield managed to get the Dutch to accept responsibility for a third of all artillery costs and all the costs related to siege operations.[34]

Cumberland's instructions were signed on 4 April and on 10 April he arrived at Brussels where he met Kőnigsegg and Waldeck. The army was not up to strength yet, but it was agreed to assemble around Brussels over the next two weeks. Intelligence of the French suggested that Louis XV had set out to the east, where an army was concentrating to take Mons. Saxe was rumoured to be dying, but was preparing to take Maubeuge.[35] Suddenly, the intelligence reports altered, and it was confirmed on 17 April that the French had not gone east, but instead had moved north to invest Tournai. However, the French

34 Lodge, *Private Correspondence*, op. cit., 31–2, Chesterfield to Newcastle, 23 March 1745 (n.s.).

35 Royal Archive Windsor, Cumberland Papers Box 2 (mfl), 83, Cumberland to Harrington, 23 April 1745 (n.s.).

army was said to be only about 55,000 strong – not large enough to maintain a siege and a covering force. The attempt seemed a desperate expedient and the confederate commanders agreed that they should move immediately to counter it. By 22 April the army was on the move towards Tournai.[36]

Naval Preparations for the New Campaign and the Toulon Enquiry, January–May 1745

If attention in Britain was focused on a decisive campaign in Flanders it was partly a reflection of the collapse of faith in the naval war during 1744. From the beginning of the war, sea control rested on keeping the Bourbon squadrons apart. Before 1744 this was done by maintaining a close watch on Cadiz and Toulon, with supporting squadrons at Gibraltar and Hyères respectively. Periodically, Ferrol and Cartagena became additional centres for Bourbon naval forces, but until France entered the war as a principal, Brest and Rochefort were less important. The policy worked imperfectly from the beginning and the French declaration of war broke the fragile control that the British had established. The probe by the Brest squadron towards the Channel in September convinced the ministry that action now had to be taken to curb this squadron's liberty of movement and it was agreed that a force of twelve ships of the line be held ready for any further incursion.[37]

However, the success of this plan rested on the old problem of getting ships home from the Mediterranean. It had to be done carefully with Sardinian support. Initially, there was to be a shift in firepower and manpower rather than numbers of ships. Rowley was to send home his three 90s and one 80, to be replaced by the smaller ships *Ipswich* (70), *Jersey* (60) and *Torrington* (44), sailing under the command of Rear Admiral Henry Medley, who was escorting out a victualling convoy.[38] Before he left, Medley was to ensure that his own ships were fully manned and provisioned, so they did not drain

---

36   Ibid., 99, Fawkener to Harrington, 28 April 1745 (n.s.); 119, Fawkener to Newcastle, 30 April 1745 (n.s.). Wade was sure that the move on Maubeuge was a feint to draw the allies away from Ghent/Ostend. See 133, Poyntz to Fawkener, 23 April 1745.

37   Woburn Archive, Bedford Mss, ix, Wolters to Bedford, 28 December 1744; *Richmond-Newcastle Correspondence*, 163, Newcastle to Richmond, 18 March 1745.

38   TNA, SP42/28, f .18, Admty to Rowley, 15 March 1745; f. 14, Corbett to Stone, 17 March 1745; BL, Add Ms 35408, .f ?, Stone to Hardwicke, 15 March 1745. The 90s were *Neptune, Barfleur* and *Marlborough*, and the 80 was *Torbay*. See TNA, Adm8/24. The run-down in ship numbers started a little later. The *Elizabeth* (70), *Dragon* (60) and *Kennington* (20) were ordered home in April.

Rowley's already strained resources. The Brest squadron was still thought to be cruising somewhere to the west of the Straits so Medley was ordered to make a passage that would avoid this force and wait for further orders from Rowley when he reached Gibraltar.[39]

Relations with the Dutch squadron had also to be sorted out. In October 1744, the States General had agreed that the squadron should continue in British pay for 1745.[40] By 18 January the last 10 of the 20 ships in the Dutch squadron had arrived at Spithead, but again they carried only two months provisions aboard, which, in Admiral Grave's words, rendered the squadron 'a dead corpse'.[41] By the end of the month the States General were pressing for the return of the their ships, which the Admiralty urged the ministers to resist. By mid-February, a compromise was agreed and ten ships were sent home, while the others remained under Grave at Spithead victualled for a full four months.[42]

The gradual adjustments to the squadrons at home and in the Mediterranean could not immediately alter the naval situation. For the moment, the British remained reactive to Bourbon moves. Dunkirk and the Channel remained quiet, but elsewhere there was intense activity. The Brest squadron was around the Straits. The Spanish treasure fleet, escorted by Admiral de Torres from Havana, was expected at any day at Cadiz. Of the Toulon squadron 15–19 were reported at Cadiz, ready to sail to provide Torres with an escort home.[43] Other reports suggested that they were preparing to go to the West Indies.[44] The French West Indian islands were said to be suffering from the break down in trade. Provisions were scarce and hunger threatened. Dutch, Danish and Swedish ships were loading victuals at Cork, ostensibly for Curaçao, but the Admiralty was sure that they were going to the French islands where prices were now soaring. An embargo on foreign shipping was ordered at Cork on 14 February.[45]

Other disturbing news arrived from North America. French expeditions

39   East Yorkshire Record Office, Grimston Mss, DDGR 39/5B, Admty to Medley, 5 February 1745.

40   TNA, Adm 1/4114, unfoliated, Granville to the Admty, 19 October 1744.

41   TNA, Adm 1/3242, unfoliated, Grave to Admty, 27 March 1745 (n.s.).

42   Ibid, f. 46, Admty to Harrington, 30 March 1745; f. 64, Admty to Harrington, 22 February 1745.

43   Ibid., f. 22, Corbett to Stone, 22 March 1745.

44   Ibid., f. 52, Admty to Newcastle, 7 February 1745.

45   Ibid., f. BL, Add Ms, 32704, f. 81, W. Winthrope to Newcastle, 22 February 1745.

up the Mississippi from Louisiana were encroaching on the Virginia back-country.[46] At the end of 1744, news had arrived from Boston that the small garrison protecting the fishing station at Canso on Nova Scotia had been over-whelmed by French forces from Louisbourg. The French now posed an imme-diate threat to Annapolis Royal on the other side of the island and Governor Shirley of Massachusetts hurried reinforcements to that place.[47] Orders were sent to Captain Warren in the Leeward Islands to take ships northwards to assist in the defence of Annapolis.[48] However, far from remaining on the defensive, Shirley was planning to attack Louisbourg itself.[49]

By early February 1745 there were grounds for serious concern regarding the navy and the colonial war. Much of the anti-Hanoverian, anti-Flanders war rhetoric rested on the supposed effectiveness of naval war. Although it had lost its lustre and force within Parliament since 1739, it remained a tenet for the Patriot opposition. Some of those opposition members now held posts in government, but joined a meeting of 229 independent Westminster electors at Vinters' Hall on 15 February to reaffirm those beliefs. Among the toasts to constitutional reform and political virtue, the prosperity of the trade, the City, the Church and King, were others to Britain 'ungermanised', English liberties over German measures, and that 'the Fleet of England may be deemed the terror of Europe'.[50] The uncomfortable reality was that not only were the 'German' measures for a European war easily passing Parlia-ment, but the fleet was plainly not the terror of Europe. Not only were the disputes within the fleet at Toulon more obvious than ever, there were growing instances of dishonourable behaviour and alarm at naval affairs.

On 6 January 1745, Captain Thomas Griffin of the *Captain* (70) was leading a small force, the *Hampton Court* (70) (Captain Savage Mostyn), the *Dreadnought* (60) and *Sunderland* (60) off Ushant. They met two French

---

46   BL, Add Ms 32704, f. 97, Strachan to Newcastle, 12 February 1745; TNA, SP 42/28 (State Papers – Naval), f. 105, Admty to Newcastle, 11 March 1745.

47   TNA, Adm 1/4114, unfoliated, Shirley to Newcastle, 22 September 1744 (in Newcastle to Admty, 7 November 1744).

48   J. Gwyn (ed.), *The Royal Navy and North America: The Warren Papers, 1736–1752*, London, 1973, 44–46, Admty to Warren, 2 March 1744/5

49   C.H. Lincoln (ed.), *Correspondence of William Shirley, Governor of Massachusetts*, New York, 1912, I, 161–165, Shirley to Newcastle, 14 March 1744/5; 173–177, Shirley to the Admty, 29 March 1744/5; H. Richmond, *The Navy in the War of 1739–48*, ii, 200–210; J. Gwyn, *An Admiral for America: Sir Peter Warren, Vice Admiral of the Red, 1703–1752*, Gainsville, 2004, 61–63.

50   BL, Add Ms 32704, f. 75, Meeting at Vinters' Hall, 15 February 1745.

ships, the *Neptune* (74) and *Florant* (74) with a captured British privateer, the *Mars*. Griffin turned to chase the *Mars*, which, soon surrendered to him. The other warships went off after the retreating French warships, but although the *Hampton Court* got up to them and trailed them for over 24 hours Mostyn did not press an attack against the more heavily armed French ships. News of this meeting caused consternation in London. Griffin seemed to have taken the most powerful ship of the squadron to seize a privateer and Mostyn seemed to have failed in his duty to attack the French ships. No action was taken against Griffin and a court martial acquitted Mostyn of all charges. Nonetheless, it reinforced a popular impression of incompetence and cowardice.[51]

This particularly aroused Vice Admiral Vernon. Vernon was still a hero without equal among the Patriot groups and a determined advocate for a maritime war. He was an old friend of Mathews and was appalled by what he considered to be Admiralty disdain for the commander in the Mediterranean.[52] He had seconded the motion to enquire into the maritime war in April 1744 and was one of the prominent MPs present at Vinters' Hall in February 1745. Mostyn was a friend of the previous First Lord of the Admiralty, the Earl of Winchelsea, whom Vernon hated and his acquittal by court martial seemed to sum up for Vernon the moral collapse within the navy. Mostyn had been acquitted because his smaller ship would have engaged to windward of the enemy.[53] This judgement infuriated Vernon, who considered that it ignored the fighting tradition of the Royal Navy. He called upon the House of Commons to make an enquiry on a simple question: 'if their ships meet others of equal force, as the weather is the same for both, Did you fight or did you not? You may tell us this or that little Advantage; it is immaterial; the Honour of your Country not only requires you should fight, but conquer, and for the contrary will admit no Excuse. We know that at Sea Men of Resolution always conquer, at almost any Odds'.[54] In a comment also probably aimed at Griffin, who had already captured several prizes while

---

51   *Gentleman's Magazine*, February 1745, 105–106.

52   BL, Add Ms 40823, f. 109, Vernon to Mathews, 19 April 1744.

53   See the correspondence of Thomas and Savage Mostyn with Winchelsea in the Leicestershire Record Office, Finch Mss, Correspondence of the 3rd Earl of Nottingham, bundle 29 November 1732 to December 1749.

54   *An Enquiry into the Conduct of Captain M---n being the Remarks of the Minutes of the Court Martial and other Incidental Matters Humbly Addressed to the Hon. House of Commons by a Sea Officer*, London, 1745, 23.

cruising, he claimed that 'the scheme of Naval commanders is chiefly to get great Estates by taking such prizes from the Enemy as are easily conquer'd'. The only remedy was to make an example of those that failed in their duty, even dearest of friends, or the nation would fall. It was almost too late and action was urgently required.[55]

Although Vernon was an outspoken Patriot, whose opinion had been effectively ignored to date, he was reflecting a growing concern with the conduct of the maritime war. In April 1744 the Commons had been reluctant to enquire into the matter, but in February 1745, the mood had changed. On 26 February, Major Charles Selwyn moved for an enquiry into the miscarriages of the British fleet in the Mediterranean. It was seconded by Velters Cornewall, brother of Captain James Cornewall of the *Marlborough*, who had been killed at the battle of Toulon. The motion seems to have come as a surprise. The Old Corps and New Allies tried to deflect the debate by pointing out that the matter was under consideration by a court martial, but the feeling in the House was irresistible and it was agreed to refer the matter to a Committee of the Whole House, with Cornewall in the chair.[56]

The Committee opened on 12 March. Mathews gave a brief account of the failures of the four captains in his division and Lestock. Philip Yorke, the son of the Lord Chancellor, noted that Mathews was clearly trying to shift any responsibility from his own division to Lestock.[57] Unease with Mathews' behaviour was already apparent.[58] As the enquiry progressed, the focus widened from the two admirals to implicate the four captains more deeply.[59]

By 22 March the detail had exhausted the interest or understanding of many members, but the evidence had confirmed that many errors were made. Mathews, particularly, seems to have suffered from the probing of his behaviour in command. Mathews and Vernon were old friends, but Vernon now told Mathews, 'in plain English that he had committed a notorious blunder'.[60] The final witnesses were examined on 4 April, and Lestock produced a final paper on 9 April. Members had had some days to examine the correspondence between the Admiralty and Mathews, which demon-

---

55   Ibid., 26–27.

56   Corbett, *Parliamentary History*, op. cit., xiii (1743–1745), 1202–1243.

57   BL, Add Ms 35337, f. 97.

58   BL, Add Ms 35351, f. 57, P. Yorke to Hardwicke, n.d. (14 March 1745).

59   BL, Add Ms 35351, f. 58, P.Yorke to Hardwicke, n.d. (19 March 1745).

60   BL, Add Ms 35351, f. 60, P.Yorke to Hardwicke, 22 March 1745.

strated the rancour that existed between the men ever since Mathews had arrived in the Mediterranean. The question was: what to do now?

After some debate, Henry Fox moved to address George II to court martial the two admirals, six of the captains, and the lieutenants of the *Dorsetshire* (80).[61] A motion was made to remove Mathews from the address, supported by the naval officers Lord Grannard and Lord George Graham, who had supported Mathews throughout the enquiry. They argued that Mathews was being associated with those charged with cowardice. His crime, if any, was lack of judgment. For Vernon this was as bad as cowardice. Mathews' neglect was unforgivable. His 'want of conduct, remissness of discipline, gross marks of incapacity' demanded investigation. The vote against the amendment was overwhelming at 218 to 75.[62]

The poor performance of the navy did not develop into a party issue. It was axiomatic that maritime commerce was the source of wealth and it was naval power that preserved and stimulated it. However, the current war in Europe had shown that there were clear limits to naval power. For France to be defeated, it had to be done by armies in Europe. For this Britain had to engage with allies. This did not negate the basic principle that British influence and ability to act in Europe rested fundamentally on naval power. The events of 1744 indicated that naval power was slipping from British hands and without it, defence of home and trade, let alone offensive action against France and Spain, were impossible. It had taken four years, but the rhetorical assumptions of British naval power were being eroded by the realities of the war.

For everyone, the key questions were; why was it happening and how was it to be reversed? The deep cause might lie in the generalised, and often remarked upon, decline of virtue and the rise of corruption, but it was the performance of individuals that absorbed the enquiry. Discipline, punishment and reward ran throughout the enquiry. The end result was to demand courts martial and for the next fifteen months the navy was going to be convulsed by trials. In the meantime, there was a new promotion of flag officers. Balchen had been drowned in October and Sir Charles Hardy had

---

61   As well as Lestock, Mathews, the four captains of Mathews' division, Williams, Burrish, Norris and Ambrose, the address included Captain Dilk of the *Chichester* and Captain Frogmore of the *Boyne*, whom the evidence of 4 April from the officers of the *Salisbury* accused of engaging at too great a distance in Rowley's division at the van. See *Votes of the House of Commons*, 1744, 398.

62   BL, Add Ms 35351, f. 67, P. Yorke to Hardwicke, n.d. (10 April 1745).

died in November. Mathews and Lestock were now suspended pending their courts martial. Anson finally accepted flag rank, but the most important promotion was that of Edward Vernon to Admiral of the White. His central role in the enquiry made him stand out as the most senior officer determined to reform the navy and re-establish its power. Vernon had actively cultivated Bedford, who was won over to his vision of maritime power.[63] The Pelhams resisted, but Bedford was adamant. They could not resist Bedford's pressure for Vernon's promotion, but 'the Duke was told he would soon have cause for Repentance'.[64] Vernon now stood almost at the pinnacle of the profession, second only to Norris. Despite Newcastle's reservations, it would be difficult now to deny him an active command (Table 8.2).

The gradual shift of ships from the Mediterranean to the Channel accelerated during 1745 and the tasks for the coming campaign were emerging. As early as October 1744 rumours reached the Admiralty that French warships were preparing to go to Cape Breton. It was assumed that these were intended to convoy home six or seven French East Indiamen that were expected at Louisbourg.[65] However, the French warships could also take munitions and supplies to Louisbourg to support an attack on Annapolis Royal. It seemed that this was part of a wider shift in Franco-Spanish naval dispositions. Since the early autumn the Brest and Toulon squadrons had been operating around the mouth of the Strait. By September there were about 41 enemy ships of the line in those waters and Rowley redeployed his squadron westward, concentrating at Mahon. Although the French forces split up during the winter, Rowley was convinced that they would re-assemble in the spring. He kept his squadron together, operating westward towards Gibraltar, leaving only a small force under Captain Osborn to intercept Spanish and French movements along the Italian coast.[66]

Manpower was still extremely scarce. On 2 March the Admiralty had informed Harrington that the manpower situation was now 'insuperable'. Of a nominal complement of 20,000 for the home ships, cruisers and convoys,

---

63   Woburn Archive, Bedford Mss, ix, f. 118, Vernon to Bedford, 19 April 1745. In this letter Vernon told Bedford that he was using his influence at Trinity House to have Winchelsea rejected as a brother in favour of Bedford.

64   RA, Windsor, Cumberland Papers, Box 2, 229, H. Etough to Fawkener, 13 May 1745.

65   East Yorkshire Record Office, Grimston, DD/GR39/6, unfoliated, Corbett to Medley, 26 October 1744.

66   TNA, SP 42/96 (State Papers – Naval), f. 80, Rowley to Newcastle, 14 February 1744/5; f. 84, Rowley to Newcastle, 21 February 1744/5.

Table 8.2 Flag ranks (new flag ranks in italics), 23 April 1745

Admiral of the Fleet	Sir John Norris	In retirement
Admiral of the White	Thomas Mathews	Suspended
	Edward Vernon	Britain
Admiral of the Blue	Nicholas Haddock	In retirement/ill
	Sir Chaloner Ogle	West Indies
Vice Admiral of the Red	James Stewart	Port Admiral (Portsmouth)
	Thomas Davers	Britain/West Indies
	Hon George Clinton	Governor of New York
Vice Admiral of the White	*William Martin*	Britain
	William Rowley	Mediterranean
Vice Admiral of the Blue	*Henry Medley*	Mediterranean
	Issac Townsend	Britain
Rear Admiral of the Red	Richard Lestock	Suspended
	Lord Vere Beauclerk	Admiralty
Rear Admiral of the White	*George Anson*	Admiralty
Rear Admiral of the Blue	*Perry Mayne*	West Indies

Source Adm 6/16 .

only 15,000 could be found. The marines that had been used to supplement crews were now too dispersed to be drafted. The big three-deckers, the 90- and 100 gun-ships, had already been drained of men to supply the smaller warships on service.[67] Pressed men deserted to merchantmen and privateers as soon as they could.[68] The Board urged Harrington to request the King to put a foot regiment on the three-deckers. However, with the Dutch pressing for more regiments in Flanders, there were few soldiers available. The Dutch auxiliary squadron of ten ships remained at Portsmouth to support the British, where they did good work providing powerful escorts

67   TNA, SP42/28, f. 70, Admty to Harrington, 2 March 1744/5. It has been assumed that the figure of 20,000 nominal complement referred to in the letter was describing the manpower requirements of the home station and cruisers and convoys.

68   See, for example, Henry Medley's correspondence with the port admiral at Portsmouth, James Stewart. East Yorkshire Record Office, Grimston, DD/GR39/19 and DD/GR39/25. The problem of desertion was not confined to warships. Transports that put into port due to bad weather could find themselves disabled as seamen deserted to join privateers. See Grimston DD/GR39/6, unfoliated, Corbett to Medley, 13 March 1745.

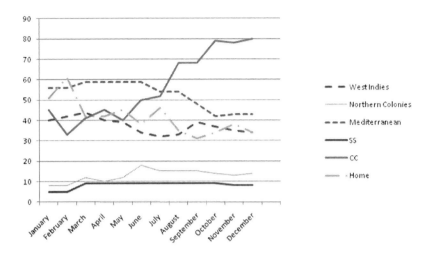

Figure 8.1 Ship dispositions,1745
Source TNA, Adm 8/24.

for coastal convoys to and from the North Sea, but continual confusion and obstruction over victualling and independent orders coming from the Netherlands made their deployment with the Royal Navy difficult.[69]

Nevertheless, the naval administration did manage to get a high percentage of ships at home ready for sea. Anson was nominated to command a small squadron to escort the King to Holland, while Vice Admiral Martin held the main battle fleet of six 70s and three 60s, cruising in the Western Approaches (Table 8.3).

Although none of the ministers committed their thoughts to paper, the importance of the coming campaign could hardly have been lost on them. The political settlement of November 1744 was still extremely fragile. The King had not given up Granville.[70] The Pelhams knew that in the longer term things could not go on.[71] Nevertheless, diplomatically, the allies had committed themselves to this final campaign. Reflecting on the situation from The Hague, Chesterfield felt that 'Things look well now everywhere and success in Flanders would be decisive'.[72]

---

69 TNA, Adm 1/3242, unbound, Grave to the Admty, 18 March 1744/5; Grave to Admty, 6 April 1745, SP 42/28, f. 188, Admty to Harrington, 3 April 1745. East Yorkshire Record Office, Grimston, DD/GR39/6, unfoliated, Corbett to Medley, 8 December 1744.

70 Newcastle to Chesterfield, 26 March 1744/5

71 BL, Add Ms 32704, f. 195, Newcastle to Cumberland, 3 May 1745.

72 Royal Archive, Windsor, Cumberland Papers, Box 2, f. 163, Chesterfield to Falkner, 11

Table 8.3 Distribution of the Fleet, spring 1745

	Home Nominal	Home Effective	West Indies	Med	North America	Cruisers Convoys
Line	20	17	12	28	2	1
Cruisers	10	6	15	18	10	17

Source: TNA Adm 8/24.

Crisis: Fontenoy

Late at night on Friday 3 May, as the King lay wind-bound at Gravesend, on his way to Hanover, the mail from Holland arrived in London. The secretaries found that there was nothing of particular note to report. However, shortly afterwards letters from Ostend reached their offices. Edward Weston, undersecretary at the Northern Department, opened a letter from the Duke of Cumberland's secretary, Sir Everard Fawkener. He reported blandly that there had been a battle in which the French held their ground.[73] However, as private letters rapidly spread the news through London, public concern and dejection mounted.[74] The Confederate Army had suffered a serious defeat at Fontenoy on 1 May, about 6 miles south east of Tournai. Although details were unclear, it was certain the British forces had suffered heavy casualties and the army was in retreat back to Ath. Newcastle received the despatches in the early hours of Saturday. He immediately sent news to the King, but the yacht had sailed. He had more luck with Hardwicke and it was agreed that the Lords Justices should meet on Monday 6 May.

It was some weeks before the full extent of the defeat was understood, but a general outline was soon known. In dismal, wet weather, the army, about 47,000 strong, advanced towards Tournai from Brussels, hoping to catch Saxe unprepared. On a slight ridge just north of the village of Fontenoy, they encountered the French army, supported by redoubts on each flank. Their right was anchored on the fortified village of Athion, on the Scheldt. Their left was covered by a wood, the Bois de Bary, and a couple of redoubts. Cumberland, Königsegg and Waldeck agreed that the British and Hanoverians would advance directly towards the centre of the French line. The Dutch on the allied left were to swing around the right of the French line

---

May 1745 (n.s.).

73   Royal Archive, Windsor, Cumberland Papers Box 2, f. 182, Weston to Falkner, 3 May 1745.

74   Ibid, f. 188, Sir William Yonge to Falkner, 5 May 1745.

and attack between Fontenoy and Athion. The battle opened at about 6.00 am on 1 May. The main advance by the British and Hanoverian infantry commenced up the slope at about 7.00 am. As they pressed on, they came under heavy fire from the redoubt and entrenchments. The cavalry, moving on the right of the infantry to cover their flank, was particularly badly handled and retired behind the line. The infantry moved on to the edge of the slope and awaited the Dutch attack on their left. The Dutch attack failed in the face of heavy fire. By 11 am both the left and right attacks had stalled. Two British battalions were sent to reinforce the Dutch for another attack, but this stalled as well and the Dutch withdrew.

At the same time as the second Dutch attack, Cumberland led the British and Hanoverian infantry forward. They advanced as far as Fontenoy village where they came within close range of the first line of French foot, which buckled and broke under volley fire. It was possible that the French centre would crumble, but Saxe took advantage of a pause in the British advance to mount a counter-attack. The attack of the French infantry was repulsed, but after another attempt to drive forward Cumberland realised that he could not break through this central position. At about 1 pm he ordered the infantry to retire down the slope. It was decided to fall back on Ath to reorganise. Total allied losses were 7,545. Thirty-two per cent of the British infantry that had engaged on the plain had been killed or wounded. The Hanoverians had suffered grievously as well. The Dutch on the left had not been so heavily engaged and lost about 6.5 per cent of their engaged force.[75]

The seriousness of the situation was clear. If the French followed up their victory by taking Tournai, the way was open for them to sweep across to Ghent and Ostend.[76] There were very few new troops left to prevent this movement (Table 8.4).[77]

Almost immediately in Britain the blame for the defeat fell upon the Dutch. Cumberland made it clear that the Hanoverians had been 'fellow labourers and fellow sufferers', but his silence regarding the Dutch was deafening. Hardwicke heard that the Dutch had only provided 12,000 men for the

---

75   Royal Archive, Windsor, Cumberland Papers, Box 2, f. 165, Cumberland to Harrington, 12 May 1745 n.s. The fullest account in English is still, F.H. Skrine, *Fontenoy and Great Britain's Share in the War of Austrian Succession, 1741–1748*, Edinburgh, 1906, 158–202.

76   BL, Add Ms 35408, f. 114, Hardwicke to Newcastle, 5 May 1745.

77   RA Windsor, Cumberland Papers, Box 2, f. 196, Harrington to Cumberland, 7 May 1745.

Table 8.4 Army disposition, May/June 1745

Squadrons/Batts	Home	Ireland	Flanders	Elsewhere
Horse	3		4	
Dragoon Gds	3	3	2	
Dragoons	6	2	6	
Foot Gds	3		3	
Foot	23	6	16	9

army, which if true was 'abominable'.[78] Nevertheless, they had to be encouraged to continue the campaign. Tournai had to hold on. Newcastle warned about publishing any aspersions on the Dutch; 'It was thought better to avoid anything that might create any uneasiness in so ticklish and necessary an Ally as the Republick is to us at present.'[79] The allies had to redouble their efforts. The British and Dutch had to reach agreement with Munster 'upon any terms' to supply troops to Luxembourg so that the Austrians would release forces from there to join the field army. Negotiations with Hesse had to be reopened as a matter of urgency.

The Lords Justices met on Monday 6 May. More British troops had to be sent. The third foot regiment that the King had refused to send to Flanders in April would be sent. Orders for regiments to embark for Nova Scotia were cancelled.[80] Reinforcements from London were ordered to bring the Guards battalions back up to strength. Drafts from Ireland would reinforce the foot. The arrangements for these movements were set in motion immediately.[81] As with the fleet, manpower for the army was becoming extremely scarce. The ministers recommended a proclamation to promise that any man who enlisted before 25 September should serve for only three years.

All this was to be communicated to the Dutch to encourage them to release their *Corps de Reserve* immediately to Flanders and put the rest of their troops on a war footing. They would be promised that the King would immediately negotiate for Hessian troops to reinforce the barrier and join negotiations for Munster troops.[82] The Dutch agreed to release five of the seven regiments in

78   BL, Add Ms 35408, f. 114, Hardwicke to Newcastle, 5 May 1745.

79   RA, Windsor, Cumberland Papers, Box 3, f. 212, Newcastle to Falkner, 10 May 1745.

80   Two regiments from the Gibraltar garrison were ordered to Cape Breton instead. See TNA, SP45/5, unfoliated, Mins of the Lords Justices, 23 May 1745.

81   TNA, SP 42/28, f.220, Admty to Newcastle, 11 May 1745.

82   TNA, SP 45/5, unfoliated, Minutes, 6 May 1745.

their *Corps de Reserve*, but insisted that Britain fulfil its promise for 40,000 troops and the Austrians send their regiments from Luxembourg as well.[83]

The campaign plan was in complete disarray, and the consequences of the catastrophe became increasingly clear over the next two weeks. Most dramatic and damaging was the news that Tournai had surrendered, which reached London on 21 May. The sudden surrender of the place came as a complete shock and as a consequence the Confederate Army could not cover both Ostend and Mons. Neither town was in a good condition for defence.[84]

The Confederate Army was in poor shape. The generals disagreed about the next move. The Dutch wanted to move to cover Mons, while Cumberland and Konigsegg favoured covering western Flanders. The allies were all demanding that the others fulfil their obligations. Despite Cumberland's entreaties for more troops it was clear that in the immediate future neither British nor German reinforcements would be adequate to rebuild the army.[85]

While the ministers contemplated the future in Flanders, more disturbing news arrived. A letter from the consul at Faro arrived on 21 May with news that a French squadron had been sighed off Cape St Vincent on 24 April heading north. This was the Toulon squadron that had come out of Cadiz and could be attempting to unite with the Brest squadron.[86] This could mean another invasion attempt. The Lords Justices met on Thursday 23 May. Admiral Martin was at sea in the western Channel with eight line of battle ships. He was ordered to look out of the approach of the French and cruise towards Brest and Rochefort for intelligence. Ships at home were to be got ready for sea and assemble at Spithead and the Downs. Admiral Vernon was given command of this force. Flanders now had to be viewed in a different light. Instead of more troops going to Flanders, British regiments had to come home (Table 8.5).[87]

---

83   Lodge, *Private Correspondence*, op. cit., 56–7, Chesterfield to Newcastle, 14 May 1745 (n.s.): RA Windsor, Cumberland Papers, Box 2, f. 206, Fagel to Konigsegg, 19 May 1745 (n.s.).

84   TNA, SP43/112, unfoliated, Newcastle to Harrington, 21 May 1745.

85   Ibid.; BL, Add Ms 32704, f.263, Cumberland to Newcastle, 20 May 1745 (n.s).

86   Ten French warships were known to be in Cadiz, believed to be covering the arrival and departure of trade and treasure ships. Rowley had moved to Mahon to cover their movements. Their move north was unexpected. TNA, SP42/96(State Papers – Naval), f. 84, Rowley to Newcastle, 21 February 1744/5.

87   TNA, SP 45/5, unfoliated, Mins of the Lords Justices, 23 May 1745.

Table 8.5 Location of naval forces, June 1745

Location	British Line of Battle	Franco-Spanish Line
West Indies	10	21
Mediterranean	35	23
Home/Channel	18	29

Source: TNA, SP 42/28, f. 359.

The Board of Admiralty reviewed the naval situation. North America had been secured. In February Warren had taken four men of war north to help defend Annapolis, despite opposition from the merchants and planters of Antigua. In March news arrived that a French squadron had gone to the West Indies. The critical waters now were the West Indies and the Channel. The Admiralty had reinforced the Leeward Islands station by two men of war and two more, the *Lennox* (70) and *Pembroke* (60), were standing ready. Warren was ordered to send back what forces he could spare without prejudice to operations in North America.[88] Nearly half the British line of battle was still in the Mediterranean, but Rowley refused to send more ships home, because he was watching for the possible return of the French squadron to Cadiz.[89] However, intelligence suggested that the French squadron from Cadiz was unlikely to be going back there. There was news that the Ferrol squadron would be ready for sea by mid-June. The French ships may go there, or one of the Biscay ports where it was thought they might unite with the Brest squadron and sail for the West Indies. If so, it posed a grave threat to Jamaica.[90] It was agreed that a large reinforcement under Vice Admiral Townshend should be sent urgently to the Caribbean, but because the invasion of the British Isles was also a possibility, the home station could not spare more than the *Lennox* and *Pembroke*. Townshend was ordered to take these two ships to Gibraltar to join five or six ships detached from Rowley's squadron for the West Indies.[91]

By mid-June, Britain had been forced on to the defensive in every theatre. The position in Flanders had collapsed. The Channel and the West Indies were under threat. In Italy, the stalemate had forced the ministry to conclude another subsidy treaty for £60,000 to keep Sardinia active in the war. The

88   TNA, SP 42/28, f. 250, Admty to the Lords Justices, 27 May 1745.

89   Ibid., f. 355, Admty to Lords Justices, 4 June 1745; f. 375, Corbett to Stone, 12 June 1745; f. 379, Orders to Rowley, 8 June 1745.

90   Woburn Archive, Bedford Mss x, f. 13, Vernon to Bedford, 10 June 1745.

91   Woburn Archive, Bedford Mss x, f. 10, Sandwich to Bedford, 6 June 1745.

news from Silesia was depressing. The Austro-Saxon army had been severely defeated at Hohenfriedburg (25 May) and the Prussian army was again moving towards Bohemia. The 1745 plan of campaign, upon which the Broad Bottom was based, was in ruins. Only in North America did an offensive option begin to emerge as news arrived of Governor Shirley's expedition from New England to Louisbourg.[92]

Newcastle, Pelham, Hardwicke and Chesterfield met, probably on the evening of 13 June, to discuss affairs. Things could not go on as they were. The French army in Flanders was at least twice as strong as the battered Confederate Army. The Austro-Saxon campaign in Silesia had ended in defeat. Getting more money for subsidies was problematic: £500,000 credit had already been granted and over £1.75 million in subsidies had not given the allies superiority in any theatre. A treaty for 6,000 additional Hessian troops with an option for 3,000 more, had been negotiated in Hanover. Pelham could get money in the form of loans, but the treaty had to be kept secret, particularly as the King was using the Hessians to avoid sending his Hanoverians to Flanders. In short, the only prospect for success was now an Austrian attack into Lorraine, but there was little chance of this while the Prussians were in Bohemia. If Prussia could be conciliated, the Prussian electoral vote might be secured for Maria Theresa's husband and 40–50,000 Austrian troops released for service on the Rhine.[93]

From London this looked like the only reasonable course of action, but in Hanover the King took a different view. He was worried that the Elector of Saxony would call on Hanover for assistance, bringing about a Hanoverian-Prussian war. This fear lay behind his reluctance to release Hanoverian troops for Flanders He wanted to force Prussia to come to terms with Austria as quickly as possible.[94] Harrington did his best both to accommodate the King's desire to curb Prussian power and to make him recognise that Vienna had to make concessions. He succeeded in neither. In the deadlock and confusion, Hardwicke confessed to his son, 'I have been long of opinion for taking that weight (Prussia) out of the scale of France, upon some terms or other, God knows how it will be brought about.'[95]

---

92   TNA, SP 42/28, f. 361, Admty to Newcastle, 9 June 1745.

93   BL, Add Ms 32704, f. 387, Newcastle to Harrington, 14 June 1745; TNA, SP 43/113 (State Papers – Regencies), unfoliated, Newcastle to Harrington, 14 June 1745 (private).

94   BL, Add Ms 32704, f. 419, Harrington to Newcastle, 4 July 1745 (n.s.) (rec 29 June).

95   BL, Add Ms 35351, f. 72, Hardwicke to P. Yorke, 22 June 1745.

Ostend and the Collapse of the Flanders Policy, July–August 1745

By the end of June the foundations of the 1745 campaign had been shattered.[96] Worse, the confidence of the allies in each other had been severely damaged.[97] Cumberland knew that Saxe could now turn in any direction. He and Kőnigsegg agreed that the most likely avenue of the French advance would be towards Brussels or Ostend and Antwerp. Accordingly, the army fell back towards Brussels, but Waldeck and many in The Hague were infuriated that Mons was being left to its own devices.[98]

By late June it was clear that Cumberland and Kőnigsegg were right and the French were advancing towards Ghent. A relief force was sent under General Molke. Molke got through with a portion of the force, but was unable to prevent the town falling to the French. Molke escaped with some Hanoverian horse and hussars, aiming to rejoin the army. However, with the war reaching their own borders, the Dutch were now in a state of intense anxiety and refused Molke passage through Dutch territory. Molke turned about and sought shelter in Ostend. This additional loss to his army exasperated Cumberland; 'a Passage through this Place could not have been with Decency refused to a neutral Prince and that even the Turks gave an hospitable reception to the King of Sweden'.[99] On 3 July news reached London that Ghent had fallen, the French had closed in on Ostend, and Bruges was under threat.

There was panic in Brussels as citizens and the Austrian administration made preparations to evacuate the city. In Antwerp they expected the French to arrive soon.[100] If Ostend fell, the shortest communication route from London to the army would be cut. A staging point for French invasion of Britain and another nest of privateering would be created. It was known that the defences were in a dreadful state and the best defensive measure would be to open the sluices and flood the surrounding countryside. This was begun on the night of 29/30 June, but as soon

---

96   RA, Cumberland Papers, Box 3, f. 133, Konigsegg to Harrington, 26 June 1745 (n.s.); BL, Add Ms 32704, ff. 438–439, Cumberland to Newcastle, 11 July 1745 (n.s.).

97   RA, Cumberland Papers, Box 3, f. 80, Pelham to Cumberland, 11 June 1745.

98   RA, Cumberland Papers, Box 3, f. 114, Trevor to Falkner, 29 June 1745 (n.s.).

99   RA, Cumberland Papers, Box 3 (microfilm 4), f. 203, Cumberland to Harrington, 19 July 1745 (n.s.). Quotation f. 205, Fawkener to Trevor, 17 July 1745 (n.s.). When Ghent fell, the Royals and the Welch Fusiliers were made prisoners, although Quarter Master Moses Ketley managed to rally 100 of Rich's dragoons and escape with them to Antwerp. See f. 166, T. Orby Hunter to Fawkener, 13 July 1745 (n.s.).

100 RA, Cumberland Papers, Box 3, f.207, Hunter to Fawkener, 19 July 1745 (n.s.).

as Count Kaunitz, who had taken over the government of the Austrian Netherlands, heard about it in Brussels, he ordered the sluices closed, which stunned the
British.[101]

Further blows were to follow. The sole remaining hope for the campaign
lay in reinforcements from Prince Charles' army in Bohemia. Although the
French still had an army in Germany under the Prince de Conti, the Austro-
Bavarian peace shifted the balance of force to Austria and made possible the
release of troops to Flanders. This hope was based on the assurance from
Vienna that their army was superior to the French. With Austrian control
secured in Western Germany it was expected that the imperial election
could be quickly held and Duke Francis elected Holy Roman Emperor.
The Austrian troops could then begin their march westwards to the Rhine.
However, two very disturbing bits of news arrived from Hanover on 9 July.
Harrington had discovered that the Austro-Saxon army in Bohemia was far
smaller than he had been led to believe and that it was the French who were
detaching forces from Germany to reinforce Saxe in Flanders.

The situation in Italy was also deteriorating. Genoa had made a treaty with
the Bourbons, which gave the latter secure access to Northern Italy and a reinforcement of 10,000 troops and heavy artillery for their campaign.[102] The Austro-
Sardinian army was already beginning to give ground under pressure and any
Austrian forces freed from Germany were likely to be directed there rather than
Flanders or the Rhine. The discovery that the Austrians had been deceiving the
British over the size of their army in Bohemia was a huge shock and indicated to
the ministry in London that effective military collaboration with Austria in Flan-
ders was becoming a remote possibility.[103]

On the night of 3 July, as soon as the news of the fall of Ghent arrived, the
Lords Justices of the Regency met to consider Ostend. With them were Lord
Vere Beauclerk and George Anson of the Admiralty. Ostend was 'the key of
Flanders'. The garrison consisted of about 2,100 troops. They were short of
provisions, had very little artillery and only six gunners to serve them.[104]

101 TNA, SP 43/114, unfoliated, Newcastle to Harrington, 19 July 1745.

102 TNA, SP 43/114, unfoliated, Harrington to Newcastle (secret), 9 July 1745.

103 BL, Add Ms 32704, f. 486, Newcastle to Harrington, (very private), 12 July 1745.

104 TNA, SP 43/114, unfoliated, Newcastle to Trevor, 12 July 1745. There were 1,080
    British, 430 Dutch and 200 in garrison under Baron Chanclos. On the state of the artil-
    lery see RA, Cumberland Papers, Box 3, f. 240, Newcastle to Cumberland, 12 July 1745;
    f. 283, Major Rainsford to Fawkener, 27 July 1745.

The Earl of Stair presented a memorial.[105] He believed that the town could be reinforced, but the rest of the Regents were not convinced. If, as Stair suggested, two Guards battalions, were sent, the entire garrison in Britain would consist of one battalion of Guards, nine regiments of foot, seven regiments of dragoons and three of horse. All the foot, apart from the Guards, would be battalions recruited since being devastated in the West Indies, or regiments raised in 1741 without campaign experience. It was considered likely that Cumberland would have to fall back to Antwerp and it was hoped that he could send five or six regiments to the town by river. The Lords Justices doubted that the troops could be evacuated from Ostend by sea if the French made a close siege. However, it was agreed to hold two battalions ready and to send Colonel Edward Braddock over to make a thorough reconnaissance. It was also agreed, as a precaution, to hold transports for 1,600 troops ready to evacuate the town.

The other matter under consideration was defence against invasion from Flanders. Beauclerk and Anson assured the Lords Justices that the seven three-deckers then in commission could be manned and brought to the Downs within the week. This would be enough to prevent any large warships covering an invasion from Flanders. These ships could be manned by taking the seamen from the ships due to depart of the West Indies and the Mediterranean. They also undertook to man as many frigates and sloops as possible, without interfering with the present convoy arrangements, to stand by to intercept smaller craft carrying troops and supplies. Overall command of this force would be given to Vernon.[106]

The Regents met again on 11 July. The Admiralty reported that Vernon's squadron and the transports would be ready soon. A report from Ostend highlighted an urgent need for small arms, so 300 muskets were added to the stores to be sent. However, Bedford and Wade concluded that the seaward approach was not secure if the French set up batteries on the coast. Despite Stair's objections, the Lords Justices decided to hold two battalions

105 RA, Cumberland Papers, Box 3, f. 186, Stair to the Lords Justices, 4 July 1745.

106 Woburn Archive, Bedford Mss, x, ff. 21–23, Sandwich to Bedford, 4 July 1745; TNA, SP 43/113, unfoliated, Newcastle to Harrington, 4 July 1745; BL, Add Ms 32704, f. 461, Newcastle to Harrington, (private) 5 July 1745: TNA, SP42/29, f.13, Corbett to Stone, 9 July 1745. The Admiralty also prepared transports for two battalions in case they were to be sent to Ostend. RA, Cumberland Papers, Box 3, f. 197, Navy Board to James Wallace, 5 July 1745.

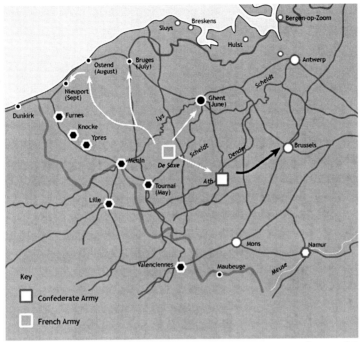

Map 11 De Saxe's move through Flanders, June–September 1745

ready, but encourage Cumberland to reinforce the garrison from his army.[107] Cumberland gave them no encouragement His focus was now on defending Antwerp, even at the cost of Brussels, and he would not guarantee sending troops.[108]

The key to resolving this crisis lay, as ever, in Berlin and Vienna. British support of Maria Theresa had done something to wipe away the stain of abandoning the Grand Alliance in 1712.[109] Nevertheless, the crisis was shifting opinion and there was now a consensus that if Austria would not give up Silesia, Britain would have to make terms with France and if this happened, the war would be over for the United Provinces and Austria as

---

107 TNA, SP 43/114, unfoliated, Report to the Lords Justice, 11 July 1745.

108 RA, Cumberland Papers, Box 3, f. 264, Cumberland to Newcastle, 14 July 1745 (n.s.); f. 272, Cumberland to Newcastle, 26 July 1745 (n.s.); f. 26, Carr and Scott to Ligonier, 25 July 1745 (n.s.).

109 BL, Add Ms 35396, f. 302, P.Yorke to T. Birch, 6 August 1745. Thomas Birch is an important observer of events in London at this time. For an overview of his life, see, A.E. Gunther, *An Introduction to the Life of the Rev. Thomas Birch D.D., F.R.S, 1705–1766*, Halesworth, 1984.

well – the spectre of 1712 could not be more clear.[110] As Newcastle wrote to Harrington, peace with Prussia 'is the universal opinion of every mortal that thinks or talks on the subject'. Austria had lost all credit and the general cry was that Flanders was being abandoned for other interests in Silesia and Italy.[111]

The problem was that the King in Hanover, supported by his Hanoverian ministers, preferred to reach an agreement with France that would leave Prussia isolated.[112] Harrington wrote despairingly of his attempts to get George to change his mind.[113] The British ministers were sure that Austria would accept terms based on the 1742 Treaty of Breslau, but the King was equally certain Maria Theresa would never accept it. On 27 July Newcastle urged Harrington to persuade the King to come home. While negotiations were taking place in Hanover, the ministry had no authority or influence. Either they must have this authority or they must resign. Harrington understood the problem and replied that George feared that an agreement with Prussia would cause an absolute break with Austria, but

> I have laid hold of every occasion of late of inculcating into the King the absolute necessity in the present circumstances of things that he should have an Administration vested with his confidence and authority and that the world should plainly see it, he has heard me with great respect and coolness upon that subject and said his servants should have no reason to complain of him on his return upon that head.[114]

Although the message seemed to be getting through, forcing the King to choose between his ministers and Austria caused great tension. Newcastle and Henry Pelham were divided on whether to force the Prussian treaty or not. In the end Newcastle's view predominated, and, at last, on 22 August, the ministers heard that Harrington had reached agreement with Andrié, the Prussian minister. By the Convention of Hanover, Britain was committed to work towards getting Austria to accept terms based of the Treaty of Breslau.

---

110 TNA, SP 43/114, unfoliated, Newcastle to Harrington, (secret), 19 July 1744.

111 BL, Add Ms 32704, f. 512, Newcastle to Harrington, 19 July 1745 (private).

112 Dann, *Hanover and Britain*, op. cit., 69.

113 BL, Add Ms 32704, f. 453, Harrington to Newcastle, 14 July 1745 (n.s.).

114 BL, Add Ms 32704, f. 527, Newcastle to Harrington, 26 July 1745; BL, Add Ms 32705, f. 10, Harrington to Newcastle, (Private), 15 August 1745 (n.s.).

George left Hanover on 24 August, unconvinced that Austria could be persuaded, and everyone suspected his compliance was dictated purely by the immediate situation.[115]

Louisbourg and the Royal Navy

Since 1739 the public had been aware that Britain was fighting a war with two potential theatres; Europe and America. However, since 1741 the War of Austrian Succession had shifted attention from Spain to France and the need to control her ambitions in Europe. Although this tangled opinions up with hostility to Hanoverian perversions of policy, it was generally accepted that France had to be restrained by supporting Austria. The fate of the Anglo-Spanish disputes would be determined by the defeat of France. No large reinforcement of forces in the West Indies was despatched after 1741. Commodore Knowles' defeat at La Guaira and Caracas in 1743 was greeted with disappointment rather than serious concern.[116] The Spanish attacks on Georgia of 1740 and 1742 had been driven off, as had the Georgian counter-invasion of Florida. Neither side had the force to make a decisive attack on the key centres of population.[117] However, war with France in February 1744 re-opened the prospect of a colonial war. French privateers immediately began to infest European and American waters.[118] On land, French forces sallied out of Louisbourg, captured Canso and threatened to go on to Annapolis. The East India Company was aware of French intentions to establish naval supremacy in eastern waters and in April 1744 four

---

115 Ibid., f. 31, Newcastle to Hardwicke, 11 August 1745.

116 J Oglesby, 'The British Attacks', op. cit., 27–40. News of the failure arrived at a time when the anti-Hanover disputes were raging, but as a case it did not serve either side in the controversy well. See also *A Journal of the Expedition to La Guaira*, London, 1744.

117 J.T. Lanning, 'American Participation in the War of Jenkins' Ear', *Georgia Historical Quarterly*, xi (1927), 191–215; J. Leitch-Wright, *Anglo-Spanish Rivalry in North America*, Georgetown, 1971); P. Spalding, *Oglethorpe in America*, Chicago, 1977. The southern frontier stretching from the Carolinas and Georgia to Louisiana was generally too sparsely populated and complicated by powerful native Indians disputes for Europeans to conduct extensive campaigns. Generally, the French managed their relations with the Indians better than the British throughout the period. See N.W. Caldwell, 'The Southern Frontier during King George's War', *Journal of Southern History*, vii (1941), 37–54.

118 A.P. Middleton, 'The Chesapeake Convoy System, 1662–1763, *William and Mary Quarterly* (3rd series), ii (1946), 182–207, especially, 192–4.

ships of the line were sent to India under Commodore Curtiss Barnett.[119] Barnett's despatch was a signal that the French global trade network was vulnerable. Small forces could inflict disproportionate damage. Louisbourg and the French West Indian islands relied on food stuffs imported from Europe, including Ireland. If these supplies were cut off, then the economic value of the islands would decline rapidly, even if they were not practically starved into submission.

By the middle of 1745, there was evidence to suggest that this maritime policy was having a significant effect, Successes at sea suggested that the French had been caught out badly. The French war had certainly seen a surge in British privateering commissions and a tactical evolution in the deployment of privateers, as groups of merchants banded together to send out 'squadrons' into the North Atlantic, which achieved some spectacular results.[120] Nearly 700 French and Spanish ships were said to have been taken between March 1744 and April 1745, amounting to almost £5 million sterling in value.[121] By August news arrived that Barnett's small force had wrecked the French East India trade.[122]

In March the ministry responded to French threats to Annapolis by preparing troop reinforcements for North America and ordering Commodore Warren to assist Shirley. In June news that Governor Shirley was mounting an expedition to Louisbourg arrived. Throughout the month there were rumours of action and on 17 July came confirmation that Canso had been recaptured. Three days later, Captain Montagu of the *Mermaid* (8) arrived in London with Warren's despatches. Warren announced that Louisbourg had fallen on 17 June to a force of about 4,000 New England volunteer soldiers, supported by Warren with four 60s, one 50, five 40s and some smaller ships.[123]

---

119 C.H. Philips, 'The Secret Committee of the East India Company', *Bulletin of the School of Oriental and African Studies*, x (1939–1942), 299–315.

120 Starkey, *British Privateering*, op. cit., 129–130, 138. The French merchant marine was caught off guard as prizes for the war peaked 1744–1745. Privateering activity in the Caribbean also peaked in these years. See, Swanson, *Predators and Prizes*, op. cit., 135. The total prize figures are very difficult to establish. Starkey notes two estimates ranging from 857 to 1246 (see. Starkey, *British Privateering*, op. cit., 137).

121 BL, Add Ms 35396, f. 228, T. Birch to P. Yorke, 1 June 1745.

122 BL, Add Ms 35396, f. 305, T. Birch to P. Yorke, 10 August 1745; *Gentleman's Magazine*, xv (August 1745), 427.

123 For the operations see, J.S. McLennan, *Louisbourg: From its Foundations to its Fall, 1713–1758*, New York, 1918 (abridged reprint, 1957), 128–180; G.S. Graham, *Empire of*

The ministry, absorbed by the crisis in Flanders and rumours of a landing in Scotland by the Young Pretender, made little comment initially. It was four days before the guns at Tower Hill were fired in celebration and the event reported in the *Gazette*. However, for the public on both sides of the Atlantic it was electric. Enthusiastic celebrations erupted on both continents and it instantly reopened the question of a maritime war.[124] For some it was essential that the city be handed over to the captors, like other prizes, so that it would be out of the power of the government to return it to France.[125] To others, tying the hands of government was unacceptable, but it should, nonetheless, be retained at a peace. Gaining Louisbourg seemed to have eliminated the greatest threat to British commerce and fisheries in the North Atlantic. The failure of the ministry to celebrate the conquest raised suspicions that they were absorbed by Hanoverian concerns and were unhappy about the event. Rifts within government began to appear.[126] The First Lord of the Admiralty, Bedford, who had championed a maritime war before joining government, and whose department was most closely concerned with it, was congratulated by Pitt on this 'national success' and he was urged by another not to give it up.[127] At this point it was critical that the town remained in British hands and two regiments were ordered from Gibraltar to reinforce the garrison of American provincials.[128]

Bedford was delighted that the navy had proved that it could cooperate with an army to deliver a victory. Warren, like Anson the previous year, became

the *North Atlantic: The Maritime Struggle for North America*, Oxford, 1958, 122–142; Gwyn, *An Admiral for America*, op. cit., 75–99.

124 Although a distinct American view can be seen in some stories concerning the war, particularly the West Indian expedition of 1740–1742, the colonial press presented a picture of world events little different from that in British newspapers. Much of the information was taken from London newspapers. See W.B. Johnson, 'The Content of American Colonial Newspapers Relative to International Affairs, 1704–1763', unpublished PhD thesis, University of Washington, 1962, 195–258. See the *Gentleman's Magazine*, xiv (1745) August and September for a series of articles on the value of Louisbourg and Cape Breton.

125 *Gentleman's Magazine*, xv (1745), 421–422 (*Westminster Journal*, 3 August 1745) The motion in the City of London Court of Aldermen on petitioning the King not to give it up was lost.

126 BL, Add Ms 35396, f. 298, T. Birch to P. Yorke, 27 July 1745.

127 Woburn Archive, Bedford Mss, x, f.33, Pitt to Bedford, 2 August 1745; 37, Leicester to Bedford, 2 August 1745.

128 TNA, SP 42/29, f. 71, Osborne to Stone, 14 August 1745.

a national hero.[129] It came at an opportune moment. The reputation of the navy remained poor as events piled on each other, diminishing 'the credit of a Fleet whose conduct has been the disgrace of our Naval power'.[130] Confidence in the valour and competence of naval officers remained low as the materials and witnesses for the Mathews and Lestock courts martial began to arrive in London. Confidence in Rowley's command had been disintegrating since the beginning of the year. Despite Commodore Osborne cruising with thirteen men of war, three Spanish register ships, carrying 700,000 pieces of eight had got into Cadiz. The Toulon squadron had got out of Cadiz.[131] In the Eastern Atlantic, five French men of war with three Spanish warships were at Ferrol. Later in the month it was discovered that a force of French warships was gathering at the Biscay ports, intended to escort a large convoy of merchantmen westwards.

Worse than this apparent loss of control, was the apparent failure of discipline. Rowley's lenient treatment at the court martial of Captain Richard Norris, son of Sir John Norris, scandalised the Admiralty. On 23 June Lieutenant Baker Philips of the *Anglesea* (40) was convicted of cowardice at court martial on the *Duke* (90). He was shot on board the *Princess Royal* at Spithead on 19 July.[132] The Rev. Thomas Birch noted that the fleet was in poor condition to resist a serious Franco-Spanish invasion attempt, but that 'even if we had equal force, the late conduct of our Sea Officers would make us uneasy for the event, But I hope that the approaching court martial will restore Discipline to our Fleets and am glad that the day for their sitting has been fixed'.[133] The lack of active flag officers was remedied in early August when Warren and the Hon. John Byng were appointed Rear Admirals of the Blue. This rewarded Warren and put a flag command in North America. Byng, who had returned from commanding at Newfoundland had a reputation as a sound, if untried, commander.[134]

---

129 Ibid., 27, Bedford to Harrington, 26 July 1745.

130 BL, Add Ms 35396, f. 287, P. Yorke to T. Birch, 13 June 1745; f. 298, T. Birch to P. Yorke, 27 July 1745

131 TNA, SP 43/113, unfoliated, Cayley to Newcastle, 15 June 1745 (n.s.); SP43/114, unfoliated, Cayley to Newcastle, 15 June 1745; 16 June 1745 (n.s.), 22 June 1745 (n.s.).

132 *Gentleman's Magazine*, xv 1745, 385. On the death of the captain, Philips had struck the colours while in battle with a French privateer.

133 BL, Add Ms 35396, f. 314, T. Birch to P. Yorke, 31 August 1745.

134 J. Charnock, *Biographica Navalis*, London, 1796, vol. iv, 145, 187. Warren's commission is dated 9 August and Byng's 8 August. Byng is described by an anonymous corre-

On 15 July Harrington reported intelligence of a French invasion plan. Two weeks later intelligence from Rotterdam indicated that 6,000 Spanish troops had been marched to Ferrol to embark for an invasion of Great Britain.[135] There appeared to be two simultaneous invasions planned; from the Channel ports to the South coast, and another from the Biscay ports to Ireland or the west of Britain. Vernon was ordered to bring as many ships together in the Downs or Spithead as possible and await further instructions. Martin, cruising out in the Western Approaches, was ordered to cruise from Brest to Rochefort for intelligence. Orders for Rowley's recall had been agreed on 15 July. He was ordered to hand command over to Henry Medley and bring whatever ships he could home with him. With this shift of Bourbon forces to the Atlantic, the war in the western Mediterranean became less critical and Medley was instructed to go east immediately to assist the Austro-Sardinian forces and attack Genoa.[136]

Throughout July the urgency of the situation increased, but there was a limit to the Admiralty's ability to react. The number of ships available was largely fixed over the summer period. Twenty ships of the line could be deployed in home waters. Martin had all the available 70s with him. There were two 80s. The *Devonshire* (80) was at Woolwich and the *Shrewsbury* (80) at Spithead. The only 60 available was the *Nottingham* at Sheerness. Once again the first rates, the 100- and 90-gun ships, had to prepared, which, as usual, put a major strain on available manpower. Five were at sea by the beginning of August, but the Admiralty had scraped the barrel to achieve this and requested a new proclamation to press to boys under 18 and men over 50 (Table 8.6).[137]

---

spondent to Bedford as 'complete an officer as any in the Navy, endowed with a great many virtues, and has been properly trained up from the cradle, his sweet disposition gets him the good will of everybody, and I flatter my self, he wont loose it by any promotion'. See Woburn Archive, Bedford Mss, ix, f. 108, MJ to Bedford, 16 March 1744/5. Nevertheless, Byng had already made some enemies as his career progressed. See C. Ware, *Admiral Byng: His Rise and Execution*, Barnsley, 2009, 25–27. I am grateful to Mr Ware for giving me sight of the manuscript prior to publication.

135 TNA, SP42/29, Intelligence from Brest, 12 June 1745 (n.s.); SP 43/114 (State Papers Regencies), unfoliated, Harrington to Newcastle, 2 August 1745 (n.s.). Intelligence from Brussels suggested that the two invasions were planned to occur together – the French in Britain and the Spanish in Ireland. See RA Windsor, Cumberland Papers, Box 4, Extract of a letter to Bedford, Brussels, 5 August 1745 (n.s.).

136 TNA, SP 43/114), unfoliated, Newcastle to Rowley, 27 July 745; Newcastle to Medley, 27 July 1745; Newcastle to Birtles, 27 July 1745.

137 TNA, SP 42/28, f. 55, Admty to the Lords Justices, 1 August 1745.

Table 8.6 Ships nominally ready for service, July–September 1745

Guns	July			August			September		
	At Sea	Martin	In Port	At Sea	Martin	In Port	At Sea	Martin	In Port
100			2	1		1	1		1
90			5	4		1	4		1
80			2	1		2			2
70		6			6			6	
60	2	2		2	1	1	2	2	1
50	4			3		1	4		1
44/40	6			6		2	8		2
24/20	12			11			13		
Others	20		10	33		9	28		12

Source: TNA Adm 8/24.

Commodore Smith commanded a small force of ships off Ostend, but Bedford pinned his hopes on Vernon to command the battle squadron assembling at the Downs.[138] Vernon, however, wanted a different plan. He argued that Admiral Martin should be recalled to the Lizard where Vernon would join him with the seven first rates and as many of the Dutch auxiliary squadron as could be mustered.[139] Vernon would then assume command of the whole fleet to cruise in the Soundings to protect trade and be ready for the Franco-Spanish squadrons should they come north. If an attempt from the Channel ports looked imminent, ships could be detached to cover that area. This was accepted by Bedford and the Lords Justices. However, 10 days later, on 14 August, Vernon was still at Spithead manning his ships and none of the Dutch ships were ready for sea. That evening the Regents received the news that Martin was back at Plymouth with half of his squadron. He had not received the orders to fall back to the Lizard and had left the other half of his squadron 20 leagues to the south west of the Scillies.

Vernon's desire to cruise with the whole fleet westward had been accepted only with reluctance. The importance of protecting trade was understood. Both the West Indies and the East Indies trade were due to return shortly. The East India Company, particularly, was concerned that seven French men of war from Brest were lurking to the west of Ireland. They feared that Vernon would not take the fleet far enough west to protect them. The Regents were concerned that Vernon would go so far west that Franco-Spanish forces coming up from the south-west, would have a free passage up the Channel. The Regents and the Board of Admiralty agreed that the East India convoy must be covered, but that sufficient force must be left in the Channel to deter invasion. Vernon was ordered to take the *St George* (90) and the *Sandwich* (90) with the Dutch auxiliaries to the Downs, where he would join the *Royal George* (100), *Duke* (90) and *Prince George* (90).[140]

Vernon obeyed, but protested that it was not the place of such a force. The ships were too large for the narrow, shallow waters of the Channel and North Sea. The Dutch were not ready to move and there were no 44s available to support the large ships. Vernon had an excellent grasp of the operational situation. He had commanded a ship during the Jacobite invasion attempt in 1708 and knew that heavy warships could not stop clean cruisers slip-

---

138 Woburn Archive, Bedford Mss x, 27, Bedford to Harrington, 26 July 1745.

139 *Richmond-Newcastle Correspondence*, 163, Newcastle to Richmond, 3 August 1745.

140 Woburn Archive, Bedford Mss x, f. 45, Legge to Bedford, 15 August 1745.

ping past. However, he also had a volatile temper and badly bruised pride. Instead of commanding the main fleet at a decisive point, he had a badly formed squadron, acting as a final barrier between Britain and invasion. He wrote constantly to Bedford and Thomas Corbett pointing out their errors, Martin's incapacity and urged a return to his plan.[141] What he did not grasp was the lack of confidence there was at the Admiralty and among the Regents. From the autumn of 1744 the Royal Navy had been wrong-footed. They had not succeeded in stopping a single significant movement of the Franco-Spanish squadrons. The force in home waters was still dangerously small and matters were moving towards crisis. Furthermore, some of the Regents had little confidence in Vernon himself. With Ostend on the verge of surrender, a small, but powerful squadron in the Channel, supported by small ships to intercept an invasion flotilla, provided more re-assurance than an unpredictable admiral cruising out to westward with almost the entire force from home waters. Vernon was right that the three deckers were inappropriate, but they were equally inappropriate for protecting the in-bound convoys. Having them close to the Medway dockyards in the winter was a good as having them at Spithead or Plymouth.

At the end of August, the disposition of the major units of the fleet in home waters was as displayed in Table 8.7.

The King and the Jacobite Rebellion

Ever since the invasion threat of February 1744, the government had been on a high state of alert over a potential Jacobite rising. Intelligence had been diligently gathered, but nothing concrete turned up until July. At the end of that month rumours reached London that Charles Edward Stuart, the elder son of the Pretender, James Stuart, had left Nantes. Two days later there was news of a battle at sea. On 9 July Captain Peircy Brett of the *Lion* (60) had encountered two French ships, the *Elizabeth* (60) and the *Du Teillay* (16), west of the Lizard. Brett bore down on the *Elizabeth*, whose decks were crowded with soldiers. For five hours the two ships fought, until, with so much damage to her masts and rigging, the *Lion* was unable to prevent the *Elizabeth* sheering away. Brett and over 100 of his crew were wounded. Forty-five were dead. The French ship had suffered badly as well, with over

---

141 Ranft, *The Vernon Papers*, op. cit., 450, Vernon to Corbett, 16 August 1745; 451, Vernon to Corbett, 17 August 1745; 454, Vernon to Bedford, 28 August 1745; 522, Vernon to Sandwich, 16 November 1745.

Table 8.7 Vessels in home waters, August 1745

Location and commander	Ships
Downs with Vernon 5 x 90, 2 x 60, 50, 44.	*Royal George* (90), *St George* (90), *Prince George* (90), *Sandwich* (90), *Duke* (90), *Nottingham* (60), *Tilbury* (60), *Gloucester* (50), *Success* (44)
Convoy to Holland under Anson 50, 4 x 40, 3 x 24, 2 x sloops Convoy George II home and then join Vernon's squadron	*Norwich* (50), *Kinsale* (40), *Ludlow Castle* (40), *Poole* (40), *Folkstone* (40), *Sheerness* (24), *Bridgewater* (24), *Glasgow* (24), *Weasel and Wolf* sloops
Spithead under T'Hooft 60, 5 x 54 (to be ready within a week) 2 others not ready: Tholen (64) and Brederode (54)	*Dortrecht* (54), *Prince Frizo* (54), *Edam* (54), *Assendoft* (54), *Tiruckzee* (60), *Leewenhout* (54)
Plymouth under Martin 4 x 70, 60.	*Yarmouth* (70), *Edinburgh* (70), *Hampton Court* (70), *Prince Frederick* (70), *Lion* (60)
20 leagues off Scillies 2 x 70, 60, 50.	*Captain* (70), *Monmouth* (70), *Princess Louisa* (60), *Portland* (50)
Irish Channel 60, 50, 40, sloop Convoy duty to Bristol and then join Martin's squadron.	*Augusta* (60), *Falkland* (50), *Saphire* (40), *Baltimore* sloop
West Coast of Scotland 24, 3 x sloops.	*Port Mahon* (24), *Serpent, Terror and Furnace* sloops

Source: TNA, SP42/29, f.95–96; Adm1/3242, unfoliated.

200 dead and wounded on her decks. The *Elizabeth* broke away for Brest, while the *Du Teillay* disappeared from sight.[142]

The battle was reported both for the bravery of Brett and the cowardice of the captain of marines, but what was rumoured immediately was that the Charles Stuart was on board the *Du Teillay*.[143] The Young Pretender had

---

142 *Gentleman's Magazine*, xv (1745), 352, 386. The *Elizabeth* was reported as the *Mercury*. See also H.H. Brindley, 'The Action between H.M.S. *Lyon* and the *Elizabeth*, July 1745', in W.G. Perrin (ed.) *Naval Miscellany, Vol.3*, Navy Records Society, lxiii (1928), 85–119.

143 BL, Add Ms 35351, f. 76, Lady Hardwicke to P. Yorke, 1 August 1745.

apparently landed alone. Nevertheless, with the other threats to Ostend and from the west of France, it was decided to make preparations for home defence. Orders were sent to Martin and Vernon. Transports were ordered for 10,000 troops to bring them back from Flanders and the King was requested to return home, should the troops be ordered back to England.[144]

On 13 August confirmation of the landing was received. In Scotland, the commander of forces there, Sir John Cope, whose army numbered about 1,400 troops, was ordered to march immediately towards the rebels, who were thought to number no more than 300.[145] Against the other threats, it seemed, in the words of the Duke of Cumberland, nothing more than a 'Romantick Expedition'.[146] The French threat dominated thinking. Wade was certain that as soon as Ostend fell the invasion would commence.[147] By this time disgust with the Austrians and Dutch was reaching a new level. The Austrian refusal to break the dykes around Ostend had been startling and their continued resistance to an accommodation with Prussia exasperating. Despite great efforts to support Ostend, its surrender on 12 August, signalled the next phase of the crisis.

The Dutch failures over the summer had also caused relations with The Hague to cool dramatically. In early July rumours of secret Dutch negotiations with France were circulating in London and Dutch behaviour in the field continued to cause concern. Nevertheless, with a crisis now looming the Dutch were called upon again to provide the 6,000 troops they were obliged to supply in case Britain was invaded.[148] On 21· Newcastle wrote on behalf of the Regents, asking the King to authorise the return of 10,000 British troops from Flanders.[149]

The King had decided to return home and landed at Margate on 31 August. Over the next week disturbing news reached London from Scotland. The

144 BL, Add Ms 32705, f. 4, Newcastle to Cumberland, 2 August 1745. Six thousand were to remain in Flanders to defend Antwerp and preserve communications with the Austro-Dutch forces. See *Richmond-Newcastle Correspondence*, 172, Newcastle to Richmond, 13 August 1745.

145 *Richmond-Newcastle Correspondence*, 172, Newcastle to Richmond, 13 August 1745.

146 RA, Windsor, Cumberland Papers, Box 4, f. 201, Cumberland to Newcastle, 30 August 1745. Woburn Archive, Bedford Mss, x, Chesterfield to Bedford, 17 September 1745.

147 *Richmond–Newcastle Correspondence*, 173, Newcastle to Richmond, 14 August 1745.

148 RA, Windsor, Cumberland Papers, Box 4, 136, Newcastle to Cumberland, 13 August 1745. The 6,000 under Lt Gen. Debitz, were ordered to embark directly for Edinburgh. See BL, Add Ms 32705, f. 106, Cumberland to Newcastle, 3 September 1745.

149 BL, Add Ms 32705, f. 100, Newcastle to Harrington, 22 August 1745.

rebel army had grown to about 3,000 and slipped past Cope near Inverness. They were marching south via Blair and Perth to Edinburgh. Orders were sent to embark the Dutch regiments from Helvoetsluys as soon as possible.[150] One regiment was to go to Leith to join Cope, the rest were to disembark in the Thames estuary. Cumberland was ordered to send home 10 British regiments under the command of Lieutenant General Ligonier. The Lords Lieutenant of the counties were ordered to form independent companies. Two additional regiments were preparing to leave Dublin for England.[151] Fortuitously, five ships of the line arrived at Plymouth from the Mediterranean.[152] Across the Channel, small craft were identified in the ports. In Brest there were six sail and in Biscay there was much larger force of two hundred sail and 13–14 warships, but it was generally agreed that this latter force was not an invasion force, but the West India trade convoy. By mid-September it looked like the threat to the west might be limited, but ships and boats were gathering in the Channel ports of France and Flanders. Byng and Vernon established a watch over them. The rebel army was marching south, but with Cope in its rear and a growing force assembling in England there was reason to believe that the danger in the north could be contained.[153] The administrative response to the crisis seems to have been smooth and effective. Troops were moving and ships positioned as quickly as anticipated. Even the Dutch, who had been the butt of frustration and anger since Fontenoy, had, after an initial diplomatic hesitation, responded well. Nevertheless, the sense of unease was growing.[154]

Arrangements had to be made for the opening of Parliament on 17 October and, as usual, policy and expenditure had to be explained. When the

---

150 The Dutch regiments had been captured during the summer campaign and had been paroled. They were constrained not to fight against the French, but could fight rebels in Britain.

151 BL Add Ms 32705, f. 173, Chesterfield to Newcastle, 12 September 1745 (rec. 18 September).

152 BL, Add Ms 35351, f. 80, Hardwicke to P. Yorke, 19 September 1745.

153 BL, Add Ms 32705, f. 155, Cumberland to Newcastle, 20 September 1745 (n.s.); *Richmond-Newcastle Correspondence*, 177, Newcastle to Richmond, 14 September 1745. On the movement of the Dutch troops and views of British officials involved, see R.A. Cumberland Papers, Box 5.

154 The only troops available were from the garrison at Tournai, whose surrender terms prohibited them from fighting against the French. There was some question as to whether they might be breach of their parole, but this was finally resolved to Dutch satisfaction. See J. Oates, 'Dutch Forces in Eighteenth Century Britain: A British Perspective', *Journal of Army Historical Research*, lxxxv (2007), 20–39, especially 28–39.

King discussed the matter with Harrington on 13 September his simmering resentment over the Convention of Hanover came to a dramatic head. The situation in Flanders and Germany was dire and the withdrawal of British troops from the Confederate Army could only make relations with Austria worse. George demanded that only five regiments be brought home, instead of the ten that the ministry wished. He insisted that, with the Dutch troops, this would be enough to quell the rebellion. Eventually he backed down, but went on to disown the Convention, claiming that Maria Theresa would never consent to it. Harrington, who had negotiated the treaty, was horrified. His position would be untenable when Parliament met, if his actions were repudiated by the King. Furthermore, the King was repudiating the policy of the entire ministry. Harrington immediately threatened to resign. The King forbade it, but Harrington insisted.[155] The next day, in the presence of Newcastle, Hardwicke and Pelham, George told the Austrian envoy, Wasner, that the Convention was not his doing, and he ordered his name struck off letters to the ambassador at Vienna, Sir Thomas Robinson. The Pelhams were devastated. Parliament was set to meet in just over a month and there was little enough to parade as fruits of the campaigning season. This denunciation of the one success that had been achieved was shattering. To them it was confirmation that they had no control over policy. Behind it they suspected that Granville was continuing to advise the King. They considered mass resignation, but in the light of the rebellion, agreed not to take the step. The result was a strange accommodation. In the Closet the King was as silent and resentful to the Pelhams as ever. Harrington alone seemed to be able to convince the King to accept ministerial policy. Newcastle was naturally resentful of Harrington's unexpected ascendancy and, as with Granville, suspected that Harrington was did not fully inform his fellow ministers of the King's mind. On 21 September news arrived that the rebels had taken Edinburgh without resistance and proclaimed the Pretender. Edinburgh castle still held out, but to all intents and purposes Scotland was lost. The rebel army was now over 5,000 and other highland clans were said to be on the march south to join Prince Charles. Yet almost nothing was said in the Closet. Afterwards Stair reproached Harrington for not disclosing information that he had, but Harrington insisted the King told him no more than he had told any of the ministers.[156]

---

155 BL, Add Ms 35408, f. 188, Newcastle to Hardwicke, 13 September 1745.
156 Ibid., f. 190, Newcastle to Hardwicke, 22 September 1745.

Amid this silence in Cabinet the rebellion unfolded. The 10 British regiments arrived at Gravesend on the 23 September and began their march north. The next day news of Sir John Cope's defeat at Prestonpans arrived.[157] Already, the London financial market was becoming unsettled, and a run on the banks began. It took a week to stabilise, but, as in 1744, the few investors who dominated the market stood by Pelham.[158] On the 24 it was agreed that Stair would assume command of forces in the south while Wade would go north to command the army to assembling at Newcastle. Lord Loudoun was to rally the new independent companies at Inverness.[159] The two regiments from Ireland were sent to reinforce the garrison at Chester in case the rebels tried to move into Wales. Initially, Cope's defeat had been baffling. He was outnumbered, but Highland armies had been defeated before. The army, like the navy, seemed infected with a lack of courage, which could only be eliminated by severe punishment.[160] In the meantime it was clear that every possible trained soldier was needed in Britain and the Cabinet requested that the King order the last British forces home from Flanders together with the Hessians in British pay.[161] However, a series of questions remained, which were referred

---

157 *Richmond-Newcastle Correspondence*, 183, Stone to Richmond, 24 September 1745. The Jacobite rebellion is one aspect of the war of 1739–1748 that has a rich and extensive literature. The campaign can be followed in detail in a number of good modern books. See for example, Duffy, *The '45*, op. cit.; F. McLynn, *The Jacobite Army in England, 1745: The Final Campaign*, Edinburgh, 1998; S. Reid, *1745: A Military History of the Last Jacobite Rising*, Staplehurst, 1996; J. Black, *Culloden and the '45*, Stroud, 1990; W.A. Speck, *The Butcher: The Duke of Cumberland and the Suppression of the 45*, Oxford, 1981. For Jacobitism in England in these years see, P.K. Monod, *Jacobitism and the English People, 1688–1788*, Cambridge, 1989; Wilson, *The Sense of the People*, op. cit. For different views of the political significance of Jacobitism during the rising, see Cruickshanks, *Political Untouchables*, op. cit. and L. Colley, *In Defiance of Oligarchy: the Tory Party, 1714–1760*, Cambridge, 1982.

158 BL, Add Ms 51427, f. 82, West to Fox, 26 September 1745: Add Ms 35396, f. 328, T. Birch to P. Yorke, 28 September 1745.

159 At this time it was expected that the remains of Cope's army would rendezvous with the reinforcements at Newcastle. On 26 September it was thought that Berwick was too important to abandon and Cope was ordered to send his dragoons there. General Huske, who commanded at Newcastle was to replace these troops by augmenting the independent companies there.

160 BL, Add Ms 32705, f. 225, Chesterfield to Newcastle, 29 September 1745.

161 TNA, SP45/5, unfoliated, 23 July 1745; 30 September 1745. On the employment of the Hessians, see J. Oates, 'Hessian Forces Employed in Scotland in 1746', *Journal of Army Historical Research*, lxxxiii (2005), 205–214. When they were deployed in February 1746, they were sent directly to Leith and marched to Perth and Stirling to prevent the rebels bypassing the main British force moving northwards at Aberdeen. Nevertheless,

to Stair, Wade, Ligonier and Prince Nassau, who came over with the Dutch troops. They were ordered to report to the Cabinet at 8 pm that evening. When the Cabinet re-assembled the officers presented the situation with a number of options. Their first task was to determine the force to be sent north. There were 29 battalions of foot and 16 squadrons of horse and dragoons in England, including eight Dutch battalions. The Dutch, one English battalion, Blakeney's, and two regiments of horse, were already on the road towards Doncaster under Lieutenant General Thomas Wentworth. The officers recommended two additional battalions be added to that force. This would leave 16 battalions, two troops of Horse Guards, a troop Horse Grenadier Guards and two regiments of dragoons in the south. The regiments being raised by nobles in the counties were ordered to assemble wherever they were needed. On the matter of whether more troops should be recalled from Flanders, the officers agreed that Cumberland should be ordered to hold ready at least six regiments of foot and nine squadrons, to be released as soon as the French in Flanders went into winter quarters. As to raising more troops, the officers suggested either raising seven new regiments, raise second battalions for seven existing regiments or add new men to every company. New regiments were already being raised by nobles and gentry in localities and these additional forces was putting a great strain on the existing pool of experienced officers, so It was agreed to augment existing companies instead.[162]

In the first week of October news was anxiously awaited in London as the shipping for the troops ordered from the Low Countries made their way to Williamstadt and Wade's army gradually assembled at Doncaster. In Flanders, Ath had fallen to the French, but intelligence from the French Channel ports indicated that all was quiet there.[163] The season for great ships cruising in the Channel was also gone and the Admiralty received permission to withdraw Vernon's 90-gun ships to Spithead.[164] In Europe, relations with Austria remained frigid. The Austro-Saxon army had been defeated again by the Prussians at the Battle of the Soor in Bohemia (19 September) and

---

within days of the initial suggestion, rumours rapidly spread that 6,000 Hessians were to coming to England. See W.J. Smith (ed.), *The Grenville Correspondence*, 4 vols, London, 1852, 39, G. Grenville to R. Grenville.

162 BL, Add Ms 33004 (Newcastle Papers), f. 84, Cabinet Council, 24 September 1745; TNA, SP 45/5 (State Papers Various), unfoliated, 24 September 1745. Ibid., unfoliated, 26 September 1746.

163 TNA, SP 42/29, f. 238, Beauclerk to Stone, 4 October 1745.

164 Ibid., f. 276, Admty to Newcastle, 8 October 1745.

Newcastle noted that even the King's sympathy for Maria Theresa was evaporating and at last he seemed reconciled to the Convention of Hanover.[165]

Austria may not accept the Convention, but rumours of peace in Germany worried the French, who hurried into more active negotiations with the Dutch and Sardinia. The French had no intention of negotiating directly with Britain, but the ministry recognised that they could not stand aside. However, one thing stood out – Louisbourg. As soon as the news of its capture had arrived, it had been exploited to juxtapose the achievements of British naval power with the recent conduct of the Dutch. Pelham was aware that resolutions were being prepared to petition the King not to give up Louisbourg at a peace.[166] Bedford and the New Allies would be immovable on this point. Peace could not be bought by returning Cape Breton to France. The Dutch, on the other hand, expected Cape Breton to be exchanged for a return to the status quo in Flanders in the interest of the common cause.[167] If Britain were to retain Cape Breton, something more had to be achieved, probably in Flanders. This required the Dutch to stay in the war for another year, but with Anglo-Austrian relations sinking rapidly and the British army leaving the Continent, the Dutch would not be convinced easily. Despite all the frustrations of the year, keeping close to the Dutch was central to ministerial policy. To this end Newcastle supported a peace congress, so long as Cape Breton was not negotiable.[168]

As the opening of Parliament approached, the ministry was in disarray. With only days to go, the Speech from the Throne was undecided. Following the King's public statements at Court, the Convention of Hanover, which could have provided the basis for explaining a continued engagement in Europe, could not now be spoken of in good faith.[169] It was finally agreed to confine the Speech entirely to the rebellion.[170]

When Parliament opened the shock of the rebellion had cooled passions. There was no division on the Speech, but most were aware that the political status quo had been shattered. Since the spring William Pitt had been patient and given his support to the ministry. However, he knew the capture

---

165 BL, Add Ms, 32705, f. 248, Newcastle to Chesterfield, 9 October 1745. See also, Smith, *Grenville Correspondence*, op. cit., G. Grenville to R. Grenville, 5 October 1745.

166 Chatsworth, Devonshire Mss, 260.50, Hartington to Devonshire, 22 October 1745

167 Ibid., 260.49, Hartington to Devonshire, 20 October 1745.

168 BL, Add Ms, 32705, f. 248, Newcastle to Chesterfield, 9 October 1745.

169 BL, Add Ms 32705, f.256, Hardwicke to Newcastle, 13 October 1745.

170 TNA, SP 45/5, unfoliated, 15 October 1745.

of Louisbourg and the collapse in Flanders threw open policy options and re-opened the maritime war theme. On the 23 September he moved to address the King to bring home all the British troops. Given that only 2,000 British cavalry remained in Flanders, it was not a major contribution to home defence, but a powerful symbolic attack on the continuation of the war in Europe. In the circumstances this motion appealed across the political spectrum and it was only by twelve votes that Pelham managed to defeat it.[171] This was a serious shock to the Pelhams. The Broad Bottom was beginning to fracture already. Their allies, Bedford and Cobham, were pushing for a withdrawal from Europe. Their own supporters in the Old Corps were willing to vote for this and the Prince of Wales' party immediately exploited the situation to propose a new alliance between the Old Corps and Leicester House to replace the existing ministry.[172]

Action had to be taken quickly. The Pelhams agreed that their best option was to consolidate their alliance with Bedford and the Cobhams rather than try to negotiate a new alliance with the Prince of Wales. Pelham immediately met with Pitt to discuss terms. Pitt demanded a place bill to exclude all junior army and navy officers from parliament. Not only would this remove ministerial patronage, but tend towards improving discipline within the services. He insisted that the last of Granville's friends be removed from office and, finally, 'The total alteration of the foreign system ... and particularly by confining all the assistance we should give to the Dutch to the bare contingent of 10,000 men; but to increase our navy and to act as principals at sea in the war against France and Spain. For peace with France at present was not to be thought of.'[173] Both Pitt and Cobham were firm on a limit of 10,000 men. They believed that a defensive war in Flanders could bring about an acceptable peace. The Dutch had never, even in the previous war, provided the quotas of troops that they promised and their behaviour in 1745 only proved that they had not changed. If Britain continued in Flanders it would be to defend Austrian Flanders. Conversely, it was possible to defeat France at sea and by this bring France to an acceptable peace. Newcastle and Pelham were convinced that such an approach would simply push the Dutch into making a separate peace and leave Britain facing France alone. They needed

---

171 Chatsworth, Devonshire Mss, 260.51, Hartington to Devonshire, 24 October 1745.

172 Contemporary letters and reports on the event are scarce. Newcastle gave the best account in a retrospective letter to Chesterfield dated 20 November 1745. See BL, Add Ms 32705 (Newcastle Papers), f. 319.

173 BL, Add Ms 32705, f. 319, Newcastle to Chesterfield, 20 November 1745.

an agreement, but their decision would be critical to the future of the war. Pitt, having made his point on 23 October, was content to refrain from further intervention during the session and Pelham does appear to have had an easier time at critical points before Parliament rose for Christmas.[174] However, what Pitt would do when Parliament reassembled in January was a matter of serious concern.

During this period the situation in the north had worsened. The rebels had probed towards Berwick where the remains of Cope's army was in garrison. It was not a serious advance, particularly as the rebels lacked artillery, but it was enough to threaten seaward communications and cause the Admiralty to ask that the provisioning base for Wade's army be situated further south at Newcastle.[175] Rebel attempts to buy up corn in Belfast were noticed. Action was taken in Ireland to prevent it, but it put the Admiralty on alert that naval action was vital to support the royal army and to interdict rebel supplies from overseas.[176]

In mid-October there were rumours that 30,000 rebels were to advance on London with the support of 20,000 Spanish and French troops. As they approached the city the French would land an army on the south coast.[177] Contrasting intelligence from Brest suggested that there were not enough men to crew the ships nor transports to embark any soldiers. Nevertheless, orders were sent to all cruisers to intercept all ships, including neutrals. If they were carrying any naval stores they were to be brought into a British port.[178] By the end of the month the Channel ports were the focus of attention. These were most likely embarkation points for an invasion.[179] Thirteen sail were counted in Flushing and near Ostend. Worse followed when prisoners from a French ship captured by the *Wolf* sloop told of a large fleet at Brest ready to sail for Torbay.[180]

So far as Cape Breton was concerned, the plan to reinforce the town before the winter ice set in became unravelled. The transports under convoy of the

---

174 Coxe, *Pelham*, op. cit., i, 276–279.

175 TNA, SP 42/29, f. 319, Admty to Newcastle, 17 October 1745.

176 BL, Add Ms 32705, ff. 286–288, Chesterfield to Newcastle, 26 October 1745 (rec. 6 November).

177 TNA, SP 42/29, f.299, Admty to Newcastle, 12 October 1745.

178 BL, Add Ms 32705, f. 260, Admty to COs of HM Ships, 16 October 1745.

179 TNA, SP 42/29, f. 339, Sandwich to Stone, 27 October 1745; f.365, Admty to Harrington, 8 November 1745.

180 Ibid., f. 367, Corbett to Stone, 15 November 1745.

Dover (44) sent to take two regiments from Gibraltar to Louisbourg, were still at Lisbon by the end of October. They could not possibly arrive in time and it was agreed that they should go to Virginia and wait there until the thaws permitted their move to Louisburg. In the meantime, Governor Shirley was ordered to provide whatever forces he could from New England.[181]

By 14 November it was known that the Jacobite army had moved south-west and crossed the border to attack Carlisle. On the 16 November the ministers met with Cobham and Pitt at Gower's house to thrash out an agreement on policy.[182] It was agreed that the Convention of Hanover must be enforced and no more support should be given to Austria unless Maria Theresa accepted the Prussian annexation of Silesia. By acting together they had achieved the treaty and they had to continue together if Granville's policy was to be defeated permanently. Where they disagreed was on the United Provinces. Cobham and Pitt repeated their view that assistance must be limited to 10,000 troops and the focus of the war must shift to a naval war against France. The Pelhams remained convinced that this would force Britain to make peace with France on bad terms because the Dutch would pull out of the war immediately. Nevertheless, they were all agreed the war must continue and the naval war must be fought to the limit of resources. However, Bedford, pointed out that it was not possible to expand the naval war without a solution to the manning problem, and Pitt and Cobham would not accept that their policy towards the Dutch would ultimately force Britain into an unfavourable peace. Newcastle urged them to reconsider. He did not believe that Parliament would accept a war policy which led to Britain fighting alone against France and Spain.[183]

The meeting concluded without agreement, leaving the Pelhams in a serious situation. They could not depend on Granville's friends in Parliament, nor could they have Pitt and Cobham without losing the Dutch. They could not work with the Dutch towards peace without losing Cape Breton. All that could be done was to open low key discussions with France in the hope that a way through the crisis would be found.

The very next day news arrived of twelve men of war fitting out at Brest. Ships were also fitting out at Dunkirk to transport troops to Scotland. The Admiralty requested that the order for troops on the second rates to be disembarked to join the camp at Dartford be deferred until confirmation of

---

181 TNA, SP 45/5, unfoliated, 14 November 1745.

182 BL, Add Ms 32705, f. 318, Newcastle to Chesterfield, 20 November 1745.

183 The same view was expressed by Chesterfield, ibid., f. 385, Chesterfield to Newcastle, 25 November 1745.

the news was received. Vernon and Martin were ordered to be ready. On 20 November it was confirmed that Carlisle had fallen to the rebels with barely a shot. Troops from the royal army were hurrying north, but the direction of the rebels' next advance was unclear. They could slip west into Wales or east into Yorkshire. The royal army was gathering at Stone, Staffordshire, in a position central enough to move east or west. However the troops were arriving in such a piecemeal fashion that it was not in a good defensive posture. The King was uneasy, but still inclined to overturn the Convention of Hanover. Hartington summed up the ministerial position when he wrote to his father, the Duke of Devonshire: 'In this situation when the Closet is so impracticable on one hand and those Gentlemen (Pitt and Cobham) so much on the other, I think we have nothing to do but to put an end to the Rebellion, as soon as possible and get out and whilst we stay in to do as little as possible in any thing but what relates to the Rebellion.'[184]

While the crisis lasted the political settlement remained on hold. On 25 November the Cabinet reconsidered the situation. Scotland had to be abandoned for the present. Glasgow, and the castles holding out at Edinburgh and Stirling, must look to their own defence. The Admiralty reported that there were only enough ships in Ostend and Dunkirk to transport about 1,500 troops from each port. To oppose them, Vernon was at the Downs with two 50s, three 44s and two Dutch men of war. Three more Dutch warships were ordered to join him. Out in the North Sea and Channel he had cruisers and sloops watching from Dogger Bank to Calais. To the north, Byng had a 50, two 44s and five sloops cruising from Leith to Montrose. Seven more small vessels and one 44 were on their way to join him. Out to the west, operating between Portsmouth and Ireland, Martin had four 70s, five 60s and one 50. One 70, three 60s and one 50 were available to join Martin or Vernon.

In the long and wild winter nights, these forces could not stop ships from getting through to the rebels. However, a serious invasion would require several lifts, which in turn relied upon daylight and a prolonged period of reasonable weather. The naval force available to contest a landing was nominally adequate, but real danger lay in prolonged north-east gales, which would enable the French to sail, but pin Vernon's force back on the Kent coast and delay any reinforcement from Portsmouth. The Admiralty believed that, given the small number of ships available to the French, they would land in Scotland. Vernon did not agree.

---

184 Chatsworth, Devonshire Mss, 182.32, Hartington to Devonshire, 21 November 1745.

He believed Suffolk or Kent was the French target. The small number of ships at Dunkirk and Ostend meant that the French would be forced to use fishing boats as transports, which were unsuited for the long trip north to Scotland. They could only land in the Thames estuary. The Dutch ships with him were due to return to Holland by the end of the year, which would leave him with very little force to oppose a landing. They only needed news of rebel success and a good north-east wind. Furthermore, there were rumours that the Brest squadron was ready for sea. If they got past Martin, which in the winter was quite possible, the French would have excellent cover for their invasion. The capture of a French privateer with Scots and Irish troops bound for England, seemed to confirm Vernon's opinion. He challenged the Admiralty to order him to Yorkshire or Edinburgh if they really believed the French intended to land in the north.[185]

The Admiralty was worried about the Brest squadron and Martin was ordered to Spithead to refresh. However, the Board refused to be drawn by Vernon and reiterated their orders for him to hinder, pursue and destroy and force that came out of the Channel ports. By the beginning of December Vernon was becoming increasingly belligerent. He had referred earlier to 'excessive malice' of Winchelsea's Board, and soon made clear his belief that malign forces were still at work against him.

In the meantime, the invasion crisis seemed to be coming to a head. On 3 December Vernon reported that all fishing boats had been gathered at Dunkirk and the invasion could start within 24 hours. In order to cover the Kent coast, he would wait until he knew they were at sea and heading towards the Thames estuary. The Admiralty ordered Commodore Smith, then at the Nore, to go north immediately to cover the coast from Norfolk to the Thames. Orders were sent to hire as many cutters as possible to reinforce Vernon.[186] Vernon accepted the instructions to Smith, but interpreted it as a further slight in that his command was now restricted to Kent and Sussex.[187]

By 10 December the fear of invasion was at fever pitch. As late as 30 November the rebel army in the north was still treated with a degree of complacency. Pelham wrote 'I cannot conceive that that 7000 such troops have any chance against a regular army commanded by person of any experience at all.'[188]

---

185 The correspondence for this and succeeding paragraphs can be followed in Ranft, *The Vernon Papers*, op. cit.

186 TNA, SP 42/29, f. 456, Admty to Newcastle, 5 December 1745; SP 45/5, unfoliated, Cabinet Minutes, 5 December 1745.

187 Ibid., 548, Vernon to Corbett, 11 December 1745.

188 RA Windsor, Cumberland Mss, Box 6, f. 212, Pelham to Fawkener, 30 November 1745.

However, within three days, the threat of a French invasion changed that view. Now, it seemed with this support, the rebels could press on to London at any risk.[189] On 6 December it was known the rebels were at Derby. They had slipped past Cumberland's army and Wade was still far behind them at Doncaster. The direction of the rebel advance was still uncertain. However, there were about 6,000 regular troops around London, which was not a despicable force when facing approximately 7,000 exhausted rebels, but more troops were needed. The militias were prepared, a regiment of 1,500 was to be raised from the workers at the Deptford dockyard.[190] However, the ministry saw that the key to the campaign was the French invasion. They did not believe the rebels would drive on for London until they knew the French had landed. Indeed, on 8 December Newcastle had news that the rebels had retired from Derby and were probably on their way to Wales. Events now turned upon the invasion, which Vernon hourly expected. Cumberland was ordered to halt at Coventry and not proceed further from London until the rebel intentions were known. He was not to move unless he knew for certain the rebels had moved to take Chester.[191]

On 9 December the Admiralty confirmed that they had enough transports to begin the move of more troops to England and on 10 December it was finally agreed that the 6,000 Hessians and the last of the English horse should be brought over. The British horse would reinforce London, but the Hessians were destined for Edinburgh. It seems that at this point (9–10 December), the ministry was calculating that the French invasion could be prevented and the rebels would continue to retire west or northwards. The eastern side of the Pennines would be blocked by Wade and Edinburgh in loyal hands. The western side would be blocked by Cumberland.

If this was the plan, it was rudely overthrown by events on the next day. Vernon wrote urgently to the Admiralty. The weather had turned fair and invasion must be imminent. Rumours immediately flashed around London that the French had landed in Pevensey Bay. It was a false alarm, but was indicative of anxiety that the point of crisis had arrived. On 12 December the

---

189 RA Windsor, Cumberland Mss, Box 7, f. 264, Newcastle to Cumberland, 3 December 1745.

190 Ibid., f. 236, Disposition of the Forces near London, December 1745. TNA, SP 45/5 (State Papers – Various), unfoliated, Minutes, 6 December 1745. On the ambiguity of the rebel advance, see *Richmond-Newcastle Correspondence*, p.195, Newcastle to Richmond, 6 December 1745.

191 TNA, SP 45/5, unfoliated, Minutes, 8 December 1745. RA Windsor, Cumberland Papers, Box 7, 347, Elizabeth Mason to Newcastle, 7 December 1745.

King and ministry agreed that the real threat lay not with the rebels in Lanca-shire, but on the south-east coast of England and it was agreed immediately to recall six battalions from Cumberland's army, to be followed by Cumber-land and the rest of the army if necessary, except for another six battalions and two regiments of horse which were to be sent to Wade.[192] It was not the unanimous view. Harrington and Hardwicke were for allowing Cumberland to pursue the rebels, but George II supported Newcastle – 'London is the great object and must be prefer'd to all other Considerations.'[193]

Two anxious days passed before the weather closed in again on the night of the 13 December without any more alarming news from the Channel. However, there was growing irritation with Vernon who continued to mix his reports with complaints about his treatment by the Admiralty. Also his intelligence seemed increasingly doubtful.[194] On 14 December, Newcastle heard from Cumberland that the rebels were in a panicked retreat and the army was in hot pursuit, intending to destroy them when they stopped to rest, probably at Preston. The King and ministry agreed that this opportu-nity should not be lost and countermanded the orders of the 12 December. The cancellation of the order arrived at Preston in less than 24 hours, but a day had been lost and it was not regained. The frustration in the army was tremendous. Cumberland was sorry 'Mr Vernon's fright should have saved the Rebel Army now at Lancaster, where we had drove them and where I hoped to have kept them at bay' till Wade arrived.[195]

On 18 December a small skirmish Clifton failed to stop the rebel with-drawal and on 20 December their main army was back in Scotland. Carlisle Castle was retaken on 30 December. However, the French invasion threat remained high. Martin was ordered to join Vernon in the Downs, where he arrived on 21 December. The activity in Calais convinced Vernon that the new line of attack would be towards Dungeness. His small craft were active

---

192 Ranft, *The Vernon Papers*, op. cit., 549, Vernon to Corbett, 11 December 1745; 551, Corbett to Vernon, 11 December 1745; 552, Stewart to Vernon, 12 December 1745. In the later letter, it is noted, besides a plan to land 15,000 troops in England and Scotland, Saxe intended to attack in Flanders towards the Dutch frontier.

193 *Richmond-Newcastle Correspondence*, 197, Newcastle to Richmond, 12 December 1745.

194 Ranft, *The Vernon Papers*, op. cit., 553, Vernon to Corbett, 13 December 1745; 554, Corbett to Vernon, 13 December 1745; 556, Vernon to Corbett, 14 December 1745; 562, Corbett to Vernon, 19 December 1745.

195 RA Windsor, Cumberland Mss, Box 8, f.44, Cumberland to Newcastle, 15 December 1745.

off Calais, managing to disrupt the convoys taking cannon and ammunition up the coast. However, the troop concentration at Dunkirk and Ostend still indicated that Scotland might be the objective. Vernon was sure Dungeness was the target. He left Martin at the Nore and went to Dungeness himself. The Admiralty continued to give Vernon freedom to dispose of his forces as he saw fit, but was increasingly concerned about his intelligence. The reports he was providing about the French Channel ports were not consistent with other intelligence.[196] At the Admiralty the picture that was emerging was that the real threat came from Dunkirk/Ostend, where 12,000 troops with artillery were nearby. There appeared to be no serious preparations at Calais and Boulogne. Furthermore, the Admiralty felt that an invasion was now was more likely to be attempted in the spring supported by the combined Franco-Spanish battle fleets.[197] The Board urged Vernon to concentrate off Dunkirk, but he insisted on focusing on Calais/Boulogne, handing over everything related to Dunkirk to Martin and Smith. On 26 December the Board decided that they had had enough and ordered Vernon to hand over his command to Martin.[198]

With hindsight, Vernon was treated very unfairly. Unknown to the British, Boulogne and Calais had been central to the French invasion plans, which were aimed at the south coast between Romney and Hythe. His cruisers had disrupted those plans and done serious damage to their ordnance convoys. They had also dissuaded the French from coming out when the winds favoured them and it was not until after Vernon's removal that the French plan was shelved.[199]

The year, which started with an ambitious plan to end the war at French expense, had been a disaster. Certain things had gone well. Cape Breton had been captured – the first significant territorial conquest after five years of war. The Broad Bottom had held together, although the future did not look good. The Convention of Hanover had split the French and Prussians and on 24 December the 'greatest event of the year' became known in England. Austria had signed a peace with Prussia based on the Treaty of Breslau (Treaty of Dresden). If Austria was to get compensation for the loss

---

196 BL, Add Ms 35705, f. 452, Hardwicke to Newcastle, 23 December 1745; TNA, SP 42/29 (State Papers – Naval), f. 523, Anson to Newcastle, 30 December 1745.

197 TNA. SP 42/29, f. 523, Anson to Newcastle, 30 December 1745; SP45/30 (State Papers – Naval), f. 5, Admty to Newcastle, 4 March 1745/6.

198 Ranft, *Vernon Papers*, op. cit., 577, Admty to Vernon, 26 December 1746.

199 The best account of the French plans in English is F. McLynn, *France and the Jacobite Rising of 1745*, Edinburgh, 1981, see especially, 143–176.

of Silesia it had now to be from France or Spain.[200] However, overall 1746 did not look promising. The rebels were in possession of almost all of Scotland. French forces occupied the Flanders coast and threatened invasion of Britain. The army and the navy had done enough to avert catastrophe, but neither had demonstrated a capability to end this war successfully. While Austria might make a more substantial contribution to the common cause against the Bourbons, the Dutch might exit from the war and peace would have to be sought with Flanders in French hands. At home the rebellion may have brought together competing and disparate elements in domestic politics around a common bond of the Protestant Succession, but there was no indication that this would stabilise the ministry. Cape Breton remained a domestic and diplomatic thorn. Without retaining Cape Breton, convincing the political nation that they had not been sold short for Hanoverian objectives would be difficult to achieve. However, something had changed. The continental alliance policy that had driven the war since 1741 had been shattered. Sympathy for Austria had evaporated. The Dutch had to be conciliated in order to keep them fighting in Britain's interest, but there was now a greater willingness to test again the rhetoric that had led to the Spanish War in 1739 – a naval war for British objectives.

---

200 BL, Add Ms 40794, f. 38. See also D.B. Horn, 'Saxony in the War of Austrian Succession, *English Historical Review*, lxiv (1929), 33–47.

9

Europe and America: the Critical Balance, January–December 1746

In mid-December 1745, two Dutch representatives, Boetslaer and Hop, arrived in London with a resolution from the States General. They proposed that the allies put a force of 95,000 into the field for the next campaign, and demanded to know what Britain would contribute to the common defence of Flanders. The Dutch had not yet declared war on France, nor had they been directly attacked at home or had their maritime commerce seriously disrupted. Thus, British ministers reasoned, a clear message had to be given to these allies. An army of 95,000 should be assembled, but no direct help could be expected from Britain while the rebellion was still alive. The Dutch should declare war on France and provide 40,000 troops. The Austrians should provide 30,000. The King would continue to supply 8,000 Hanoverians in Flanders and the 6,000 Hessians would be sent back there as soon as the rebellion was over. Britain would join the Dutch in providing a subsidy for 10,000 Saxons.[1] This was very much in line with Cobham's views, who 'owned (it) was much more reasonable than he imagined we could have made it, and that, if we would support the continent at all, it could not be in a better or cheaper manner'[2]. He agreed to come into government with the Pelhams on condition that Pitt became Secretary at War, William, Viscount Barrington joined the Admiralty and James Grenville had a post of £1,000 a year.

George II agreed to all these demands, except the appointment of Pitt. He accepted that the continental war could not be won without a fundamental shift in Dutch or Austrian commitment to it. The Speech from the Throne, opening Parliament on 14 January, echoed the response to the Dutch representatives. He acknowledged that the Anglo-Dutch alliance was essential

---

1   RA Windsor, Cumberland Papers, Box 9, 25, Harrington to Boetslaer and Hop, 3 January 1746.

2   BL, Add Ms 32706, f. 164, Newcastle to Chesterfield, 18 February 1746.

to containing French ambition and that he would do 'the utmost of my power, according to the circumstances of my own dominions'. There was no mention of troops returning to Flanders. Support would concentrate on helping the Dutch to augment their own forces. Most importantly, the role of the navy was stressed.

> The great advantages which we have received from our naval strength, in protecting the commerce of my subjects, and intercepting and distressing that of my enemies, have been happily experienced by the former and severely felt by the latter. I am therefore determined to be particularly attentive to this important service and to have such a fleet at sea early in the spring as may be sufficient to defend ourselves and effectually annoy our enemies.[3]

The message seems to have hit precisely the right note in Parliament. The Commons address re-emphasised the support to the Dutch 'as far as the circumstances of the kingdom would permit'.

Just three days later, on 17 January, Marshall de Saxe moved his army out of winter quarters and advanced on Brussels. The Confederate Army was taken by surprise and fell back to Antwerp. By 19 January the French had surrounded Brussels. Halle, Malines, and Vilvoorde quickly fell to the French.[4] This news arrived in London on 2 February and it is impossible to tell how far it influenced the King's sudden change of plan. He secretly approached Lord Bath to form an administration. He depended on his friend Harrington to stand by him and hoped that Granville would be able to construct support for the new administration in the Commons. Although unprepared, Bath went to work on it with Granville. After having assured himself that the usual City financiers would not withdraw their credit, Bath openly challenged the ministry on 6 February by declaring he had advised the King against employing Pitt. The King's apparent acceptance of this advice and his revived complaints against the foreign policy so recently agreed, made the ministry's position impossible and they concerted a plan for mass resignation. Harrington, upon whose support the King had relied, and Newcastle, resigned on 10 February. The King was furious with Harrington, but was less surprised or upset about Newcastle. On 11 February Henry Pelham, Bedford, Gower and

---

3   Corbett, *Parliamentary History*, op. cit., xiii (1743–1747), 1395–1396.
4   TNA, SP87/20, f. 57, Dunmore to Harrington, 31 January 1745/6.

Pembroke resigned. Richmond, Hardwicke and Winnington gave notice of their intention to go. Hardwicke was to tender his resignation on Friday 14 February.

On 11 February Bath was appointed First Lord of the Treasury and Granville Secretary of State for the Northern Department. Winchelsea returned as First Lord of the Admiralty. However, within 24 hours it was clear that Bath could not get enough support in the Commons for an administration. The Patriot opposition detested him and Granville. No major figure in the Commons would lead the administration in that House and the King, besieged by resignations, realised it was a hopeless stratagem. He ordered Thomas Winnington to ask Pelham to return to office. Over the next four days compromises had to be worked out. The Pelhams returned to their old posts and demanded that Bath, Granville and the Finches be purged from any office. The King felt particularly betrayed by Harrington and tried to hold out against his return to office, but the Pelhams insisted. The Pelhams pressed the opportunity to bring in Cobham's 'Cubs'. Viscount Barrington was appointed to the Admiralty Board in the place of Lord Archibald Hamilton, who had refused to resign with the Pelhams. During this crisis an old and experienced member of the Board of Trade, Colonel Martin Bladen, had died, providing a place for James Grenville. Finally, Pitt was allowed in as Vice Treasurer of Ireland.[5]

The whole affair was over in eight days. The Pelhams had reinforced the Broad Bottom, although the effective part of the ministry had not changed much. Cobham's 'Cubs' were untested. Their power lay in their ability to articulate popular concepts which had a disturbing and inherently uncontrollable effect on parliament. Now in office, no one could be sure how they would use that power.[6]

The Winter Campaign, 1746

This ministerial re-organisation had been taking place against a vigorous winter campaign. The rebellion looked as though it had been contained. Edinburgh had been re-occupied on 4 January, but General Hawley's

---

5   The best account of this change is BL, Add Ms 32706, f. 164, Newcastle to Chesterfield, 18 February 1746. William Coxe provides this narrative and a similar one from the correspondence of Lord Bath, see *Pelham*, op. cit., i, 288–297.

6   BL, Add Ms 32706, f. 221, Chesterfield to Newcastle, 27 February 1746.

advance to Stirling had ended in defeat at Falkirk on 17 January.[7] By the end of the month it was clear that the battle had made little difference to the balance of force. Cumberland was in Edinburgh. Contrary winds held up the Hessian reinforcements, but British regulars were making their way northwards. On 5 February news arrived in London that Stirling Castle had been relieved. The advance into the Highlands continued over the winter and into early spring. The coastal routes led via Aberdeen and Montrose, from where supplies could be provided by sea. Finally, on 24 April news arrived that Cumberland had won a decisive victory over the Jacobites at Culloden. The rebel army was shattered and Cumberland turned his attention to a brutal pacification of the Highlands.

From mid-January most intelligence indicated that a French invasion was no longer imminent.[8] In contrast the situation in Flanders was steadily deteriorating. On 3 February news arrived that Louvain had fallen and that Brussels was invested. News that Brussels had fallen arrived on the 18 February. Flanders had to be supported, and the orders were given to return the Hessians from Scotland as soon as possible.[9] Meanwhile, the ministers agreed to revise their support to the Dutch. If the Dutch would put 50,000 troops into the field and Maria Theresa put 50,000 troops into Flanders, Britain would increase the subsidy to Austria by £100,000 and pay two-thirds of the subsidy to Saxony for 15,000 troops.[10]

At the end of February there was a welcome respite as the French army went into winter quarters. Louvain was recaptured and the Confederate Army was drawn up in quarters to protect Antwerp. During April an Austrian corps arrived from Bohemia, under the command of Marshal Batthyány. The army now consisted of between 30–40,000 Austrians, 10,000 Hanoverians and about 2,000 British cavalry. The Dutch mustered about 10,000 and were negotiating for 8,000 additional Munster and Hessian troops. The generals still pressed for additional Austrian troops, but with about 50,000 troops,

7   RA Windsor, Cumberland Papers, Box 10, 43, Hawley to Newcastle, 7 January 1746; 99, Hawley to Cumberland, 17 January 1746. For the battle see, G.B. Bailey, *Falkirk or Paradise! The Battle of Falkirk Muir, 17 January 1746*, Edinburgh, 1996.

8   TNA, SP 42/30, f. 60, Admty to Newcastle, 21 January 1746. It was believed that the French focus was now to infiltrate reinforcements into Scotland rather than mount an independent invasion.

9   RA Windsor, Cumberland Papers, Box 10, 275, Ligonier to Cumberland, 18 February 1746.

10 Lodge, *Eighteenth Century Diplomacy*, op. cit., 144–145.

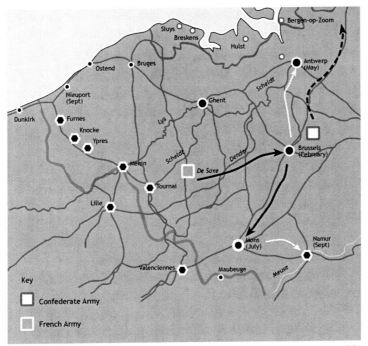

Map 12 De Saxe's campaign in Flanders, February–September 1746

the force on hand was far more respectable than the allies had cause to hope for in January.[11]

As the allies began to plan for the coming campaign, diplomatic initiatives continued. The fall of Brussels led the Dutch to renew their negotiations with France. For the restitution of the barrier, France demanded the return of Cape Breton, the refortification of Dunkirk as well as territorial concessions by Austria which would cut Austrian Flanders off from the United Provinces. While this was potentially attractive to the Dutch, it was impossible for Britain to accept and only worsened Anglo-Dutch relations.[12] For the present war would continue.

Britain and the Plans of the 1746 Campaign

In Britain, the resources for the new campaign were being examined. By early March Cumberland was convinced he had enough force in Scotland to subdue the rebellion. The Dutch and Hessians covered the lowlands,

---

11   RA Windsor, Cumberland Papers, Box 10, 184, Ilten to Cumberland, 7 April 1746.

12   Lodge, *Eighteenth Century Diplomacy*, op. cit.,145–149.

while the royal army was gathering strength in Aberdeen, supported from the sea.[13] These troops constituted the main force of the British army and would not be available elsewhere until any pacification of Scotland had been completed. In England, seven battalions of Guards and 13 regiments of foot had been held in case of a French invasion and to man warships if required.

The army was still clearly stretched. The navy, conversely, had found its resources in British waters growing and the naval balance in all theatres had quietly but significantly shifted.

Since the rebellion had erupted the numbers of all types of vessels in home waters had been rising (Figure 9.1). Line of battle ships from the Mediterranean had, at last, come back home and been refitted for service. The same was true of the cruisers (50- to 20-gun ships). Numbers of smaller vessels had been expanded by purchase, hire or building. The smaller vessels cruising around the coast of Britain hindered French support for the Jacobites and ensured communications from the south to Scotland and to Holland. By April 1746, the naval network across the North Sea and into the Channel, while not impervious, was tight. Ships patrolled around the coast, provided escorts for transports, provision ships and victuallers and made possible an abortive attempt to bombard the shipping in Dunkirk.[14] It was now possible for the Admiralty to consider putting three significant squadrons to sea – Martin's Channel force, an escort for an expedition to Canada and a Western Squadron to cruise in search of the returning French West Indian trade.[15]

Meanwhile, the other stations were stable. In the Mediterranean, the concentration of Bourbon naval forces in Cadiz/Cartagena and the Atlantic ports enabled Vice Admiral Henry Medley to cover the eastern coast of Spain with his main squadron. The news from the West Indies was good, even over-optimistic, as false rumours spread of Vice Admiral Townsend having starved Martinique into surrender.[16] He had, nonetheless, seriously disrupted the French West Indies trade by scattering a convoy and capturing

---

13 RA Windsor, Cumberland Papers, Box 12, 108, Cumberland to Newcastle, 14 March 1746.

14 This last was a plan proposed by Captain Charles Knowles. It was not a success as the shot landed well short of the assembled shipping. See BL Add Ms 15956, f. 125, Knowles to Anson, 11 January 1746.

15 Woburn Archive, Bedford Papers, xi, f. 58, Sandwich to Bedford, 24 April 1746; f. 111, Sandwich to Bedford, 7 May 1746.

16 RA Windsor, Cumberland Papers, Box, 10, f. 127, Stephen Poynitz to Fawkener, 27 February 1746.

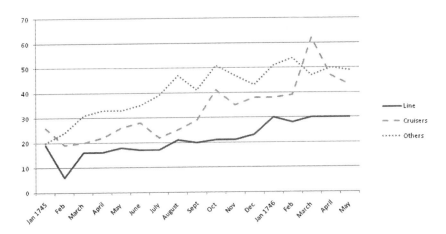

Figure 9.1 Ships in home waters, January 1745–May 1746
Source: TNA, Adm 8/24 and Adm8/25.

over 30 merchantmen. The latest reports from the East Indies indicated that Commodore Barnett still dominated those waters.

The naval war was looking brighter. The peripheries seemed to be stable and for the first time since the opening of the war with France, the re-disposition of naval forces towards Britain had placed the most powerful element of the fleet in home waters, significantly reducing the strain of supplying manpower, provisions and stores to distant stations. This coincided with important changes at the Admiralty. The removal of Lord Archibald Hamilton in February had left Anson and Beauclerk as the only naval officers on the Board. However, with their experience, the political weight of Bedford and Sandwich and the enthusiasm of Henry Bilson Legge, George Grenville and Viscount Barrington, it was an exceptionally powerful Board that was well placed to encourage change within the navy and present a new image to the political public at large.[17]

---

17   Henry Bilson Legge was an ambitious, well-connected and able politician. He joined the Admiralty Board on 25 April 1745 on the resignation of Lord Baltimore, who had lost precedence to Lord Vere Beauclerk in the re-organisation of December 1744 and was never reconciled to this fact. Legge was a staunch Walpole Whig, who was dismissed as junior Secretary to the Treasury Board on the fall of Walpole in 1742. He maintained good relations with the Pelhams and the Duke of Bedford, who supported him regaining a minor office in July 1742. Bedford later brought him into the Admiralty. Legge had served as a volunteer at sea between 1728 and 1731, including voyages under the command of Lord Vere Beauclerk in the *Kinsale* (32) and the *Oxford* (50) See P.J.D.J. Kulisheck, "'The Favourite Child of the Whigs'": The Life and Career of Henry Bilson Legge, 1708–

This was needed as public perception of the navy was still quite negative. In September Captain Henry Russane of the marines had been sentenced to death for cowardice during Brett's action against the *Elizabeth* in July.[18] The courts martial resulting from the battle of Toulon continued to hang over the navy. The trials of the lieutenants of the *Dorsetshire* opened on 23 September 1745 and the charges were rapidly dismissed.[19] On 25 September the trial of Captain George Burrish of the *Dorsetshire* opened. Although found guilty of not doing his utmost to engage with the enemy, he was cleared of the specific charge of not covering the approach of the fireship *Anne*, as a result of which she caught fire prematurely and was lost. The court rejected both the death penalty and imprisonment in favour of disqualifying Burrish from further service in the navy.[20] The trial of Captain Williams of the *Royal Oak* resulted in a similar conviction and sentence after mitigation for long service and disability. Five more captains stood trial during November and December and were acquitted.[21] Lestock's trial finally opened on 12 March, but was not to conclude until 3 June. In the meanwhile, the simmering hostility between Vernon and the Admiralty exploded. Even before Vernon returned from the West Indies in January 1743, he had ensured that his version of events was put into the public domain by encouraging Captain Charles Knowles to circulate a pamphlet on the defeat at Cartagena, placing blame entirely on the army. This was published in 1743 and during 1744 Vernon published edited versions of his correspondence to present his case to the public. The ministers, who had seen Wentworth's and Trelawney's correspondence had a more balanced view of events and were extremely suspicious of Vernon, but Bedford, who had not been in office at this time, was more enamoured with Vernon's apparent strait talking and clear vision for a maritime war. Bedford championed Vernon's return to command in August 1745, but by December had learned how difficult the admiral could be and dismissed him. Vernon reacted by publishing his correspondence with the Admiralty Board during

---

1764', unpublished PhD thesis, University of Minnesota, 1996, 11–14; 18–52.

18   TNA, Adm 1/5285, unfoliated, Courts Martial on Capt. H. Russane, 10 September 1745.

19   TNA, Adm 1/5285, unfoliated, Courts Martial on lieutenants of the *Dorsetshire*, 24 September 1745.

20   TNA, Adm 1/5285, unfoliated, Court Martial of Captain Burrish sentence 9 October 1745.

21   Ibid., these were Ambrose of the *Rupert* (27 November), Pett of the *Princessa* (27 November), Dilke of the *Chichester* (5 Dececmber), West of the *Warwick* (13 Dececmber) and Sclater of the *Somerset* (24 Dececmber).

his period of command in the Channel. This was the last straw, even for Bedford, and he was removed from the flag list on 11 April (Table 9.1).[22]

This left the list of available and active flag officers very thin. Although there were significant successes against French shipping, it was impossible to prevent supplies getting through to the rebels, nor could a French invasion of southern England be entirely discounted.[23] There was a real fear that when the British ships were forced to return to port for refit the Brest fleet would emerge and French troops march back to the Channel ports.[24] It was against this background that the plans for the new campaign were laid.

The Expedition to Canada, March–June 1746

By the beginning of March the rebellion was fading, but Flanders was in dire straits. The news from Italy was also bad. During the latter part of 1745 the Bourbons had advanced into the Milanese and had captured Milan itself in December. Sardinia had begun talks with France.[25] By March the principles of an agreement between them were known in London and it looked as if Sardinia might soon be out of the war. Overall the situation was very worrying. With Spain and France dominating Italy, and Silesia lost, at least in part because of British pressure, the Austrians might have little appetite for continuing the alliance with the Maritime Powers. The Dutch, under pressure from the French and with even less hope of Austrian support, would be more inclined to make peace.

The British ministry was faced with three stark choices. It could persevere with the policy spelt out in January of supporting the Dutch with subsidies to German allies. The navy was now well positioned to carry out its role of defending the home islands. However, it was not clear if this was enough to keep the Dutch in the war or to bring France (and Spain) to an acceptable peace. It was possible to concentrate entirely on a naval war. The assertion in the King's Speech in January that the navy and privateers had damaged the Bourbons was an attractive, if unproven, claim. Like the fall of Louisbourg,

---

22   Ranft, *The Vernon Papers*, op. cit., 587, Corbett to Vernon, 11 April 1746. The pamphlets were *A Specimen of Naked Truth* and *Some Seasonable Advice from an Honest Sailor*, both published in the early part of 1746.

23   For a summary of French reinforcements see, F.J. McLynn, 'Sea Power and the Jacobite Rising of 1745', *Mariner's Mirror*, xlvii (1981), 163–172, especially 171.

24   TNA, SP42/30, f. 5, Admty to Newcastle, 4 January 1746.

25   Browning, *The War of Austrian Succession*, op. cit., 257–260.

Table 9.1 Flag list (new flag tanks in italics), May 1746

Admiral of the Fleet	Sir John Norris	In retirement
Admiral of the White	Thomas Mathews	Suspended
Admiral of the Blue	Nicholas Haddock	In retirement/ill
	Sir Chaloner Ogle	Britain
Vice Admiral of the Red	James Stewart	Port Admiral (Portsmouth)
	Thomas Davers	West Indies
	Hon George Clinton	Governor of New York
Vice Admiral of the White	*William Martin*	Britain
	William Rowley	In retirement
Vice Admiral of the Blue	*Henry Medley*	Mediterranean
	Issac Townsend	West Indies
Rear Admiral of the Red	Richard Lestock	Suspended
	Lord Vere Beauclerk	Admiralty
Rear Admiral of the White	*George Anson*	Admiralty
Rear Admiral of the Blue	Perry Mayne	Britain
	Sir Peter Warren	North America
	Hon John Byng	Britain

the capture of the French East Indies trade by Barnett, Townsend's success in the West Indies and rumour that Martinique had fallen, it played to the popular perception that British naval power should be able to achieve great things with a real impact on diplomatic decisions. Another option was to renew the military commitment to Flanders in the hope that the Dutch and Austrians would commit more fully to a plan recapture the Austrian Netherlands. Politically, this would be the most difficult as it challenged the evidence of three years of fighting. Whichever of the three policies was adopted, it had to bring about decisive results in 1746 for there was by now a growing consensus that the war had to be brought to an end soon. This could not happen at present because the French would not make peace without the return of Cape Breton and its surrender would be fatal to the ministry.

A way had to be found to break the deadlock. If Prussia could be induced to join the allies, Newcastle believed it might breathe some new life into the Flanders campaign, but this was improbable. The advantages of a naval war, on the other hand, began to take real shape. In January, Admiral Peter Warren had written from Louisbourg on the possibility of an expedition to capture Quebec. Newcastle had passed this proposal on to Bedford. The King was enthusiastic and even before the operation had been fully considered, agreed to release five regiments from England for the purpose under the command of Lieutenant General James St Clair, the Quarter Master General of the army in Flanders.[26] The whole matter was considered on 28 March by Bedford, Wade and St Clair. They concluded that, with the two regiments of foot already on their way to Louisbourg from Gibraltar, a useful force could be assembled at Louisbourg to advance up the St Lawrence. The naval and transport requirements could be assembled within the month and Warren's squadron at Louisbourg would be more than adequate to meet any French attempt to re-conquer the city. The critical requirement was for more soldiers and the committee concluded that a minimum of 3,500 additional troops would have to be added to the existing American troops and a new garrison regiment should be raised in North America.

On 3 April the plan was approved. The experience of organising the West Indian operation of 1740 was fresh in the minds of the ministers and orders were on their way to the Admiralty the next day. Newcastle wrote to the governors of the Northern Colonies exhorting them to prepare. The plan of campaign hardly differed from the two other expeditions to Quebec in 1690 and 1711. The American levies from New York, New Jersey, Pennsylvania, Maryland and Virginia were to rendezvous at Albany on the Hudson. From there they were to advance north to Montreal. This force was to be under the command of Lieutenant Governor William Gooch of Virginia, who had commanded the American regiment in the West Indies. The troops from Massachusetts, Rhode Island, Connecticut and New Hampshire were to rendezvous at Louisbourg with the regular battalions coming from Britain. Together they would go up the St Lawrence to attack Quebec. The commander of the naval escort, Commodore Thomas Cotes, was provided with a force of one 80, three 60s, two 44s and a bomb ketch.

While offensive operations were being prepared, news of a French naval expedition from Brest was filtering through. In March Admiral Martin had taken the main fleet to cruise off Ushant. By 17 May information was circulating that the Brest squadron had sailed under the command of the Duc

---

26   TNA, SP 42/98, f. 27, Warrant for St Clair, 26 March 1746.

d'Anville with 2,000 soldiers aboard.[27] His destination was unknown. It could be to Britain, Italy, North America or the West Indies. If it was the last, Admiral Townsend had an inferior force in the Caribbean, so it was agreed that St Clair and Cotes were to follow him. To this degree the initiative had already been lost as the expedition was now tied to the destination of the French operation.

On 28 May, Martin's report from Ushant arrived. The Brest squadron had sailed.[28] It had gone to Aix roads off Rochefort to rendezvous with transports awaiting convoy. Preparations for the expeditionary force were hurried forward. It had been agreed that the force must be at Quebec by mid-July for any chance of success before the ice set in at the end of September. For this, Anson calculated that they must leave England by 10 May. Bedford's committee believed that this was quite practicable, but delays began to creep into the schedule, and embarkation only began on 22 May. Throughout the first half of June, reports from ships off Rochefort suggested that the Brest squadron and transports were still in the Aix roads and hopes were high that Martin would be able to destroy them before they sailed.[29] On 15 June Cotes gave the orders for the expeditionary force to make sail from Spithead, but light winds delayed departure. St Clair was already having doubts about the practicality of the plan as it was well past the latest date on which Anson had claimed it was necessary to get into the St Lawrence. St Clair had also been troubled by the plans he had received from Gooch in America.[30] As the expeditionary force lay at anchor at Spithead waiting for a change of wind, more news arrived from Martin. A Swedish ship had seen the French fleet at sea, 30 leagues to the west of Bordeaux. Martin had missed them by less than 24 hours.[31] There was still a chance of a battle and St Clair's expeditionary army, well to the north, was at last making sail in fresh east-south-easterly gales. However, four days later, on 25 June, it was concluded that D'Anville was almost certainly on his way to Cape Breton and the threat to the expedition was too great. Cotes was ordered to return to Spithead until his escort could

---

27   For an excellent study of this expedition, see J. Pritchard, *Anatomy of a Naval Disaster: The 1746 French Expedition to North America*, Montreal, 1995.

28   TNA, SP 42/30, f. 414, Admty to Martin, 29 May 1746 (copy).

29   Bedford Mss, xi, f. 39, Sandwich to Bedford, 14 June 1746.

30   TNA, SP 42/98, f. 86, St Clair to Newcastle, 15 June 1746.

31   TNA, SP 42/31, f. 43, Admty to Newcastle, 21 June 1746. The French left Rochefort on the 9‑10 June (o.s.). Martin arrived on the 10 June.

be reinforced.[32] Two days later orders arrived to disembark three regiments at Portsmouth and take the other two to Newcastle. The immediate cause of this cancellation was confirmation that the French expeditionary force was at sea, but in reality the purpose and significance of the expedition had been gradually changing over the preceding weeks.

The Return to Flanders and the Western Squadron, April–July 1746

At the beginning of May Saxe had re-opened the Flanders campaign. The allies had less than 25,000 troops in the field and the allied commander, Batthyány, fell back before them. As the French advanced on Antwerp, the Confederate Army retreated northwards towards Breda. Further south, Marshal d'Estrees surrounded Maubeuge. On 20 May, Antwerp surrendered and within days Mons was under threat. The question of whether the Dutch would continue the war was becoming daily more critical. Even before Culloden the situation in Flanders had forced the ministry to reconsider their policy.[33] The rebellion had forced Britain practically to abandon Flanders. Only three British regiments of dragoons, the Hessian horse and 8,000 Hanoverians in British pay in remained in Flanders. The ministers agreed that Britain would pay the King for an additional 10,000 Hanoverian troops for service in Flanders until the end of November 1746. On 28 April they also agreed to send the Hessian infantry back to Flanders and that four battalions of British regulars should be ready on transports at Newcastle to send across to Flanders in an emergency.[34]

It was known that the opposition lords intended to move that the war in Flanders be abandoned in favour of a purely maritime war. Given the history of the previous 12 months, this had the potential to re-ignite the old debate about Hanover influence, the duplicity of the allies and the natural way of British naval war. The behaviour of Cobham's 'Cubs' could not be taken for granted.[35] However, a fortuitous event intervened. On 24 April, two weeks before the expected debate, the Paymaster General, Thomas Winnington, died and it was inevitable that Pitt would renew his claim for promotion. Given the circumstances, even the King saw that changes were necessary. He accepted Pitt as Paymaster. Sir William Yonge, the long-serving, but ailing

---

32   TNA, SP 42/98, f. 90, Newcastle to St Clair, 25 June 1745.

33   TNA, SP 45/5, unfoliated, 4 April 1746.

34   Ibid., 28 April 1746.

35   Woburn Archive, Bedford Mss, xi, f. 53, Newcastle to Bedford, 22 April 1746.

Secretary at War was moved into Pitt's old office as Secretary to the Lord Lieutenant of Ireland. Bedford was satisfied by the promotion of Henry Fox to Secretary at War and Henry Legge's move from the Admiralty to the Treasury. Legge's place on the Admiralty Board was taken by William Ponsonby, a son-in-law of the Old Corps Whig magnate, the Duke of Devonshire. The re-organisation maintained the political balance, marginally embedding the New Allies and their commitment to maritime war in the ministry. It was enough to consolidate the ministry and defuse any fragmentation generated by the renewed commitment to the Flanders war. When, on 2 May, the Earl of Oxford moved in the Lords to petition the King not to continue the war in Flanders, it was heavily defeated.

During May the continuing bad news from the field was made worse by reports of the Dutch negotiations with the French. The latest French proposal was extremely moderate. They demanded the return of Cape Breton and the right to fortify Dunkirk. Austria must hand over Tuscany to Don Philip. In return the French would evacuate all their conquests in Flanders. Louis XV would renounce support for the Pretender and recognise Maria Theresa's husband as Holy Roman Emperor. However, they also wanted a treaty of perpetual neutrality for the Low Countries. It was a highly attractive set of proposals to the Dutch, who undertook to consider them seriously, but they posed a deadly threat to Old Corps Whigs in the British ministry. If Britain were forced to make peace by the restitution of Cape Breton it was unlikely the ministry would survive. Furthermore, with the Low Countries neutral, the old Grand Alliance of Britain, the United Provinces and Austria would be dead and the future defence of Hanover far more problematic. Such a peace would destroy the Old Corps' relationship with the King and the New Allies, and, almost certainly, lead to a humiliating peace with France and Spain.

Everything now hinged on whether the Dutch would make a separate peace. For this reason, the expedition going to Quebec had to handled with care. These issues were discussed with the King on 21 May. Newcastle wanted the expedition to Canada to continue, but also argued that six or seven British regiments had to be sent to Flanders. The expedition would consolidate the support of the New Allies and make the French fear for their colonies. The reinforcements to Flanders would give the Dutch confidence. Harrington, Chesterfield and Pelham argued, no doubt playing to the King's fears, that the Dutch would make peace. Britain would be alone and French armies free to advance through Westphalia to Hanover. Regardless of her navy, Britain would be powerless to stop the occupation of Hanover and forced to accept French terms. Newcastle's counter argument rested on his conviction that the Dutch would not make a separate peace, particularly if Britain showed willingness to support them. He argued strongly for the expedition and reinforcement of Flanders. In the end it was agreed that the expedition should continue to assemble. Quebec remained the objective, but until it sailed the force was to be considered as a mobile expeditionary army. If the Brest squadron went to the West Indies, St Clair would follow it. If the situation in Europe demanded it, St Clair's expeditionary force would go to Flanders. It was agreed to leave open the question of how many troops would go to Flanders or North America as events unfolded.[36]

At this point, British policy was committed to North America and to Europe. Both were critical to the future of the war. This ran counter to the deeply held rhetoric of maritime war that had run through debates for years and had crystallised recently into the idea that war could be carried on by naval power alone. Before the British regiments returned to Flanders, Newcastle decided to test parliamentary sentiment. Lord Lonsdale agreed to propose a motion not to send any troops out of Britain.[37] The debate was held on 12 June and the motion was heavily defeated. The same motion was proposed in the Commons on 18 June and crushed, 103 to 12 votes. Newcastle could now rest assured that the parliamentary support for both commitments remained intact.[38] On 22 June orders were signed for Lieutenant General Ligonier to go to Flanders with four British battalions and take command of all troops there in British pay.[39]

The Hessian foot arrived back in Holland on 24 June and joined the army about Breda on 4 July. Ligonier reached the army with the four battalions on 11 July. His initial optimism faded quickly. The Hessians had no powder. There were no horses or carriages for the field artillery. Ligonier found his relationship with the allies extremely discomforting. Having such a small force and a relatively recent commission as lieutenant general, he found neither the Austrians nor the Dutch would accord him or his troops the seniority he expected. Even Prince Waldeck, the commander of the Dutch, separated his forces from the British to avoid any idea that he or his troops should cede seniority to Ligonier.[40]

---

36 BL, Add Ms 35408, f. 224, Newcastle to Hardwicke, 21 May 1746.

37 BL, Add Ms 32707, f. 296, Hardwicke to Newcastle, 9 June 1746.

38 Corbett, *Parliamentary History*, op. cit., xiii (1743–1747), 1413–1416; Coxe, *Pelham*, op. cit., i, 317.

39 R. Whitworth, *Field Marshal Lord Ligonier: A Story of the British Army*, Oxford, 1958, 120–121.

40 Ligonier's lengthy correspondence on this issue can be found in TNA, SP87/20.

Thus, when orders were sent to stop the Canadian expedition on 25 June, it was certainly in response to the news that the Brest squadron was heading for Cape Breton, but behind the decision on 27 June to disperse the expedition also lay the need to reinforce the army in Flanders. The King and Harrington were in favour of abandoning the expedition, but Newcastle was against this.[41] He worried that if d'Anville re-captured Cape Breton or Newfoundland, he might make it impossible for Britain to secure an acceptable peace.[42] Bedford, who had been out of London, disbanding his volunteer regiment in Berwick on Tweed during this period, was furious when he heard that the expedition had been cancelled.[43] He insisted that it proceed to protect Cape Breton if not to attack Quebec. He had no difficulty in getting Newcastle's support to restore the expedition, and orders to re-embark the troops were sent almost immediately.[44] To counter the Brest squadron, the naval escort was increased from four to eight ships of the line, three 44s and a sloop. St Clair, who had come to London from Portsmouth, was sent back again and with the new enlarged escort a new naval commander was appointed – Richard Lestock.

Lestock's appointment caused a few ripples of comment. His court martial had sat from March until 3 June. The evidence in the trial was contradictory and the court found that it was insufficient to support the charge. He was acquitted on all charges and restored to his rank, which made him the senior sea-going flag officer of the fleet. His instructions were to pursue d'Anville. On 6 August the expeditionary force came under sail, but unfortunately as the ships passed Bembridge Ledge, off the Isle of Wight, Lestock's flagship, the *Princessa* (70), grounded and the fleet was delayed while repairs were made.

---

41   Anson's role can only be inferred, but he was insistent that the expedition had to be at the mouth of the St Lawrence by mid-May and he later to write to Bedford about the lack of ships in home ports if the Brest and Ferrol squadrons were still in European waters. See Woburn Archive, Bedford Papers, xii, f. 72, Anson to Bedford, 17 July 1746.

42   *Richmond-Newcastle Correspondence*, 227–228, Newcastle to Richmond, 28 June 1746; BL, Add Ms 32707, f. 390, Newcastle to Cumberland, 3 July 1746.

43   *Gentleman's Magazine*, xvi (1746), 439–440.

44   *Richmond-Newcastle Correspondence*, 228, Pelham to Richmond, 1 July 1746; Woburn Archive, Bedford Mss, xii, f. 66, Newcastle to Bedford, 5 July 1746; TNA, SP 42/98, f. 98, Newcastle to St Clair, 17 July 1746. The restoration of the expedition received enthusiastic support from William Pitt, who hoped that the recent news of the death of King Philip V of Spain would revive attempts to resolve the war in America. See Woburn Archive, Bedford Mss, xii (1746), f. 72, Pitt to Bedford, 19 July 1746.

On 9 August Anson arrived at Portsmouth to take command of the Channel squadron. On the same day a letter reached St Clair and Lestock from Knowles at Louisbourg. Knowles described the utterly ruinous state of the town and it was quickly concluded that this was not appropriate to over-winter in this fortress. Anson, who had raised his flag on the *Yarmouth* (70) agreed. St Clair and Lestock requested permission to spend the winter season in the British Northern Colonies. Warren had confirmed that an attack on Canada was impossible for 1746. Too little time remained to raise the American troops expected to cooperate with the expeditionary army.[45] The King approved, but the confusion this generated soon became apparent. St Clair claimed he had no knowledge of America and deferred to Lestock's judgement. Lestock suggested that they go to Boston. Anson believed that if d'Anville had gone to Cape Breton, he would be back to Europe within a month. This would leave Lestock in America, and too few forces in Britain to meet the concentration of Bourbon naval forces on the Atlantic coast, thereby re-creating the disastrous naval situation of 1744–1745.

Anson's fear of naval inferiority in home waters was understood and shared within the ministry.[46] On 16 July, Newcastle had instructed the Admiralty to prepare a squadron for the defence of Great Britain.[47] Anson discussed Newcastle's order with the King the next day, who asked if there would be enough force left in home waters, should the Bourbon squadrons unite. Anson assured the King that there were.[48] However, it prompted him to consider immediately recalling more of the cruising ships to ensure that a sufficient squadron was available for later in the season. The idea of sending a large squadron out to the west to counter the movement of a large Bourbon fleet had been briefly implemented under Vernon in 1745. The reason for countermanding the order was partly a fear that the main squadron would be too far to westward if a Bourbon fleet slipped past and entered the Channel, and partly a general distrust of Vernon. However, now, Bedford completely agreed with Anson. He told Anson:

---

45   TNA, CO 5/44, f. 43, Warren to Newcastle, 6 June 1746 (rec. 31 July).

46   Woburn Archive, Bedford Mss, xiii (1746), ff. 25–26, Anson to Bedford, 22 August 1746. He believed that d'Anville might detach ships to provide an escort for the transports to Canada. TNA, SP 42/30, f. 412, Admty to Newcastle, 30 May 1746; f. 421, Sandwich to Newcastle, 30 May 1746.

47   TNA, SP 42/31, f. 117, Admty to Newcastle, 6 August 1746.

48   Woburn Archive, Bedford Mss, xii, f. 72, Anson to Bedford, 17 July 1746.

You know my opinion has long been that we ought to unite all the ships cruising to the westward, whether in the Bay or off the Isle of Batz and St Maloes, or off Cape Clear, into one squadron; and I am the more strongly confirmed in that opinion at present, because by the sending away of so great a force to America as is now designed to be put under the command of Admiral Lestock we are incapacitated from dividing our force to the westward, which, when collected together is not more than sufficient to withstand the Brest or Rochefort fleets, if united with that of Ferrol. I am moreover confident that these are the sentiments of his Majesty, as well as of the Ministers, who, I think, very justly agree that no little <u>Agreements</u> of making prizes on the enemy ought in any measure to be put in competition with the keeping an ascendancy over them in the Channel.[49]

Clearly, the reasoning at this time was not solely related to the movements of enemy squadrons. The need to impose greater discipline upon the navy was also apparent. Sandwich agreed, but was not convinced about the urgency and argued that some cruisers should be kept out to intercept the Spanish treasure fleet.[50]

Active forces in home waters were now divided between the Channel Squadron under Anson, Lestock's escort of the expedition, Commodore William Mitchell's small ships off Ostend and Commodore Smith's squadron patrolling Scottish waters. Anson's orders were signed on 6 August. They allowed him to operate where he felt best 'for intercepting and destroying the ships of the enemy, their convoys outward and homeward bound, and for suppressing their privateers and annoying their trade and for protecting the trade of his Majesty's subjects'. He was free to cruise as long as he could and detach ships for special duties or to refit as he saw necessary. Anson had nominal command of 17 ships of the line, 10 cruisers (50s-40s) and

---

49   BL, Add Mss, 15955, f. 133–134, Bedford to Anson, 18 July 1746, original emphasis.

50   BL, Add Ms 15957, f. 5, Sandwich to Anson, 20 July 1746. Richmond presents the opinions of Bedford and Sandwich as far more dichotomous and principled. However, it seems that both men were responding to a specific question of what to do at this point. As Bedford's reply to Anson indicates, the view that the squadron should be united, given the departure of Lestock's squadron, was just about universally held by king and ministry. Richmond also suggests that Anson was raising the matter autonomously as a result of his succession to command the Channel Squadron. He noted that he had not found Anson's original letter. He had missed Newcastle's initiation of the process and Anson's letter to Bedford on the 17 which provides the background to the matter.

two sloops, but found organising his squadron difficult as the demands of Lestock's ships conflicted with his own.[51] It was not until 4 September that Anson got to sea.

While these preparations were in hand, concern that the Dutch would make peace continued. On 4 August it was known that the French and Dutch had agreed to a conference at Breda. However, the French position was not as strong as it had been. The death of King Philip V of Spain (9 July [n.s.]) gave hope that the new king, Ferdinand VI, would abandon the dowager Queen's obsession for territory in Italy for her sons. News from Italy in June also indicated that the Bourbon position there was beginning to crumble. The Franco-Spanish army had been heavily defeated by the Austrians at Piacenza and was in a headlong retreat towards Nice.[52] It was now even possible that the Austro-Sardinian forces would be able to launch an offensive into Provence. This opened the prospect of negotiations with Spain to detach her from France and, using Portuguese channels, Newcastle, sent a Spanish exile and the last ambassador to Madrid, Sir Benjamin Keene, to Lisbon to open negotiations with Spain.

In the mean time, the situation in Flanders deteriorated. In July the French invested Charleroi. If this city fell, Namur would be next and the French would be able to threaten the United Provinces from the east as well as the south. Marshal Batthyány and the allied council of war agreed to march the army south-east to protect both cities. Prince Charles of Lorraine and two Austrian corps had crossed the Rhine and would join the Confederate Army on its march. Ligonier believed that this would bring the allies up to about 65,000 men in the field, as opposed to about 130,000 French.[53] Although the Confederate Army successfully ranged itself in front of Namur, Saxe denied them any chance of relieving Charleroi, which surrendered on 22 July.[54] Despite his numerical superiority, Saxe refused to give battle and throughout August the armies stood watching each other as provisions dwindled.

---

51 Woburn Archive, Bedford Mss xiii f. 21, Anson to Bedford, 17 or 21 (?) August 1746; f. 25, Anson to Bedford, 22 August 1746.

52 Wilkinson, *The Defence of Piedmont*, op. cit., 252–263.

53 TNA, SP 87/20, f. 232, Ligonier to Harrington, 20 July 1746 (n.s.); f. 237, Ligonier to Harrington, 24 July 1746 (n.s.).

54 Ibid., f. 246, Ligonier to Harrington, 3 August 1746 (n.s.).

The End of the Canadian Expedition and the Coastal Raids on France, August–October 1746

The Dutch had to be kept in the war if Flanders was to be retrieved. The Earl of Sandwich was sent to Breda to join the negotiations, but with firm instruction not to concede to French terms. He was to keep the negotiations going until further news was received from Lisbon and Provence.[55] Like the capture of Quebec, the defection of Spain or the invasion of Southern France made it possible that peace might be made without returning Cape Breton.

On the morning of 21 August a meeting of ministers was called to consider the future of St Clair's expedition. Seven regiments of foot were already headed for Flanders and it was possible that Cumberland himself might go to command them.[56] If St Clair's additional six regiments were sent to Flanders something considerable might be achieved before the winter set in. Newcastle was opposed to this. Although the Dutch might be reassured, it would give France hope that Cape Breton might be recovered and strike anxiety into the hearts of Bedford, Cobham and the New Allies for the same reason. An alternative would be to send the expedition to attack the coast of France. Such an operation had been considered for a while. The prospect of the Provence operation had revived memories of Protestant insurrection in southern France during a similar operation in 1707 and the west of France had its own history of Protestant resistance that might be encouraged.[57] There were a number of other attractions as well. It kept the expeditionary force together and, if it wintered in Ireland after operations, it would be ready for an early start in 1747. Thus it retained its political and diplomatic weight. It had an additional popular appeal in that it was a direct riposte to the French invasion threats since 1744. It might do great damage to French maritime commerce and infrastructure if it attacked some ports. This coincided with the popular belief that France could be badly damaged by sea power. Also, operating in the eastern Atlantic, rather than America, it gave some comfort to the Dutch. It provided the possibility that French forces might be diverted from Flanders and eventually, the whole force might be sent as reinforcement to Flanders. Finally, it was a great relief to those in the ministry, like Anson and Pelham, who feared that the French invasion

---

55 Lodge, *Eighteenth Century Diplomacy*, op. cit., 165–171; BL, Add Ms 32708, f. 101, Newcastle to George II, 18 August 1746.

56 TNA, SP 45/5, unfoliated, Newcastle to George II, 21 August 1746. For the dispositions of the British regiments, see *Gentleman's Magazine*, xvi (1746), 440.

57 TNA, SP 42/98, f. 122, Newcastle to St Clair, 22 August 1746.

threat was not yet dead. It kept a substantial naval force in home waters.[58] The ministers were unanimous; the expedition would be directed to attack the western coast of France.[59]

The sudden change in plan shocked St Clair who had no plans or information regarding that part of the world. Although opinion had been unanimous at the meeting on 22 August, one important voice had not yet been heard – that of the Duke of Cumberland. Cumberland had arrived back in London from Scotland on 25 July. He was feted by the public and honoured by his father as a martial hero. The King had approved the plan to attack the French coast on the 21 July, but seems to have been having second thoughts, perhaps under the influence of St Clair's reaction and Cumberland's preference for reinforcing Flanders. Newcastle arranged for the inner cabinet to meet on Monday 25 August with Cumberland and Wade. On the Sunday, Newcastle met the King, Bedford and Beauclerk to rehearse the arguments. Anson gave his approval of the expedition. With all these names behind him, Newcastle vigorously defended the plan at the meeting with Cumberland. At the end of it Cumberland was won over. He agreed that six more regiments in Flanders would not make much difference so late in the campaign and even suggested reinforcing the expedition with two battalions of Guards and two regiments from the Irish establishment under Major General Read. The King approved these reinforcements and the addition of Huske's Welch Fusiliers.[60]

In the meantime, Lestock and St Clair had decided to attack Lorient, the home port of the French East India Company. At 8.00 am on 15 September Lestock set the signal to unmoor and the expeditionary force set sail from Portsmouth[61]. They reached the French coast at Quimperlé Bay on 18 September and the troops landed on 20 September with complete success, despite the lack of surprise. By the evening of 21 September the

58 BL, Add Ms 32708, f. 108, H. Pelham to Newcastle, 22 (?) August 1746; Woburn Archive, Bedford Mss, xiii (1746), f. 29, Anson to Bedford, 24 August 1746.

59 BL, Add Ms 32708, f. 120, Newcastle to George II, 21 August 1746. The full attendance list of this meeting is not known. Harrington, Newcastle and Bedford were there, Hardwicke, Pelham and Anson were not. Others are not known.

60 BL, Add Ms 32708, f. 150, Newcastle to Pelham, 26 August 1746; f. 164, Newcastle to George II, 27 August 1746.

61 Details of this expedition can be found in R. Harding, 'The Expedition to Lorient, 1746', in N. Tracy (ed.) *The Age of Sail: The International Annual of the Historic Sailing Ship*, I, (London, 2002), 34–54. The French side of the campaign is covered more fully in P. Diverres, *L'Attaque de Lorient par les Anglais (1746)*, Rennes, 1931.

army was before Lorient. The French authorities were urgently building batteries and calling in the militia from the surrounding countryside, but decided to offer St Clair negotiations. St Clair refused, but after two days of building batteries, the engineers concluded that, given the state of the road back to the landing beaches, they could not bring up enough ammunition and shot to break the walls or French batteries. By the afternoon of the 26 September St Clair and his three brigadiers agreed to abandon the attempt. St Clair blamed his engineers for failing to site the batteries effectively and inform him accurately of the general situation in relation to a siege. The ammunition was fired off and the heavier cannons and mortars spiked up. By 29 September all the troops were back aboard the transports.

On 30 September a majority of officers on the council of war held on Lestock's flagship, the *Princessa*, agreed that they should make for Ireland as their instructions ordered. Neither Lestock nor St Clair were in favour of this, but were constrained by the requirement to concede to the majority. However, as they made sail they received two important pieces of information. The first was from Captain Thomas Lake of the *Exeter* (60), whom Lestock had sent out to sound Quiberon Bay. He reported that he had found an excellent channel for large ships to enter the bay. The second was a letter from Captain Wickham of the *Panther* (50), who informed Lestock that two battalions of Guards had arrived at Portsmouth and would soon be sent to him as reinforcements. St Clair and Lestock realised that as they could now be sure of being able to lie safely in wait of these additional troops, and agreed that they should make for Quiberon, where they arrived on 2 October. After a day reconnoitring, the army landed on the Quiberon peninsula and established a battery across its neck. Reconnaissance around the bay yielded some small prizes and confirmed that there were other good landing places. However, the army was now reduced to about 2,600 fit troops and no further news of the missing transports or reinforcements arrived. A council of war on 7 October considered the situation and agreed that as the campaign in Flanders must now be over, the value of the expedition as a diversion was probably at an end. It was agreed to ravage the Brittany islands of Houet and Hedic and return to Ireland. On 17 October the expeditionary force sailed. The force split up on the 23 October, with the transports heading for Cork, where they arrived on 31 October. Lestock's squadron dropped anchor at Spithead on the 27 October.

The impact of the expedition was ambiguous. In its final form it had been intended to draw off French forces from Flanders. There was no evidence that it had done this. Throughout September the Confederate Army had been harried by Saxe. His rapid move to capture Huy cut the allies off from their supply at Maastricht and the countryside beyond. Rather than give battle to a superior force, Prince Charles decided to cross to the eastern bank of the Meuse and move down stream to reopen communications with Maastricht. This was successfully achieved, but Saxe pushed up and held the allies in a confined territory in front of the city, subsisting on a diminishing stock of provisions. Meanwhile, unprotected by the army, Namur surrendered on 14 September. The allies moved south again to protect Liege, which was seen as Saxe's next objective. Saxe moved to attack the allies on 30 September. Before the engagement properly opened, the French got into Liege and opened up the allied left flank. The Dutch had to turn to re-establish the flank, while Ligonier defended the centre, including the village of Roucoux, from which this battle took its name.[62] It was a stubborn contest in which the centre under Ligonier and the left under Waldeck bore the brunt of the fighting. At nightfall, the allies withdrew back over the Meuse, leaving about 5,000 dead, wounded and prisoners. Saxe did not press them, but prepared for winter quarters and a new campaign that would aim to capture Maastricht. The Confederate Army fell back into Dutch territory for winter quarters around Venlo.

Although the coastal expedition did not decisively alter events in Flanders, it had an impact. It came near to success and information from Holland suggested that it had given the French a serious fright. Particularly, they were worried about Belle Ile.[63] The cost had been remarkably low. The expeditionary force remained generally healthy and in a position to sail for North America early in the new year.[64] On the other hand, the shock and damage caused to France made the ministry fear that the French would mount small coastal raids from Dunkirk or even revive their invasion plans to exact revenge.[65] Originally, the expeditionary force was ordered to sail for Ireland on completion of operations, to leave for America early in the new year. However, fear that French attention would turn away from the Meuse to the Channel and another invasion plan caused the orders to be revised. The whole force was ordered back to Britain.[66]

---

62 TNA, SP 87/21, f. 21, Ligonier to Harrington, 6 September 1746. Just before the battle the three British battalions, long expected from Scotland, finally arrived in camp under Brigadier Houghton.

63 TNA, SP 42/98, f. 208, Newcastle to Lestock and St Clair, 22 October 1746.

64 Woburn Archive, Bedford Papers, xv, f. 24, Bedford to Stone, 10 November 1746.

65 BL, Add Ms 35408, f. 276, Newcastle to Hardwicke, 19 October 1746.

66 TNA, SP 42/98, f. 253, Newcastle to St Clair, 18 November 1746. *Grenville Correspond-*

The Crises and the Duke of Newcastle

The preceding eighteen months had been the most dramatic and turbulent of the entire war.[67] The relatively bright prospects of 1745 had rapidly unravelled in the face of defeat at Fontenoy and the Jacobite rising in Scotland. The Confederate Army was weak and ill prepared for 1746. Before the campaign had properly opened, Antwerp and Brussels had fallen. In Italy the change in fortune after the Battle of Piacenza in June 1746 was equally dramatic and the Austro-Sardinian forces were prepared to invade Provence. All the while, Britain could contribute little to the Confederate Army The attempt to regain the initiative by an invasion of Canada was well conceived but hindered by bad weather and a French expedition to recover Louisbourg. The shift to attacking the French coast was largely aimed at doing some material damage to France and maintaining a credible threat from the sea.

On the whole, so far as the public was concerned, the naval war was a mixed affair. The list of French and Spanish merchantmen captured by warships and privateers was impressive.[68] However, there was no clear evidence that this activity was having a crucial impact on either France or Spain. The courts martial in the wake of the Battle of Toulon had done little to restore public confidence. At sea, the navy had played a crucial role in deterring a French invasion and restricting support to the rebels in Scotland and supporting the royal army's advance. However, it had not stopped d'Anville's expedition and although Anson went to sea with all the ships available in home waters in September, with freedom to use this naval power as he saw fit, he returned to Spithead on 28 October with no obvious success.

Neither the Flanders campaign nor the naval war produced results that promised a good peace, and splits within the ministry had begun to open. The most serious split was between Newcastle and his brother Henry Pelham. From the early summer of 1746, Pelham had become convinced

---

ence, op. cit., 55–6, Bedford to G. Grenville, 24 November 1746.

67 Inevitably, most histories focus on the Jacobite Rebellion as the central feature in this period. A hostile army on British soil, under one hundred miles from London, is solid justification for that focus. Most of the interest is in debates around the counter-factual proposition that the Jacobite army could have toppled the Hanoverian state by a swift advance on London from Derby. Whether or not they would have been successful cannot be explored here, but it can be asserted that the rebellion did create a crisis of policy. It shattered the Flanders campaign for over a year, with repercussions that echoed to the end of the war.

68 See *Gentleman's Magazine* for monthly lists of prizes taken.

that the Dutch negotiations with the French would lead to a separate peace. He was also disgusted with the consistent failure of Austria to use the subsidies effectively. In sum, he believed that Britain could not carry on the war with such allies and Britain had to make serious efforts to conclude peace with France.[69] He was supported by Harrington and the Earl of Chesterfield. They differed on the value of Dutch neutrality. Harrington feared for Hanover, but Chesterfield saw great advantages as he did not believe the French could campaign as easily in Western Germany as they did in the Low Countries. However, they agreed that a naval war would not have any effect on France.[70] Newcastle, Bedford and Hardwicke fundamentally disagreed. So long as the Dutch could be kept fighting, another campaign in North America or Europe, or both, could force a better peace and, crucially, the King was inclined to agree with this view.

This fundamental split on the practicality of continuing the war was bad enough, but it coincided with a changing approach to government within the ministry. Since the beginning of the war the ministry had worked with open discussion among an inner group of ministers. Newcastle had shone in this environment, balancing the views of colleagues and Parliament to create a working war ministry that was capable of generating trust in Parliament and, eventually, from the King. With that trust it was capable of absorbing new allies and adjusting policies to meet new diplomatic realities. It was because of this approach to government that Newcastle, the Old Corps and the New Allies had eventually expelled Granville from government. In the early summer of 1746 it seemed the King had finally accepted his ministry could conduct a war policy in which he had faith. Parliament seemed supportive of measures that took the war to France in Europe and North America. At this point, it suddenly was threatened from within. Chesterfield had urged Newcastle to exploit his victory over Granville, and Newcastle was beginning to see himself as the driver of policy. With the King's support, his

---

69 Coxe, *Pelham*, op. cit., ii 329, Pelham to H. Walpole, 12 June 1746; 330, Pelham to Robinson, 18 July 1746; 331, Pelham to H. Walpole, 29 July 1746; BL, Add Ms 32709, f. 9, H. Pelham to Stone (?), 4 October 1746.

70 Dobrée, *Letters of Philip Dormer Stanhope*, op. cit., iii, 749, Chesterfield to Newcastle, 20 March 1745/6.; 762, Chesterfield to Trevor, 20 May 1746. Chesterfield's speculation on the logistical problem posed to France by campaigning in Germany, have been given support by H.M. Scott's work on the campaign of 1757. See H.M. Scott, 'Hanover in Mid-Eighteenth Century Franco-British Geopolitics', in B. Simms and T. Riotte (eds) *The Hanoverian Dimension in British History, 1714–1837*, Cambridge, 2007, 275–300, especially 291–296.

behaviour increasingly resembled that of Granville. Regardless of colleagues, he was busy pushing negotiations with Austria and the United Provinces. He was conducting private correspondence with Sandwich over the Dutch negotiations and politics. The situation appalled Henry Pelham and deepened the rift with his brother.[71]

The war was at a critical point. Negotiations had started at Breda and Britain had to chose between accepting terms with the Dutch or making it difficult for the Dutch to make a peace. Newcastle wanted the impression of British negotiation to encourage the Dutch, but the objective was to string out the talks so that another campaign could be organised. He gained the King's agreement to send the Earl of Sandwich to Breda as Britain's representative, with these private instructions. Harrington knew that Newcastle corresponded with Sandwich, but, as the responsible Secretary of State, assumed that he had control of the official negotiation.[72]

However, Harrington's relations with the King had never recovered from the resignations of February 1746 and it was increasingly clear that, with the King's support, Newcastle was directing the negotiations. On 28 October 1746 Harrington brought draft letters he had prepared for Sandwich and Trevor to a meeting of ministers. He had previously discussed them with the King and was staggered to find that Newcastle and Hardwicke objected to them. Harrington fumed against the interference and the private correspondence and, when he realised that the King had connived at this, resigned his post.[73] The King's approval of Newcastle's position was made clear by his immediate acceptance of the Earl of Chesterfield as Harrington's successor. Chesterfield had been *persona non grata* to George only a few years ago, but was now quick to have him installed as Secretary of State for the Northern Department, one of the most senior posts in the realm.[74]

Chesterfield had long expressed his doubts about the practicality of continuing the war, but, since returning to England from Ireland in July, seems to have been convinced that another campaign was worthwhile. Chesterfield had spent some time at the Duke of Bedford's seat, Woburn Abbey, and it might have been here that he came to accept that Canada still offered oppor-

---

71 BL, Add Ms 32709, f. 35, Newcastle to George II, no date (probably October 1746); f. 65, H. Pelham to Stone, 18 October 1746.

72 Coxe, *Pelham*, op. cit., ii, 332, Pelham to H. Walpole, 29 July 1746; Dobree, *Chesterfield*, 769, Chesterfield to Trevor, 5 August 1746.

73 BL, Add Ms 32709, f. 117, Newcastle to George II, 28 October 1746.

74 BL, Add Ms 35408, f. 280, Newcastle to Hardwicke, 28 October 1746.

tunities.[75] While Lord Lieutenant of Ireland, Chesterfield had entered into the regular, open and discursive style of correspondence that was the mark of Newcastle's communication with political allies of all kinds. Newcastle clearly felt that he had convinced Chesterfield of his views and had him ready to assume Harrington's post. Henry Pelham continued to argue for peace, and where possible prevented Newcastle meeting other ministers alone, but Newcastle, now had the confidence of the King and the Duke of Cumberland, the support of Bedford and Chesterfield. Newcastle wrote to the Duke of Grafton about Pelham's constant attendance 'I am now, with all my faults, plainly the Favourite Secretary with Mr Pelham, who, last night, in a very sly way said "My Brother and Lord Chesterfield's plan is to attack France on all sides etc.'[76] That summed up accurately the initial plan for 1747, but it barely lasted a month.

---

75 For his long opposition to continuing the war, see Dobree, *Chesterfield*, op. cit.

76 BL, Add Ms 32709, f. 192, Newcastle to Grafton, 8 November 1746, original emphasis.

10

Newcastle's War: the End in Europe and America, January 1747–October 1748

Revival of the Flanders War

Newcastle's domination of the cabinet reflected the political realities of the moment. First, he had the support of the King. As Granville had demonstrated, with royal support it was possible for any minister to stand apart from his colleagues in Cabinet. However, as Granville's fate also demonstrated, it was not enough. If a minister chose to stand separately, he had to command a majority in parliament. For this, party support was vital. Granville never achieved it, but, for a short period, Newcastle did. Newcastle could depend on the Broad Bottom alliance.

America was crucial to Newcastle's position. He insisted that Cape Breton would not be surrendered and Bedford was satisfied that the war in America had not been given up, but would be revived in 1747.[1] Bedford was also pragmatic enough to see that the rebellion and the continued danger of French invasion could intervene and deflect resources from North America.[2] Cape Breton united the New Allies to the Old Corps and stood in the way of peace. However much Pelham and Chesterfield wanted peace, only another campaign could shift the diplomatic balance while preserving the domestic political settlement.

Cumberland's victorious campaign against the Jacobites had raised him and the army to great heights. Even allowing for exaggerated relief by the

---

1 Woburn Archive, Bedford Mss xv, f. 20, Beauclerk to Bedford, 10 November 1746; f. 24, Bedford to Stone, 10 November 1746.

2 Woburn Archive, Bedford Mss, xv, f. 43, Newcastle to Bedford, 20 November 1746; *Grenville Correspondence*, 55–6, Bedford to G. Grenville, 24 November 1746. Bedford's frustration with this, might account for the reports that he was increasingly testy in relations with those who did not fully support his views.

destruction of a frightening army of Jacobites and deference to his royal person, high expectations about this young general were strongly held by people in Britain and Europe. The Brittany campaign had done nothing to dampen regard for the army and although the British contribution to the Confederate Army in Flanders had been small, it was asserted that it was British and German troops that had averted disaster at Roucoux.[3] The animosity between British and Hanoverians that marked the 1743–1744 campaigns had disappeared. The King's troops, with Hessian auxiliaries, were now seen as a core around which a larger and more effective Confederate Army might take the field. Nevertheless, the key to the new plan lay not in Flanders but in Italy. The year 1746 had shown that French forces could be diverted from Flanders. The attack on the Brittany coast was intended to do just this, but it was the Austro-Sardinian advance towards Provence after the Battle of Piacenza in June that was most interesting. Newcastle believed that 88 battalions had been withdrawn from Flanders to face the new threat.[4] If this pressure could be maintained, there was no chance of the French fielding a major force in Flanders during 1747. It was calculated that if the allies could get into the field first with a large army of about 100,000 the losses of the previous years could be regained in a single campaign.[5]

There was also reason to believe that the allies would make greater efforts in a new campaign. The losses of 1746 had brought the war closer to the United Provinces. Likewise, the Austrians had lost most of Flanders, and could lose in a peace the land communication between Flanders and their Rhenish territories. Negotiations with the allies at The Hague found them surprisingly willing to contribute to a revived Confederate Army in Flanders.[6] The original plan, discussed by ministers in October, concluded that they would need a field army of at least 100,000 to recapture Flanders. It was expected that the Dutch could provide 20,000 troops. The Austrians would

---

3 TNA, SP87/21, f. 169, Ligonier to Harrington, 31 October 1746 (n.s.).

4 BL, Add Ms 32709, f. 369, Newcastle to Cumberland, 23 December 1746.

5 BL, Add Ms 35409, f. 13, Projet (undated, but before 18 November 1746). One of the frustrating aspects of Newcastle's domination of the cabinet, is the absence of papers that record how decisions were made. Exactly how the new plan emerged, what professional advice was sought and how close to unanimity the ministers were, is unknown. Sir Richard Lodge considered the plan as Newcastle's own and dismissed it because the Duke was 'profoundly ignorant of all military affairs'. See Lodge, *Eighteenth Century Diplomacy*, op. cit., 215. See also, TNA, SP87/21, f. 203, Ligonier to Chesterfield, 1 December 1746 (n.s.).

6 BL, Add Ms 32709, f. 352, Newcastle to Cumberland 19 December 1746.

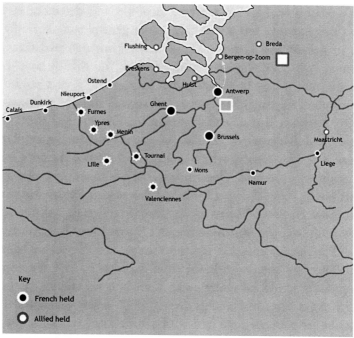

Map 13 Flanders, Spring 1747

provide 50,000, and Britain 34,000. The Confederate Army in Flanders would therefore be 104,000. As the invasion of Provence was central to the campaign, the Austrians were also expected to provide 50,000 for that invasion, in conjunction with 30,000 Sardinian troops. However, as negotiations proceeded throughout November and into January 1747, the Dutch were induced to agree to 40,000, the Austrians to 60,000 in Flanders and 60,000 in Provence and the British increased their contingent to 40,000. This would enable the allies to field 140,000 troops against a weakened French army in Flanders. Command of the army was also settled with surprising ease. The Dutch and Austrians accepted the Duke of Cumberland as supreme commander for the campaign.[7]

Part of the reason for the success of the negotiations was the expansion of British subsidies. Unlike 1742–1745, the issue of subsidies to allies created hardly a ripple of dissent in Parliament. This was partly because of the rebellion, but also because from 1746 the employment of Hanoverians was

---

7   TNA, SP87/12, f.203, Ligonier to Chesterfield, 1 December 1746.

serving British interests.[8] The end of the war in Germany in December 1745 removed the suspicion that British money was paying to defend the borders of Hanover against Prussia. Instead, they were the largest single contingent in the British contribution to the Flanders war.

Record sums were provided to Hanover (£410,000), Austria (£433,000) and Sardinia (£300,000). Additional subsidies to Hesse, Bavaria, Cologne and Mainz took the sum to over £1.2 million.[9] The second critical feature of the subsidy policy and, indeed, the whole war plan, was the availability of credit. The rebellion had shaken the financial confidence of the City, but the willingness of the small number of large investors to stand by the regime rapidly stabilised the markets and government credit. However, the backlash against the 'Trafffickers' or moneymen, who had certainly profited handsomely from their investments, was a demand that in future loans should be placed on the open market. Henry Pelham was extremely anxious about a loan of £4 million. The new system was unknown, but within four hours, £6 million had been subscribed. The success shocked ministers, but gave them confidence that credit was no longer an issue for prosecuting the war.[10]

As 1746 drew to a close, Newcastle reflected that 'I think it impossible for things to look everywhere better than they do.'[11] He was being optimistic, but news that the Austro-Sardinian forces had crossed the River Var into Provence between 17 and 19 November (o.s.), was a sign that one of the fundamentals of the campaign was in place.[12] It was now important that the allies got their troops into the field early and ministers at The Hague, Turin and Vienna were ordered to press those courts to get their forces together, with a clear threat that George II expected the numbers to be precisely what was bargained for with the subsidy.

---

8   Harris, *A Patriot Press*, op. cit., 213–222.

9   Corbett, *Parliamentary History*, op. cit., xiii, 1432–1433; Coxe, *Pelham*, op. cit., i, 350. The total sum required for 1747 was just under £9.5 million.

10   The open subscription was a return to an older method of raising credit that also had its problems. See Dickson, *The Financial Revolution in England*, op. cit., 223–228. See also BL, Add Ms 32709, f. 352, Newcastle to Cumberland, 19 December 1746; Dobrée, *Chesterfield*, op. cit., iii, 833, Chesterfield to Robinson, 19 December 1746.

11   BL, Add Ms 32709, f. 369, Newcastle to Cumberland, 19 December 1746.

12   For a narrative of the campaign, see Spencer Wilkinson, *The Defence of Piedmont*, op. cit., 279–287.

The Naval War and North America

Despite three years of failure, expectations of the campaign in Flanders remained high. However, it is striking how low were the expectations of the war at sea. It is true that the navy had done a good job in deterring French invasion and although the expedition to Canada had not taken place, it had been effectively organised and had operated in European waters with very little trouble. Nothing had happened to indicate that, from a naval perspective, operations in Canada were impracticable, and exploiting North America remained firmly in the minds of ministers. However, there were few voices being heard that now that claimed Bourbon power could be destroyed by sea power. The war against Bourbon trade continued to yield a large number of prizes, but French and Spanish privateers in turn continued to take a toll of British trade. Damage was being done, but there was ample evidence that French trade had shifted to neutral shipping, which was entangling diplomatic relations with countries such as Denmark, Prussia and, most frustrating of all, the United Provinces.[13]

Since 1742, the British had expected the French war effort to show signs of exhaustion owing to the fundamental financial fragility of the French crown. The continuing campaigns had left spectators in London mystified as to why this weakness had not manifested itself more clearly.[14] However, masked by the continued ability to put squadrons to sea, the financial core of French naval strength was rapidly draining away. D'Antin's expedition to the West Indies in 1740 had cost about one-third more than anticipated.[15] It was fortunate for France that the expedition did not provoke war with Britain as it had seriously depleted the naval budget which took almost three years to recover. D'Anville's expedition to Cape Breton in 1746 took another huge financial effort. The concern these expeditions caused the British also masked the extreme levels of operational complexity and damage to the naval resources that they imposed on France. Loss of manpower by desertion, death and sickness and damage to ships made the Brest squadron almost inoperable when it limped back to that port in April 1741. D'Anville's force experienced devastating levels of sickness

---

13   The diplomatic impact upon neutrals of the war on French and Spanish trade can be followed in R. Pares, *Colonial Blockade and Neutral Rights, 1739–1763*, Oxford, 1938.

14   Corbett, *Parliamentary History*, op. cit., xiii, 1437, 5 December 1746.

15   R.D. Bourland, 'Maurepas and His Administration of the French Navy on the Eve of the War of Austrian Succession (1737–1742)', unpublished PhD thesis, University of Notre Dame, 1978.

and straggled back to France in the autumn and early winter of 1746 in a shattered condition.[16]

Although the British did not know it, by the beginning of 1745 the French navy was strained to breaking point. The Minister of Marine, Maurepas, decided that it was impossible to keep the great squadrons of Brest and Toulon together. He could not see how these squadrons, combined with the Spanish, pinned the British fleet in its over-stretched and inflexible deployment. Instead he believed that they were better used protecting France's oceanic trade. The squadrons were broken up to form escorts and cruising squadrons for merchant convoys.[17] These large convoys, which formed up in the Bay of Biscay, were soon noted by the British and attempts to intercept them were made on both sides of the Atlantic. On 31 October 1745, Vice Admiral Townsend, cruising out of Antigua, managed to intercept a large westbound convoy of over 200 merchantmen under escort of four warships and captured 20 of them before they got into Martinique. However, his successor, Commodore Lee, failed to meet the next large convoy which arrived safely at Fort Royale, Martinique, on 15 June 1746.[18] Likewise, the homeward bound convoys evaded Anson's Western Squadron.[19] Anson's first cruise from early September to late October achieved little. Bad weather that drove him off station and the continuous presence of French privateers and neutral shipping to warn the French of his presence, made it a difficult and frustrating cruise.[20] Nevertheless, Anson sailed

---

16 Pritchard, *Anatomy of a Naval Disaster*, op. cit., 197–203. It would not have been possible to mount D'Anville's expedition at all without an additional 13 million livres being granted for the naval budget in December 1745. For a study of the fragility of French naval manpower in the Seven Years War, see, T.J.A. Le Goff, 'Problémes de Recrutement de la marine française pendent la Guerre de Sept Ans', *Revue Historique*, 283 (1990), 208–233.

17 C. Buchet, *La Lutte pour l'Espace Caribe et la Façade Atlantique de l'Amerique Centrale du Sud (1672–1763)*, 2 vols, Paris, 1991, i, 300; E. Taillemite, 'Une Bataille de l'Atlantique au XVIIIe Siecle: La Guerre de Succession d'Autriche, 1744–1748', in *Guerres et Paix*, Paris, 1987, 131–148.

18 Buchet, *La Lutte*, op. cit., 291.

19 Anson missed the return of D'Anville's squadron from Cape Breton and was off station, returning to Portsmouth, when Conflans arrived back at Brest with the West Indies convoy on 6 Nov 1746 (n.s.). In January 1747, in the Eastern Atlantic, Commodore Fox intercepted Dubois de la Motte escorting a convoy back from the West Indies, but failed to prevent him getting his 64 charges safely into Brest. See, M. Verge-Franceschi, *La Marine Francaise au xviiie Siecle*, Paris, 1996, 99.

20 BL, Add Ms 35409 (Hardwicke Papers), f.26, Anson to Newcastle, 11 May 1747.

again in early November and stayed out on station cruising from Brest to Ushant, until mid-February. Winter gales wrought serious damage to his ships. Apart from capturing a French hospital ship the cruise yielded nothing but discomfort and anxiety.[21] Anson confessed the cruises had been unsuccessful. He had not been able to move in response to intelligence as effectively as he hoped and that the damage his squadron had received being at sea for so long in the winter was far greater than he anticipated, but he had learned a great deal.[22] The attrition of the weather, the need for frigates, cruisers or friendly privateers to act as scouts, had to be resolved for a Western cruising squadron to be a success.

Although British policymakers were only dimly aware of it, the balance of effective naval force had swung decisively in favour of Britain.[23] In 1746, France had 35 effective line of battle ships and 16 frigates. At the same time, Britain had 63 line of battle ships and 96 frigates, but the number of ships returning to home waters is a clue to the naval situation at the beginning of 1747. While French and Spanish forces were scattered around the Atlantic ports to act as local escort squadrons, and others were in the West Indies as convoy escorts, the British fleet had been concentrating at home. The need to do this had been recognised in 1743, but it was only during 1745 that the fruits of the policy began to become evident. The growing number of ships of all types made the employment of a Western Squadron more practicable. It also made the support of that squadron by smaller ships more possible. The number of ships active in home waters had risen from 60 in January 1745, to 119 (+98 per cent) by January 1746 and 123 by January 1747, a cumulative rise of 105 per cent.[24] The importance of this was not just that providing larger squadrons was now possible, but that the supply, manning, maintenance and victualling of ships became simpler. The stresses that hit the victualling service in 1740 and 1744 were not repeated. The undermanning was chronic and accepted, but in home waters the situation was easier.

---

21   Bedford Archive, Bedford Mss xv, f. 64, Anson to Bedford, 4 Dec 1746; f. 74, Anson to Bedford, 13 December 1746.

22   Bedford Archive, Bedford Mss xvi, f. 30, Anson to Bedford, 6 February 1746/7.

23   Pritchard, *Anatomy*, op. cit, 39. The British figure is taken from the 1 June report in TNA, Adm 8/25 (Ship Dispositions).

24   TNA, Adm 8/25. The definition of active is calculated by adding those ships listed as convoys and cruisers to those listed as at Home, minus those listed as fitting out.

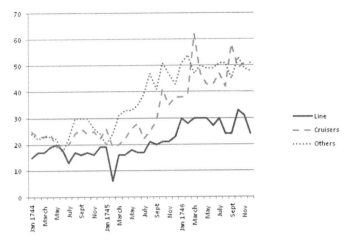

Figure 10.1 Ships in home waters, January 1744–December 1746
Source: TNA, Adm 8/24 and Adm 8/25.

The reverse was now true for the French fleet. A larger percentage of the fleet was forced to spend time overseas in the Americas, in ports that were nowhere near as highly developed as the British ports, which had seen continuous, if generally low level, investment since 1714.[25] The relative levels of stress and degradation as a result of overstretch, which had been very much in favour of the Bourbon squadrons from 1740 to 1745, was gradually but decisively shifting in Britain's favour during 1746–1747.

However, the lack of dramatic success at sea masked this shift and there were other tensions within the Admiralty and naval establishment at this time. When Bedford became First Lord of the Admiralty in December 1744, he brought with him a new generation of politician administrators, Sandwich, George Grenville and Anson, who were eager to exercise power and rapidly became frustrated by the apparent negligence of the Navy Board. The Board was dominated by the Comptroller, Captain Richard Haddock, who had been in office since 1734 and the Surveyor, Sir Joseph Ackworth, who had held his post since 1715.[26] Ackworth was the key technical expert

---

25   The British were also unaware that the trans-Atlantic convoy system was imposing heavy costs on French merchants. See Taillemite, 'Une Bataille de l'Atlantique', op. cit.

26   The other four members of the Board had not been so long in post. The Clerk of Acts, John Clevland, since April 1743, the Comptroller of the Treasurer's Account, William Corbett, since December 1743, the Comptroller of the Victualling Accounts, Francis Gashry, since June 1744, and the Comptroller of the Storekeeper's Accounts, George Crowl, since March 1741.

on the Board and thus the principal figure in the dispute with the Admiralty. As Surveyor he was responsible for dockyards, buildings and supply, building, repair and maintenance of all warships. He was not popular among shipbuilders or naval officers, but his long service had, according to Henry Legge, given him 'so much the nature of Pompey the Great about him that he cannot bear an equal'.[27] The Admiralty felt offended by the advice of the Board and the Board felt itself fully qualified to challenge, resist or make counter-proposals to these new Admiralty Commissioners. Very soon the clashes began. The Admiralty was aware that criticism of British warships had been mounting within the navy over the years. British ships were smaller in dimensions and tonnage for the number of guns they carried, compared to their Bourbon adversaries. The result was the ships were less stable (particularly the 80s) and seaworthy than there enemies. They had also ceased to be built to a single pattern or design laid down for such vessels. The Admiralty initiated an examination of the design of line of battle ships by a committee of flag officers under Sir John Norris in June 1745.

The result was not entirely what the Admiralty expected. The committee supported the increase in dimensions for ships, but retained the three-deck 80 against the two and half deck 74. The committee also increased the fire-power of the ships by restoring the weight of guns of the ships of the line to the pre-1743 position. The Admiralty had to accept the committee's advice, but took the opportunity to reduce the discretion of the Surveyor or shipbuilders by strengthening the demand of standardisation of each rate of ship. The Admiralty also retained the right to cut down existing 90s and 80s to 74s.[28] The result was delays and bad feelings, but little real change.[29]

The tension continued during 1745 and 1746, particularly after a new Admiralty commissioner, Henry Bilson Legge, joined the Board in April 1745. Legge's attempts to remove Ackworth came to nothing and the energy in the dispute gradually dissipated. Legge moved on to the Treasury in June 1746. Bedford had hinted he was ready to resign and Sandwich was despatched to The Hague in August, where he was increasingly drawn into speculations as to whether he would succeed Bedford as First Lord or

---

27   Baugh, *British Naval Administration*, op. cit., 87–92, quote 89–90. For a recent revision of Ackworth's reputation, see P. Hemmingway, 'Sir Jacob Ackworth and Experimental Ship Design during the Period of the Establishments', *Mariner's Mirror*, xcvi (2010), 149–160.

28   Lavery, *The Ship of the Line*, op. cit., i, 90–95.

29   Ibid.

Table 10.1 Flag ranks (new flag ranks in italics), January 1747[a]

Admiral of the Fleet	Sir John Norris	In retirement
Admiral of the White	Thomas Mathews	Dismissed
Admiral of the Blue	Sir Chaloner Ogle	In retirement
Vice Admiral of the Red	James Stewart	Port Admiral (Portsmouth)
	Thomas Davers	West Indies
	Hon George Clinton	Governor of New York
Vice Admiral of the White	William Martin	In retirement
	William Rowley	In retirement
	Issac Townsend	Britain (app 14 July 1746)
Vice Admiral of the Blue	Henry Medley	Mediterranean
Rear Admiral of the Red	Richard Lestock	Died October 1746
	Lord Vere Beauclerk	Admiralty
Rear Admiral of the White	George Anson	Admiralty
Rear Admiral of the Blue	Perry Mayne	Britain
	Sir Peter Warren	Britain
	Hon John Byng	Mediterranean

Note: [a] Admiral of the Blue, Nicholas Haddock had died on 26 September 1746

Chesterfield as Secretary of State for the Northern Department. Grenville was awaiting his promised move to the Treasury. Anson was at sea from the early autumn and Lord Vere Beauclerk was increasingly tired of his post and pressing for preferment. As the year ended, only Anson could be considered to be fully engaged in the higher direction of navy.

The senior professional ranks of the navy had also been thinned out. Mathews had been dismissed in October and in the same month, Lestock died. Townsend had returned rich from his command in the Leewards in 1746. If Anson remained in London, only Rear Admiral Perry Mayne would be available for home service, and he was rumoured to be bound for Jamaica to replace Davers (Table 10.1).[30]

---

30 Woburn Archive, Bedford Mss xvi, f.23, Sandwich to Bedford, 31 January 1747 (n.s.). Davers remained in the West Indies until his death in September 1747.

With only four sea-going flag officers in Britain, there was a need for promotions, but none were made. The reason for this is not clear, but public opinion may have played a part. Certainly, after the disputes between officers and the highly publicised courts martial of 1745–1746, there was a feeling that promotion ought to be handled with care. The public perception of the flag officers was not generally complementary. When Byng was ordered out to join Medley in the Mediterranean, 'People begin already to say I wish the two Chiefs of the Sea agree together, for they are both pretty hasty, you see sir, how it is. (N)o sooner is a man sent from hence but the Squibs are preparing to be flung at them.'[31] It was also a time when ambitious families were aware that the war would not last much longer and advancement or profit to a relative in the service had to grasped quickly.[32] An anonymous correspondent, styling himself 'Britanicus' cautioned Bedford that 'People will lose that Great Opinion they have at present of you' if he went ahead with promotions of some of the most likely candidates, whom he listed with their bad characters. Osborne was 'a pusillanimous fretful, poor and uneasy wretch'. Temple Smith, a 'very worthy sensible man', but 'so indolent and easy in command that even his very friends hardly wish it him'. Stapleton, 'commonly drunk and then Mad, a stranger to his profession and of such bad principles that wherever he commands he must be despised'.[33] Naval officers themselves were by now very careful about their reputations. Fanny Boscawen, writing to Captain Edward Boscawen, urged her husband not to consider taking a command in the West Indies: 'any man will risk his reputation extremely that goes there; and yours is so high I don't think it worth while to hazard the loss or diminution of it for any profit whatever. A rich sea officer is not now an uncommon thing, but one approved of by all his countrymen is extremely so.'[34] Before the promotions were considered there might have been the wish to record some success at sea and base those decision upon its results.

Although the immediate situation of the war at sea did not look particularly promising, the British navy had successfully re-deployed. North

---

31   East Yorks Record Office, Grimston Mss, DDGR 39/3, unfoliated, J. Le Keuse to Medley, 18 November 1746.

32   Woburn Archive, Bedford Mss xvi, f. 63, Anson to Bedford, 7 June 1747.

33   Woburn Archive, Bedford Mss xvi, f. 21, 'Britanicus' to Bedford, 30 January 1746/7.

34   Fanny Boscawen to Edward Boscawen, 19 March 1747, quoted in C. Aspinal-Oglander, (ed.), *Admiral's Wife: Being the Life and Letters of the Hon. Mrs Edward Boscawen from 1719 to 1761*, London, 1940, 25–26.

America still remained at aspiration. On 24 December 1746, Vice Admiral Sir Peter Warren arrived back in England from Louisbourg. Warren's advice had been central to the Canadian scheme of 1746 and within the week he was summoned to meet Newcastle and Bedford. His appreciation of the situation was staggering. He was, according to Newcastle:

> strongly of Opinion, that except we can have force of Regular troops and North Americans amounting to 30,000 Men, it will be in vain to attempt the Conquest of Quebeck and Canada and such a force I doubt is impracticable to be got at present. If this comes out so, we shall probably only send two or three Regiments to fortifie and secure Nova Scotia and Cape Breton. But as nothing is yet determined I beg you would say nothing of it.[35]

If this was true, then any prospect of an American plan was dead.

The Cabinet met on 12 January to consider this report. Of those present only Bedford was unreservedly committed to such an operation and it was no surprise that the meeting agreed that a further expedition was impracticable and the troops from St Clair's expedition should be redeployed to European operations. Warren was asked to prepare a paper on the forces required to secure Cape Breton and Nova Scotia.[36] For the foreseeable future, Bedford and his allies had to accept that offensive American operations would lack credibility in the face of any determined scrutiny. Warren would be sent back to Louisbourg with four ships of the line, eight cruisers and two sloops to provide naval support.

Opening of the Campaign in Flanders: Objective Antwerp, January–May 1747

The allies had been forced to seek winter quarters for a large proportion of their troops on Dutch soil. Apart from the logistical difficulties this posed, it gave the opportunity for the French to step up their pressure on the Dutch, justifying an invasion of Dutch territory in pursuit of their enemies.[37]

Cumberland arrived at The Hague in early December 1746 and for the next three months supervised the assembly of the Confederate Army. Dutch

35 *Richmond-Newcastle Correspondence*, 238, Newcastle to Richmond, 1 January 1746/7.
36 Gwyn, *The Royal Navy and North America*, op. cit., 377, Meeting of the Cabinet Council, 12 January 1747; 378, Warren to Newcastle, 17 January 1747.
37 TNA, SP87/21, f. 174, Cresner to Ligonier, 28 October 1746 (n.s.).

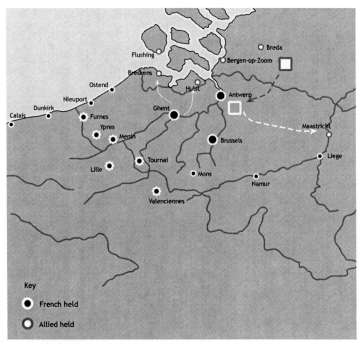

Map 14 The campaign, March–May 1747

anxiety was growing, and Cumberland knew he had to get into the field early to strike a decisive blow which would put an end to any Franco-Dutch negotiations. He planned to attack Antwerp as soon as possible. Throughout January and February information from France fed his belief that the French would abandon western Flanders to concentrate their smaller forces on trying to take Maastricht. Cumberland was sure that as long as the defence of Maastricht was determined, he would have enough time to take Antwerp and then relieve Maastricht.[38] By the end of March, Cumberland's army was coming together. Reports from France suggested that the country was suffering. Trade was at a standstill, the countryside depopulated. Royal finances were creaking and the defection of Spain was anticipated.[39] A good, early campaign might be just enough to make a decisive shift in the diplomatic balance.

However, as early as mid-February worrying news was reaching London and Cumberland's head quarters. The most significant was that the Austro-

---

38   Ibid., f. 58, Cumberland to Chesterfield, 24 February 1747 (n.s.); f. 91, Cumberland to Chesterfield, 21 March 1747 (n.s.), f. 129, Cumberland to Chesterfield, 14 April 1774 (n.s.).

39   Ibid., f. 46, Report, undated.

Sardinian advance into Provence had not only come to a halt, but the army had retreated back across the Var. Having that army in Provence was an essential element in the campaign and it did not take long for reports to reach Cumberland that French battalions were on the march back north.[40] They could not possibly reach Flanders for weeks, and if pressure could be re-applied the French would have to counter-march back to Provence. Intense diplomatic pressure was immediately applied to Vienna and Turin to return across the Var. However, it soon became clear that the Austro-Sardinians had neither the ability nor the will to do this. The immediate cause of the withdrawal was a popular rising in Genoa, which ejected the Austrian garrison, cutting off the main land supply line. While Genoa remained in revolt, there was no possibility of a renewed invasion of Provence. The Austrian response also indicated that they had not provided the number of troops specified in the subsidy treaty and, despite being explicitly stated that the subsidy was for the invasion of Provence, they had plans to use the forces to invade Naples. Austrian culpability for this debacle was clear in British minds and it was decided to send Lieutenant General Thomas Wentworth to Vienna and Turin to report precisely on the application of the subsidy treaty.

The second worrying development was news from Maastricht. The attack on Antwerp was predicated on stout resistance at this city. However, the Dutch garrison commander, General Aylua, claimed that he could not hold out more than a fortnight. Cumberland immediately despatched Lieutenant General Albemarle to investigate.[41] Albemarle's report in late April made sobering reading. Aylua's garrison, said to be 7,000 was in fact only 5,000 and it was estimated 12,000 were needed for an effective prolonged defence.[42] However, by this time the third and most devastating event was unfolding and would completely change the face of the campaign.

French Counter-move: The Invasion of Dutch Flanders and the Battle of Laffelt, April–July 1747

Ever since the Peace of Westphalia (1648) the Dutch had jealously guarded their possession of the left bank of the Western Scheldt below Antwerp. This area, Cadsand, also known as Dutch Flanders, was the key to ensuring that Antwerp never rivalled the Dutch ports for the Atlantic trades. The Dutch

---

40 Ibid., f. 24, Ligonier to Chesterfield, 23 February 1747 (n.s.). (rec. 17 o.s.).
41 Ibid., f. 131, Cumberland to Chesterfield, 3 April 1747 (o.s.) (rec. 6 [o.s.]).
42 Ibid., f. 152, Cumberland to Chesterfield, 25 April 1747 (n.s.) (rec. 17 [o.s.]).

maintained a series of forts just down river from Antwerp to enforce their treaty rights. Near the mouth of the Western Scheldt they also had batteries at Breskens, opposite Flushing, to command the mouth of that great waterway. From the military point of view, it provided the Maritime Powers with a secure line of communication to Antwerp. Even when Antwerp fell to Saxe in 1745, the waterway was open to the great fortress port of Bergen-op-Zoom. Rivers and canals radiating from the Scheldt closer to Antwerp were protected by the forts lining the river, which provided good communications inland to Brabant.

Cumberland's advance on Antwerp took him through barren, over-foraged land and the siege of the city relied on supplies brought up the Scheldt, reaching him from the magazines at Breda and Bergen-op-Zoom.[43] Suddenly, two French columns under Count Lowendahl and Count Contades erupted into Dutch Flanders in early April rapidly isolating the various forts and besieging Sluys. Cumberland was not convinced that Lowendahl's army, said to be 30,000, was half that number, but he hurried to The Hague, where near panic had struck.[44]

The importance of reassuring the Dutch was understood in Britain and three regiments coming from Ireland were diverted immediately to reinforce the defences of Cadsand, and placed under the commander there, General de la Roque. Commodore Mitchell was sent to reinforce the Dutch squadron in the Scheldt.[45] Cumberland remained sanguine, thinking that the successful attack on Antwerp would soon cause the French to abandon any gains they were making.[46]

By the end of April the Scheldt forts had fallen and Sluys had been captured. The whole of Cadsand was in French hands, apart from Hulst, where the Dutch General Roque held out. The French now overlooked the entire length of the Western Scheldt, and just over the river was Zealand and Flushing. Preparations for a French landing on Zealand were reported anxiously from Flushing. On the positive side, the panic in Zealand had brought about a popular rising in favour of the election of the Prince of Orange as stadtholder of the province. By mid-May the rising had spread across the provinces and Prince William was elected stadtholder of all

---

43   TNA, SP 87/22, f. 137, Cumberland to Chesterfield, 18 April 1747 (n.s.) (rec 10 [o.s.]).

44   Ibid., f. 144, Cumberland to Chesterfield, 21 April 1747 (n.s.) (rec 14 [o.s.]).

45   Ibid., f. 142, Newcastle to Fuller, 10 April 1747.

46   Ibid., f. 152, Cumberland to Chesterfield, 25 April 1747 (n.s.) (rec. 17 [o.s.]).

provinces, and captain and admiral of all their forces.[47] This was a move long wished for in London. Prince William was the husband of George II's eldest daughter, Anne, and it was felt that this princely couple could galvanise the Dutch into a more active war effort. To encourage them, despite the King's great concerns, three additional battalions of foot were sent to Zealand.[48]

Unfortunately, resistance in Dutch Flanders was crumbling. The defence of Hulst disintegrated on the night of 5–6 May and the last positions were lost. Cumberland conceded that the siege of Antwerp was now impossible, and that the only chance of decisive action in Flanders was to tempt Saxe out of his positions for a battle in the open field.[49] This immediately worried the King and ministers. Chesterfield warned Cumberland that to lose a battle now would be 'the most fatal and decisive blow that could possibly be given to the interests of the republic in particular and indeed to those of the Common Cause in general'. The King ordered him not to give battle unless there was a more than equal chance of success.[50]

In less than four weeks, Saxe had destroyed the offensive plans of the Confederate Army. Cumberland still believed his force was large enough to prevent Saxe exploiting this victory.[51] For a while, the armies appeared immobilised by each other. In the allied camp, it was thought that Saxe would not dare move to Maastricht with Cumberland's army threatening their rear. Cumberland could not move towards Antwerp or Maastricht, without exposing the whole Dutch border to invasion.[52] Saxe broke the deadlock by moving a corps under Clermont towards Maastricht, threatening to cut the city off from the Confederate Army. Cumberland saw the opportunity to cut Clermont off from the main French army and moved his own army towards the Meuse.[53] At the very least, Cumberland reasoned, Clermont would be forced to fall back, but if the allies got between him

---

47 A.C. Carter, *Neutrality or Commitment: The Evolution of Dutch Foreign Policy, 1667–1795*, London, 1975, 74.

48 These were a battalion of Foot Guards from London, the 2 batt of the 1 Foot and Loudoun's Highlanders.

49 TNA, SP 87/22, f. 173, Cumberland to Chesterfield, 5 May 1747 (n.s.) (rec 1 May [o.s.]); f. 186, Cumberland to Chesterfield, 12 May 1747 (n.s.) (rec 4 [o.s.]).

50 Ibid., f. 230, Chesterfield to Cumberland, 5 May 1747.

51 TNA, SP 87/22, f. 258, Cumberland to Chesterfield, 26 May 1747 (n.s.).

52 BL, Add Ms 35363, f. 161, J. Yorke to P. Yorke, 25 May 1747 (n.s.).

53 TNA, SP 87/22, f. 356, Cumberland to Chesterfield, 26 June 1747 (n.s.) (rec 19).

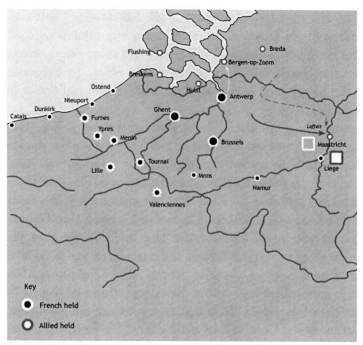

Map 15 The campaign, May–October 1747

and Saxe, he might even be forced away from Saxe, across the Meuse. Throughout the early part of the year, the allies seem to have been confident in their intelligence about Saxe's camp, but now, as they prepared to advance against Clermont, there was a growing sense of unease. Bad intelligence or simply no news clouded their view. As they moved into position towards Tongres, they suddenly realised that were faced not with a detached corps under Clermont, almost the entire French army. Saxe had moved up behind Clermont and on 21 June launched a ferocious attack on the British, German and Dutch troops of the left wing. As at Roucoux in 1746, the Austrians on the right could not send support and after nearly five hours of attack and repulse the Confederate Army began to fall back. Seeing the danger of collapse, Ligonier led a series of cavalry charges that stalled the French advance, giving Cumberland time to retire the army across the Meuse. What Cumberland had hoped to do to Clermont was done to him. Cumberland took up position along the Meuse between Maastricht and Liege, which prevented Saxe from bringing up the heavy artillery by water from Liege to besiege Maastricht, but the Confederate Army had been pushed to the east of the Meuse, opening up the whole southern Dutch frontier to French operations.[54] Any hopes for a decisive campaign to alter the diplomatic balance during 1747 had expired that day at the Battle of Laffelt.

Reaction in Britain

News of the defeat arrived in London on 27 June. The City was quiet. Parliament had been dissolved and members were in the country in the midst of General Election and their usual local business. Newcastle was at Bishopstone, one of his estates in Sussex, when he received news of Laffelt. Initially, he thought that Saxe had over-stretched himself, but very quickly realised that this battle had had a decisive impact on the situation and returned to London, urging his friend Hardwicke to join the ministerial meeting.[55]

With the collapse of Dutch Flanders, even the limited reinforcement of Louisbourg looked too ambitious. Warren's orders were cancelled and the troops were sent to Flushing instead. Warren was appointed second in command to Anson who was to take the home squadron to cruise into Biscay in search of the great convoys assembling at Aix.[56] It is difficult to establish where in the Admiralty this change in plan was instigated, but it was probably a consensus that an American operation was not practicable during 1747.

Short of a dramatic victory, the only prospect of bringing about change in the diplomatic positions was to break down the opposing alliance. French efforts were channelled towards getting the Dutch to make a separate peace. British efforts focused on avoiding this while encouraging Spain to split from France. This was complicated by inter-allied disagreements. Austria and Sardinia were determined that the other would not make gains in Italy at their expense. Neither would support any peace that gave territory in Italy to Don Philip, which was a Spanish condition for coming to terms with Britain. Britain had no great interest in that matter and was willing to accept some form of settlement for Don Philip, if it were agreeable to Austria and Sardinia. However, Britain could not accept the other Spanish condition – the return

---

54   Ibid., f. 368, Cumberland to Chesterfield, 3 July 1747 (n.s.) (rec. 27 June); SP87/23 (Military Operations), f. 1, Cumberland to Chesterfield, 6 July 1747 (n.s.). For a narrative of the battle see, E. Charteris, *William Augustus, Duke of Cumberland: His Early Life and Career*, London, 1913, 2 vols, i, 299–321.

55   BL, Add Ms 35409, f. 29, Newcastle to Hardwicke, 28 June 1746; f. 32, Newcastle to Hardwicke, 8 July 1747.

56   Ibid., 387, Cabinet Council, 30 March 1747; f. 388, Newcastle to Shirley, 30 May 1747.

of Gibraltar or Minorca in exchange for agreeing trading rights in America. These Anglo-Spanish negotiations continued throughout the first five months of 1747 without agreement. The Austrians, fearing that Britain might assent to Don Philip's settlement in Italy, did what they could to defeat this negotiation and by May the whole effort had ground to a halt with a final rejection from Madrid.[57] At the same time the Franco-Dutch negotiations got nowhere with the British using whatever device they could to hinder Dutch moves to a separate peace. The British exploitation of procedures finally caused the Breda conference to break down in March and although discussions continued at The Hague, the momentum gradually wound down.

News from the East Indies was worrying. On 25 April news arrived that, at Madras, had surrendered on 10 September 1746 to a French and Indian force. Two Indiamen in the roads had been captured and the fate of the outward bound and returning China trade now lay in the balance.[58] The governor was condemned as was the commander of the ships on station, Captain Thomas Griffen, who was away refitting at Bengal.[59]

In March Newcastle was still hoped for success in Flanders during 1747, but was clear in his own mind that whatever the outcome of the campaign, next year in Parliament was going to be more difficult. Whatever the ministry did over the next 12 months it would provide grist to the opposition. As he informed Hardwicke:

> as to the dissolution of Parliament I must adhere to my opinion that in every natural light, that that measure can be considered; it appears to me absolutely necessary. Tho in the present circumstances I hardly see any event that can happen but must cause a muddle for clamour and opposition an other year which may possibly even cause a Tory, or at least (must I say) a very disagreeable Parliament. Let the ministry be ever so united as to the cession of Cape Breton the nation will be displeased with it and if the Tories that I think this campaign not so desperate should any ways prove in the right and should (it) (as I think it will not) become and thought

---

57   The outline of the Anglo-Spanish negotiations can be followed in Dobrée, *Chesterfield*, op. cit., iii. See 922, Chesterfield to Sandwich, 5 May 1747; 927, Chesterfield to Robinson, 8 May 1747.

58   BL, Add Ms 3 5363, f. 156, P. Yorke to J. Yorke, 25 April 1747.

59   Ibid., f. 159, P. Yorke to J. Yorke, 12 May 1747. For Griffin's account of the loss, in which he places the blame on treachery of the son of the local Nabob, see TNA, Adm1/160, f. 13, Griffin to Corbett, 6 November 1746.

absolutely necessary to risk another campaign rather than submit to such conditions as can only be obtained this year, the continuation of the war may create as much or more dissatisfaction. So that in all events the dissolution of the Parliament seems to be to be absolutely necessary.[60]

On this the ministers agreed and Parliament was dissolved on 13 June. It was, according to Newcastle, universally agreed among the supporters of the ministry 'who think the King will have a good parliament when the nation is in good humour, retains a grateful sense of late deliverance owing (under God) to His Majesty's care and your Royal Highness's signal services, and when no foreign transactions either of peace or war has happened to blow up, or perverted, the minds of weak people capable of being seduced'.[61]

Their judgement was excellent. The news of the dissolution was greeted by the opposition as evidence that the ministry intended to surrender Cape Breton soon, but the issue did not catch the public imagination.[62] The 1741 election had taken place against a background of intense anti-Walpole agitation that had built up particularly since 1738 and the war had played an important part. The election of 1747 was one of the quietest recorded, with only 67 contested seats. Taking advantage of the post-rebellion quiet in anti-Hanoverian sentiment and going to the electorate before the critical decisions had to be made over restoring Cape Breton or continuing the war another year, the war itself seems to have had little impact on the result. The ministerial support was calculated to have barely altered from about 340 to 338 members. The Tories were reduced to 115 from 136. The opposition in Scotland was halved. It also disrupted the Tory-Leicester House collaboration.[63] It was not until after the definitive peace treaty had been signed that significant parliamentary opposition revived.

The First Battle of Cape Finisterre (3 May) and the General Election of 1747

Before Parliament rose, there was some good news, which lightened the mood before the elections.[64] Anson's cruise into Biscay had met with great success. The French had gathered two convoys together near the isle of Aix. The first

---

60   BL, Add Ms 35409, f. 10–11, Newcastle to Hardwicke, 22 March 1746/7.

61   BL Add Ms 32711, f. 232, Newcastle to Cumberland, 7 June 1747.

62   BL, Add Ms 35397, f. 43, T. Birch to P. Yorke, 13 June 1747.

63   Sedgwick, *The House of Commons*, op. cit., 56–57, 75–6.

64   BL Add Ms 32711, f. 71, Grafton to Newcastle, undated.

consisted of 46 French East India Company ships bound for Pondicherry. The second was a convoy of 30 ships under an escort commanded by Chef d'Escadre, de la Jonquiere, who was to be the new governor of Canada. The combined escort consisted of two ships of the line, seven cruisers and a small frigate. They were to sail together until well out into the Atlantic, where they would separate to go their own way. The convoys sailed on 30 April on a bearing to take them clear of Cape Finisterre.[65]

Anson was by this time patrolling at precisely this point with his squadron of eleven line, four cruisers, a sloop and a fireship. On the morning of 3 May Anson was about 24 leagues north-west of Cape Finisterre before a NNW wind, when the sails of the French convoy were sighted bearing almost dead ahead to the south east. It was noted that nine of the French ships immediately shortened sail and formed line of battle, while the rest of the fleet crowded on sail bearing away to the south-west. Warren, in the van was anxious to get to close quarters by a general chase, but Anson preserved the line. This was what La Jonquiere wanted Anson to do. He was not trying to evade the British, but awaiting their attack, forcing them to form line, thus allowing his convoys to escape. When the British line was preparing to cross his van, La Jonquiere filled his sails and turned to leeward. Thus began a chase action. The British ships were able to come up to the French and, by 7 pm, they captured the six French warships and four of their powerful East Indiamen. La Jonquiere and the French crews behaved gallantly, but were seriously outnumbered. They lost between 700 and 800 killed and wounded, including La Jonquiere himself who was seriously wounded in the back. The British lost no ships but about 520 killed and wounded. The pursuit of the convoy yielded six merchantmen to add to the prizes.[66]

To the ministry it was certainly welcome news. Pelham was delighted not just with the prizes, but 'a total defeat of their projects both in India and America, is an event which no one could have expected and seems reserved for the fortunate and able hand of our friend Anson'.[67] It was a revival of the old belief that a single action at sea could have a decisive impact out of all proportion to the men and ships engaged. The ability to do this was not accredited to the Royal Navy, but to Anson personally. As in 1744, when

---

65 The French considered 50s to be capable of standing in the line during this period.
66 W. Beatson, *Naval and Military Memoirs of Great Britain*, London, 1790, i, 336–342.
67 Woburn Archive, Bedford Mss xvii, f. 111, Pelham to Bedford, 15 May 1747

Anson returned from China, it was the prize money that attracted public attention. Besides the ships and their cargoes, the warships carried about £200,000 in money, which was ostentatiously paraded to the Tower of London.[68] Anson received a peerage and prize money worth nearly £63,000. Warren was knighted and had over £30,000. Beyond this, the reaction was mixed. The navy was not suddenly restored to being the darling of the nation.[69] Rumours were spread that Anson had not done enough and that the victory was owing to Warren rather than Anson, although Warren strongly denied any resentment.[70] It followed on the stories that the fall of Madras was owing to the negligence of Griffin and only just preceded other stories, reported from foreign newspapers, that Sir John Byng had been so useless in the Mediterranean, that he had actually been arrested by Lieutenant General Wentworth.[71] Yet, this was mixed with news that was definitely improving. Captain Fox had sailed from Spithead in the *Kent* (70) with three other ships of the line, two cruisers and two fireships. They were sailing in response to rumours that a large convoy of merchantmen was on its way home from St Domingue, under escort of Du Bois de la Mothe. After over six weeks cruising near Cape Ortegal, Fox sighted the convoy on 20 June. Mothe had one 74, one 64, one 54 and one 36, a far more balanced force than that with which La Jonquiere faced Anson. Fox chased all day and by nightfall was barely two leagues behind the convoy. On the evening of the 21 June Fox was almost up with the escorts covering the rear of convoy, but instead of engaging, Mothe ordered his ships to put on all sail and ordered the convoy to shift for themselves. Despite thick weather, nearly fifty out of a convoy of about 120 ships fell victim to Fox's or Warren's ships, before the survivors got into various ports on the coast of Western France.[72]

Reaction to Laffelt: Neither Peace nor War, July–December 1747

The shocking news of Laffelt brought the ministers back to earth and quickly back to London. There were two surprising results of the defeat. Rather than

---

68   Ibid., 342; BL, Add Ms 35409, f. 25, Anson to Newcastle, 11 May 1747.

69   For an example of attitudes to the navy in the wake of the courts martial, see *Gentleman's Magazine*, xvii (1747), 88.

70   BL, Add Ms 35363, f. 163, P. Yorke to J. Yorke, 29 May 1747; Add Ms 35397, f. 43, T. Birch to P. Yorke, 13 June 1747.

71   BL, Add Ms 35397, f. 56, T. Birch to P. Yorke, 18 July 1747.

72   Beatson, *Naval and Military Memoirs*, op. cit., 343–344.

pushing the Dutch into immediate negotiations, the Prince of Orange urged his countrymen and allies to greater effort. The other surprising event was a peace proposal from Saxe to Cumberland, brought to his head quarters by Ligonier, who had been captured in the action.[73] It was the first time the French had approached the British directly. There was little that was new in the proposal, but it hinted at French willingness to abandon Spain and so was enough to reopen tentative negotiations.

There was also little doubt that Saxe would now move on either Breda or Bergen-op-Zoom. Cumberland could not move west while Saxe's main army threatened Maastricht. If the city was lost the allies in Flanders would be cut off from reinforcement and supply from Germany. While Cumberland stayed on the right bank of the Meuse, between Liege and Maastricht, he believed he preserved this last link.[74] He also believed that Lowendahl's corps, which marched north west after Laffelt, was too small to carry Bergen or Breda.[75] While the Dutch held the forts on the right bank of the Scheldt below Antwerp and the Royal Navy patrolled those waters, Lowendahl could not expect significant reinforcement or re-supply from Antwerp.[76] He prepared to reinforce those areas. However, no more troops could be spared from Britain and despite the Prince of Orange's bellicosity, it was obvious that the Dutch financial situation could barely support an expansion of their forces. The French success had also worried the Rhineland princes who broke off negotiation for additional troops.[77] The arrangements for the 30,000 Russians that had been hired had not progressed far enough for them to be of use in the west this campaign. However, George II quickly approved the transfer of five more Hanoverian battalions from Germany.[78]

During July and August there was little that could be done in London but follow the resistance of Bergen-op-Zoom. This fortified port city stood at the border of Zealand and Brabant, commanding the waterway of the Eastern

---

73   TNA, SP 87/23, f. 6, Cumberland to Chesterfield, 10 July 1747 (n.s.).

74   Ibid., f. 44, Cumberland to Chesterfield, 20 July 1747 (n.s.).

75   Cumberland was unsure of the size of Lowendahl's corps, which was about 35,000 strong. See, J.M White, *Marshal of France: The Life and Times of Maurice de Saxe*, Chicago, 1962, 223.

76   Ibid., f. 37, Cumberland to Chesterfield, 17 July 1747 (n.s.).

77   Woburn Archive, Bedford Ms xvii, f. 84, Hardwicke to Bedford, 15 August 1747.

78   Dobrée, *Chesterfield*, op. cit., iii, 952, Chesterfield to Dayrolles, 3 July 1747; 958, Chesterfield to the Prince of Orange, 10 July 1747.

Scheldt.[79] Command of the fortress was in the hands of the 90-year-old Swede, Count Cronstram, with an Austrian garrison of 16,000. The design of the fortifications meant that Lowendahl's force was too small to invest the city, which remained open to re-supply during the whole siege. Lowendahl opened siege works around the 17 July and the general feeling in London was that like every other Dutch fortified place it would soon fall. However, as the weeks passed, confidence that the city would hold out returned and with Saxe immobile before Maastricht, Lowendahl might have to raise the siege with the onset of winter.

The campaign looked as if it would draw to a close with little change and attention was turning to winter quarters and the peace negotiations. Neither side was willing to compromise on its key demands and neither the Confederate allies nor the Bourbons looked like splitting. Similarly, there was no clear way forward with the war, now that the diversion from Provence looked stalled. Chestefield reflected the mood in a letter to Solomon Dayrolles, the British representative at The Hague:

> Things are now, in my opinion, in a most miserable situation and the taking of Bergen-op-Zoom y mettrait le comble. I wish a could see a plan either for a vigorous war or a tolerable peace, or rather a plan eventually for each. I see many things which I will not mention, that make me despair of seeing the war carried on another year with that vigour superior, or at least equal, force, which is absolutely necessary for success and as I think no state so bad as that which we have been in these three years, of neither making war nor peace.[80]

Bedford had similar views. He believed that with the fall of Bergen 'this must at last become a sea war', but how long Britain could hold out at sea against a France rampaging triumphant on land was unknown. He concluded that the only course was to make as much noise arming for the next campaign in order to make a peace during the winter.[81]

The Confederate allies were buoyed up by events outside Flanders. Against all expectations, the Austro-Sardinian forces won another crushing victory against the Bourbons in Italy. After relieving Genoa, the Chevalier de Belle Ile had led the Bourbon army back into Piedmont, where, at the Battle of Assieta, on 8 July, his army was heavily defeated. Belle Ile was killed and the

---

79 For a description of Bergen-op-Zoom see *Gentleman's Magazine*, xvii (1747), 328–329.

80 Dobrée, *Chesterfield*, op. cit., iii, 965, Chesterfield to Dayrolles, 17 July 1747.

81 BL, Add Ms 15955, f. 143, Bedford to Anson, 13 August 1747.

new commander, Villemur, withdrew back to Provence.[82] The balance of force had swung back in favour of the Austro-Sardinians and, for a few weeks it looked as if the Austro-Sardinian army might renew its offensive.[83]

At sea the victories and prizes of the early summer had improved the mood, and the Admiralty was in a position to reinforce and exploit the situation. The navy seemed at last capable of countering the convoys. Anson was determined to keep pulling ships back from the Mediterranean to reinforce the home station, as he told Bedford, 'I know your opinion and I am persuaded that the French cannot be annoyed so much, nor the kingdom secured as by keeping a strong squadron at home, sufficient to make detachments, whenever we have intelligence that the French are sending ships either to the East or West Indies.'[84] Expressed in this way, Admiralty policy was reactive, providing a defensive shield and responding to French initiatives. However, this reserve of ships made it possible to provide an almost continuous cruise by the Western Squadron. Warren relieved Anson and then Hawke succeeded Warren in command of the squadron cruising from Ushant to Aix in the Bay of Biscay. In April the Directors of the East India Company requested six ships of the line and three smaller ships to reinforce Captain Griffin after the loss of Madras.[85] This news had followed hard on the heels of Anson's victory over La Jonquiere, which had nonetheless, permitted the remains of the East India convoy, under Bouvet de Lozier, to escape to reach Madras with men, money and munitions. In May it was agreed that the ships would be sent in September. The command was contentious. Bedford's wish that Captain Edward Boscawen should go was thought doubtful, as it was believed Boscawen would refuse if he were not in command. By August the problem had been resolved with the decision to recall Griffin, leaving Boscawen senior commander on station.[86] During August Boscawen was preparing four ships of the line, three cruisers and

---

82   Spencer-Wilkinson, *The Defence of Piedmont*, op. cit., 305–317.

83   Woburn Archive, Bedford Mss xvii, f. 57, Newcastle to Bedford, 22 July 1747.

84   Ibid., f. 65, Anson to Bedford, 2 August 1747. In this letter Anson tells Bedford that in a meeting to be held with Newcastle in a few days, he would insist that six more ships are returned from the Mediterranean. It is not clear if Newcastle had any intention of resisting such a move. Indeed, he had already approved it, but he may have been questioning the order as Bedford had already earmarked ships from the Mediterranean for the East Indies. See f. 74, Anson to Bedford, 5 August 1747.

85   Ibid., Bedford Mss xvi, f. 86, Memo of the Directors of the East India Company, 24 April 1747.

86   TNA, Adm 1/160, f. 59, Griffin to Corbett, 15 August 1748.

three small vessels, together with an East India convoy with 1,200 troops, but it was not until 4 November that Boscawen finally got out of Spithead for the east.

It was at this time that the thinned out ranks of the flag officers were replenished. The army had already had a general promotion of major and lieutenant generals, largely in response to a similar action that was undertaken by the States General at the beginning of the 1747 campaign. There was no pressure like this in the navy, but the reduction in numbers by death and courts martial greatly reduced the options for the Admiralty in supplying admirals to significant commands. On 15 July seven new rear admirals received their flags and there was a general promotion through the ranks to fill the vacant admiral of the white positions. By this measure the growing number of ships and flag officers on the home station gave the Admiralty greater flexibility in maintaining a Western Squadron and responding to expeditions sent out by the French (Table 10.2).

Fall of Bergen-op-Zoom and the end of the policy options, September 1747–March 1748

In the first days of September 1747, the position in London was reasonably clear. The ministry was united on continuing with warlike measures, but split on their purpose. Newcastle and Hardwicke were now even more isolated in their belief that if peace was not made during the winter another campaign should be conducted.

The army and the navy were both in good condition and well disposed for a campaign. It could be that Saxe had been checked in Flanders and with renewed vigour in the United Provinces and Austro-Sardinian pressure on Provence, there may have been little to fear in a new campaign. Indeed, there were still possibilities that might shift the diplomatic balance, at least marginally, in favour of the allies. Direct naval pressure had been more successful in 1747 than at any time since 1742, when naval action had forced Naples to withdraw temporarily from the war. As yet these successes had been without discernible impact on French diplomacy. Despite this, it was natural that British ministers should plan to build on this maritime advantage. During 1747 North America had been neglected in order to shore up Flanders, but this did not mean that no action could be taken. Nova Scotia and Louisbourg had to be defended and it was agreed that Philips' regular battalion that garrisoned Nova Scotia and two new regular regiments, raised under the command of Governor William

Table 10.2 Flag ranks, 15 July 1747[a]

Admiral of the Fleet	Sir John Norris	In retirement
Admiral of the White	*Sir Chaloner Ogle*	In retirement
	James Stewart	Port Admiral (Portsmouth)
	Hon George Clinton	Governor of New York
Admiral of the Blue	*William Martin*	In retirement
	William Rowley	In retirement
	Issac Townsend	In retirement
Vice Admiral of the Red	*Lord Vere Beauclerk*	Admiralty
	George Anson	Admiralty
Vice Admiral of the White	*Perry Mayne*	Britain
	Sir Peter Warren	Britain
Vice Admiral of the Blue	*Hon John Byng*	Mediterranean
Rear Admiral of the Red	*Henry Osborne*	Britain
	Thomas Smith	Britain
	Thomas Griffin	East Indies
Rear Admiral of the White	*Edward Hawke*	Britain
	William Chambers	Britain
Rear Admiral of the Blue	*Hon. John Forbes*	Britain
	Edward Boscawen	Britain

Source: TNA, Adm 6/17, f. 246.

Note: [a] Vice Admiral of the Red, Thomas Davers had died in Jamaica on 16 September 1747. Henry Medley was promoted to Admiral of the Red on 15 July, but had died on the Mediterranean station on 5 June that year.

Shirley and William Pepperell from Massachusetts, should be completed from the levies enlisted for the Canadian expedition of the previous year.[87] By September Bedford, Anson and Warren had agreed to Shirley's plan to drive the French and their native Indian allies completely out of Cape Breton island.[88] If the island was secured and the French driven out it would make it more difficult for the French to negotiate its return. There were also clear signs of discontent between the French and Spanish, permitting hopes that this alliance might crack first.

---

87   Lincoln, *Correspondence of William Shirley*, op. cit., i, 386–388, Newcastle to Shirley, 30 May 1747.

88   Ibid., 401–404, Newcastle to Shirley, 3 October 1747; Woburn Archive, Bedford Mss, xviii, f. 20, Newcastle to Bedford, 26 Sept 1747.

The problem with this optimistic projection was that it was based on a series of assumptions that fell apart over the autumn. On 8 September, news reached London that Bergen had fallen. Lowendahl knew that his time was limited and stormed the outworks as soon as the breach looked practicable. The French assault broke into the works and an exceptional slaughter of the defenders shocked Europe. Before Lowendahl withdrew his main force to Antwerp, he captured the remaining forts along the right bank of the Scheldt.

The French options for 1748 were now far greater. They could push into Dutch Brabant or Zealand or they could concentrate on Maastricht. Dutch fears of invasion were again heightened, so the chance of building an offensive army was proportionately reduced. The Austrians could not be relied upon. Their disputes with the Sardinians had been reported back to London by Lieutenant General Wentworth and by October his reports made it clear that any movements towards Provence were little more than posturing.[89] There was fury in London that once again the Austrians had not fielded the numbers that they had promised. Despite all the inspecting and checking it was rumoured that no more than 40,000 of the promised 60,000 were in Flanders.[90] As Chesterfield told Dayrolles, 'Give the Austrians what we please, they will always be grossly deficient; and let the Dutch take what vigorous measures they please, I fear they have not the means of enforcing them. Our means fall short, and our capacity still shorter.'[91]

After the fall of Bergen, George II called his ministers together to consider what was to be done. Chesterfield opened with a long list of problems. There were no resources for another campaign. The negotiations with Russia had stalled and plans to hire Danes were extremely doubtful. Jacobitism was rearing its head again both in England and Scotland. French diplomacy had secured Swedish support and the possibility of buying more men of war. Only a peace would save Britain from 'utter destruction'. Newcastle replied that these difficulties were overdrawn. Besides how should a peace be secured? Only by preparing for the next campaign could new proposals be generated or accepted. If necessary Britain had to accept the financial burden if, as seemed probable, the Dutch would not and pay the subsidies to Russia and Denmark. Pelham supported Chesterfield and particularly feared that France was preparing an invasion. He wanted 10 to 12 regiments imme-

---

89   TNA, SP87/23, f. 379, Wentworth to Cumberland, 22 September 1747 (n.s.).

90   Dobrée, *Chesterfield*, op. cit., iii, 968, Chesterfield to Cumberland, 21 July 1747 (n.s.).

91   Ibid., 966, Chesterfield to Dayrolles, 17 July 1747 (n.s.).

diately brought home. Newcastle acknowledged that if the French took Zealand they would be well placed to risk invasions of England or Scotland. Hardwicke and Bedford argued that a peace plan had to be concerted with the Prince of Orange. How this was to be done was not clear. The King concluded the meeting at that point. Peace plans would be pursued in conjunction with plans for a new campaign.[92] In 1747 the plan relied heavily on the Austro-Sardinian invasion of Provence. The objective for 1748 was less ambitious – to hold on until new proposals were on the table – but it relied on the Prince of Orange being able to make good his promises and put 60–70,000 men into the field.

As the armies went into winter quarters, there was no slacking of the preparations for war. One piece of good news was another naval victory. Rear Admiral Hawke had taken over command of the Western Squadron when Warren fell sick. Intelligence had reached London that another large convoy was assembling in Aix roads, to be escorted to the West Indies by the ships of the Brest squadron. This convoy, of over 250 ships, left the French coast on 6 October, with an escort of eight ships of the line and one frigate under the command of L'Estenduère. The French were not under any illusion that such large convoys would get out unnoticed. Hawke had been cruising between Ushant and Finisterre with a squadron of 12 line (64s and 60s) and two 50s for over seven weeks. At 7 am on morning of the 14 October, Hawke's squadron was about 140 miles west of Ushant when lookouts sighted sails to the south-west. Hawke immediately signalled the chase. L'Estenduère ordered the convoy to leave under the escort of a powerful East Indiaman, *Content*, and formed his squadron of eight ships in line to receive Hawke. A fierce battle raged from about 11.30 until 8.30 pm. The volume and accuracy of fire from the British squadron overwhelmed the French ships. The French fought gallantly, inflicting serious damage and relatively heavy casualties on the British, but by nightfall, six of the eight French warships were severely damaged and in British hands.[93] The convoy had escaped, but Hawke sent a warning to Captain George Pocock, commanding in the Leeward Islands, of their approach. Forty of the merchantmen fell into Pocock's hands.

It was more evidence that the British were becoming dominant in the Western Approaches. They had enough ships to keep scouts out and to keep a standing squadron at sea that was large enough to make small detachments and still be more than a match for any escort that the French gave to their convoys. On the

---

92   BL, Add Ms 35409, f. 105, Newcastle to Cumberland, 12 September 1747.

93   For an excellent account of the battle see, Mackay, *Admiral Hawke*, op. cit., 69–88.

whole, in fleet actions or single ship encounters the training and sea experience of the British seamen was increasingly taking its toll on the French. By the end of 1747, the French navy had lost seven ships of the line and six cruisers in a single year, more than all the ships of those classes taken since the war began.[94] The convoy system had all but collapsed and the French had to turn to Sweden to replace their lost warships.[95]

Although these facts were known in London, and the strain on French maritime commerce was assumed, it was not clear that it would have a decisive impact on thinking in the French court. It was also known that Saxe had fallen out with other powerful factions at the French court, who would prefer to make peace. From the beginning of the war, French war objectives had been unclear. To reduce Austria had been the opening objective, but when the Prussian alliance turned sour and Bavaria collapsed, more attention was paid to reducing Great Britain. Throughout, French policy was not particularly consistent or effective. Assisting Spain was a means of damaging Britain and Austria, but the Italian campaigns did little or nothing to harm Britain and only irritated Spain by disputes with Madrid. France did nothing after 1740 to assist Spain against British interests in the West Indies, Gibraltar or Minorca. Even her policy towards the United Provinces was confused. Unwilling to invade and slow to take advantage of Dutch fears, the French failed to capitalise on their many victories in Flanders. France was becoming war weary as a result of its own confused policy.

As the winter progressed both sides were preparing for another campaign, which neither side really wanted. The question would be which side would be the first to move the negotiations forward. Eventually, this fell to the Britain. Only Newcastle had much faith in another campaign and this crumbled away over the winter as it became clear that the five elements of policy; a breech between Spain and France; the Confederate Army, the navy, the subsidy regime and the diversion in Provence, would not add up to anything substantial during 1748. So far as the French breach with Spain was concerned, this had been hoped for since the death of Philip V in July 1746. The arrival of a new Spanish envoy, Major General Wall, an Irish émigré, promised some movement on the part of Spain. Unfortunately, the loss of Bergen changed Spanish perceptions and the negotiations quickly stalled and did not resume.[96]

---

94 Beatson, *Naval and Military Memoirs*, op. cit., i, appendix 65.

95 Dobrée, *Chesterfield*, op. cit., iii, 1079, Chesterfield to Titley, 1 January 1747/8.

96 BL, Add Ms 35409, f. 136, Stone to Hardwicke, 3 October 1747.

The foundation of the 1746 campaign, the diversionary attack into Provence, looked dead. There were continuing strains between the Austrians and Sardinians. Genoa still blocked the coastal route to Provence. Austria was anxious for a campaign against Spanish-held Naples.[97] Sardinia could be expected to resist that, but there could be little confidence to suggest that a realistic diversion from Flanders would be mounted.

In September 1747 the subsidy treaties then being negotiated for additional forces from Russia, Denmark and the German princes, gave Newcastle hope that the Confederate Army would be about 180,000 troops in the spring.[98] This would have been the largest force the allies had ever managed to field, but experience should have told him the paper figure was unlikely to be realised. Practically before the ink was dry on the ratifications, the hope of getting additional Russians or Danes in Flanders faded. It became clear that the Dutch did not have the financial resources to support their quota of the Confederate Army in the coming year let alone a portion of the subsidy to Russia or Denmark and subsistence for the troops when they arrived. Whether the Russians would ever arrive also began to become doubtful as Prussia began making difficulties over their march across Europe.[99] Cumberland was at The Hague at the end of the 1747 campaign where he saw just how fragile the Dutch situation was. He had just completed the arrangements for winter quarters that covered Maastricht and Breda and Boisleduc. Intelligence arrived that Lowendahl was on the move with 25,000 troops to escort a convoy to Bergen. The allies saw that with this scale of movement the convoy was a cover and Lowendahl was probably aiming to attack Oudenbosch or Roosendaal, towards Breda. However, in response the Dutch could not assemble more than 10,000 troops. Even this Cumberland thought was no more than a 'paper list'. Eleven battalions and 11 squadrons that should have gone to Maastricht, had to be recalled, leaving that place more vulnerable than before.[100] Of equal concern was the command of the army. Cumberland returned to The Hague expecting to take command of the Confederate Army. He found that this presumption noted on his passport caused annoyance. The new status of the Prince of Orange demanded, according to Dutch ministers, that Cumberland share command with the

---

97   BL, Add Ms 32713, f. 95, Newcastle to Hardwicke, 21 Sept 1747.

98   BL, Add Ms 32713, f. 95, Newcastle to Hardwicke, 21 September 1747.

99   Ibid., 1082, Chesterfield to 1082, Chesterfield to Sandwich, 12 January 1748; BL, Add Ms 35409, f. 150, Stone to Hardwicke, 28 December 1747.

100 BL, Add Ms 35409, f. 150, Stone to Hardwicke, 28 December 1747.

Prince. Cumberland soon realised that the matter was not going to be resolved easily.[101]

The subsidy regime held out few prospects for 1748. Although the Hanoverians, Hessians and Sardinians had proved good value for money, the Dutch and Austrians had not fulfilled their obligations and there was little chance of that changing in 1748. Disputes over adjusting the inspection and payment schedules delayed signatures and did not give the ministry any more confidence that the full quotas would be provided. However, if realistic preparations for a campaign were to be made in order to influence the peace negotiations, continuing the subsidies was essential. The cost of these subsidies had risen to £1.83 million out of a total estimated expenditure for the year of £10.4 million. To meet this demand, the ministry agreed to borrow £6.3 million – 'the Great Loan'. The credit market had proved buoyant in 1747 and Pelham had managed to get two loans, amounting to £5 million filled by open subscription without difficulty. When the new loan was announced in November 1747, it met with no parliamentary opposition and subscriptions came in quickly. However, over the winter the deteriorating situation in Holland began to hit the market. The crucial Dutch money market began to lose confidence after the fall of Bergen-op-Zoom and by January the scarcity of credit was noticeable even in Britain.[102] By increasing the interest offered and creating a linkage to the lottery, Pelham managed to keep government debt attractive to investors, but willingness to subscribe in one set of market conditions did not mean ability to pay in another. Subscribers were required to make their payments in tranches of 10ths. However, by January Pelham was aware that the lack of credit in the market might mean that subscribers would not be able to make the due payments. Rather than see the debt unpaid, he agreed to defer the April/May payments to October/November. Despite this, the value of government stock on the market fell towards the extreme low it had experienced at the height of the Jacobite Rebellion.[103]

In contrast to the war in Flanders, the maritime war was still going remarkably well over the winter of 1747/8, but the results had not changed the French

---

101 BL, Add Ms 32714, f. 311, Cumberland to Newcastle, 8 March 1748.

102 By 1746 the war had taken its toll on Dutch commerce and credit. Maritime trade was depressed by the war and the threat of French invasion caused anxiety. Dutch investment capital seems to have been attracted to the British public debt, which was seen as being more secure at this time. See C. Wilson, *Anglo-Dutch Commerce and Finance in the Eighteenth Century*, Cambridge, 1941, 136–150.

103 Dickson, *The Financial Revolution in England*, op. cit., 226–228.

diplomatic position and there was still a great lack of public confidence in the navy. In early October rumours spread of the French bringing forces together at Ostend and Calais.[104] Jacobite disturbances had been experienced around the country during the election period. The suggestion that six regiments come home to garrison southern England was accepted, despite the fact that the Royal Navy had achieved a huge measure of superiority over the French in home waters by this time. Cumberland protested that withdrawing the troops would signal a desertion to the Dutch and might trigger a unilateral peace with France. A compromise was reached and the Prince of Orange agreed to allow five British regiments to go to England for the winter on condition they returned in spring, although the cost was a further weakening of Dutch confidence and probably the defeat of the Prince's attempts to get the United Provinces to declare war on France.[105]

By March 1748 Newcastle's optimism of the previous September had proved completely unrealistic and the realities of the looming campaign began to close in on him. Cabinet understanding was that the preparations for a campaign were an element in the negotiation to bring the war to a close before the campaigning season opened. However, the erosion of trust between Newcastle and his colleagues was such that the failure to see concrete moves towards peace was attributed to Newcastle's underhand instructions to Sandwich. In late January Chesterfield decided to resign as Secretary of State for the Northern Department for this very reason.[106] Sandwich had hoped to take the post, but among many positive reasons for keeping him at the negotiations and thinking him well suited to be First Lord of the Admiralty, which he had long canvassed, he was also distrusted as being too willing to continue the war.[107] Newcastle took over as Secretary for the Northern Department, and Bedford accepted the seals for Newcastle's old post in the Southern Department on the understanding that peace was going to be pursued. However, both the Old Corps and Bedford's New Allies remained restive. If Bedford deserted, the Broad Bottom would rapidly collapse. Newcastle was warned by Pitt, that a leading figure in the Old

---

104 BL, Add Ms 32711 f. 201, Hardwicke to Newcastle, 2 October 1747; TNA, SP87/23 (Military Expeditions), f. 423, Chesterfield to Cumberland, 20 October 1747.

105 TNA, SP87/23, f. 426, Cumberland to Chesterfield, 31 October 1747 (n.s.).

106 See the letters to Dayrolles in Dobrée, *Chesterfield*, op. cit., iii, culminating in 1088, Chesterfield to Dayrolles, 26 January 1748.

107 Corbett, *Parliament History*, op. cit, xiv, 151, Fox to Hanbury Williams, 17 February 1748; BL, Add Ms 32714, f. 223, Richmond to Newcastle, 13 February 1748.

Corps, Horace Walpole, was working with the Tory Lord Gower 'to possess His Grace against the King's measures and Those of <u>Him</u>, whom he supposes the authors of them'. According to Pitt, Bedford (only one month into his new post) now believed that Newcastle had '<u>singly</u> obstructed the Making the Peace this winter, contrary to the declared opinion of every other member of the Cabinet Council and that Personal Regard for me had been the single occasion that no notice had been taken of it in the House of Commons'. Newcastle was plainly feeling his isolation; 'pursued in every corner, by busy and uninformed men, loaded with all the omissions of others and supposed to have obstructed measures of Peace, which others never, or but till very lately, had the courage to propose'.[108]

The only person who had remained confident of another campaign was the Duke of Cumberland, but after his return to Holland in February, even he could not maintain any illusion that the grand Confederate Army would be parading in Brabant in the coming months. The inability of the Dutch to field their quota was apparent in February. Charles Bentinck, the Prince of Orange's emissary, came to London to try to arrange a loan for £1 million. Bentinck wanted at least £100,000 of this to be provided immediately by the British government and his unwillingness to offer security or interest above the existing 4 per cent return made any appeal to City improbable. By 11 March Newcastle had to accept that 'We cannot any longer alone pursue Measures with vigour' and he asked Cumberland to press Sandwich to conclude the peace.[109] Sandwich signed the preliminaries with France on 8 April. The pressure to end the war increased over the next few weeks. Saxe was determined to take Maastricht before the end of the war, and there was no prospect of the Confederate Army marching to relieve the city. At Roermonde, Cumberland could muster about 60,000 men (possibly 80,000 at the extreme limit), but facing him were 140,000 French. On the evening of 7 May the inner cabinet met. Newcastle urged them sign an armistice before Maastricht fell. The ministers needed little prodding and agreed that there was no option.

Chesterfield's resignation in February had led to Sandwich replacing Bedford as First Lord of the Admiralty on 26 May. Chesterfield parted from the ministry with a promise not to oppose and his brother, John Stanhope, was rewarded with the vacant place on the Admiralty Board. Despite fears

---

108 BL, Add Ms 32714, 304, Newcastle to Cumberland, 4 March 1748, original emphasis.

109 Ibid., f. 326, Newcastle to Cumberland, 11 March 1748.

in the ministry of an invasion, British naval forces dominated the waters of the Channel and Eastern Atlantic. Hawke was out cruising in January with a squadron of six line, when on 31 May a large damaged warship was sighted. After a battle of six hours Captain Harland of the *Nottingham* (60) brought in the battered *Magnanime* (74), which, after being disabled by weather, had been forced to leave a convoy bound for the East Indies and was on her way back to Brest. In March Captain Cotes' squadron of four line met a Spanish convoy that had come out of Cadiz. The escort commander had given the usual orders, forming his nine escorts into line of battle and ordering the convoy to scatter. Cotes was too weak to take on the Spanish line, but put on sail to chase the convoy instead. He took five prizes, while the Spanish escorts remained in line of battle. Rear Admiral Warren kept up the cruises until news of the peace preliminaries reached him.

Ships were heading for the East Indies to redress the naval balance there. However, there was no prospect of reviving a major campaign in North America. Significant success in North America required a substantial body of regular troops; 8,000 by the last calculation, but every military resource was needed in Flanders to prevent catastrophic collapse there. In the West Indies, on the other hand, where the war began, there were echoes of the very earliest campaign. As in 1740, Spanish naval force was concentrated at Havana. This Barlovento Squadron was only of use to provide a secure escort for convoys leaving the Caribbean though the Gulf of Florida. Also as in 1740, there was no militarily significant permanent French naval presence in the region. In 1745, Commodore Townsend had found that attempting to take the French Leeward Islands without land forces was impracticable, but by 1747 Captain Pocock with a small force of four line and seven cruisers was able to maintain a continuous threat to French trade and supply routes. In mid 1747, Captain Knowles, commanding at Louisbourg, got his wish to return to the West Indies and command at Jamaica. Knowles had been with Vernon in 1740 and now resurrected Vernon's plans to attack Port Louis, St Domingue, and Santiago de Cuba. The attack on Port Louis was a success, the town capitulating on 11 March 1748. Like Vernon at Chagres and Porto Bello, Knowles blew up the fortifications and withdrew. The attack on Santiago de Cuba on 29 March miscarried as the light breezes made it difficult for the ships to break through the narrow entrance into the bay. To Knowles fell the honour of the last significant squadron action of the war. After news of the peace with France was received at Jamaica on 29 June, there was still no news of a peace with Spain, so Knowles took his squadron of six line and a cruiser to the north coast of Cuba hoping to intercept the treasure ships coming from La Vera Cruz to Havana. On 1 October he ran into Admiral Reggio's Barlovento

Squadron, also of six ships of the line and a cruiser, which had been out in search of the British homeward bound trade. From late afternoon until into the night a confused action raged, in which signals were misunderstood and Knowles railed against the performance of his captains The Spanish *Conquistador* (64) was badly damaged and surrendered. Reggio's flagship, the *Africa* (74), was driven ashore and burned by her crew, but the rest of the Spanish ships got back to Havana. The war in the West Indies, ended with a small victory, but not one that united the navy. Knowles and his captains were at loggerheads with accusation and counter-accusation, which did not end until they were back in England.[110]

All this was in the future or unknown to the ministry in London in the early spring of 1748. At sea Britain was more than holding her own, but there was not yet any evidence that the naval war would make a significant difference to the diplomatic balance by changing the attitudes of either France or Britain. However, in Britain the old ideas of maritime power had been revived. It was taken for granted that the disruption of the convoy system was destroying French and Spanish trade and ruining their towns.[111] The mystery was why France had not been more evidently diminished by the crushing of trade. One reason, it was asserted in Parliament, was that British insurers were willing to provide insurance for French ships. A bill to prohibit British subjects from insuring the ships of enemies was passed without division. Prohibit this, so the proposers argued, and only the merchants with the largest capital reserves would be able to bear the risk to carry on overseas trades. From then on, within a year or two, the French colonies would starve and be willing to surrender. Despite a counter case by the Solicitor General pointing out that similar prohibitions, since the 1660s, had only driven the enemy to get services from elsewhere or compete more vigorously in different markets, the logic of the situation that demanded that French commerce be put under the greatest pressure, won out.[112]

However, this did not mean naval victories in 1747 had caused a huge shift in opinion. Although the Great Loan and supply passed through the new Parliament without difficulty, the measures for funding the loan, taxes on imports, revived the debate over the importance of trade and the maritime war with which the conflict had begun in 1739. Pelham reminded

---

110 The best narrative of these actions is in Richmond, *The Navy in the War*, op. cit., iii, 117–147.

111 BL, Add Ms 32714, f. 326, Newcastle to Cumberland, 11 March 1748.

112 Cobbett, *Parliamentary History*, op. cit., xiv, 108–133.

members that they were engaged in two wars, which Parliament had advised the King to undertake. The important point was that the outcome of the war to preserve trade and navigation was now dependent on the outcome of the war against France for the liberties of Europe. The wars and the money to fight them could not be separated. However, it encouraged reflections on the quixotic policies that had got Britain 'environed with rocks, whirlpools and quicksands, from whence it will be a miracle if we escape without shipwreck'. Velters Cornewall, the brother of Captain James Cornewall, killed at the Battle of Toulon in 1744, expatiated widely on the madness of European engagements and the impossibility of French successes on land to force Britain to ignominious peace, if 'British' counsels were taken and the naval war maintained: 'If we leave the continent to take care of itself, and confine ourselves to a naval war, we may carry it on with little expense and great success both against France and Spain, till they shall be glad to give up all the conquests we made in America, for the sake of preserving what they may then have remaining.' Henry Fox conceded that in any war with a power with the most extensive maritime commerce, Britain, ought to destroy the trade of the enemy, which would enrich Britain and starve the enemy of resources for a land war. However, Britain could never stand aside where one power threatened the liberties of Europe – it was not 'for the sake of the Queen of Hungary, or from a pure principle of generosity, in assisting the distressed, though even that would not have been a bad motive? No, Sir, we engaged in it for our own safety, as well as the safety of Europe'. If France succeeded in reducing Austria, none in Europe, would dare to disobey Versailles and when Britain engaged in war with Spain it would, in reality, be a war against all the maritime powers of Europe, marshalled by French instructions.[113] The debate went back and forth, but there was no division.

After nine years of war, the passion in debates that had torn apart parliamentary politics from 1738 seemed to rekindle as the war drew to a close. The intense hostility to Hanover, that peaked during Granville's attempt to dominate policy in 1743–1744, started to manifest itself again. However, neither the maritime nor the anti-Hanover rhetoric regained intensity of its appeal. The apparent inability of naval power to break up the Spanish empire or force the French to moderate their terms for peace had done a great deal of damage, at least temporarily, to that ideology. In 1746, the Jacobite revolt, the peace in Germany and the fall of Granville

---

113 Ibid., 164, 168.

had exposed the vulnerability of Britain to French attack and diminished the fears that British taxes were funding the defence of the King's Hanoverian electorate. Newcastle' domination of policy was not the same as Granville's, but to some it still seemed to fly in the face of obvious British interests.

The Treaty of Aix-la-Chapelle and the End of the War, May–October 1748

From Britain's perspective a great deal had to be given up. The signature for the preliminaries had to be given without Austrian and Sardinian approval, a slight reminder of Britain's unilateral negotiation of 1711. The mutual restoration of conquests had to be accepted, which meant that Cape Breton was returned to France in exchange for Madras and the French evacuation of Flanders. Dunkirk, whose fortifications were supposed to have been removed by the Treaty of Utrecht, was permitted to be refortified on the landward side. In return, France restated its 1718 commitment not to support the Stuarts. Louis XV recognised the Pragmatic Sanction and the current Emperor, Francis, husband of Maria Theresa. Both powers committed themselves to working towards articles that primarily affected other nations. Austria was angered that Britain and France guaranteed Silesia and Glatz to Prussia and a patrimony of Parma, Piacenza and Guastella to Don Philip. Sardinia's territorial gains promised under the Treaty of Worms were accepted. Genoa and Modena were to be restored to their pre-war boundaries. By 17 June the powers had signed the preliminaries and notification of the ceasefire could be sent around the world. It was be another four months before the details could be incorporated into a definite Treaty of Aix la Chapelle in October 1748.

The only article that related to the Anglo-Spanish dispute promised Britain the renewal of the *Asiento* for four years. It would take two more years for an Anglo-Spanish commercial treaty to settle the issues that had led to war in 1739 to be ratified. The *Asiento* was ended, past claims adjusted and British rights clarified, but no new commercial rights were conceded by either nation.[114] The expectation of quick and fruitful conquests in Spanish America had long faded and for Britain in 1750 it was far more important that the treaty provided good future relations with Spain, which dissuaded a new Franco-Spanish alliance, than it attempt to salvage the dreams of 1739.

---

114 McLachlan, *Trade and Peace with Old Spain*, op. cit., 139.

11

Conclusion: The Peace and British Naval Power

In October 1748 most Europeans were content that the war that had ravaged the continent for more than seven years was over. During this period Britain had been fighting three wars. The Anglo-Spanish War had been subsumed into the War of Austrian Succession, from which the Anglo-French War emerged as the most vital to Britain's survival as a Protestant power. They were inseparable in so far as the Anglo-French struggle and naval power linked them all.

The eventual British victory in that crucial struggle for maritime supremacy with France has provided the dominant perspective for historical interpretations of the events of 1739 to 1748. Looking back in the knowledge of that victory the navalist ideology and rhetoric that preceded the war and the contentions of the Patriot opposition throughout its course looked prescient when compared to the dominant Old Corps attachment to the continental campaign. From this perspective, the war appears to have been mismanaged and misdirected, wasting the true potential of British sea power. However, by looking closely at the political and diplomatic conditions of the time, a different picture emerges.

In 1739 Britain had confidently expected to make great and permanent changes to the commercial and colonial environment in the West Indies by the application of naval power. From the beginning it was understood that French intervention could alter the prospects of success dramatically, but it was a risk that had to be taken and, despite growing French activity, the ministry did not allow itself to be deflected from what it saw as the decisive expedition to the Caribbean. Fleury's behaviour and attitude suggested that he was not enthusiastic for war and rapid, dramatic success could enable the British to make peace from a position of strength before France intervened decisively in favour of Spain. When the Brest and Toulon squadrons were finally known to be steering for the West Indies in September 1740, the

British ministry was forced to delay the expedition in order to reinforce the naval escort. For the next six months Britain's fate lay in the balance. If the French and Spanish squadrons joined in the West Indies, Vernon's squadron, the expedition and even Jamaica were under threat. The British were always confident that if Ogle joined Vernon in time, British naval forces would be more than a match for the Bourbons, but there was still a possibility that rather than quick and easy victory, a naval campaign might end in Franco-Spanish domination of the West Indies, severe damage to the British fleet, and the eclipse of British maritime trade.

In the event, French naval operations in the West Indies proved remarkably ineffective. The British knew almost immediately that the French and Spanish had not joined forces and Vernon was able to operate, with his force concentrated, far to leeward of Jamaica, on the Spanish Main. The defeat of the British expedition was, ultimately, less to do with French naval power than local Spanish resistance. Both sides were fully aware that operations in the West Indies had to be conducted quickly, before yellow fever inevitably decimated the ranks of non-immune Europeans. At Cartagena in 1741, La Guaira and Caracas in 1743, static fortifications provided the effective defensive structures that enabled militias and small numbers of Spanish regulars to hold the British at bay. By the time the British landed at Guantanamos in 1741 and Panama 1742, they were too weak to advance through the wilderness or break through prepared positions in the hills. From the beginning of the war, the British dominated the waters of the Caribbean. Naval force was never lacking as the British were always able, rapidly, to despatch and maintain ships to counter Bourbon naval moves, but the ambitious claims for maritime power foundered on the lack of the other critical resource; soldiers. Without large military forces the decisive re-balancing of power in the region was impossible.[1] The British had only managed to raise enough forces for the 1741 operations by the use of American levies. By 1742 events in Europe made the despatch of further significant land forces to the region impossible. Nevertheless, this did not entirely puncture the claims for maritime war. Naval protection ensured that regional trade remained stable during the war.[2] The destruction of the fortifications protecting smaller Spanish and French ports, such as Chagres and Porto Bello in 1739 and Port Louis (Hispaniola) in 1748, achieved the ambition of opening trading opportuni-

---

1   It was not until 1760 when armies of about 10,000 effective troops could be sustained in the region that significant operations were maintained in the West Indies.

2   B.R. Mitchell, *British Historical Statistics*, Cambridge, 1988, 492–493.

ties in those territories. Over the course of the war the blockade of enemy ports seriously disrupted their colonial commerce and enriched the British war effort by a regular supply of prizes. The regular publication of the lists of prizes kept the impact of maritime war in public view. By the end of the war, the disruption of the large French colonial convoys was providing examples of spectacular success.

By mid-1742 the high expectations from a colonial war with Spain had evaporated and the longer-term advantages of naval domination in the region had yet to be realised. Yet there was no immediate rejection of the maritime war. There was no enquiry into the failures. Attention was focused on Europe. Speculation over the causes of defeat became subsumed in the general political debate over Walpole's fall and the perception of growing Hanoverian influence in British policy. Before Walpole's fall the delays and misadventures on operations were often attributed to his pro-French influence. Although this was entirely untrue and ministers knew that the organisation and administration of the expedition had worked reasonably well, there was no value in countering the assertions of the opposition by detailed reference to events. Walpole's fate did not hinge on this argument and without resorting to laying papers before Parliament, which they did not wish to do, their arguments were no stronger than the claims of the opposition. It was also clear to ministers that Vernon's behaviour was partly to blame for the failure of the West Indian expedition, but they did not counter the pamphlet literature which appeared in 1743–1744, heaping blame upon the army commander, Major General Wentworth, the soldiers, the engineers and artillery. Vernon's professional standing and popularity in the country made challenging his role in the West Indian operation politically dangerous with few advantages, but they resisted employing Vernon again until 1745. The public perception of the failure was allowed to rest upon Walpole, the administration and the army, leaving the reputation of the navy intact.

If the Royal Navy and ideology of maritime war emerged from the disasters of the West Indian operations with their reputations largely undamaged, events in Europe began to undermine them. Early in the war Haddock's failings were attributed to Walpole's dealings with France in order to protect Hanover.[3] The political settlement in the wake of Walpole's fall reinforced the probability that naval failings would be attributed to political incompetence. The political balance of power between the competing Whig group-

---

3   For example see Chesterfield's assertions in the debate on the King's speech, in Cobbett, *Parliamentary History*, op. cit., xii (1741–1743), 225, 4 December 1741.

ings and the King led to a failure to rebuild ministerial unity in the wake of Walpole's fall. Even Winchelsea had concerns over his capability when he was appointed First Lord of the Admiralty in March 1742. Without significant professional advice or support and politically excluded as far as possible by the dominant Old Corps ministers. Winchelsea's' Admiralty was unable to assert itself during 1743–1744. It could not overrule Mathews' demands in the interests of the wider war. Against the rising furore over Hanoverian influence on British policy, and the attrition on flag officers in London, Mathews and the Mediterranean fleet were seen as a distinctly British contribution to supporting Austria. Any failure in this theatre could be easily attributable to the incapability of Winchelsea's Admiralty or the Hanoverian leaning of Carteret. Again, the Pelhams, balancing their parliamentary power with their influence in the King's Closet, were willing to accept the public perception of the problem as one of incompetence rather than challenge those assumptions too vigorously.

The events of 1744 began to change this. In February the French invasion attempt in the Channel and the disappointing results of the Battle of Toulon shook public confidence in the navy. Senior naval officers, like Norris and Mathews, who had put some distance between themselves and the Admiralty, had been found wanting at the critical time. Norris's instance on commanding all ships in home waters had not been a great success either for the defence of the realm or the needs of commerce. Mathews disputes with Lestock and some of the captains of his squadron provided growing cause for concern as the details of that command became public. During the year, the failure of navy to re-assert control in the Mediterranean or the Western Approaches worried informed observers. Only Vernon among the senior officers of the navy, who was excluded from command in this year and so untainted by failures, retained his popular appeal.

As with the West Indies expedition, there was no attempt during 1744 to examine the reasons behind the performance of the navy. The problem of overstretch into the Mediterranean was understood with the Admiralty. It tried to remedy the situation, but lacked the political or professional support to implement the re-distribution of the fleet during 1743. The shock of the Brest squadron appearing in the Channel in February 1744 and the removal of Carteret, Winchelsea and the New Whigs from government at the end of the year changed that situation. There were no reasons for those left in government to challenge the presumption of Winchelsea's incompetence or Carteret's Hanoverian preferences. A new political start was promised with the Duke of Bedford at the head of the Admiralty and a revived commitment to maritime war. A new professional start was also possible. Vernon was not only the established popular voice of maritime war and professional naval standards, but he was now almost the most senior active flag officer. He was the voice of the tradition at the head of the profession. Equally important was the inclusion of Anson on Bedford's new Board of Admiralty. A hero in his own right and undamaged by the disappointments of 1739–1744, he was the promise for the future. It was a powerful political and professional combination.

Matters did not improve immediately during 1745. The courts martial over Toulon and Mostyn's cruise, and the Admiralty's dispute with Vernon at the end of the year, kept public concern about the navy high, but by this time the shift of the fleet into home waters, the change in French maritime strategy and the capture of Louisbourg, provided the basis for a more reassuring, effective and direct challenge to the Bourbons at sea. The threat of invasion during the last half of 1745 dominated naval policy, but the French did not re-appear in the Channel and the navy proved capable of dominating the waters from the Western Approaches through to the North Sea. By the beginning of 1746 there was even the hope that another trans-Atlantic operation, this time to Canada, might provide the decisive victory needed to bring this war to an end.

The fact that Canada and the maritime war became the focus of British efforts in 1746 was not just owing to the revival of faith in the power of the Royal Navy. It was directly related to the collapse of the Flanders campaign. From 1741 it was accepted that containing France in Europe depended upon Austria. Until the home islands came under direct French threat, supporting Austria was the key to British policy. Specifically, Britain needed Austria to continue to defend the Austrian Netherlands and not draw its resources in to protect her Central European and Italian domains. Subsidies were a traditional means of achieving this objective. However, given the crisis Austria faced, only an army in Flanders, or even Germany, could ensure Austrian commitment to the Low Countries. It was not just a defensive reaction. Throughout the war, British ministers and soldiers thought that a large Confederate Army in Flanders could inflict decisive damage upon the French. The Earl of Stair was the most ambitious in this regard, but also Cumberland hoped for significant advances into France. It was the collapse of these hopes in 1745 and 1747 that forced a refocusing of attention on the maritime war. As early as 1743 concerns were rising that Britain's need to keep the Austrians fighting in Flanders was leading to a war in which Britain was forced to fight on Austrian terms for Austrian objectives. The military collapse of 1745 was so complete that the army's fortunes could not be revived in 1746. In Flanders the Confederate Army seemed incapable of holding back, let alone defeating the French. On the upper Rhine the Austrians seemed unable to make headway and hope that subsidies would induce the Austrians and Sardinians to make a dramatic diversion from Italy into southern France in 1746 proved illusory. By 1746, disengagement from the Flanders campaign became an attractive proposition. The campaign of 1747 demonstrated that there was now little hope that Austria or Sardinia would apply the subsidies as demanded by Britain. Although belatedly the Dutch were taking a more active part in the war it was too late.

By the beginning of 1748 it was clear that there would be no effective army in Flanders for the coming year. In Britain it was increasingly clear that an acceptable peace had to be made with France in the near future and therefore that it had to come about through the exercise of naval power. Unfortunately, it was not clear how effective this naval pressure would be. The victories of Cape Finisterre had showed how disruptive British naval power could be. French maritime commerce was suffering and their West Indian colonies, particularly Martinique, were beginning to experience severe shortages. British forces were on their way to India to redress the loss of Madras. However, it was unclear if this would have an impact on French attitudes and, if so, how long this would take. In 1747 a renewed attack on Canada was abandoned as it was thought it would take too long to have an impact on France. In 1748, with Flanders almost all in French hands, it would be far too late to prevent the collapse of the alliance. Once the situation in Flanders was understood, it did not take the British ministry long to agree that, despite the promise of naval power, peace had to be sought immediately.

By May 1748 Britain had survived and the Austrian Succession was largely intact. The great ambitions harboured in 1739 had been defeated. Yet there were reasons to believe that Britain had won the war at sea, which had been in the balance ever since 1740. British sea power dominated the North Atlantic, the Caribbean and the Mediterranean. The shift in power and its potential had only become evident during 1747, and, given the overall situation this sea power could not be converted into the diplomatic leverage commonly anticipated in 1738–1739.

By the time the peace was concluded in October 1748, the gap between the exaggerated expectations of 1739 and the realistic potential of British sea power in a global context was still unclear. There was still room for debate and disagreement. However, the lack of agreement at the end of the war is indicative not of a deeply entrenched and unchanged ideological split between the Patriot enthusiasts for maritime war and the proponents of continental campaigns who inhabited the Court. Rather, it was simply that politicians and statesmen were still trying to understand the practical possibilities of sea power in the wars that had been evolving since 1740. There were deeply held views on the unique efficacy of sea power, but they were not consistently held. There were very few in Britain who were ever deeply ideologically committed to the efficacy of continental campaigns. For most statesmen and politicians it all depended on the particular situation. The pressure for a naval and colonial war against Spain in 1739 was irresistible because of the apparent logic of the case, built up over ten years. That kind of pressure was never replicated during the war. Fears that military and financial resources would be misused in defence of Hanover were real and deep, but those fears were clearly differentiated in most MPs' minds from the need to use those same resources in Europe for British interests. MPs were not well informed, nor particularly interested in the detail of military policy. Their beliefs rested on assumptions which had a superficial logic or truth. Enthusiasts for maritime war might confuse a European war with a war for Hanover, but MPs were sophisticated enough to see the difference. Despite intense press campaigns against Hanoverian influence, the hostility did not translate into rejecting action in Europe in support of British interests. The arguments for a maritime and colonial war against France were posed and occasionally accepted, but they never overwhelmed the dominant logic that France had to be defeated in Europe. From 1745 military defeat in Flanders meant that this logic was beginning to crumble – it was becoming clear that France could not be defeated there – but maritime war did not provide the obvious alternative. In 1746 a move to a campaign in Canada suited the domestic political need to shore up the Broad Bottom by bringing in Cobham and his allies and was a reasonable response to Dutch and Austrian failure to commit themselves to the Flanders campaign. However, within months the consequences of the collapse of the Dutch on British interests were too great to bear and the British position was revised to encompass campaigns in both America and Flanders. A campaign against Canada alone could not reap rewards quickly enough to compensate for imminent Dutch neutrality. Abandoning the European alliance system, although temporarily attractive in 1746, was not an answer to the problem. That Britain emerged from the war relatively unscathed was partly due to French diplomatic ineptitude, particularly after Fleury's death in January 1743, but it was also due to the fact that the alliances bonded by British subsidies and assisted by naval and land operations, held together well enough at critical points to convince

France and Spain that the cost of continuing would exceed the rewards. Neither France nor Spain gained by the war and in that regard Britain, if not Austria, could be said to have achieved its objectives. But France had not been defeated and by early 1748 neither European nor colonial and naval campaigns offered convincing prospects for defeating France.

Thus, it cannot be claimed that the experiences of war between 1739 and 1748 produced a clear path for statesmen that led to the great successes of 1759–1762. The making of war and the peace suggested that colonial campaigns produced modest results and without being able to defend Flanders or Hanover these would almost certainly be lost in an exchange at a peace conference. Although there were clear signs in the growth and development of the Royal Navy that naval and colonial campaigns might be becoming more effective, there was nothing to suggest that defending Flanders or Hanover would be any easier in the future.[4]

However, although only six years separated the Peace of Aix-la-Chapelle and the outbreak of the Anglo-French conflict in North America which broke out in 1754, the military context altered dramatically. This was clearly an Anglo-French struggle, not an Anglo-Bourbon war. It was dominated by the colonial dimension, as the war against Spain had started in 1739, but unlike the 1740s Britain was not faced with the problem of dealing with French and Spanish naval forces at the same time. Attention could be focused on the Channel and the Western Approaches, rather than the Atlantic seaboard from Dunkirk to Cadiz. The policies that had evolved between 1743 and 1746, particularly the development of the Western Squadron, to contain French naval power could be re-introduced quickly and effectively.

The defence of Hanover remained an important factor in British calculations, but the defence of the Habsburg territories did not. It was a very different diplomatic constellation in which the Diplomatic Revolution of 1754–1756 completely changed the dynamic of British involvement in a European war. Until the middle of 1756 the British tried to ensure that the colonial war did not spill over into a European conflict. Hanover was protected by treaties with Russia and Prussia, but Austrian Flanders remained vulnerable to French attack. The French attack on Minorca in April 1756 signalled that the war would be fought in Europe, but almost immediately the threat to Flanders was lifted. An Austro-French treaty (Treaty of

---

4   S.B. Baxter, 'The Myth of the Grand Alliance in the Eighteenth Century', in P.R. Sellin and S.B. Baxter (eds) *Anglo-Dutch Cross Currents in the Seventeenth and Eighteenth Centuries*, Los Angeles, 1976, 43–59.

Versailles, 1 May 1756) was concluded under which France accepted the neutrality of the Austrian Netherlands in a future conflict. This was soon followed by the Dutch firmly declaring their neutrality (declaration of 25 May 1756). [5] Although invasion of the British Isles might be attempted and Hanover threatened and Austria was now an ally of France, French occupation of the Low Countries was no longer a danger.

Hanover still posed a problem. British involvement in European campaigns of the 1740s was determined by the need to keep the Low Countries out of French hands and to preserve the Austrian Habsburgs as a balance to the House of Bourbon. These were undisputedly British interests and understood as such. Hanover had to be defended if attacked as a result of her attachment to Britain, but ministers had to be constantly on guard to present any support to Hanover as a contribution to the Common Cause. Between 1741 and 1745 the disputes between the King and his ministers over how this was to be done was foundation of so much of the political instability that followed Walpole's fall. The fact that the ministers achieved this against a background of continuing operational disappointment is testimony to their political and diplomatic skills. The Jacobite Rebellion in July 1745 and the acceptance by George II of the Broad Bottomed Administration in February 1746 brought matters to a head in Britain and the Treaty of Dresden in December 1745 brought peace in Germany, which enabled the subsidised Hanoverian forces to be employed unambiguously for the defence of Flanders. Together they quietened anti-Hanoverian agitation in Parliament until the final months of the war. By 1756, in alliance with Prussia and Russia, Hanover still had to be protected or, if lost, redeemed at a peace. When the Austro-Prussian war broke out in August 1756, with France as an ally of Austria, willing to intervene directly in Germany, the threat to Hanover was clear. British intervention in Germany to counter this threat would not be self-evidently serving British rather than Hanoverian purposes. As in 1741–1742, the old fears of Hanoverian influence would be revived with a vengeance and not easily countered by any ministry. While it remained uncertain as to whether France had to be defeated in Europe or could be decisively beaten by colonial campaigns alone, the question of how to support Hanover against French attacks remained as a critical point of contention in British politics.

If the experience of 1739 to 1748 did not provide clarity in how a future war

---

5   A.C. Carter, *The Dutch Republic in Europe in the Seven Years War*, London, 1971, 31–68.

should be fought, the experiences, nonetheless, fed into the eventual successes of the Seven Years War. Many of the key actors who had been forced to learn hard lessons in the 1740s were still active eight years later. Newcastle, Pitt, Hardwicke, the Grenvilles, remained in politics and office. They knew how the political and administrative machinery worked. The situation was very different in 1756, but they understood where their power lay and the limits on the military machinery they commanded.[6] The administrative machinery of government worked well throughout the war. The naval, military and fiscal administration all proved adaptable and generally effective. The large scale movements of men, ships, stores and victuals, sometimes strained systems and capacity, but the methods proved sound models for the Seven Years War.[7] The methods of mobilising American manpower, which were so important in the conquest of Canada, were developed and proven in 1740 and 1746. Not all the lessons were learned. Experience was painfully gained by the colonial expeditions in the 1740s, but the vast effort required for successful colonial operations was still not fully appreciated until 1758–1759.

Most of all, the navy, which had gone through turmoil ranging from wildly unrealistic expectations to a dramatic collapse of confidence, had emerged with its political and professional reputation at least partially recovered. With hindsight, this was probably the most important outcome of the war. If the war had ended in 1745 there would have been almost nothing to show for the enormous hopes of 1739. British policy based on continental or naval campaigns would have appeared equally bankrupt. The recovery during 1746 – 1748 was slow and limited, but enough was achieved for the public to believe that the navy could capitalise on its superiority over the Bourbon fleets and have an impact on French commerce, decision-making and war-making capability. The French and Spanish navies were beaten. Their commerce was heavily disrupted. Spanish and French operations in Italy and Flanders were influenced by events at sea. It was not enough to prove the validity of the expectations of 1739, but it was enough to give British political society confidence that they could win a naval war against the Bourbon powers. A new

---

6   R. Middleton, *The Bells of Victory: The Pitt-Newcastle Ministry and the Conduct of the Seven Years War, 1757–1762*, Cambridge, 1985; E.S.J. Frazer, 'The Pitt-Newcastle Coalition and the Conduct of the Seven Years War', unpublished DPhil thesis, University of Oxford, 1976.

7   To compare the administrative machinery of this period and the Seven Years War, see C.R. Middleton, 'The Administration of Newcastle and Pitt: The Departments of State and the Conduct of the Seven Years War', unpublished PhD thesis, University of Exeter, 1968 and Morgan, 'The Impact of War', op. cit.

generation of naval officers emerged from this war with experience failure and success. Anson was the most significant of this group, but Hawke, Boscawen, Howe, Keppel, Saunders, also understood how the navy had salvaged its reputation between 1746 and 1748. They knew what the public expected and what had to be done. Public confidence was not entirely restored and naval discipline was reinforced in 1749 by the promulgation of revised, more draconian, Articles of War.[8] The consequences of failing to meet those political expectations were made transparent when, under the provisions of the revised Articles, Admiral the Hon. John Byng was executed on 14 March 1757 for failing to do his utmost. The British Army never laboured under such expectations as the navy, and the victory at Culloden seems to have eliminated any discontent with the army's performance in Flanders. As in the navy, a new generation of army officers had learned their trade through failure and success.[9]

An important fact is that the naval war retained its political hold in Britain despite the failures of 1739 to 1745. Partly this was because the public displaced the failures on to the politicians and administrators until 1744 when the short-comings of naval officers, or naval power were too glaring to be dismissed. Thereafter, new officers were emerging, such as Anson, who were untainted by the inefficiency or cowardice of his colleagues, appeared to breath a new spirit into the navy. This view was highly attractive to the naval historians of the early twentieth century and underpins Admiral Richmond's narrative of the war. Civilian incompetence dominates the navy's fall, to be saved by professional naval officers like Anson and Hawke. The reality was more complex.

Richmond's broad conclusions are sound. Anson and Hawke's contributions to the revival of naval reputation were vital. Newcastle's instructions to Norris in 1740–1741 were sometimes confused. Winchelsea was, by his own admission, unsuited to be First Lord. The disposition of the fleet was inappropriate when war with France broke out, especially when seen with hindsight. Supplies to overseas stations were often dangerously low. However, to conclude that this was due entirely to the 'amiable but ineffectual' Duke of Newcastle, or 'one of the most incompetent Board of Admiralty that ever held office' under Winchelsea, is to ignore both the context of their actions and the results.[10]

---

8   N.A.M. Rodger, *Articles of War*, Havant, 1982, 21–34.

9   G. Plank, *Rebellion and Savagery: The Jacobite Rising of 1745 and the British Empire*, Philadelphia, 2006.

10   Richmond, *The Navy in the War*, op. cit., ii, 145.

Newcastle is a particular target of Richmond's contempt. He dominated this war and its historiography because of his position as Secretary of State, his political power and because of the survival of the great collection of his papers provides a central core of evidence related to decision-making with which the historian can work. Those papers show a man often tormented by anxiety and jealousy. He does not fit the heroic mould of William Pitt, whose rhetoric and public image fitted more closely the ideal of the war leader. There is no doubt that Newcastle made mistakes, founded both on naivety and hubris, but over nine years of war, he balanced dramatically changing domestic political and diplomatic priorities to create a war policy that worked. Winchelsea's assumption of the post of First Lord of the Admiralty coincided with the political and professional isolation of the Admiralty. This was partly caused by Winchelsea's appointment, but was also coincidental with the decline of the professional leadership of the navy. Wager had retired. Haddock was suffering a nervous breakdown. Norris was completely alienated by what he perceived an insufferable personal slight. Winchelsea had to cope with weaknesses in his relations with the Inner Cabinet, with commanders like Mathews, Norris and, on the margins, Vernon, as well as the subordinate Navy and Victualling Boards. Although much was done to restore the situation, starting while Winchelsea was First Lord, it was not completed until after the war ended. On the whole, the politicians that ran the war effort between 1739 and 1748 presided over policies and an administrative machine that worked well. They were beset by problems including disunity and conflict within the ministry and with the Crown. They had to handle a war that escalated within a year to an Anglo-Bourbon conflict and within two years encompassed the need to preserve the Austrian monarchy. They had to move rapidly to a state of war whose intensity was unmatched since 1710. Things did not all go well, but the ministers' achievements were also enormous. Incompetence at that level was not as widespread or significant as Richmond believed.

Furthermore, the political and professional leadership of the navy was not so distinctly separated that failure and success can be attributed to one or the other. They were closely linked. The political collapse of the navy in 1744–1745 was the result of operational failures from the West Indies to the Channel, as well as political compromises that placed the Admiralty outside the inner circle of decision-making. Likewise the recovery, in which Anson played such an important operational part, was only possible because the political settlement, following Carteret's final dismissal in February 1746, brought the Admiralty back into the inner circle. The Pelhams, Bedford and the New Allies had confidence in each other and, finally, the confidence of the King. Anson provided the vital link which reunited the political and professional leadership of the navy and with that the power of the Admiralty to impose itself on naval administration and operations was gradually restored. At the same time, French naval power was withering through over-extension and lack of resources. It still took time to show results, but during 1747 the Royal Navy was an effective offensive force against greatly diminished French and Spanish squadrons.

Britain had entered the war in 1739 with an ideological commitment to the power of naval force. It was profoundly shaken by events in the West Indies, the Mediterranean and eventually in the Channel. Once engaged in the War of Austrian Succession key decisions were made in Vienna and Berlin, which also challenged the relevance and effectiveness of sea power. However, for Britain the war ultimately focused on the old struggle with France, and in this context the navy eventually demonstrated its ability to inflict damage on the enemy which, if not decisive, was far in excess of the Flanders campaigns. Despite everything, some conquests had been made, prizes brought in, victories gained and a naval war effectively won. It was enough to ensure that the ideology of sea power and the British commitment to its navy was restored. By 1748 the war had demonstrated that British naval power was capable of making an impact from the North Atlantic to the Indian Ocean. The political and operational infrastructure was in place for Britain to use naval power across the globe. The Seven Years War was to demonstrate that with more denign diplomatic conditions and with more intense effort over time this naval power could be converted into decisive military action and achieve results that fundamentally changed Britain's relations with Europe and the rest of world.

Bibliography

Manuscripts

British Library

Additional Manuscripts (Add. Ms), 19033 (Wager Papers), 19036 (Wager Papers), 22536 (Carteret Papers), 28132 (Journal of Sir John Norris), 28133 (Norris Journal), 32692 (Newcastle Papers), 32693, 32694, 32695, 32697, 32698, 32699, 32700, 32701, 32702, 32703, 32801, 32982, 32993, 33004, 33048, 35337 (Journal of P. Yorke), 35351 (Hardwicke Papers), 35354, 35363, 35396, 35406, 35407, 35408, 35506, 35860, 35870, 40823 (Vernon Papers), 51390 (Holland House), 51427, 57036 (Weston Papers), Egerton Mss, EG 2529, EG 2539, EG 2530.

Chatsworth House, Derbyshire

Devonshire Mss, 245.9, 260.32, 260.42.

East Yorkshire Record Office

Grimston Mss, DDGR 39/5B.

India Office Library

East India Company, B/65 (Court Minutes).

Leicestershire Record Office

Finch Mss.

The National Archive

Adm 1/904, Adm 1/4111-4114, Adm 1/4154, Adm3/43, Adm8/20-26, Adm 106/2179, Adm 6/16, CO 5/41, CO 5/42, CO137/19, CO137/56, SP 36/51 – 53 (State Papers –Domestic), SP 41/12 (War Office), SP41/36, SP42/22-3 (State Papers – Naval), SP42/69, SP 42/85, SP 42/86, SP 42/87, SP 42/90, SP 42/91, SP 42/92, SP 42/93, SP42/94, SP42/95 (State Papers – Regencies), SP 43/25, SP 43/27, SP 43/28, SP 43/34, SP 43/100, SP 43/101, SP43/112, SP 43/114, SP44/181(State Papers Military), SP44/225, SP45/2 (State Papers – Various), SP45/3, SP45/4, SP45/5, SP78/220 -228 (State Papers – France), SP 87/9-24 (Military – Low Countries), SP89/40 (State Papers – Portugal), WO26/19 (Sec. at War's Miscellany Book).

Library of Congress
Vernon-Wager Mss (microfilms).

Royal Archives, Windsor
Cumberland Papers, Boxes 1–10 (microfilmed copies).

Scottish Record Office
Stair Muniments GD135/141/25-27.

University of Nottingham
Cumber Mss.

Woburn Estate Archive
Bedford Mss, ix–xv.

Printed Works

A Bill for the Speedy and Effectual Manning of His Majesty's Fleet as it was Engrossed and Ordered for a Third Reading, London, 1744.
A Journal of the Expedition to La Guiara, London, 1744.
Acts of the Privy Council.
Admiral V----n's Opinion upon the Present State of the British Navy, London, 1744.
Aiton, A.S., 'The Asiento Treaty as Reflected in the Papers of Lord Shelburne', *Hispanic American Historical Review*, viii (1928), 167–177.
Aldridge, D. 'Sir John Norris and the British Naval Expeditions in the Baltic Sea, 1715–1727', unpublished PhD thesis, University of London, 1972.
Aldridge, D.D., *Admiral Sir John Norris and the British Naval Expeditions to the Baltic Sea, 1715–1727*, Lund, 2009.
An Enquiry into the Conduct of Captain M---n being the Remarks of the Minutes of the Court Martial and other Incidental Matters Humbly Addressed to the Hon. House of Commons by a Sea Officer, London, 1745.
Anderson, M.S., *The War of Austrian Succession, 1740–1748*, London, 1995.
Anon., *An Account of the Expedition to Cartagena*, London, 1743.
Anson, W.V., *The Life of Lord Anson*, London, 1912.
Asher, E.L., *The Resistance to the Maritime Classes: The Survival of Feudalism in the France of Colbert*, Berkeley, 1960.
Aspinal-Oglander, C. (ed.) *Admiral's Wife: Being the Life and Letters of the Hon. Mrs Edward Boscawen from 1719 to 1761*, London, 1940.

Authentic Papers Relating to the Expedition Against Cartagena. Being the Reslutions of the Councils of War, both of the Sea and Land Officers London, 1744.

Avery E.L. and Scouton, A.H., 'The Opposition to Sir Robert Walpole, 1737–1739', *English Historical Review*, lxxxiii (1968), 331–336.

Bailey, G.B., *Falkirk or Paradise! The Battle of Falkirk Muir, 17 January 1746*, Edinburgh, 1996.

Ballantyne, A., *The Life of Lord Carteret*, London, 1887.

Barnes, D.G., 'Henry Pelham and the Duke of Newcastle', *Journal of British Studies*, i (1962), 62–77.

Bassett, W.G., 'The Caribbean in International Politics, 1670–1707', unpublished PhD thesis, University of London, 1934.

Baudrillart, A., *Philippe V et la Cour de France*, 5 vols, Paris, 1890–1900.

Baugh, D., *British Naval Administration in the Age of Walpole*, Princeton, 1965.

Baugh, D., 'Naval Power: What gave the British Navy Superiority?', in L. Prados de la Escoura (ed.) *Exceptionalism and Industrialisation: Britain and its European Rivals, 1688–1815*, Cambridge, 2004, 235–257.

Baxter, S.B., 'The Myth of the Grand Alliance in the Eighteenth Century', in P.R. Sellin and S.B. Baxter (eds) *Anglo-Dutch Cross Currents in the Seventeenth and Eighteenth Centuries*, Los Angeles, 1976, 43–59.

Beatson, W., *Naval and Military Memoirs of Great Britain*, 6 vols, London, 1790.

Beckett, J., *The Rise and Fall of the Grenvilles: Dukes of Buckingham and Chandos, 1710 to 1921*, Manchester, 1994.

Bennett, G.V., 'Jacobitism and the Rise of Walpole, in N. McKendrick (ed.) *Historical Perspectives: Studies in English Thought and Society*, London, 1974, 70–92.

Béthencourt, A., *Patino en la Politica Internacional de Felipe V*, Valladolid, 1954.

Black, J., *America or Europe? British Foreign Policy, 1739–63*, London, 1998.

Black, J., *Britain as a Military Power, 1688–1815*, London, 1999.

Black, J., *British Foreign Policy in the Age of Walpole*, Edinburgh, 1985.

Black, J., 'British Intelligence in the Mid-Eighteenth Century Crisis', *Intelligence and National Security*, ii (1987), 209–229.

Black, J., 'British Neutrality in the War of Polish Succession, 1733–1735, *International History Review*, vii (1986), 345–366.

Black, J., *Culloden and the '45*, Stroud, 1990.

Black, J., *George II: Puppet of the Politicians?*, Exeter, 2007.

Black, J., 'Hanoverian Nexus: Walpole and the Electorate', in B. Simms and T. Riotte (eds) *The Hanoverian Dimension in British History, 1714–1837*, Cambridge, 2007, 10–27.

Black, J., 'Hanover and British Foreign Policy, 1714–1760, *EHR*, cxx (2005), 303–339.

Black, J., 'Jacobitism and Foreign Policy, 1731–5, in E. Cruickshanks and J. Black (eds) *The Jacobite Challenge*, Edinburgh, 1988, 142–160.

Black, J., *Natural and Necessary Enemies: Anglo-French Relations in the Eighteenth Century*, Athens, Georgia, 1986.

Black, J., *Parliament and Foreign Policy in the Eighteenth Century*, Cambridge, 2004.

Black, J., *The Collapse of the Anglo-French Alliance, 1727–1731*, Gloucester, 1987.

Black, J., *The Continental Commitment: Britain, Hanover and Interventionism, 1714–1783*, 2005 .

Black, J., *Walpole in Power*, Stroud, 2001.

Bourland, R.D., 'Maurepas and His Administration of the French Navy on the Eve of the War of Austrian Succession (1737–1742)', unpublished PhD thesis, University of Notre Dame, 1978.

Brewer, J and Hellmouth, E., (eds), *Rethinking Leviathan: The Eighteenth Century State in Britain and Germany*, Oxford, 1999.

Brindley, H.H., 'The Action between H.M.S. *Lyon* and the *Elizabeth*, July 1745', in W.G. Perrin (ed.) *Naval Miscellany, Vol.3*, Navy Records Society, lxiii (1928), 85–119.

Brown, P.D., *William Pitt, Earl of Chatham*, London, 1978.

Brown, V.L., 'Contraband Trade: A Factor in the Decline of Spain's Empire in America', *Hispanic American Historical Review*, viii (1928), 178–189.

Brown, V.L., 'The South Sea Company and Contraband Trade', *American Historical Review*, xxxi (1925–6), 662–678.

Browning, R., 'The British Orientation of Austrian Foreign Policy, 1749–1754', *Central European History*, i (1968), 299–323

Browning, R., *The Duke of Newcastle*, New Haven, 1975.

Browning, R., *The War of Austrian Succession*, Sutton, 1995.

Buchet, C., *La Lutte pour l'Espace Caribe et la Façade Atlantique de l'Amerique Centale du Sud (1672–1763)*, 2 vols, Paris, 1991.

Butel, P., 'France, the Antilles and Europe in the Seventeenth and Eighteenth Centuries: Renewals of Foreign Trade', in J.D. Tracy (ed.) *The Rise of the Merchant Empires*, Cambridge, 1990, 153–173.

Butler, R., *Choiseul*, 2 vols, Oxford, 1980.

Caldwell, N.W., 'The Southern Frontier during King George's War', *Journal of Southern History*, vii (1941), 37–54.

Campbell, P.R., *Power and Politics in Old Regime France, 1720–1745*, London, 1996.

Capp, B., *Cromwell's Navy: The Fleet and the English Revolution, 1648–1660*, Oxford, 1989.

Carswell, J., *The South Sea Bubble*, 2nd edn, Stroud, 1993.

Carter, A.C., *Neutrality or Commitment: The Evolution of Dutch Foreign Policy, 1667–1795*, London, 1975.

Carter, A.C., *The Dutch Republic in Europe in the Seven Years War*, London, 1971.

Chandler, D., *Marlborough as Military Commander*, London, 1973.

Charnock, J., *Biographica Navalis*, London, 1796, vol. iv.

Charteris, E., *William Augustus, Duke of Cumberland: His Early Life and Career*, 2 vols, London, 1913.

Clark, G.R., 'Swallowed Up', *Earth*, iv (1995), 35–41.

Clark, J.C.D., 'Protestantism, Nationalism and National Identity', *Historical Journal*, xliii (2000), 249–276.

Clark, J.C.D., *Revolution and Rebellion: State and Society in England in the Seventeenth and Eighteenth Centuries*, Cambridge, 1986.

Coad, J., *Historic Architecture of the Royal Navy*, London, 1983.

Coad, J., *The Royal Dockyards, 1690–1815: Architecture and Engineering Works of the Sailing Navy*, Aldershot, 1989.

Cobbett, W., *Parliamentary History*, x (1737–1739) to xiv (1747–1748).

Colin, J., *Louis XV et les Jacobites: Le Project de Débarquement en Angleterre de 1743–1744*, Paris, 1901.

Colley, L., *Britons: Forging the Nation, 1707–1837*, Yale, New Haven, 1992, 17.

Colley, L., *In Defiance of Oligarchy: the Tory Party, 1714–1760*, Cambridge 1982.

Conn, S., *Gibraltar in British Diplomacy in the Eighteenth Century*, New Haven, 1942.

Connors, R., 'Pelham, Parliament and Public Policy, 1746–1754', unpublished PhD thesis, University of Cambridge, 1993.

Conway, S., 'Continental Connections: Britain and Europe in the Eighteenth Century', *History*, xc (2005), 353–374.

Conway, S., *War, State and Society in Mid-Eighteenth Century Britain and Ireland*, Oxford, 2006.

Coombs, D., *The Conduct of the Dutch: British Opinion and the Dutch Alliance during the War of the Spanish Succession*, The Hague, 1958.

Corbett, J.S., *England in the Mediterranean: A Study of the Rise and Influence of British Power within the Straits, 1603–1713*, 2 vols, London, 1904.

Corbett, J.S., *England in the Seven Years War*, 2 vols, London, 1907.

Corbett, T., *An Account of the Expedition of the British Fleet to Sicily in the Years 1718, 1719 and 1720*, London, 1739.

Coxe, W., *Memoirs of the Administration of Henry Pelham*, 2 vols., London, 1829.

Coxe, W., *Memoirs of the Life and Administration of Sir Robert Walpole, Earl of Orford*, 4 vols, London, 1816.

Crewe, D., *Yellow Jack and the Worm: British Naval Administration in the West Indies, 1739–1748*, Liverpool, 1993.

Crowhurst, P., *The Defence of British Trade, 1689–1815*, Folkstone, 1977.

Cruickshanks, E., '101 Secret Agent', *History Today*, April (1969), 273–276.

Cruickshanks, E., *Political Untouchables: The Tories and the '45*, Edinburgh, 1979.

Danley, M.H., 'Military Writings and the Theory and Practice of Strategy in the Eighteenth Century British Army', unpublished PhD thesis, Kansas State University, 2001.

Dann, U., *Hanover and Great Britain, 1740–1760*, Leicester, 1991.

Davies, D. *Pepy's Navy:Ships, Men and Warfare, 1649–1689*, Barnsley, 2008.

Davis, R., 'English Foreign Trade, 1660–1700', in W.E. Minchinton (ed.) *The Growth of English Overseas Trade in the Seventeenth and Eighteenth Centuries*,

London, 1969, 78–98.

Denman, T.J., 'The Political Debate over Strategy, 1680–1712', unpublished PhD thesis, University of Cambridge, 1985.

Devine, J.A., *The British North American Colonies in the War of 1739–1748*, unpublished PhD thesis, University of Virginia, 1968.

Dickinson, H.T., *Liberty and Property: Political Ideology in Eighteenth Century Britain*, London, 1977.

Dickinson, H.T., *Walpole and the Whig Supremacy*, London, 1973.

Dickson, P.G.M., *The Financial Revolution in England: A Study of the Development of Public Credit, 1688–1756*, London, 1967.

Diverres, P., *L'Attaque de Lorient par les Anglais (1746)*, Rennes, 1931.

Dobrée, B. (ed.), *The Letters of Philip Dormer Stanhope, 4th Earl of Chesterfield*, 6 vols, London 1932.

Dousdebes, P.J., *Cartagena de Indias: Plaza Fuerte*, Bogata, 1948.

Duffy, C., *The 45: Bonnie Prince Charlie and the Untold Story of the Jacobite Rising*, London, 2003.

Duffy, C., *The Wild Goose and the Eagle*, London, 1964.

Duffy, M., 'The Establishment of the Western Squadron as the Linchpin of British Naval Strategy, in M. Duffy (ed.) *Parameters of British Naval Power, 1650–1850*, Exeter, 1992, 60–81.

Dunthorne, H., *The Maritime Powers, 1721–1740: A Study of Anglo-Dutch Relations in the Age of Walpole*, New York, 1986.

Earle P., *Sailors: English Merchant Seamen, 1650–1775*, London, 1998.

Ellis, K., *The Post Office in the Eighteenth Century: A Study in Administrative History*, Oxford, 1958.

Fayle, C.E., 'Economic Pressure in the War of 1739–48, *Journal of the Royal United Services Institution*, 1923, 434–446.

Floyd, T.S., *The Anglo-Spanish Struggle for Mosquitia*, New Mexico, 1967.

Foord, A., *His Majesty's Opposition, 1714–1830*, Oxford, 1964.

Frazer, ES.J., 'The Pitt-Newcastle Coalition and the Conduct of the Seven Years War', unpublished DPhil thesis, University of Oxford, 1976.

Fritz, P.S., 'The Anti-Jacobite Intelligence System of the English Ministers, 1715–1745', *Historical Journal*, xvi (1973), 265–289.

Gardiner, R. (ed.), *The Line of Battle: The Sailing Warship, 1650–1840*, London, 1992.

Geikie, R. and Montgomery, I.A., *The Dutch Barrier, 1705–1719*, Cambridge, 1930.

Gentleman's Magazine Vols 9–18 (1739–1748).

George, M.D., *English Political Caricature to 1792*, Oxford, 1959.

Gerrard, C., *The Patriot Opposition to Walpole*, Oxford, 1994.

Gibbs, G.C., 'Accession to the Throne and Change of Rulers: Determining Factors in the Establishment and Continuation of the Personal Union', in R. Rexhauser (ed.) *Die Personalunionen von Sachen-Polen 1697–1763 und Hannover-England 1714–1837: Ein Vergleich*, Wiesleben, 2005, 241–274.

Gibbs, G.C., 'English Attitudes towards Hanover and the Hanoverian Succession in the First Half of the Eighteenth Century', in A.M. Birke and K.Kluken (eds) *England und Hannover*, Munchen, 1986, 33–51.

Gibbs, G.C., 'Newspapers, Parliament and Foreign Policy in the Age of Stanhope and Walpole, in *Melanges Offerts á G. Jaquemyns*, Brussels, 1968, 293–315.

Gibbs, G.C. 'Parliament and Foreign Policy, 1715–1731', unpublished MA thesis, University of Liverpool, 1953.

Gibson, J.S., *Ships of the '45*, London, 1967.

Glete, J., *Navies and Nations: Warships, Navies and State Building in Europe and America, 1500–1860*, 2 vols, Stockholm, 1993.

Goldsmith, M.M., 'Faction Detected: Ideological Consequences of Robert Walpole's Decline and Fall', *History*, lxiv (1979), 1–19.

Gould, E.H., 'To Strengthen the King's Hands: Dynastic Legitimacy, Militia Reform and Ideas of National Unity in England, 1745–1760, *HJ*, xxxiv (1991), 329–348.

Graham, D.S., *British Intervention in Defence of the American Colonies, 1748–1756*, unpublished PhD thesis, London, 1969.

Graham, G.S., *Empire of the North Atlantic: The Maritime Struggle for North America*, Oxford, 1958.

Graham, G.S., 'The Naval Defence of British North America, 1739–1763', *TRHS* (4th Series), xxx (1949), 95–110.

Graham, J.M. (ed.), *Annals of the Viscount and the First and Second Earls of Stair*, 2 vols, Edinburgh, 1875.

Gunther, A.E., *An Introduction to the Life of the Rev. Thomas Birch D.D., F.R.S, 1705–1766*, Halesworth, 1984.

Guy, A., *Oeconomy and Discipline: Officership and Administration in the British Army, 1714–63*, Manchester, 1985.

Gwyn, J., *An Admiral for America: Sir Peter Warren, Vice Admiral of the Red, 1703–1752*, Gainsville, 2004.

Gwyn, J., 'British Government Spending and the North American Colonies, 1740–1755', in P. Marshall and G. Williams (eds) *The British Empire Before the American Revolution*, London, 1980, 74–84.

Gwyn, J., 'French and British Naval Power at the Two Sieges of Louisbourg; 1745 and 1758, *Nova Scotia Historical Review*, x (1990), 63–73.

Gwyn, J. (ed.), *The Royal Navy and North America: The Warren Papers, 1736–1752*, London, 1973.

Haas, J., 'The Rise of the Bedfords, 1741–1757: A Study in the Politics of the Reign of George II', unpublished PhD thesis, University of Illinois, 1960.

Haas, J.M., *A Management Odyssey: The Royal Dockyards, 1714–1914*, New York, 1994.

Harding, N., 'Sir Robert Walpole and Hanover', *Historical Research*, lxxvi (2003), 164–188.

Harding, R., *Amphibious Warfare in the Eighteenth Century: The British Expedition to the West Indies, 1740–1742*, Woodbridge, 1991.

Harding, R., 'A Tale of Two Sieges: Gibraltar, 1726–7, and 1779–1783', *Transactions of the Naval Dockyards Society*, vol. 2 (2006), 31–46.

Harding, R., 'Lord Cathcart, the Earl of Stair and the Scottish Opposition to Sir Robert Walpole', *Parliamentary History*, ll (1992), 192–117.

Harding, R., 'The Expedition to Lorient, 1746', in N. Tracy (ed.) *The Age of Sail: The International Annual of the Historic Sailing Ship*, I, London, 2002, 34–54.

Harris, B., *Politics and the Nation: Britain in the Mid-Eighteenth Century*, Oxford, 2002.

Harris, R., 'A Leicester House Political Diary, 1742–3', *Camden Miscellany*, xliv (1992), 375–411.

Harris, R., *A Patriot Press: National Politics and the London Press in the 1740s*, Oxford, 1993.

Hattendorf, J.B., *England and the War of Spanish Succession; A Study of the English View and Conduct of Grand Strategy, 1702–1712*, New York, 1987.

Hayter, T., *The Army and the Crowd in Mid-Georgian England*, London, 1978.

Hayton, D., 'The "Country" Interest and the Party System, 1689–c1720', in C. Jones (ed.) *Party and Management in Parliament, 1660–1784*, Leicester, 1984, 36–85.

Henderson, A.J., *London and the National Government, 1721–1742: A Study of City Politics and the Walpole Administration*, Durham, North Carolina, 1945.

Henretta, J.A., *Salutary Neglect: Colonial Administration under the Duke of Newcastle*, Princeton, 1972.

Hertz, G., *British Imperialism in the Eighteenth Century*, London, 1908.

Hildner, E.G., 'The Role of the South Sea Company in the Diplomacy Leading to the War of Jenkins' Ear, 1729–1739', *Hispanic American Historical Review*, xviii (1938), 322–341.

Hill, B.W., 'Oxford, Bolingbroke and the Peace of Utrecht', *Historical Journal*, xvi (1973), 241–263.

Hill, B.W., *Sir Robert Walpole*, Hamish Hamilton, London, 1989.

Hill, B.W., *The Growth of Parliamentary Parties, 1689–1742*, London, 1976.

Historical Manuscripts Commission: Du Cane Mss, London, 1905.

Historical Manuscripts Commission: Egmont Diary 3 vols. London 1923.

Historical Manuscripts Commission: Trevor Manuscripts, London, 1895.

Horn, D.B., *The British Diplomatic Service, 1689–1789*, Oxford, 1961.

Horn, D.B., 'Saxony in the War of Austrian Succession', *English Historical Review*, lxiv (1929), 33–47.

Horsfall, L., 'British Relations with the Spanish Colonies in the Caribbean, 1713–1739', unpublished MA thesis, London, 1936.

Houlding, J.A., *Fit for Service: The Training of the British Army 1715–1795*, Oxford, 1981.

Ibáñez, I.R., 'Mobilising Resources for War: The British and Spanish Intelligence Systems during the War of Jenkins's Ear (1739–1744)', PhD University of London 2009.

John, A.H., 'War and the English Economy, 1700–1763', *Ec.HR*, vii (1955), 329–344.

Johnson, E., 'The Bedford Connection: The Fourth Duke of Bedford's Political

Influence between 1732 and 1771', unpublished PhD thesis, University of Cambridge, 1979.

Johnson, J.A., 'Parliament and the Navy, 1688–1714', unpublished PhD thesis, University of Sheffield, 1968.

Johnson, W.B., 'The Content of American Colonial Newspapers Relative to International Affairs, 1704–1763', unpublished PhD thesis, University of Washington, 1962.

Jones, D.W., *War and Economy in the Age of William III and Marlborough*, Oxford, 1988.

Joslin, D.M., 'London Bankers in Wartime, 1739–1784', in L.S. Pressnal (ed.) *Studies in the Industrial Revolution*, London, 1960, 156–177.

Journal of the House of Commons, xxiii (1737–9).

Kamen, H., *Philip V of Spain: The King who Reigned Twice*, New Haven, 2001 .

Kemp, B., *Sir Robert Walpole*, London, 1976.

King, C., *The British Merchant*, London, 1720.

Kramnick, I., *Bolingbroke and his Circle: The Politics of Nostalgia in the Age of Walpole*, Ithaca, 1968.

Kulisheck, P.J.D.J., '"The Favourite Child of the Whigs": The Life and Career of Henry Bilson Legge, 1708–1764', unpublished PhD thesis, University of Minnesota, 1996/

Lanning, J.T., 'American Participation in the War of Jenkins' Ear', *Georgia Historical Quarterly*, xi (1927), 191–215.

Laprade, W.T., *Public Opinion and Politics in Eighteenth Century England to the Fall of Walpole*, New York, 1936.

Lavery, B., *The Ship of the Line, Volume 1: The Development of the Battlefleet*, London, 1983.

Le Fevre P. and Harding, R. (eds), *Precursors of Nelson: British Admirals of the Eighteenth Century*, London, 2000.

Le Goff, T.J.A., 'Problémes de Recrutement de la marine française pendent la Guerre de Sept Ans', *Revue Historique*, 283 (1990), 208–233.

Leitch-Wright, J., *Anglo-Spanish Rivalry in North America*, Georgetown, 1971.

Lincoln, C.H. (ed.), *Correspondence of William Shirley*, 2 vols, New York, 1912.

Lodge, R., *Great Britain and Prussia in the Eighteenth Century*, Oxford, 1923.

Lodge, R., *Private Correspondence of Chesterfield and Newcastle, 1744–1746*, London, 1930.

Lodge, R., *The Private Correspondence of Sir Benjamin Keene, K.B.*, Cambridge, 1933.

Lodge, R., *Studies in Eighteenth Century Diplomacy, 1740–1748*, London, 1930.

Lodge, R., 'The Continental Policy of Great Britain, 1740–60, *History*, xvi (1932), 298–304.

Lodge, R., 'The So-Called Treaty of Hanau of 1743', *English Historical Review*, xxxviii (1923), 384–407.

Lodge, R., 'The Treaty of Seville, 1729', *Transactions of the Royal Historical Society*, xvi (1933), 1–43.

Lodge, R., 'The Treaty of Worms', *English Historical Review*, xlv (1929),

220–255.

Luff, P.A., 'Mathews v. Lestock: Parliament, Politics and the Navy in the Mid Eighteenth Century', *Parliamentary History*, x (1991), 45–62.

Luff, P.A., 'The Noblemen's Regiments: Politics and the "Forty-Five"', *BIHR*, lxv (1992), 54–73.

Mackay, R.F., *Admiral Hawke*, Oxford, 1965.

Marchena Fernández, J., *La Institucion Militar en Cartagena de Indias, 1700–1870*, Seville, 1982.

Marshall, D.W., 'British Military Engineers, 1741–1783: A Study of Organisation, Social Origin and Cartography', unpublished PhD thesis, University of Michigan, 1976.

Massie, A.W., 'Great Britain and the Defence of the Low Countries, 1744–1748', unpublished DPhil thesis, University of Oxford, 1987.

McCann, T.J. (ed.), *The Correspondence of the Dukes of Richmond and Newcastle, 1724–1750*, Lewes, 1984.

McGill, W.J., 'The Roots of Policy: Kaunitz in Vienna and Versailles', *Journal of Modern History*, xliii (1971), 228–244.

McLachlan, J.O., 'The Seven Years Peace and the West Indian Policy of Carvajal and Wall', *EHR*, liii (1938), 457–477.

McLachlan, J.O., *Trade and Peace with Old Spain, 1667–1750*, Cambridge, 1940.

McLeish, J., 'British Activities in Yucatan and on the Moskito Shore in the Eighteenth Century', unpublished MA thesis, London, 1926

McLennan, J.S., *Louisbourg: From its Foundations to its Fall, 1713–1758*, London, 1918 (abridged reprint, 1957).

McLynn, F.J., *France and the Jacobite Rising of 1745*, Edinburgh, 1981.

McLynn, F.J., 'Seapower and the Jacobite Rising of 1745', *Mariner's Mirror*, lxvii (1981), 163–172.

McLynn, F.J., *The Jacobite Army in England, 1745: The Final Campaign*, Edinburgh, 1998.

McNeill, J.R., *Atlantic Empires of France and Spain: Louisbourg and Havana, 1700–1763*, Chapel Hill, 1985.

Merino Navarro, J.P., *La Armada Española en el siglo XVIII*, Madrid, 1981.

Middleton, A.P., 'The Chesapeake Convoy System, 1662–1763, *William and Mary Quarterly* (3rd series), ii (1946), 182–207.

Middleton, C.R., 'The Administration of Newcastle and Pitt: The Departments of State and the Conduct of the Seven Years War', unpublished PhD thesis, University of Exeter, 1968.

Middleton, R., *The Bells of Victory: The Pitt-Newcastle Ministry and the Conduct of the Seven Years War, 1757–1762*, Cambridge, 1985.

Minchinton, W.E., (ed.), *The Growth of English Overseas Trade*, London, 1969.

Mitchell, B.R., *British Historical Statistics*, Cambridge, 1988.

Mitchell, B.R. and Deane, P., *Abstract of British Historical Statistics*, Cambridge, 1962.

Monod, P.K., *Jacobitism and the English People, 1688–1788*, Cambridge, 1989.

Morgan, G.W., 'The Impact of War on the Administration of the Army, Navy and Ordnance in Britain, 1739–1754', unpublished, PhD thesis, University of Leicester, 1977.

Murray, J.J., *George I, the Baltic and the Whig Split of 1717*, London, 1969.

Nelson, G.H., 'Contraband Trade under the Asiento, 1730–1739', *American Historical Review*, li (1945), 55–67.

Nerzic, J.-Y. and Buchet, C., *Marins et Flibustiers du Roi-Soleil – Cartagena 1697*, Paris, 2002.

Newton, L.W., 'Caribbean Contraband and Spanish Retailiation', *Mededelingen Nederlandse Vereniging voor Zeegeschiednenis*, xxix (1974), 22–27.

Oates, J., 'Dutch Forces in Eighteenth Century Britain: A British Perspective', *Journal of Army Historical Research*, lxxxv (2007), 20–39.

Oates, J., 'Hessian Forces Employed in Scotland in 1746', *Journal of Army Historical Research*, lxxxiii (2005), 205–214.

Oates, J., 'Sir Robert Walpole after his Fall from Power, 1742–1745', *History*, xci (2006), 218–230.

Oates, J., 'The Crisis of the Hanoverian State?' *Journal of Army Historical Research*, lxxxi (2003), 308–329.

Oglesby, J.C.M., 'The British Attacks on the Caracas Coast, 1743', *Mariner's Mirror*, lviii (1972), 27–40.

Ogelsby, J.C.M., *War at Sea in the West Indies, 1739–1748*, unpublished PhD thesis, Uni of Washington, 1963.

Original Papers Relating to the Expedition to Cartagena, London, 1744.

Original Papers Relating to the Expedition to the Island of Cuba London, 1744.

Owen, J.R., 'George II Reconsidered', in A. Whiteman, J.S. Bromley and P.G.M. Dickinson (eds) *Statesmen, Scholars and Merchants*, Oxford, 1973, 113–134.

Owen, J.B., *The Rise of the Pelhams*, London, 1957.

Owen, J.B., 'The Survival of Country Attitudes in the Eighteenth Century House of Commons', in J.S. Bromley and E.H. Kossmann (eds) *Britain and the Netherlands*, iv, Hague, 1971, 42–69.

Pajol, C.P.V., *Les Guerres sous Louis XV*, 6 vols, Paris, 1883.

Pares, R., 'American versus Continental Warfare, 1739–1763', *English Historical Review*, li (1936), 429–465.

Pares, R., *Blockade and Neutral Rights, 1739–1763*, Oxford, 1938.

Pares, R., *Colonial Blockade and Neutral Rights, 1739–1763*, Oxford, 1938.

Pares, R., *War and Trade in the West Indies, 1739–1763*, Oxford, 1936.

Parry, C. (ed.), *Consolidated Treaty Series*, New York, 1969, vols 32–35.

Pencak, W., 'Warfare and Political Change in Eighteenth Century Massachusetts, in P. Marshall and G. Williams (eds) *The British Empire Before the American Revolution*, London, 1980, 51–73.

Peters, M., *Pitt and Popularity: The Patriot Minister and London Opinion during the Seven Years War*, Oxford, 1980.

Philips, C.H., 'The Secret Committee of the East India Company', *Bulletin of the School of Oriental and African Studies*, x (1939–1942), 299–315.

Plank, G., *Rebellion and Savagery: The Jacobite Rising of 1745 and the British Empire*, Philadelphia, 2006.

Plumb, J.H., *Sir Robert Walpole*, 2 vols, London, 1956 and 1960.

Pool, B., *Navy Board Contracts, 1660–1832*, London, 1966.

Pressnal, L.S., 'The Rate of Interest in the Eighteenth Century', in L.S. Pressnal (ed.) *Studies in the Industrial Revolution*, London, 1960, 178–214.

Pritchard, J., *Anatomy of a Naval Disaster: The 1746 French Expedition to North America*, Montreal, 1995.

Ranft, B. Mc, *The Vernon Papers*, London, 1958.

Reese, T.R., 'Britain's Military Support of Georgia in the War of 1739–1748', *Georgia Historical Quarterly*, xliii (1959), 1–10.

Reid, S., *1745: A Military History of the Last Jacobite Rising*, Staplehurst, 1996.

Rexheuser, R., *Die Personalunionen von Sachen-Polen 1697–1763 und Hannover-England 1714–1837*, Wiesbaden, 2005. .

Richmond, H.W., 'English Strategy in the War of the Austrian Succession', *JRUSI*, lxiv (1919), 246–254

Richmond, H.W., *The Navy in the War of 1739–1748*, 3 vols, Cambridge, 1920.

Rodger, N.A.M., *Articles of War*, Havant, 1982.

Rodger, N.A.M., 'George, Lord Anson', in P. Le Fevre and R. Harding (eds) *Precursors of Nelson: British Admirals of the Eighteenth Century*, London, 2000, 177–199.

Rodger, N.A.M., *The Command of the Ocean: A Naval History of Britain, 1649–1815*, London, 2004.

Rodger, N.A.M., 'The Continental Commitment in the Eighteenth Century', in L. Freedman, P. Hayes and R. O'Neil (eds) *War, Strategy and International Politics*, Oxford, 1992, 39–55.

Rodger, N.A.M., *The Insatiable Earl: A Life of John Montagu, 4th Earl of Sandwich*, London, 1993.

Rogers, N., *The Press Gang: Naval Impressment and its Opponents in Georgian Britain*, London, 2007.

Rogers, N., *Whigs and Cities: Popular Politics in the Age of Walpole and Pitt*, Oxford, 1989.

Rose, G.H. (ed.), *A Selection from the Papers of the Earls of Marchmont*, 3 vols, London, 1831.

Roseveare, H., *The Treasury, The Evolution of a British Institution*, London, 1969.

Sainty, J.C., *Officials of the Secretaries of State, 1660–1782*, London, 1973.

Schumpeter, E.B., *English Overseas Trade Statistics, 1697–1808*, Oxford, 1960.

Schwoerer, L.G., *No Standing Armies!*, Baltimore, 1974.

Scott, H.M., '"The True Principles of the Revolution": The Duke of Newcastle and the Idea of the Old System', in J. Black (ed.) *Knights Errant and True Englishmen: British Foreign Policy, 1660–1800*, Edinburgh, 1989, 54–91.

Scott, H.M., 'Hanover in Mid-Eighteenth Century Franco-British Geopolitics', in B. Simms and T. Riotte (eds) *The Hanoverian Dimension in British History, 1714–1837*, Cambridge, 2007, 275–300.

Sedgwick, R.R., 'The Inner Cabinet from 1739 to 1741', *English Historical*

Review, 34 (1919), 290–302.

Sedgwick, R.R. (ed.), *Memoirs of the Reign of King George II by John Lord Hervey*, 3 vols, London, 1931.

Sedgwick, R.R., *The House of Commons, 1715–1754*, 2 vols, London, 1970.

Simms, B., *Three Victories and a Defeat: The Rise and Fall of the First British Empire, 1714–1783*, London, 2007.

Simms, B. and Riotte, T., *The Hanoverian Dimension in British History, 1714–1837*, Cambridge, 2007.

Skinner, Q., 'The Principles and Practice of Opposition: The Case of Bolingbroke versus Walpole', in N. McKendrick (ed.) *Historical Perspectives: Studies in English Thought and Society*, London, 1974, 93–128.

Skrine, F.R., *Fontenoy and Great Britain's Share in the War of Austrian Succession, 1741–1748*, Edinburgh, 1906.

Smith, H., *Georgian Monarchy: Politics and Culture, 1714–1760*, Cambridge, 2006.

Smith, H., 'The Court in England, 1714–1760: A Declining Political Institution?', *History*, xc (2005), 23–41.

Smith, W.J. (ed.), *The Grenville Correspondence*, 4 vols, London, 1852.

Sommers, S.M., *Parliamentary Politics of a County and a Town: General Elections in Suffolk and Ipswich in the Eighteenth Century*, London, 2002.

Sosin, J.M., 'Louisburg and the Peace of Aix-la-Chapelle, 1748', *WMQ*, xiv (1957), 516–535.

Spalding, P., *Oglethorpe in America*, Chicago, 1977.

Speck, W.A., *The Butcher: The Duke of Cumberland and the Suppression of the 45*, Oxford, 1981.

Speck, W.A., '"Whigs and Tories Dim their Glories": English Political Parties under the First Two Georges', in J. Cannon (ed.) *The Whig Ascendency: Colloquies on Hanoverian England*, London, 1981, 51–76.

Stallybrass, P., 'Time, Space and Unity: The Symbolic Discourse of the Faerie Queene', in R. Samuel (ed.), *Patriotism: The Making and Unmaking of British National Identity*, London, 1989, iii, 199–214.

Starkey, D.J., *British Privateering Enterprise in the Eighteenth Century*, Exeter, 1990.

Steele, I.K., *Politics of Colonial Policy: The Board of Trade in Colonial Administration, 1696–1720*, Oxford, 1968.

Steele, I.K., *The English Atlantic, 1675–1740*, Oxford, 1986.

Sutherland, L., 'Samson Gideon and the Reduction of Interest, 1749–1750', *Economic History Review*, lxx (1955), 229–257.

Sutherland, L., 'Samson Gideon: Eighteenth Century Jewish Financier', *Transactions of the Jewish Historical Society of England*, xvii (1953), 79–90.

Swanson, C.E., 'American Privateering and Imperial Warfare, 1739–1748', *WMQ*, xlii (1985), 357–382.

Swanson, C.E., *Predators and Prizes; American Privateering and Imperial Warfare, 1739–1748*, Chapel Hill, 1991.

Taillemite, E., 'Une bataille de l'Atlantique au XVIIIᵉ siècle: la guerre de Succession d'Autriche, 1744–1748', in *Guerre et Paix*, Paris, 1987, 131–148.

Targett, S., 'Government and Ideology during the Age of Whig Supremacy: The Political Argument of Sir Robert Walpole's Newspaper Propagandists', *HJ*, xxxvii (1994), 289–317.

Taylor S. and Jones, C. (eds), *Tory and Whig: The Parliamentary Papers of Edward Harley, 3rd Earl of Oxford and William Hay, M.P. for Seaford, 1716–1753*, Woodbridge, 1998.

Temperley, H.W.V., 'The Inner and Outer Cabinet and Privy Council, 1679–1783', *English Historical Review*, 27 (1912), 682–699.

Thomson, M.A., *The Secretaries of State, 1681–1782*, Oxford, 1932.

Trevelyan, G.M., *England under Queen Anne*, 3 vols, London, 1934.

Tunstall, B., *William Pitt: Earl of Chatham*, London, 1938.

Vaucher, P., *Robert Walpole et la Politique de Fleury (1731–1742)*, Paris, 1924.

Verge- Franceschi, M., *La Marine Francaise au xviiie Siecle*, Paris, 1996.

Villalabos, R.S., 'Contrabando Frances en el Pacifico, 1700–24', *Revista Historica Americana*, li (1961), 49–80.

Walker, G.J., *Spanish Politics and Imperial Trade, 1700–1789*, London, 1979.

Walpole, H., *Memoirs of the Reign of George II*, 4 vols, London, 1846.

Ware, C., *Admiral Byng: His Rise and Execution*, Barnsley, 2009.

Wells, J. and Wills, D., 'Revolution, Restitution and Debt Repudiation: The Jacobite Threat to England's Institutions and Economic Growth', *Journal of Economic History*, lx (2000), 418–441.

West, J., *Gunpowder, Government and War in the Mid-Eighteenth Century*, Woodbridge, 1991.

Wheeler, J.S., *The Making of a World Power: War and the Military Revolution in Seventeenth Century England*, Stroud, 1999.

White, J.M., *Marshal of France: The Life and Times of Maurice de Saxe*, Chicago, 1962.

Whitworth, R., *Field Marshal Lord Ligonier: A Story of the British Army*, Oxford, 1958.

Whitworth, R., *William Augustus, Duke of Cumberland*, London, 1992.

Wickham Legg, L.G., 'Newcastle and the Counter Order to Admiral Haddock, March 1739', *English Historical Review*, xlvi (1931), 272–274.

Wiggins, L., M., *The Faction of Cousins : A Political Account of the Grenvilles, 1733-1763*, New Haven, 1958.

Wilkes, J., *A Whig in Power: The Political Career of Henry Pelham*, Evanston, 1964.

Wilkinson, C., *The British Navy and the State in the Eighteenth Century*, Woodbridge, 2004.

Wilkinson, H.S., *The Defence of Piedmont, 1742–1748: A Prelude to Napoleon*, Oxford, 1927.

Williams, B., *Carteret and Newcastle: A Contrast in Contemporaries*, Cambridge, 1943.

Williams, B., *The Life of William Pitt, Earl of Chatham*, 2 vols, London, 1915.

Williams, G., *The Prize of All the Oceans: The Triumph and Tragedy of Anson's*

Voyage round the World, London, 1999.

Willis, S., *Fighting at Sea in the Eighteenth Century: The Art of Sailing Warfare*, Woodbridge, 2008.

Willis, S., 'The High Life: Topmen in the Age of Sail', *Mariner's Mirror*, xc (2004), 152–166.

Wilson, C., *Anglo-Dutch Commerce and Finance in the Eighteenth Century*, Cambridge, 1941.

Wilson, K., 'Empire, Trade and Popular Politics in Mid-Hanoverian Britain: The Case of Admiral Vernon', *Past and Present*, cxxi (1988), 74–109.

Wilson, K., *The Sense of the People: Politics, Culture and Imperialism in England, 1715–1785*, Cambridge, 1998.

Winfield, R., *The 50-Gun Ship*, London, 1997.

Woodfine, P., 'Horace Walpole and British Relations with Spain, 1738', *Camden Miscellany*, xxxii (1994), 277–311.

Woodfine, P., *Britannia's Glories: The Walpole Ministry and the War with Spain*, Woodbridge, 1998.

Woodfine, P., Ideas of Naval Power and the Conflict with Spain, 1738–1742', in J. Black and P. Woodfine (eds) *The British Navy and the Use of Naval Power in the Eighteenth Century*, Leicester, 1988, 71–90.

Woodfine, P., 'The Anglo–Spanish War of 1739', in J. Black (ed.) *The Origins of War in Early Modern Europe*, Edinburgh, 1987, 186–205.

Yorke, P. (ed.), *Life and Correspondence of Philip Yorke, Earl of Hardwicke*, 3 vols, Cambridge, 1913.

Zapatero, J.M., *Historia de las Fortificaciones de Cartagena de Indias*, Madrid, 1979.

Index

Lightning Source UK Ltd.
Milton Keynes UK
UKOW031407100513

210508UK00004B/37/P